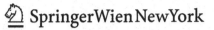

Schahram Dustdar

Fei Li

Service Engineering

European Research Results

SpringerWienNewYork

Schahram Dustdar
Vienna University of Technology
Information Systems Institute
1040 Wien, Austria
dustdar@infosys.tuwien.ac.at

Fei Li
Vienna University of Technology
Information Systems Institute
1040 Wien, Austria
li@infosys.tuwien.ac.at

SpringerWienNewYork is a part of Springer Science + Business Media
springer.at

Typesetting: Camera ready by the authors
Printing: Strauss GmbH, Mörlenbach, Germany

Printed on acid-free paper
SPIN 80014801

With 106 Figures

ISBN 978-3-7091-1727-9   ISBN 978-3-7091-0415-6 (eBook)
DOI 10.1007/978-3-7091-0415-6
SpringerWienNewYork

Preface

Service-oriented Computing (SOC) is posing increasing challenges to traditional software engineering methodologies including specification, modeling, architecture, and verification, just to name a few. On the other hand, the latest advancements in software engineering are continuously leveraged in SOC research, especially in the design and implementation of service-oriented systems. The mutual impacts between SOC and software engineering have been seen in the last decade, and great research efforts have been devoted to the field. These research efforts are generally referred to as *Service Engineering*.

In Europe, many research projects have been funded to address a large spectrum of research challenges in service engineering. However, in spite of the considerable efforts and significant contributions, few have attempted to summarize the research results systematically. To provide a coherent and consolidated view on the European community in service engineering, the European Commission has established a collaboration working group on Service Engineering, which is lead by Schahram Dustdar. This book is a joint contribution of this working group.

This book aims at introducing the state of the art of service engineering based on the research results achieved in European projects. Given the broadness of research aspects in SOC and the rich selection of software engineering methods, a coherent vision of service engineering is critical to the readability of the book. To this end, a series of use cases from the telecommunication field have been carefully designed and serve as a motivating case study for all contributions, which address different aspects of these use cases in their own ways. Because of the crosscutting nature of the research challenges, classifying the contributions into several themes would only give readers an over-simplified vision of the field. Instead, we employ the S-Cube Conceptual Research Framework to identify the research domains and cross-cutting issues addressed by each contribution.

Since the initiation of this book, some noticeable trends in service engineering have been observed. In contrast to the varieties of research problems, two areas in software engineering emerge to be the main sources of methodologies employed in this book: a) Model-driven Engineering and b) Adaptive Software Architectures. At design-time, Model-driven Engineering facilitates different phases of service development. At runtime, with model management systems, models are also exploited for service compliance checking. In the area of adaptive software architecture, the key features of SOC, such as loose-coupling, late-binding, service discovery, and dynamic composition, have already ensured adaptability of service-oriented systems. Services are the means to implement adaptability, as well as a result of past achievements in adaptive software architecture.

By extensively summarizing the state of the art of service engineering, this book offers a view on how SOC research is in line with the latest development of software engineering. One can expect more interactions between SOC and software engineering to enrich service engineering methodologies in the future.

Vienna, August, 2010   *Schahram Dustdar*
                                                                          Fei Li

Contents

Acronyms

A@P   Attribute-oriented Programming

AgWS   Agentified Services

AO   Aspect-oriented the encapsulation of crosscutting concerns.

AOM   Aspect-oriented Modeling

AOSD   Aspect-oriented Software Development

API   Application Programming Interface

ASR   Automatic Speech Recognition

BAM   Business Architecture Model

BI   Business Intelligence

BMM   Business Motivation Model

BPEL   Business Process Execution Language

BPEL4SWS   Business Process Execution Language for Semantic Web Services

BPM   Business Process Management

BPMN   Business Process Modeling Notation

CD   Context Diagram

CEP   Complex Event Processing

CIM   Computational independent model

CPO   Cell Phone Operator

CRM   Customer Relationship Management

ASM   Abstract State Machines

CWA   Closed World Assumption

DBMS   DataBase Management System

DDD   Domain Driven Design

DSPL	Dynamic Software Product Line
ECA	Event Condition Action
EPC	Event-driven Process Chain
EPF	Eclipse Process Framework
EPL	Event Processing Language
ERP	Enterprise Ressource Planning
ESB	Enterprise Service Bus
GReQL	Graph Repository Query Language
IM	Instant Messaging
IDE	Integrated Development Environment
IOPE	Inputs, Outputs Preconditions and Effects (IOPE)
IRF	Integrated Research Framework
JDO	Java Data Objects
JEE	Java Enterprise Edition
JMX	Java Management Extensions
JSP	Java Server Pages
LSA	Latent Semantic Analysis
M2M	Model to model
M2T	Model to text
MAS	Multi-agent system
MDA	Model-driven Architecture
MDD	Model-driven Development
MDE	Model-driven Engineering
MDSD	Model-driven Software Development
MDSE	Model-driven service engineering
MicroWSMO	Micro Web Service Modeling Ontology
MORSE	Model-aware Repository and Service Environment
MPSP	Mobile Phone Service Portability
MSOAM	Mainstream SOA Methodology
MVC	Model-View-Controller
NLP	Natural Language Processing
OMG	Object Management Group
OOAD	Object-oriented Analysis and Design

OSS   Operations Support System

OWA   Open World Assumption

OWL   Ontology Web Language

P2P   Peer-to-peer

PIM   Platform-independent model

PSM   Platform-specific model

POJO   Plain Old Java Object

POTS   Plain Old Telephony Services

PROSA   PRO-Active Self-Adaptation

QoS   Quality of Service

RDF   Resource Description Framework

RDFS   RDF Schema

RE   Requirements Engineering

REST   Representational State Transfer

RMC   Rational Method Composer

RPC   Remote procedure call

RUP   Rational Unified Process

SAM   System Architecture Model

SAWSDL   Semantic Annotations for WSDL

SBA   Service Based Application

SCR   Service Communication Router

SDD   Strategic Dependency Diagram

SerDiQueL Service Discovery Query Language

SIMS   Semantic Interfaces for Mobile Services

SLA   Service Level Agreement

SMS   Short Message Service

SOA   Service-oriented Architectures

SOAD   Service-oriented Analysis and Design

SoaML   Service-oriented Architecture Modelling Language

SOAP   Simple Object Access Protocol

SOC   Service-oriented Computing

SOMA   Service-oriented Modeling and Architecture

SOMF   Service-oriented Modeling Framework

SWS	Semantic Web Services
SyBM	System Behavioural Model
SL	Second Life
SySM	System Structural Model
UDDI	Universal Description Discovery and Integration
UML	Unified Modeling Language
VMF	VRESCo Mapping Framework
VO	Virtual Operator
VoIP	Voice over IP
VQL	VRESCo Query Language
WADL	Web Application Description Language
WCF	Windows Communication Foundation
WF-nets	Workflow nets
WS-BPEL	Web Services Business Process Execution Language
WSDL	Web Services Description Language
WSML	Web Service Modeling Language
WSMO	Web Service Modeling Ontology
WSMO-Lite	Web Service Modeling Ontology Lite
WSMX	(Web Service Modeling eXecution environment
XMI	eXtensible Markup Interchange
XML	Extensible Markup Language
XPath	XML Path Language
XQuery	XML Query Language
XSD	XML Schema Definition

Chapter 1
Describing Case Studies and Classifying Research Approaches

Antonio Bucchiarone, Raman Kazhamiakin, Valentina Mazza, and Pierluigi Plebani

Abstract This initial chapter aims at providing a useful introduction and reference point to the research described in the following chapters. First of all, to provide a homogenous description of the existing approaches on service engineering, we introduce a common case study referring to the telecommunication domain. This case study will be used in the other chapters of this book to motivate and describe the presented approaches. The way in which the case study is described follows the approach developed in the S-Cube Network of Excellence. In addition, we also provide a classification of the research results proposed in the rest of the book, by relying on the S-Cube Integrated Research Framework. Such a classification allows the reader to have an idea about how the contributions deal with research in the service engineering field.

1.1 Introduction

Case studies can be described in various ways depending on their purposes. For instance, they can describe a specific development or proof of concept using a specific technology, or they can simply describe an application case without offering a specific implementation solution. Of course, while in the first case the case study description contains also design, implementation, and even deployment and operation details, in the second case it should be implementation and technology agnostic. Since, of course, we are thinking of case studies supported by software, the descrip-

Antonio Bucchiarone and Raman Kazhamiakin
FBK-IRST
Via Sommarive 18 - 38050 Trento, Italy
e-mail: [bucchiarone,raman]@fbk.eu

Valentina Mazza and Pierluigi Plebani
Dipartimento di Elettronica ed Informazione, Politecnico di Milano
Via Ponzio 34/5 - 20133 Milano, Italy
e-mail: [vmazza,plebani]@elet.polimi.it

1

tion should focus on *what* expectations the software should address more than on *how* these should be addressed. In other terms, the description should be focusing on eliciting those *goals* and *assumptions* that the software should address.

As the term case study has been used in the literature to mean a problem together with a specific solution, the goal of this chapter is to introduce two results from the S-Cube Network of Excellence [1]. On the one hand, in Section 1.2 we introduce the case study description approach proposed in the S-Cube project [4]. By relying on this approach, this chapter describes a common case study that will be referred by the contributions in this book presented in the next chapters. On the other hand, in Section 1.3 we discuss the S-Cube Integrated Research Framework (IRF): a coherent holistic framework that integrates the principles, techniques, methods and mechanisms provided by the research activities done in the S-Cube project. Using the IRF, we are able to classify and compare the solutions about the described case study [5].

1.2 Mobile Phone Services Portability Case Study

The case study introduced in this chapter and used all along the book is about *mobile phone services portability*.

Voice and data services are provided by a set of mobile telecommunication companies around Europe. There companies are usually called Cell Phone Operators (CPOs). Some of these CPOs operate in a single country, whereas some others are big CPOs that have branches in several countries. Inhouse services are offered by the CPO to manage all the customers and the stipulated contracts. Moreover the customers can view personal information about their contracts accessing to a suitable services made available by the telephone operator, or some user could query all the services offered by the CPO accessing its public services. Not all the CPOs have their own telecom infrastructures; some of them rent the network services from big telecom companies and provide a service to the users. Such operator are called Virtual Operators (VOs).

The case study presented in this chapter is about the additional services that a company support to allow the portability of the phone number and the portability of services.

The possibility to change a mobile phone operator without changing the mobile phone number is one of the mandatory services that a mobile phone operator must provide. National and European laws regulate this procedure with the aim of allowing the customers to freely select the best company according to their requirements to be advantaged by the more suitable or cheapest services offered by the new phone operator, without advising his contacts of a new telephone number.

It might also happen that the portability is only about the services on which a customer is subscribed. For instance, a customer might move from an European Coun-

---

[1] S-Cube NoE Web site: http://www.s-cube-network.eu

try to another for a limited period, e.g., one year, but keeping his subscription, even with a new phone number, with the company and using the same services already available but not by roaming. At the end of such period, the customer could move back to his home country again, picking up his original telephone number and subscription. Starting from this description of the case study, we could identify the following stakeholders:

- Cell Phone Operators (CPOs)
- Customers

In order to make case studies comparable and easy to understand, S-Cube has defined a case study description approach that leverages the results achieved by NEXOF-RA [2] and from the Requirements Engineering literature [6]. The usage of such an approach for revising and describing all cases has been very useful to highlight inconsistencies and to identify those aspects in the case study that cover the elements considered relevant for the research.

The proposed approach is adopted in this chapter to describe in a more systematic way the mobile service portability case study that is used along the book. In more detail, the case study is described in terms of:

- A list of *Business Goals* and *Domain Assumptions* for the case study.
- A *Case Study Domain Description*.
- A list of *Scenario Descriptions*.

1.2.1 Business Goal and Domain Assumptions

Business Goals and the Domain Assumptions define the functionalities and the properties of both the machines and the environment where the systems operate. Whereas the business goals state the functionalities of the product, the domain assumptions report properties or restrictions of the system. For each Domain Assumption and Business Goal a table reports a description of it, the stakeholders involved, the rationale, the priority and the material supporting the description, if any.

To better understand the domain of the case study, we use a glossary to explain some specific terms that could be unknown outside the specific domain. Often the glossary is not enough, consequently the description should be enriched using UML diagrams [3], or Entity-Relationship diagrams, and so on.

1.2.1.1 Business Goals

Business Goals report all the functionalities of the system; referring to this case study we could define the following goals:

- To provide mobile phone number portability
- To provide mobile services portability

- To satisfy national and european rules
- To make the portability as transparent as possible to the customer
- To provide new added-value services

The following tables describe each listed business goal.

Table 1.1: To provide mobile phone number portability

Field	Description
Unique ID	TELCO_BG_01
Short Name	To provide mobile phone number portability
Type	Business Goal
Description	The system shall offer some capabilities to permit the portability of a mobile phone number across different CPOs. Service portability makes possible to the customers change the telephone operator keeping their old phone numbers. The customer could decide to move to a certain CPO, since the charges it has for a particular service are more convenient for him. The customer would avoid to have a new telephone number, since he should have to notify all his contacts of the changed number.
Rationale	Satisfy the need of a customer that want to take advantage of the services of a certain CPO without change his old telephone number.
Involved Stakeholders	CPOs and customer
Priority of accomplishment	Must have

Table 1.2: To provide mobile services portability

Field	Description
Unique ID	TELCO_BG_02
Short Name	To provide mobile services portability
Type	Business Goal
Description	The system shall enable a customer moved to another country to use the service already subscribed in the former country. Maybe not all services are available, but services could be composed by existing ones or even, if no other options are available, the customer could be linked to his home country for this service (with an extra-fee).
Rationale	Satisfy the need of a customer that want to take advantage of the services of a certain CPO when moving in the countries where CPO operates.
Involved Stakeholders	CPOs and customer
Priority of accomplishment	Must have

Table 1.3: To satisfy national and european rules

Field	Description
Unique ID	TELCO_BG_03
Short Name	To satisfy national and european rules
Type	Business Goal
Description	European and National governments strictly regulate some of the services provided by the CPO. As a consequence, several regulations had been approved especially for making the change of a mobile operator as simple and economic as possible. Since these rules change during the time, the system should be able to promptly react.
Rationale	Enable a quick reaction in case of new European and National regulations.
Involved Stakeholders	CPO
Priority of accomplishment	Must have

Table 1.4: To make the portability as much transparent as possible to the customer

Field	Description
Unique ID	TELCO_BG_04
Short Name	To make the portability as much transparent as possible to the customer
Type	Business Goal
Description	To improve the customer satisfaction the portability of services and numbers should be transparent to the user. As a consequence, the user can interact either directly to the system by a Web application or supported by a company employee to apply for the number portability. The customer should realize that the number portability occurred only at the end of the process. Only in case of problems, the customer will be contacted.
Rationale	To improve the customer satisfaction
Involved Stakeholders	CPOs and customer
Priority of accomplishment	Should have

Table 1.5: To provide new added-value services

Field	Description
Unique ID	TELCO_BG_05
Short Name	To provide new added-value services
Type	Business Goal
Description	The system shall enable CPOs to easily provide new services. Mainly regarding on the evolution of the Web and the spread of new application under the 2.0 umbrella, CPOs need to increase the number of services by considering all the users that consume this kind of applications.
Rationale	Increase the market rate.
Involved Stakeholders	CPOs and customer
Priority of accomplishment	Should have

1.2.1.2 Domain Assumptions

Domain assumptions report all the properties and the constraint of the system. For the considered case study we could define the following domain assumptions:

- Distributed companies

* Service provisioning

Table 1.6: Distributed companies

Field	Description
Unique ID	TELCO_DA_01
Short Name	Distributed companies
Type	Domain assumption
Description	The CPO consists of multiple departments, possibly spread over multiple nations. In-house Services are shared among departments: e.g., CRM, Billing, and so on.
Rationale	
Involved Stakeholders	CPO
Priority of accomplishment	Must have

Table 1.7: Service provisioning

Field	Description
Unique ID	TELCO_DA_02
Short Name	Service provisioning
Type	Domain assumption
Description	The system shall provide some useful services the customer could access. After an authentication phase the customer should access to personal data and get information about the contracts, the billing and so on. He could decide to change his contract choosing a more suitable telephone charges, or he could have a service to pay the billings.
Rationale	Make available services to the customers.
Involved Stakeholders	CPO and customer
Priority of accomplishment	Must have

1.2.2 Domain Analysis

For the domain descriptions of the case study, Strategic Dependency Diagrams (SDDs) [1] and/or Context Diagram (CD) [6] are used. In particular, the SDDs are used to model the dependencies among the actors involved in the organisational context. Dependency edges in the diagram link the actors with needs (dependers) to actors with the capability of satisfying those needs (dependees). The needs are expressed in terms of goals (positioned on the edges). In addition to the SDD it could be useful to enhance the description with the CD. In such a diagram the boxes represent all the active entities of the case study, while the direct arrows represent the phenomena between the agents. The source of the edge is the controller of the phenomena, while the destination is the agent monitoring the phenomenon. In the diagram, the system under study represents a particular agent.

1.2.2.1 Strategic Dependency Model and Context Diagram

Figure 1.1 illustrates the strategic dependency diagram of the case study. The diagram puts in evidence the business goals (the ellipses in the diagram) shared among the actors (the yellow circles in the diagram) of the scenario, showing the dependencies among them. The CPOs offer their services satisfying the national and the european rules; their goal is the provisioning of services useful to the customers in order to get information about the status of their contracts and/or to change them. In particular the current case study focuses on the provisioning of the telephone number portability service; such service should be offered to the customer in a transparent way.

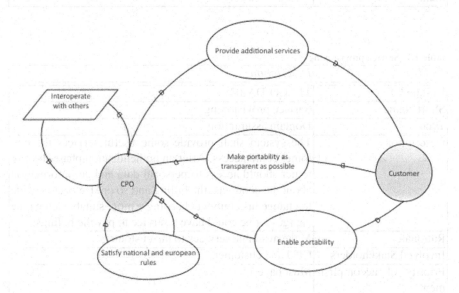

Fig. 1.1: Strategic dependency diagram

Figure 1.2 illustrates the context diagram of the current case study. In the context diagram, all the actors that appear in the business goals and scenarios are agents.

1.2.2.2 Domain Model

Figure 1.3 illustrates the domain model of the current case study. A UML notation is used to represent the entities and the actors involved in the case study and the relationships among them. The CPO stipulates a *Contract* with a *Customer*. A contract is characterized by the particular *Fares* to pay for the service usage; it could include

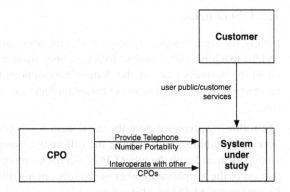

Fig. 1.2 Context diagram

the basic *Voice Service* or some additional service (*Value Added Service*) provided by the CPO, such as e-mail services, SMS services and so on. When a Customer requires a *Telephone Number Portability* of his telephone number moving from a CPO to another one, such portability is associated to a contract. Moreover, the diagram illustrates the possibility of a Customer to access to different type of *Services* provided by the CPO.

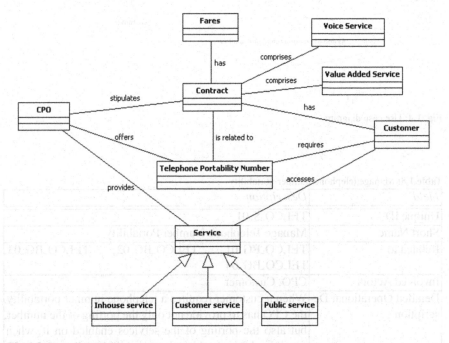

Fig. 1.3: Domain model

1.2.3 Scenarios

Finally, the scenarios description includes the phenomena shared between the world and the machine. Here, a scenario is described using a table containing information about the business goals or the domain assumptions they refer to, the operational description of the scenario, the eventual problem involved and the supporting material.

The following scenarios describe the system for the management of Mobile Phone Service Portability; they assume the different departments of a CPO cooperating among them and with the other CPOs. Scenarios report the basic process behind the request of the telephone number portability among different CPOs and the portability for the same CPO in different countries.

Figure 1.4 shows the general use-case diagram for the case study we are considering.

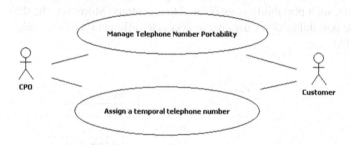

Fig. 1.4: Use case diagram

Table 1.8: Manage telephone number portability

Field	Description
Unique ID	TELCO_S_01
Short Name	Manage Telephone Number Portability
Related to	TELCO_BG_01, TELCO_BG_02, TELCO_BG_03, TELCO_BG_04
Involved Actors	CPO, Customer
Detailed Operational Description	When a customer requires a telephone number portability, the CPO has to provide not only the porting of the number, but also the porting of the services enabled on it, when possible. After checking the portability of the number the CPO executes the porting. At the end of the process the number is activated and bound to the new CPO.

continued on next page ...

Table 1.8: Manage telephone number portability (continued)

Field	Description
Problems and Challenges	Problems and challenges in this scenario are mainly related to the integration among the CPOs and the departments.
Additional Material	The following diagram describes the process:

Table 1.9: Temporary mobile services portability

Field	Description
Unique ID	TELCO_S_02
Short Name	Temporary mobile services portability
Related to	TELCO_BG_01, TELCO_BG_02, TELCO_BG_03, TELCO_BG_04
Involved Actors	CPO, Customer
Detailed Operational Description	It could be happen that, for a limited period, a customer has to move to another country. During the stay, the customer would avoid to pay the roaming charges when receive or make a phone call, maintaining his CPO; so he would have assigned, from the CPO, a new temporal telephone number in the new country. When, at the end of such period, the customer comes back to his home country, he would take possession of the original telephone number and subscription. In addition to the new telephone number, the customer can also port additional services as, for instance, SMS service and UMTS service. The porting of all of these services are independent each other. So, the customer can ask to port only some of them.

continued on next page ...

Table 1.9: Temporary mobile services portability (continued)

Field	Description
Problems and Challenges	Problems and challenges in this scenario are mainly related to the integration of the departments of the same CPO, located in different countries.
Additional Material	The following diagram describes the process where: • In order to port a number to another subsidiary of the CPO, the customer, first, has to file a request. • The CPO checks whether it is possible to port the number and any additional services and calculates the associated costs. In this case, the CPO calculates 10 € for porting the phone number and the SMS service and 50€ for porting the UMTS service. • The customer decides that he only wants to port his phone number since the porting of the UMTS service seems to be too expensive for him. • In parallel to the execution of this porting a bill is issued and the money arrival is monitored. • At the end of the process, the customer receives a report, which confirms the complete-ness of this transaction. 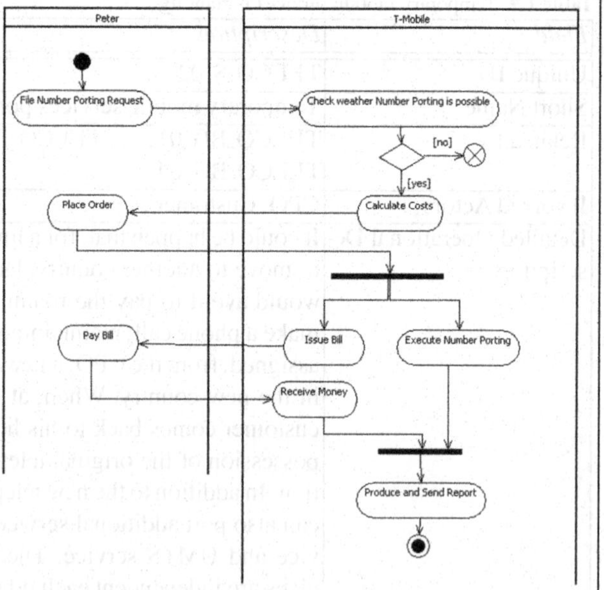

Table 1.10: Social network integration

Field	Description
Unique ID	TELCO_S_03
Short Name	Social network
Related to	TELCO_BG_03, TELCO_BG_05
Involved Actors	CPO, Customer
Detailed Operational Description	The innovation department of the telecom company decides to launch a new service which offers their customers a promotion to see free pay-per view movies. Customers can send up to 10 invitations to their friends of a social network to watch one free movie per invitation. Customers can customise the invitation, selecting the friend from the social network, one movie and including some text. Friends can accept the invitation, which includes providing some marketing info. Once the friends accepts the invitation, the customer is also allowed to see the film. The service will provide valuable information about the success of the promotion, providing different reports based on the collected marketing data.
Problems and Challenges	Problems and challenges in this scenario are mainly related to the integration of CPOs and social network applications
Additional Material	none

1.3 Research Results Classification

As a second main contribution of this chapter, we introduce the S-Cube IRF as a way for organizing the research challenges and results about Service-based Applications (SBAs). Focusing on the Service Engineering perspective, this approach will be used in Section 1.3.3 to classify the results that are introduced in the next chapters.

1.3.1 S-Cube Integrated Research Framework

The IRF for SBAs of S-Cube, aims to integrate, align, and coordinate the joint research activities undertaken within the project. To achieve this, IRF provides a coherent and holistic view on the principles and mechanisms for SBAs. In particular, the IRF should encompass those aspects of the research that are cross-cutting and defines proper interfaces among the research components of the overall conceptual network architecture. To continuously coordinate and align the research roadmap of the project as a whole, the framework is continuously validated with the help of the industrial case studies. The ultimate goal of the validation is to revise and improve the IRF.

More specifically, the IRF may be represented with the eight macro elements that are clustered into four conceptual blocks as represented in Figure 1.5:

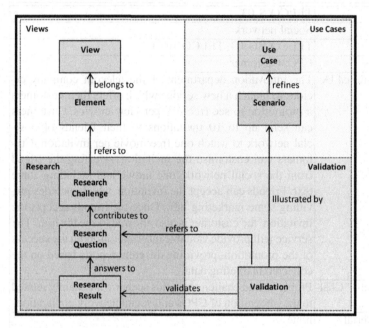

Fig. 1.5: Structure of the IRF

- The "Views" block represents the different perspectives that are considered by the S-Cube research activities and cover various aspects of the latter with respect to the SBAs. These views, namely "Conceptual Research Framework", the "Reference Life-cycle", "Logical Run-time Architecture", and "Logical Design Environment", are the most stable elements of the IRF. They also define the key *elements* of the framework, such as the blocks of the conceptual framework and their relations, phases of the SBA life-cycle, or modules of the logical run-time architecture.

- The "Research" block defines the objectives and results of the S-Cube research activities layered in *Research Challenges* (i.e., long-term research goals to form the S-Cube roadmap), *Research Questions* (i.e., specific short-term research objectives), and the *Research Results* (outcomes and achievements of the research efforts that aim to answer those questions).

- The "Use Cases" block defines the industrial case studies developed by the S-Cube consortium in a strong synergy with the industrial partners of the project. These case studes are the essential elements for the continuous validation of the research efforts of the project. On the one hand, the case studies are used to illustrate the research challenges of the IRF and to motivate specific research problems. On the other hand, they are exploited to validate the research outcomes. This is achieved through the definition and evaluation of the specific scenarios emerging from those use cases and industrial application domains.

- Finally, the "Validation" block defines the actual process of the IRF validation. Specifically, the validation captures the specific goal of the validation activity, the scenario used in that activity, the set up, the validated result, and the outcome of the validation process. Based on those outcomes, the research activities, as well as the IRF, are continuously revised and improved.

1.3.2 S-Cube Research Challenges

The research agenda of S-Cube covers a wide range of the long-term objectives in the area of the SBAs, in general, and of Service Engineering in particular. To illustrate those objectives, namely research challenges in the terminology of the S-Cube IRF, we present the S-Cube Conceptual Research Framework that corresponds to one of the IRF views. We classify the research challenges according to the elements of this framework.

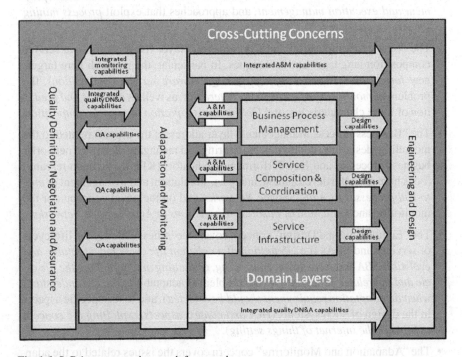

Fig. 1.6: S-Cube conceptual research framework

As it is shown in Figure 1.6, the conceptual research framework consists of six related blocks, where horizontal components define "traditional" domain layers of

SBAs (Service Infrastructure, Service Composition and Coordination, and Business Process Management) and the vertical components defines the cross-cutting issues (Engineering and Design, Adaptation and Monitoring, Quality Definition, Negotiation and Assurance) crucial for the SBA research udertaken in S-Cube. In this way, the framework systematically addresses cross-cutting issues making explicit the knowledge of the horizontal layers that is relevant for these issues, and that currently is mostly hidden in specific and isolated languages, standards, and mechanisms. To do this, the used approach is that the domain layers offer (design, monitoring, adaptation, verification) capabilities that are relevant for the cross-cutting issues. The vertical components define over-arching principles and methodologies by exploiting in suitable ways the capabilities exposed by the horizontal components.

With respect to the S-Cube research agenda, these components define a wide range of the research challenges, where the Service Engineering holds a primary role:

- The "Service Infrastructure" layer studies a high-performance execution platform supporting adaptation and monitoring of SBAs (e.g., self-* mechanisms). Specifically, the challenges addressed here include the problem of *multi-level and self-adaptation*, novel mechanisms and techniques related to the *deployment and execution management*, and approaches that exploit *process mining for service discovery*.

- The "Service Composition and Coordination" layer focuses on novel service composition languages and techniques. In particular, the research here targets new *formal models and languages for QoS-aware service compositions*, the problem of *monitoring of quality characteristics*, as well as *analysis and prediction* of these characteristics, and *QoS-aware adaptation in service composition*.

- The "Business Process Management" layer addresses the aspects related to the modelling, designing, deploying, monitoring and managing of service networks, business processes and Key Performance Indicators (KPIs). The main research focus here is on the development, analysis, simulation, and management of *end-to-end processes in Agile Service Networks*, and on the novel concepts for the monitoring and validation of *business transactions in Agile Service Networks*.

- The "Engineering and Design" concern covers the issues related to the life-cycle of services and SBAs (i.e., *definition of a coherent life cycle for adaptable and evolvable SBA* and *measuring, controlling, evaluating and improving the life cycle and the related processes*), to the problem of adaptability (i.e., to *understand when an adaptation requirement should be selected*), and to the specific aspects in the design of such systems (*HCI and context aspects, exploiting the concept of SBAs in the internet of things setting*).

- The "Adaptation and Monitoring" concern covers the issues related to the adaptation of a SBA. Addressing the problem that is cross-cutting to the technology layers, here the research challenges include *comprehensive and integrated adaptation and monitoring principles, techniques, and methodologies*, the problem of *proactive adaptation and predictive monitoring*, studying the role of human actors in the adaptation process (*context and HCI aspects in the monitoring and adaptation, mixed initiative SBA adaptation*).

- The "Quality Definition, Negotiation and Assurance" concern involves principles and methods for defining, negotiating and ensuring quality attributes and Service Level Agreements (SLAs). Starting from the definition of comprehensive, *end-to-end quality reference model* and *rich and extensible quality definition language*, this component addresses such problems as *exploiting user and task models for automatic quality contract establishment, proactive SLA negotiation and agreement, run-time quality assurance techniques* and *quality prediction*.

1.3.3 Research Results in Service Engineering

In this section we introduce briefly the research results in Service Engineering that will be described in detail in the rest of the book, by relying on the IRF presented in the section above. The classification has been done using the research challenges introduced before and the output is depicted in Figure 1.7. It shows which aspect of the S-Cube research framework is covered by the approaches. In the following paragraphs we better explain this coverage.

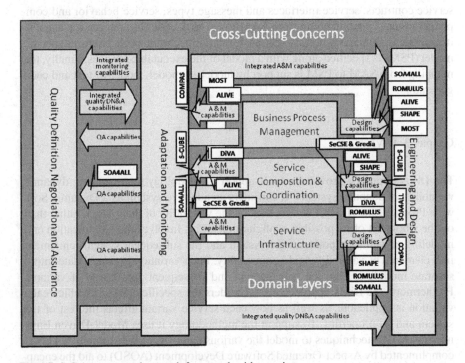

Fig. 1.7: S-Cube conceptual research framework with mappings

Chapter 2. SHAPE

The goals of Chapter 2 are to support the activities of service modeling and design and to fit into an overall model-driven development approach. In it a UML profile has been defined to support the range of modeling requirements for service-oriented architectures, including the specification of service implementations. This is done using an automatic artifacts generation following an Model-Driven Architecture (MDA) based approach. The main objective was to provide a foundation for Model-Driven Service Engineering (MDSE) based on the MDA approach. A MDSE supports the activities in service engineering by developing models and performing activities on them such as transformations, simulation and validation. Its main challenge was to define a consistent and comprehensive top-down approach which supports service modeling starting from higher models such as goal models, requirements models or business process models down to the modeling of services and their realization. The methodology guides developers through different phases of modeling to identify services within a service-oriented architecture, covering aspects such as service contracts, composition and integration. Starting from the Business Architecture Model (BAM) which includes goals, business processes, business informations and organization modeling the approach proceeds identifying the Service Architecture Model (SAM). The latter specifies the services architecture, the service contracts, service interfaces and message types, service behavior and component models. The mapping from BAM to SAM is done through service capabilities modeling and/or using model transformation techniques. A platform-specific model (PSM) is specified along with a model of the executable services. Finally, the mapping from SAM to PSM is support by model-to-model, model-to-text and code generators.

Chapter 3. DiVA

The DiVA approach provides a tool-support methodology for managing dynamic variability in adaptive systems. It considers an adaptive system as a Dynamic Software Product Line (DSPL) and focuses on the variability of the system, rather than on the whole set of its possible configurations. This involves the identification and modeling of variation points in the system and the subsequent system refinement into elements of variability and commonality. Each variation is consolidate into a separate module to ease the management and subsequent application of variants. Furthermore, the DiVA approach also considers the specific context to which each variation is applicable, as well as how each service variant affects the rest of the system and its properties. To support the methodology it uses Model-Driven Engineering (MDE) techniques to model the various elements of the variability. This is complimented by Aspect-Oriented Software Development (AOSD) to aid the encapsulation of the variants identified.

Chapter 4. ALIVE

In Chapter 4 an architecture for the deployment and management of dynamic, flexible and robust service-based applications is proposed. Its main challenge is to create a framework for services engineering addressing the new reality of open systems of active services. The proposed architecture is composed of three layers for the design and management of distributed systems, namely: *services, coordination* and *organization*. The *service layer* extends existing service models to make them aware of their social context and of the rules of engagement with other services. It is concerned with the description of services, the selection of appropriate services for a given task and the execution and monitoring of services associated with a given organization. The *coordination layer* provides the means to specify, at a high level, patterns of service interactions using a variety of powerful coordination techniques based on agent technology. The *organizational layer* resides above coordination, providing a social context for the coordination and service levels. This level specifies the rules that govern interaction and defines the system on the basis of goals and results, abstracting away from the specific actions used to accomplish them. This engineering approach does not provide a coherent life-cycle to design, realize and maintain services and SBA but only a set of modeling approaches for each layer with the support to transform a model in another model or models into text using the Model Driven Development principles. Unlike the organizational layer, the coordination and service layers of the system are supposed to adapt to the current situation. Regarding the adaptation challenge the framework proposes a way to monitor the service level and adapt it at run-time. Other levels react to this adaptation with restructuring but they do not provide separate monitoring and adaptation strategies and mechanisms. No cross-layers monitoring and adaptation approaches are provided.

Chapter 5. COMPAS

In Chapter 5 the authors propose an approach to monitor business processes with the objective to check the conformance of an organization's business activities and practices with existing laws, regulations and its own internal policies. This is a result in the COMPAS project that aims to design and implement novel models, languages, and an architectural framework. By achieving these goals, the project ensures dynamic and on-going compliance of software services to business regulations as well as stated user service-requirements. The main result of this project is an event-based monitoring framework for business processes at runtime. The monitoring proposed is model-aware, in the sense that it can access and reflect on process models at runtime. High-level events (that correspond to business events), containing references to the process models, are recognized from low-level process events using complex event processing techniques. The model references enable runtime retrieval and reflection on the original process models. As a consequence, the size of the events is kept small and (new) models and model elements can be considered during monitoring.

Chapter 6. S-CUBE

The adaptation of a service-based application (SBA) can address various goals, such as corrective and perfective adaptations. In the first case the objective is to recover or even prevent potential failures of the SBA functioning, while in the second case the SBA is adapted in order to better meet its requirements. When the adaptation deals with the replacement of services in a workflow realizing the application, corrective adaptation aims at removing the service with unsatisfactory behavior, and perfective adaptation aims at promoting new service with better characteristics.

In Chapter 6 a framework to integrate and align perfective and corrective adaptations is presented. In this framework, requirements engineering techniques are used to realize and to trigger perfective adaptations. More specifically, it uses goal-driven design approach based on Tropos methodology to define the SBA requirements and to decompose them into plans corresponding, e.g., to service binding. The analysis techniques based on the goal models are applied in order to see whether the newly available services suit better the requirements of the SBA. If this is the case, requirement engineer can promote the usage of such a service instead of the ones currently exploited by the enterprise.

To realize the corrective adaptation, the framework exploits online testing techniques. Specifically, based on the SBA model (i.e., its workflow and constituent services), a set of test cases is generated and executed in different moments of time in order to see whether the executed SBA instance satisfies its requirements. In case of test failure adaptation is triggered and the violating services are replaced. It is important to note that both of the above techniques share the characteristics that they are pro-active in nature, i.e., both techniques trigger adaptation (suggest service replacement) before the possible problem (or inefficient service use) takes place.

Finally, the framework integrates both perfective and corrective adaptation within the same architecture. For this purpose, an enterprise service registry is exploited. New services are added to the registry as an outcome of the requirement engineering analysis, while the old services may be removed from the registry if suggested by the online testing results. The execution of the SBA workflow based on dynamic binding techniques ensures that the proper services are then used by the SBA at run-time. Targeting primarily adaptation based on the service replacement and binding, the framework mostly operates at the domain layer of service composition and coordination, providing the corresponding design capabilities (based on goal-driven requirements engineering) and adaptation and monitoring capabilities (based on online testing and service replacement).

Chapter 7. ROMULUS

In Chapter 7 a service development approach, based on Domain Driven Design (DDD), has been proposed. Principally it uses a common language which describes the application model, assisted by graphical notations, and maintaining the model very close to its implementation. It proposes a precise method to develop services that is organized in layers where each layer depends only on the layers below. These layers are: User Interface, Service, Domain and Infrastructure. The *Infrastructure Layer* provides support to the rest of layers such as persistence of the domain, messaging, logging or network I/O. The *Domain Layer* represents the business logic of the application. The *Service Layer* exposes services of the domain layer while the *User Interface Layer* is responsible for showing the information to the user. Moreover a precise design approach is defined that starts from the service identification to the end user programming and customization of services through the domain design of services and aspect identification, development and testing. The main challenge of this project is to use the DDD approach to develop a Service and how to compose, customize and extending services using mashup technology. A Mashup Builder has been developed and provides a graphical user interface for building mashups easily, allowing the user to develop mashups faster. It allows the user to combine information obtained from different services.

Chapter 8. MOST

In Chapter 8 authors consider the business process management (BPM) discipline where a service is seen as an encapsulation of a business process. They provide a *refinement technique* of business processes. A refinement can be generally seen as a technique which allows to add more information to a model on a certain abstraction level while preserving the original information and constraints on a more abstract level. The refinement technique is especially useful when several people with different expertise and responsibilities work on the same business process. In this paper two kinds of refinement have been defined: horizontal and vertical. *Horizontal refinement* is a transformation from an abstract to a more specific process which contains the composition of activities. It is also called decomposition. *A vertical refinement* is a transformation from a principle behavior model (i.e., BPMN processes) of a component to a process model.

Chapter 9. SOA4ALL

The main purpose of the idea proposed in Chapter 9 is to create complex and distributed systems by seamlessly combining Web services. Using semantic-based technologies, an adaptive process, able to provide adaptive late-binding capabilities within workflows has been defined. The approach is based on the use of Semantic Web Services, that is of semantic annotations of services that support the application of automated machinery in order to reason about the functional and non-functional characteristics of services. In particular, it advocates that workflow definitions use service template as internal activities instead of concrete and prefixed services whenever flexibility in service selection is desired. At run-time, these services templates can be bound to specific services selected on the basis of the existing conditions and informed by contextual knowledge which may include monitoring data, user location or other aspects that may affect which service is the most appropriate. Since that service templates are described semantically, both the required functional and non-functional properties have clear semantics. This enhances the interpretation of services by humans, and more importantly, it allows service selection and data mismatches to be resolved at runtime as supported by Semantic Web Services middleware. Non functional information about cost, QoS, trust, legal constraints, etc.. can be taken into account so that the selected service is the most suitable from a business perspective. The overall approach relies on the provisioning of semantic annotation for services and the corresponding storage and querying system, on the replacement of workflow activities by service templates, and on the adaptation of execution environments in order to take service templates into account and trigger the selection of appropriate services automatically.

Chapter 10. SeCSE and Gredia

In Chapter 10 authors present main results of the two projects SeCSE and Gredia. More precisely they introduce a framework to design and adapt service-based systems. From the design point of view they show the iterative design process supported by the framework. It uses structural and behavioral design models of service-based systems to support discovery of services that can fulfill the models. The identified services are used to reformulate the design models and trigger new service discovery iterations. Finally, UML class and sequence diagrams are used to define structural and behavioral models. From the adaptation point of view it supports execution time adaptation using special servers and listeners to allow notifications of changes in services and application environment. To adapt service-based applications a process is used that allows services to be identified based on both pull and push modes of query execution. The pull mode of query execution is performed to identify services while the push mode is performed when the application is running and a service needs to be replaced.

Chapter 11. VreSCO

VreSCO the Vienna Runtime Environment for Service-oriented Computing has in part been developed within the FP7 Network of Excellence project S-Cube. It provides a solution for some issues and shortcomings that are prevalent in current SOA research and practice. First and foremost it constitutes a service registry that is used by providers to store information about services in a (meta-)data model. The distinction between abstract features (metadata model) and concrete service implementations (service model) allows to group service instances that provide an identical functionality. Moreover, it enables clients to query the stored information using the specialized query language VQL in order to dynamically select an endpoint for their invocations. The selection may be based on functional criteria which concern the interface (or service contract), but also on non-functional criteria in the form of QoS attributes. The Daios framework employs an abstracted message format and is used in VreSCO to realize dynamic and protocol-independent invocations. The VreSCO data model supports explicit visioning of service revisions, operations and parameters. User-defined and default tags describe the features of a service revision and its position in the version graph. With the aid of mapping functions, the VreSCO runtime mediates between service instances which perform the same task but differ in their technical interface.

Acknowledgements The research leading to these results has received funding from the European Community's Seventh Framework Programme FP7/2007-2013 under grant agreement 215483 (S-Cube).

References

1. i-star software formalism. `http://www.ics.uci.edu/~alspaugh/software/istar.html`
2. NESSI Open Framework - Reference Architecture (NEXOF-RA): Scenarios and Requirements for Open Framework Construction. `http://www.nexof-ra.eu/?q=rep/term/200`
3. Abdullah, M.S., Benest, I.D., Paige, R.F., Kimble, C.: Using unified modeling language for conceptual modelling of knowledge-based systems. In: Conceptual Modeling - ER 2007, 26th International Conference on Conceptual Modeling, Auckland, New Zealand, November 5-9, 2007, Proceedings, pp. 438–453 (2007)
4. S-Cube Consortium: Deliverable CD-IA-2.2.2 - Collection of Industrial Best Practices, Scenario and Business Cases (2009)
5. S-Cube Consortium: Deliverable CD-IA-3.1.1 - Integration Framework Baseline (2009)
6. Jackson, M.: Software requirements & specifications: a lexicon of practice, principles and prejudices. ACM Press/Addison-Wesley Publishing Co., New York, NY, USA (1995)

Chapter 2
Model-driven Service Engineering with SoaML

Brian Elvesæter, Cyril Carrez, Parastoo Mohagheghi, Arne-Jørgen Berre, Svein G. Johnsen and Arnor Solberg

Abstract This chapter presents a model-driven service engineering (MDSE) methodology that uses OMG MDA specifications such as BMM, BPMN and SoaML to identify and specify services within a service-oriented architecture. The methodology takes advantage of business modelling practices and provides a guide to service modelling with SoaML. The presentation is case-driven and illuminated using the telecommunication example. The chapter focuses in particular on the use of the SoaML modelling language as a means for expressing service specifications that are aligned with business models and can be realized in different platform technologies.

Brian Elvesæter
SINTEF ICT, P. O. Box 124 Blindern, N-0314 Oslo, Norway, e-mail: `brian.elvesater@sintef.no`

Cyril Carrez
SINTEF ICT, P. O. Box 124 Blindern, N-0314 Oslo, Norway, e-mail: `cyril.carrez@sintef.no`

Parastoo Mohagheghi
SINTEF ICT, P. O. Box 124 Blindern, N-0314 Oslo, Norway, e-mail: `parastoo.mohagheghi@sintef.no`

Arne-Jørgen Berre
SINTEF ICT, P. O. Box 124 Blindern, N-0314 Oslo, Norway, e-mail: `arne.j.berre@sintef.no`

Svein G. Johnsen
SINTEF ICT, P. O. Box 124 Blindern, N-0314 Oslo, Norway, e-mail: `svein.g.johnsen@sintef.no`

Arnor Solberg
SINTEF ICT, P. O. Box 124 Blindern, N-0314 Oslo, Norway, e-mail: `arnor.solberg@sintef.no`

2.1 Introduction and Overview

2.1.1 Background and Motivation

There are two major trends in modern service engineering. Firstly, service-oriented architecture (SOA) has emerged as a direct consequence of specific business and technology drivers that have materialized over the past decade. Trends such as the outsourcing of non-core business operations, the importance of business process re-engineering and the need for system integration have been key influences in pushing SOA as an important architectural approach to information technology (IT) today. Secondly, modelling has become an integral part of software engineering approaches. Business process models are ideally used to describe how work is done within an enterprise, while various technical models describe the IT systems. There are several approaches to model-driven engineering (MDE) such as the OMG Model Driven Architecture (MDA)[1] [12] and efforts around domain-specific languages which have recently gained much popularity.

In MDA, business models are described as computational independent models (CIMs). For the IT models, MDA separates platform-independent models (PIMs) from platform-specific models (PSMs) in order to abstract the implementation technologies. It is also common to model a system from different views or perspectives such as its structure and behaviour. In addition to models, MDA includes the mechanism of transformations to provide mappings between representations of the system on different abstraction levels. Due to the powerful concepts of abstraction and refinement, MDA is being increasingly applied in various domains and for different types of applications, thus making it also an attractive solution for implementing the new wave of applications based on service-oriented architectures. In order to do so, new methodologies and languages with concepts required for modelling of services are required.

SOA has been promoted for some years without a specific language that supports modelling services. In order to meet this requirement the Service oriented architecture Modelling Language (SoaML) [16] was specified. The goals of SoaML are to support the activities of service modelling and design and to fit into an overall model-driven development approach. The SoaML profile defines extensions to UML 2 [17] to support the range of modelling requirements for service-oriented architectures, including the specification of systems of services, the specification of individual service interfaces, and the specification of service implementations. This is done in such a way as to support the automatic generation of derived artefacts following an MDA based approach.

The role of the SoaML specification is to specify a language, i.e., a metamodel and a UML profile, for the design of services within a service-oriented architecture. However, developing services requires a language and a process. It is not the role of the specification to define a methodology, but rather to provide a foundation for model-driven service engineering (MDSE) based on the MDA approach that can be adopted

---

[1] OMG Model Driven Architecture (MDA), http://www.omg.org/mda/

in different software development processes. The aim of this chapter is to provide a methodology for the SoaML language. This methodology was developed as part of the 7th Framework Programme research project SHAPE (ICT-2007-216408)[2].

2.1.2 Solution Idea

The business requirements of real-world applications require a flexible development approach to service-based IT landscapes that enables the businesses to exploit the benefits of the SOA paradigm in an efficient manner. We assume that there should be a systematic approach to service development which we refer to as service engineering. Service engineering should ideally cover all phases of a service life-cycle: from collecting requirements to the stages of development or identifying services, composition, operation, monitoring and evolution. A challenge is therefore to identify activities in software engineering related to the concept of services and SOA.

Generally speaking, a methodology describes a regular and systematic way of how to accomplish something. The term methodology here denotes a set or collection of methods and related artefacts needed to support the model-driven engineering of SOA-based systems. Our view of methodology aligns with [5] who defines methodology as a "body of methods, meant to support all software development phases" and with [7] who defines methodology in the context of model-based systems engineering as the "collection of related processes, methods, and tools used to support the discipline of systems engineering in a model-based or model-driven context".

To address this need we present a model-driven service engineering (MDSE) methodology based on the OMG MDA approach [12]. The methodology guides solution architects in how to specify services that are aligned with the business process models. The focus of the MDSE methodology presented here is on the analysis and design of service-oriented architectures. Rather than providing a comprehensive methodology for supporting the engineering process for SOA systems, the aim is to define SOA modelling guidelines that can be included in existing model-driven methodologies. The MDSE methodology takes advantage of the SOA concepts defined in SoaML which allows to:

1. **Identify services** and the requirements they are intended to fulfil, and the anticipated dependencies between them.
2. **Specify services**, including the functional capabilities they provide, what capabilities consumers are expected to provide, the protocols or rules for using them, and the service information exchanged between consumers and providers.
3. **Define service consumers and providers**, what requisition and services they consume and provide, how they are connected and how the service functional capabilities are used by consumers and implemented by providers in a manner consistent with both the service specification protocols and requirements.

---

[2] Semantically-enabled Heterogeneous Service Architecture and Platforms Engineering (SHAPE), http://www.shape-project.eu/

4. **Define policies** for using and providing services.

5. **Define architectural classification schemes** having aspects to support a broad range of architectural, organizational and physical partitioning schemes and constraints.

2.1.3 Outline of the Approach

Our MDSE methodology aims to integrate with existing business modelling practices within an enterprise, allowing building upon and extending existing modelling practices rather than replacing them. The methodology assumes that modern business modelling practices take advantage of business modelling tools that adopts the OMG MDA specifications Business Motivation Model (BMM) [13] and Business Process Modeling Notation (BPMN) [14]. From these models we will drive the specification of services as a set of SoaML model artefacts.

The MDSE methodology provides guidelines for how to use SoaML to define and specify a service-oriented architecture from both a business and an IT perspective. The methodology prescribes building a set of model artefacts following the iterative and incremental process paradigm. Figure 2.1 depicts the overall process and identifies the set of model artefacts to specify. The figure shows the set of work products prescribed by the methodology and the overall workflow. The icons indicate the associated BMM, BPMN or SoaML diagram(s) for each work product and the arrows show the most common path through the set of work products within an iteration.

Starting from the upper left we have the *Business Architecture Model (BAM)* which includes the business goals, business processes, capabilities, services architectures, and service contracts and choreographies. The *System Architecture Model (SAM)* specifies the service interfaces, interfaces and message types, service choreographies and software components. The *model-to-model (M2M) transformation* consists of transformation rules and procedural guidelines to support a semi-automated mapping from BAM to SAM.

The *Platform-Specific Model (PSM)* contains the design and implementation artefacts of the specified service-oriented architecture in the chosen technology platforms, e.g. cloud, Web Services, Java Enterprise Edition (JEE), multi-agent systems (MAS), peer-2-peer (P2P), grid and Semantic Web Services (SWS). We consider PSM-level modelling guidelines out of scope for the presentation of the methodology in this chapter and focus on the business architecture and system architecture modelling. PSM-level extensions to the methodology would involve defining further modelling guidelines and *model-to-text (M2T) transformation* rules for the technology platforms.

We use and extend the Eclipse Process Framework (EPF)[3] for implementing the methodology. EPF is a process framework that allows to define methodology and process content that can be customized and integrated with other engineering

---

[3] Eclipse Process Framework (EPF), http://www.eclipse.org/epf/

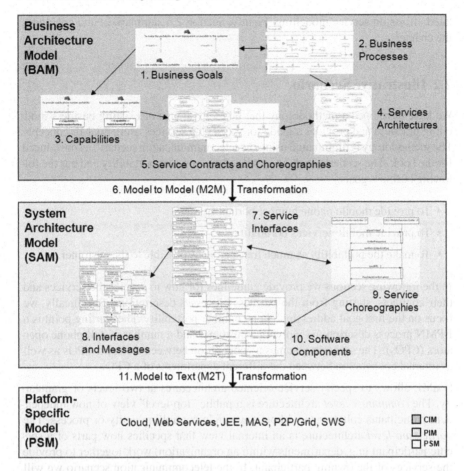

Fig. 2.1: The overall model-driven process

methodologies. The methodology presented here is dependent on modelling tools that support the OMG specifications BMM, BPMN and SoaML. In the example presented in this chapter we have used the UML modelling tool Modelio[4].

2.1.4 Structure of the Chapter

The remainder of this chapter is organized as follows: In Section 2.2 we introduce the telecommunication scenario that we use to illustrate our model-based service engineering methodology. Section 2.3 presents the business architecture modelling guidelines to describe the business perspective of an SOA, and Section 2.4 presents the system architecture modelling guidelines to describe the IT perspective of an SOA. Section 2.5 contains a discussion of our results in comparison with other re-

---

[4] Modeliosoft, http://www.modeliosoft.com/

lated efforts on service modelling. Finally, Section 2.6 summarizes and concludes the chapter.

2.2 Illustrative Scenario

We have developed a methodology that takes advantage of existing business modelling practices and provides a guide for specifying services using SoaML concepts. The methodology is illuminated using the telecommunication scenario as introduced for the book. The scenario is about mobile phone services portability and has the following business goals:

- To provide mobile phone number portability.
- To provide mobile services portability.
- To make the portability as much transparent as possible to the customer.

In the following sections we provide guidelines for how to specify the services and their contracts, starting from the business processes descriptions. Specifically, we focus on the first goal addressing phone number portability. The starting point is a BPMN process description involving a customer and a number of cell phone operators (CPOs). The scenario assumes a cooperation between different CPOs as well as internal cooperation between the different departments of a CPO.

SoaML allows to specify service-oriented architectures at two levels of granularity. The *community-level* architecture is a public "top-level" view of how independent participants collaborate without any single controlling entity or process. The *participant-level* architecture is an internal view that specifies how parts of a specific participant (e.g. departments within an organization) work together to provide the services of the owning participant. In the telecommunication scenario we will show how to apply SoaML to specify a *community-level* architecture and how this is refined into a *participant-level* architecture and further mapped to a software architecture for a specific CPO named *AcmeCPO*.

The BPMN process diagram shown in Figure 2.2 describes the request and assignment of mobile services portability. When a *Customer* requires a telephone number portability, the *AcmeCPO* has to provide not only the porting of the number, but also the porting of the services enabled on it, when possible. After checking the portability of the number the CPO executes the porting. At the end of the process the number is activated and bound to the new CPO.

2.3 Business Architecture Modelling

This part of the methodology covers selected areas of CIM-level modelling resulting in a *Business Architecture Model (BAM)* that describes the business perspective of a service-oriented architecture. The BAM is used to express the business operations

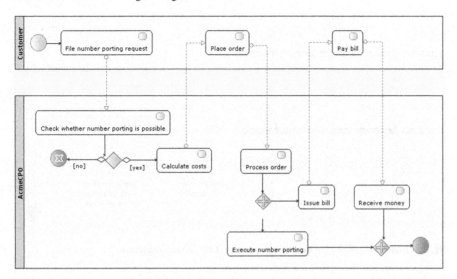

Fig. 2.2: Request and assignment of mobile phone services portability (BPMN diagram)

and environment which the service-oriented architecture is to support. The BAM includes business goals (Section 2.3.1), business processes with associated organisation roles and information elements (Section 2.3.2), and capabilities (Section 2.3.3) that are relevant for capturing business requirements and identify services within a service-oriented architecture. The BAM further describes the services architecture (Section 2.3.4) of the business community and the service contracts (Section 2.3.5) between the business entities participating in the community. Figure 2.3 depicts an activity diagram that shows the modelling tasks involved in the specification of the Business Architecture Model.

2.3.1 Business Goals

Business Motivation Model (BMM) [13] is a business-level modelling technique that supports the modelling of the business goals and objectives, the means and policies to achieve them, and the influencing factors that drive and control the work involved. This is typically used to define the overall business strategy in early phases of an engineering project.

The purpose of the BMM is to agree with the business stakeholders the business goals that will be met by implementing the service-oriented architecture, so that a set of required high level business processes can be identified for further analysis. BMM provides a scheme or structure for developing, communicating, and managing business plans in an organized manner. In particular, the BMM supports the following:

- It identifies factors that motivate the establishment of business plans.

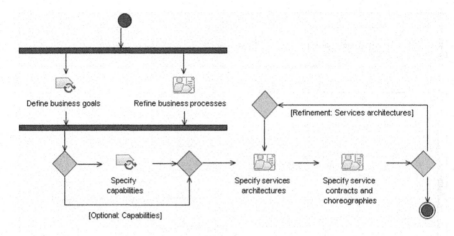

Fig. 2.3: Business architecture modelling activities (EPF activity diagram)

- It identifies and defines the elements of business plans.
- It indicates how all these factors and elements inter-relate.

Among these elements, business policies and business rules provide governance for and guidance to the business. Once produced and agreed, the BMM serves as a reference that ensures that a full assessment may be made of all the business implications of any proposed changes to the service-oriented architecture.

2.3.1.1 Modelling of Business Goals

Business goals are discovered by a process of workshops and interviews involving relevant stakeholders. The BMM describes a loose hierarchy of goals of the business within the particular area of concern, from the goals of a business stakeholder in developing a product to the business goals met by the product or its users.

The goals are created as classes containing motivation-related information. The name is expressed in a natural language and has properties such as scope, quantitative/qualitative value, etc. Relationships between goals such as "part of", "positive influence", "negative influence", "guarantee" and "measure" can be specified. Figure 2.4 shows the goals specified for the telecommunication example.

2.3.2 Business Processes

Business Process Modeling Notation (BPMN) [14], is designed to communicate a wide variety of information on business processes to a wide variety of audiences, providing a standard notation that is readily understandable by all business stakeholders. Business process descriptions bring real business vision and constitute an excellent formalization and analysis tool when constructing systems. In the context

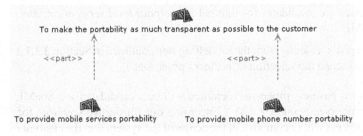

Fig. 2.4: Business goals diagram (BMM diagram)

of a development project they are used in business-oriented activities related to requirements, specifications and analysis.

Business processes may be at a number of levels of detail, from a high level description of the business processes down to task flows which comprise a set of detailed specifications for the business services to be realized in the service-oriented architecture. BPMN is designed to cover many types of modelling and allows the creation of end-to-end business processes. It allows the specification of private processes (both non-executable and executable), public processes, choreographies and collaborations.

Typically, BPMN is used to define business processes on the CIM level. The definitions are then mapped to more technical models on the PIM and PSM level. Our methodology does not address the full scope of business modelling at the CIM level, but rather assumes that some kind of business process models or descriptions already exist that have been developed using existing BPMN guidelines. However, typically these models must be further refined and mapped to SoaML concepts for describing the business perspective of an SOA.

2.3.2.1 Modelling of Business Processes

The BAM should contain refined descriptions of the business processes which are relevant to the service-oriented architecture to be defined. These are the business processes that will enable the goals to be met and include the roles which collaborate through services that are to be specified and developed.

The first step is to identify the relevant business processes for the service-oriented architecture, following these guidelines:

- Identify public and collaborative business processes that involve interactions and potential usage of software services between different business organizations. These processes are candidates for public *community-level services architectures* in SoaML.

- Identify private business processes for the business entities under your ownership control that are involved in the services architecture under consideration.

These processes are candidates for internal *participant-level services architectures* in SoaML.

- The business goals resulting from the modelling steps outlined in Section 2.3.1.1 can be used to scope the selection of business processes.

Each of the selected business processes identified will be a candidate for a SoaML services architecture (see Section 2.3.4). Concerning our illustrative scenario, the public business process will encompass all the actors of the system (i.e. the customer and the different CPOs, as it will be exemplified hereafter); the private business process will encompass the *AcmeCPO*.

Once the business processes have been identified, their specification can begin. Each business process will be specified in a business process diagram and refined with respect to participants, their tasks, and information flow between the participants.

Participants represent the business units or organization roles that are involved in the execution of a process. Participants are specified using the BPMN constructs: *pools*, *participants* and *lanes*. Pools represent business organizations and lanes represent internal business units within an organization.

Each participant will perform different tasks and exchange information with other participants. The next step is to focus on the tasks which describe the interaction points between the business entities. These interaction points will be associated with service contracts in SoaML (see Section 2.3.5). Each task will possibly create, manipulate and use some information items. The following BPMN constructs are used for information modelling: *data objects*, *data inputs and outputs*, *data associations* and *messages*.

Figure 2.5 shows the refined business process model for the request and assignment of mobile phone services originally depicted in Figure 2.2. Three different participants take part in this process: *Customer*, *AcmeCPO* and *OtherCPO*. The interaction points between the participant tasks have been further revised by modelling data objects that are typed as specific message types, e.g. *PhoneNumberPortabilityRequest*. The tasks in the *OtherCPO* participant are considered private, thus from the perspective of *AcmeCPO* we only model the public information exchange.

Since the focus of our modelling refinement is on *AcmeCPO*, we can also specify an internal process that details the *AcmeCPO* pool. As can be seen in Figure 2.6 we have introduced two new roles represented by the lanes *CustomerManager* and *CPOManager* and assigned the tasks specified in the pool to these two roles according to whether the task is oriented towards the customer or another CPO. The figure only shows a partial left view of the BPMN diagram to illustrate the refinements with regards to the lanes.

2.3.3 Capabilities

Capabilities identify or specify a cohesive set of functions or resources that a service provided by one or more participants might offer. Capabilities can be used by

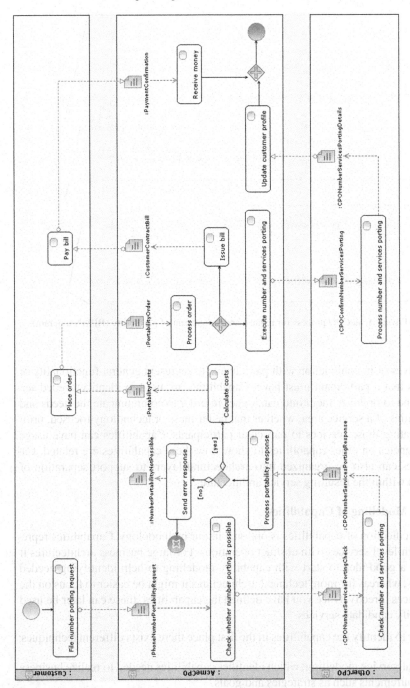

Fig. 2.5: Public community process for request and assignment of portability (BPMN diagram)

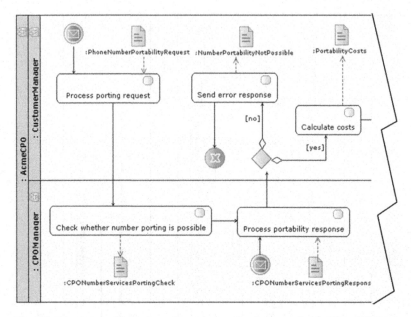

Fig. 2.6: Private *AcmeCPO* process for request and assignment of portability (BPMN diagram)

themselves or in conjunction with participants to represent general functionality or abilities that a participant must have. Capabilities are used to identify needed services, and to organize them into catalogues in order to communicate the needs and capabilities of a service area, whether that be business or technology focused, prior to allocating those services to particular participants. Capabilities can have usage dependencies on other capabilities to show how these capabilities are related. Capabilities can also be organized into architectural layers to support separation of concern within the resulting service architecture.

2.3.3.1 Modelling of Capabilities

The specification of capabilities is optional in our methodology. Capabilities represent high-level services with abstract operations. For large business architectures it may be a good idea to start with capability modelling to help identifying needed services, whereas for more technical architectures it might be easier to focus on the IT services directly. Once you have defined the capabilities, these can later be used to identify candidate services.

In order to identify the capabilities in the first place there exists different techniques:

- Goal-service modelling, which identifies capabilities needed to realize business requirements such as strategies and goals.
- Domain decomposition, which uses activities in business processes and other descriptions of business functions to identify needed capabilities.

• Existing asset analysis, which mines capabilities from existing applications.

Figure 2.7 shows a simple example of two capabilitites that were derived from the business goals (Figure 2.4).

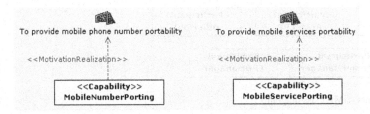

Fig. 2.7: Capabilities (UML class diagram)

2.3.4 Services Architectures

A *services architecture* is a high level description of how participants work together for a purpose by providing and using services expressed as *service contracts*. The services architecture defines the requirements for the types of *participants* and service realizations that fulfill specific roles. A *role* defines the basic function (or set of functions) that an entity may perform in a particular context. In contrast, a participant specifies the type of a party that fills the role in the context of a specific services architecture. Both service contracts and participants can be reused when composing different services in other services architectures.

2.3.4.1 Modelling of Services Architectures

Services architectures are modelled as UML collaborations with the stereotype ≪ServicesArchitecture≫. A services architecture has components at two levels of granularity: The *community services architecture* is a "top level" view of how independent participants work together for some purpose. The services architecture of a community does not assume or require any single controlling entity or process. The public process described in Figure 2.5 maps to a community-level services architecture for the telecommunication scenario.

A participant may also have a *participant services architecture*, which specifies how parts of that participant (e.g., departments within an organization) work together to provide the services of the owning participant. Participants that realize this specification must adhere to the architecture it specifies. The internal process described in Figure 2.6 maps to a participant-level architecture for *AcmeCPO*.

Participants are modelled as UML classes stereotyped ≪Participant≫. Participants are identified from pools, participants and lanes specified in the BPMN processes (see Section 2.3.2.1). Figure 2.8 shows the participants identified from the two BPMN process diagrams: the three pools in Figure 2.5 map to the three participants

Customer, *AcmeCPO* and *OtherCPO* for the community-level services architecture. The two lanes in the Figure 2.6 map to the two participants *CustomerManager* and *CPOManager* which are internal roles in the *AcmeCPO* participant-level services architecture.

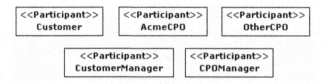

Fig. 2.8: Participants (UML class diagram)

The next step is to identify the possible interactions between the different participants. The interactions are represented as service contracts. A service contract is a UML collaboration with the stereotype ≪ServiceContract≫. In this step, only an empty UML collaboration is specified. The detailing of the service contracts will be further elaborated in Section 2.3.5.1.

Once all service contracts and participants have been identified, the service designer can use them to build the service architecture. Roles in the UML collaboration are typed by the identified participants, while UML collaboration uses are linked to the service contracts. The modeller has to bind the different roles to the appropriate collaboration uses, hence specifying how participants will interact.

Concerning the scenario, Figure 2.9 shows the two resulting services architectures. The *CommunityMobilePhoneServicesPortability* specifies the community-level architecture with its three participants that are connected together by four collaboration uses which are linked to the service contracts *NumberPortingRequest*, *PlaceOrder*, *CheckNumberServicesPorting* and *ProcessNumberServicesPorting*. The *AcmeCPOMobilePhoneServicesPortability* shows how *AcmeCPO* is organized internally to provide services. Two additional participants *CustomerManager* and *CPOManager* have been specified, connected by the service contracts *AcmeCheckMobileServicesPorting* and *AcmeExecuteMobileServicesPorting*. These two participants represent internal roles that are connected to the existing, external roles and the corresponding service contracts specified in the community-level services architecture.

2.3.5 Service Contracts and Choreographies

SoaML allows different approaches to specify services. In our methodology, we have chosen to combine two different approaches, as we see one fits more at the business level (service contract approach) and the other at the IT level (service interface approach). In the business architecture modelling we suggest to use service contracts that are further refined to service interfaces in the system architecture modelling.

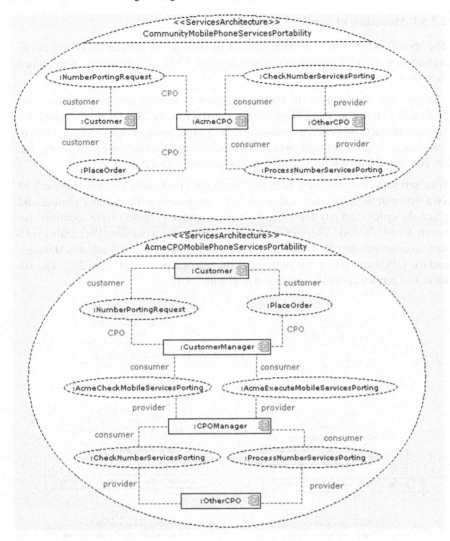

Fig. 2.9: Services architecture (UML collaboration diagram)

A *service contract approach* defines service specifications (the service contract) that define the roles each participant plays in the service (such as provider and consumer) and the interfaces they implement to play that role in that service. The service contract represents an agreement between the involved participants for how the service is to be provided and consumed. This agreement includes the interfaces, choreography and any other terms and conditions. Service contracts are frequently part of one or more services architectures that define how a set of participants provide and use services for a particular business purpose or process.

2.3.5.1 Modelling of Service Contracts

The specification of service contracts can be seen as the refinement of a services architecture. Service contracts are specified as UML collaborations stereotyped ≪ServiceContract≫.

The first step is to analyse the BPMN diagrams to identify service contracts. This is a design-choice as there is no single construct in the BPMN that resembles a service contract. However, a certain pattern of objects can reveal service contracts, for instance when two single tasks follow one after another across a pool or lane and are connected with a sequence flow and associated with a data object.

Four services contracts were identified from the community process (Figure 2.5). Two between the *Customer* and *AcmeCPO*: requesting a file number porting and place the order (and pay the bill). Two other service contracts were identified between *AcmeCPO* and *OtherCPO*: checking and actually processing the number porting. Another two service contracts were identified between the *CustomerManager* and the *CPOManager* in the analysis of the internal process (Figure 2.6). The six identified service contracts are shown in Figure 2.10.

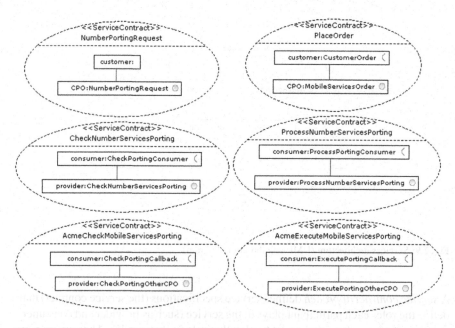

Fig. 2.10: Service contracts (UML collaboration diagram)

Once the service contracts are identified, one has to specify the consumer and provider roles. These roles are typed by corresponding UML interfaces stereotyped ≪Consumer≫ and ≪Provider≫ respectively. At this modelling step we only identify the names and possibly some high-level operations in the interfaces. These interfaces will be further elaborated and refined as part of the system architecture modelling. Figure 2.10 shows the six service contracts, with their interfaces. The first one, *NumberPortingRequest*, represents a simple service where any consumer can use the service without any contractual obligations. It has two roles: *customer* and *CPO*, but only the *CPO* role has an interface type, namely *NumberPortingRequest*. The five other service contracts specify that there are contractual obligations on both the consumer and provider side, which means that both roles must have an interface type. For example, the service contract *PlaceOrder* specifies the interface *CustomerOrder* for the *consumer* role and the interface *MobileServicesOrder* for the *CPO* role.

Each interface will define (business) operations. The arguments of those operations specify the information elements that are exchanged. These information elements can be derived from the business processes, where the information items map to a message type or a data entity in SoaML. Message types and data entities are defined as stereotypes on a UML class. So a first step would be to create these information items as regular UML classes, and then refine them to either message types or data entities as part of the system architecture modelling (see Section 2.4.2.1). The information modelled here does not need to be complete. It may be sufficient to just link the class to a particular information standard or just describe the most important properties of the data objects. For instance Figure 2.11 shows a partial view of the data objects identified in the BPMN process (Figure 2.5). These data objects are represented as SoaML message types and have been linked with the BPMN data objects.

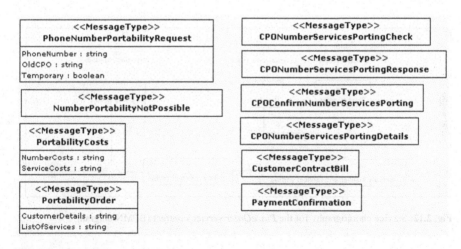

Fig. 2.11: Message types (UML class diagram)

2.3.5.2 Modelling of Service Choreographies

A choreography is a specification of what is transmitted and when it is transmitted between participants to enact a service exchange. The choreography defines what happens between the provider and consumer participants without defining their internal processes - their internal processes do have to be compatible with their service contracts.

We recommend to model the behaviour of any complex service contract in order to get a better understanding of the interaction between the roles. A starting point for specifying the behaviour of the service contracts are the BPMN process diagrams. Thus, BPMN may be the preferred formalism to use for describing service choreographies at the business level. Figure 2.12 shows the part of the BPMN process related to the service contract *PlaceOrder*. Modelling the service choreographies also gives you an opportunity to revise and further refine the information exchange between the two parties. This model will later be refined at the IT level as part of the modelling of the corresponding service interface and its service choreography (see Section 2.4.3).

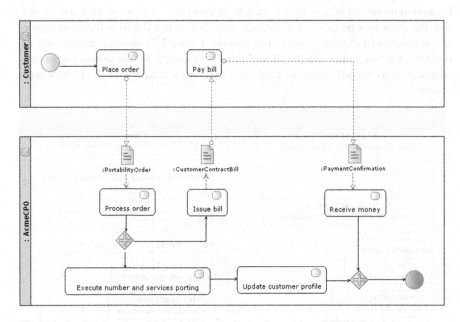

Fig. 2.12: Service choreography for the *PlaceOrder* service contract (BPMN diagram)

2.4 System Architecture Modelling

The *System Architecture Model (SAM)* describes the IT perspective of a service-oriented architecture. The SAM is a refinement of the BAM, and is used to express the overall architecture of the system at the PIM level. It partitions the system into components and defines the components in terms of what interfaces they provide, what interfaces they use, and how these interfaces should be used (protocol). Two aspects of component collaborations are described: the static model (structure) and dynamic model (behaviour). The structural model describes the components, their dependencies, and their interfaces; the dynamic model describes the component interactions and protocols.

The methodology first starts by refining the service contracts of the BAM by defining service interfaces (Section 2.4.1) with the associated interfaces and messages (Section 2.4.2) and service choreographies (Section 2.4.3) which define the protocols to use when accessing those interfaces. Software components are then specified and composed in a component architecture (Section 2.4.4). Figure 2.13 depicts an activity diagram that shows the modelling tasks involved in the specification of the System Architecture Model.

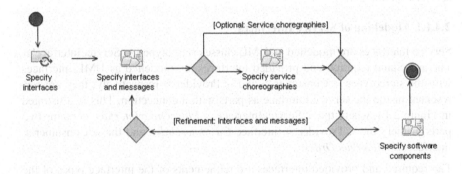

Fig. 2.13: System architecture modelling activities (EPF activity diagram)

2.4.1 Service Interfaces

The service contracts specified in the business architecture modelling (Section 2.3.5) are refined to *service interfaces* in the system architecture modelling. The service interfaces specify the interactions between the software components of the service-oriented architecture: service interfaces will serve as port types on software components (Section 2.4.4). SoaML allows for two approaches:

- **Simple interface based approach:** A *simple interface* specifies a unidirectional service, focusing on a one-way interaction provided by a participant on a port. The participant receives operations on this port and may provide results to the caller. A simple interface can be used with "anonymous" callers where the participant makes no assumptions about the caller or the choreography of the service. The one-way service corresponds most directly to simpler remote procedure call (RPC) style Web services.

- **Service interface based approach:** A *service interface* specifies a bi-directional service, where "callbacks" exist at the provider's side (in addition to the usual operations at the consumer's side), allowing an exchange from the consumer to the provider as a part of a conversation between the two parties. A service interface defines the interface and responsibilities of the provider and the consumer of a service, by including commands and information by which actions are initiated (Section 2.4.2), and by optionally including specific protocols (Section 2.4.3).

A service interface will type the service port of a software component, hence specifying that this component provides the service on that port (Section 2.4.4). SoaML also defines a *conjugate service interface*, where the consumer and provider are inverted from the associated service interface; the name of a conjugate service interface is the same as the associated service interface, with a tilde '~' in front. A conjugate service interface will type the request port of a software component consuming the service (Section 2.4.4).

2.4.1.1 Modelling of Service Interfaces

Service interfaces are modelled as UML classes stereotyped ≪ServiceInterface≫. The associated required and provided interfaces are modelled as UML interfaces with the stereotypes ≪Consumer≫ and ≪Provider≫ respectively; they are represented inside the service interface as parts with a connection. This is illustrated in Figure 2.14, where the ≪ServiceInterface≫ *PlaceOrderInterface* contains two parts, namely the ≪Provider≫ interface *CustomerOrder* and the ≪Consumer≫ interface *MobilServiceOrder*.

The required and provided interfaces are refinements of the interface types of the consumer and provider roles defined in the service contracts. However, in the service contracts these interfaces were primarily defined as business-level interfaces. These interfaces can be refined directly, or possibly mapped to a new set of interfaces that will be used to detail the IT-level artefacts. Figure 2.14 shows such a refinement, where each service contract maps to a corresponding service interface with a new set of consumer and provider interface types. These interfaces will be used to further detail the specification for the software components (see hereafter).

2.4.2 Interfaces and Messages

The provided and required interfaces of the previous section are refined with operations and callbacks, hence specifying how to interact with a component that provides or uses such interfaces. The operations are specified in the provided interface, while the callbacks are specified as part of the required interface, hence allowing a conversation between provider and consumer of a service.

Arguments of operations and callbacks can make use of messages, which specify the kind of data expected. There are several SOA interaction paradigms in common use, including document centric messaging, remote procedure calls (RPC),

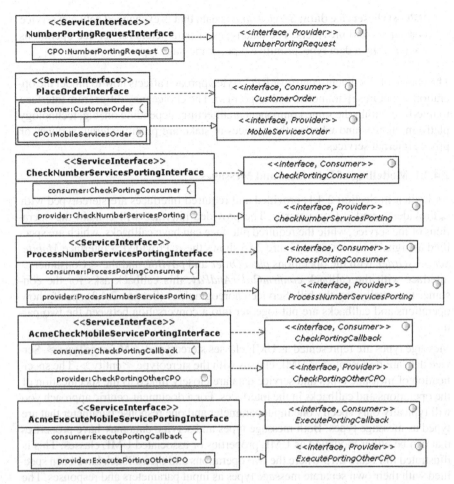

Fig. 2.14: Service interfaces (UML class diagram)

and publish-subscribe. The decision depends on cohesion and coupling, state management, distributed transactions, performance, granularity, synchronization, ease of development and maintenance, and best practices. SoaML supports document-centric messaging and RPC-style service data:

- **Document-centric messaging:** *Message types* specify the information exchanged between service consumers and providers. Message types represent "pure data" that may be communicated between parties – it is then up to the parties, based on the SOA specification, to interpret this data and act accordingly. As "pure data" message types may not have dependencies on the environment, location or information system of either party. A message type is in the domain or service-specific content and does not include header or other implementation or protocol-specific information.

- **RPC-style service data:** *Service data* is data that is exchanged between service consumers and providers. The data types of parameters for service operations are typed by a data type, primitive type, or message type.

The choice of document-centric or RPC-style approach affects how to model the operation signatures (parameters and responses). The choice may differ from interface to interface within the same component architecture, depending on, e.g. technology platform choices and whether the services at stake are public external services or private internal services.

2.4.2.1 Modelling of Interfaces and Messages

As written in Section 2.4.1, provided and required interfaces are stereotyped with ≪Provider≫ and ≪Consumer≫. The provided interface will contain the operations of the service, while the required interface can have callbacks, which are specified as signals. For instance Figure 2.15 shows the ≪Provided≫ interface *Mobile-ServicesOrder* with the operations *placeOrder* and *payBill*, and the ≪Consumer≫ interface with the callback *confirmOrderAndPay*; this callback asks for the consumer to actually pay the bill. Service choreographies (Section 2.4.3) specify how operations and callbacks are put together into a conversation between the two parties.

Message types are represented as UML classes stereotyped ≪MessageType≫. Service data are represented as UML classes with the stereotype ≪entity≫. The specification of message types and service data are closely linked to the specification of the operations and callbacks in the interfaces. For a document-centric approach you will typically only specify one input parameter and one response parameter that are typed as message types. Both message types and service data may have properties that can be either modelled as UML properties or associated UML classes. This is illustrated in Figure 2.15 where the two operations and the callback have been specified with their own separate message types as input parameters and responses. The message types *OrderRequest* and *OrderResponse* have both properties and associated classes that contain additional information to support the customer in browsing the cost of the services before selecting the ones to be ported and enabling whether a temporary or fixed porting should be enabled.

2.4.3 Service Choreographies

The behaviour of a service interface expresses the expected interaction between the consumers and providers of services. It is a refinement of the behaviour of service contracts (Section 2.3.5), and is mostly used in association with bi-directional services, where operations and callback need to be sequenced in a specific manner. The components taking part in the service at stake will then have to act according to the protocol specified by the service choreography.

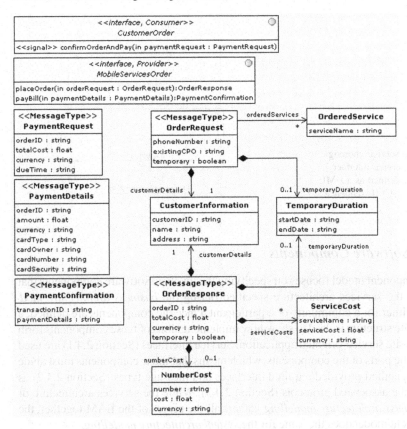

Fig. 2.15: Interfaces and message types (UML class diagram)

2.4.3.1 Modelling Service Choreographies

Service choreographies can be specified as any UML behavior, the most common ones being activity, interaction or state machine. One has to specify the message sequence between the consumer and provider interfaces. The sequence should be linked to operations defined in the interfaces. The modelling of the service choreography is an iterative process that is linked to revising the interfaces and messages (Section 2.4.2), until a complete service choreography can be specified.

Figure 2.16 specifies the behaviour of the service interface *PlaceOrderInterface* using an interaction diagram. The service interface describes a bi-directional service with a call-back at the client-side (see Figure 2.15). The *customer* invokes the operation *placeOrder* on the interface *MobileServicesOrder*. A message type *OrderResponse* is returned to the customer. Then the *CPO* invokes the callback *confirmOrderAndPay* on the interface *CustomerOrder* at the customer-side which triggers a signal forcing the customer to confirm and pay for the order and invoke the operation *payBill*.

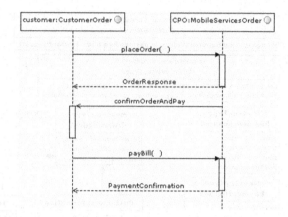

Fig. 2.16 Service choreography or service interface behaviour defined as a UML interaction (UML sequence diagram)

2.4.4 Software Components

The component model focuses on specifying the involved software components that realizes the services architecture specified during the *business architecture modelling*, either for a community or a participant. Once the components are defined, a composite structure is used to show how implementations of these components form a composite service-oriented application. Service interfaces (Section 2.4.1) are used to type the ports of the components, which means that those components must abide by the specified provided/required interfaces and message types (Section 2.4.2) as well as the associated protocols (Section 2.4.3). While the services architecture of the *business architecture modelling* gathers all the pieces of the BAM together, the component model does the same for the *system architecture modelling*.

2.4.4.1 Modelling Software Components

Software components are modelled as components with composite structures using class diagrams in UML. Each participant in the services architecture of the BAM can be refined into SoaML participant in the SAM. SoaML participants of the SAM represent software components that realize the service contracts specified for the business organizations (specified as SoaML participant) in the Business Architecture Model. For instance the three participants of the community services architecture of Figure 2.9 are refined and assembled in the component model of Figure 2.17 (i.e. components *CustomerWeb*, *AcmeCPOServices* and *OtherCPOServices*).

The next step is to connect the software components together, through their ports. Each port of a component is either a ≪Service≫ port or a ≪Request≫ port. The former will provide a service, and is typed by a service interface; the latter is a consumer of a service, and is typed by the conjugate service interface. A ≪Service≫ port will then have to implement the operations specified in the associated ≪Provider≫ interface, while the ≪Request≫ port will have to implement the callbacks specified in the associated ≪Consumer≫ interface. The ports can then be connected such that they have matching types. This is exemplified in

Figure 2.17, where the three components are connected using request and service ports. For instance, the component *CustomerWeb* has a port which is typed by the conjugate service interface *~PlaceOrderInterface*, which means that it has to implement the callback *confirmOrderAndPay* specified in the ≪Consumer≫ interface *CustomerOrder*. Similarly the component *AcmeCPOServices* has a port which is typed by the service interface *PlaceOrderInterface*, which means the component has to implement the operations defined in the ≪Provider≫ interface *MobileServicesOrder* (see Figure 2.14). As the two ports are typed by matching interfaces, they can be connected together.

Finally, the internals of the software components can be further refined. The two components *CustomerManager* and *CPOManager* inside the *AcmeCPOServices* corresponds to the participants defined for the participant-level services architecture of Figure 2.9. These two internal components are interconnected through the *AcmeCheckMobileServicesPortingInterface* and *AcmeExecuteMobileServices-PortingInterface* request (conjugate service interface) and provider (service interface) port types.

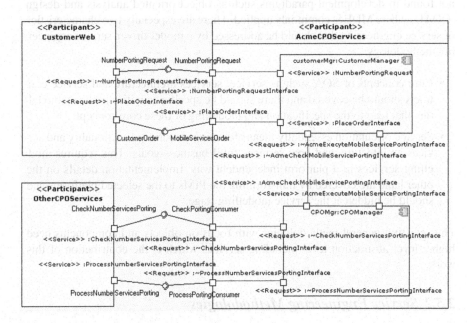

Fig. 2.17: Software components (UML class diagram)

Note that not all software components can be specified fully in this manner. Indeed some components are provided or developed by third parties, which means that their internal structure may be unknown. However, such component must behave according to the service interfaces that type their ports, possibly including the corresponding service choreographies. This is why the system component *OtherCPOServices* of Figure 2.17 has no internal structure and is specified as a "black-box".

2.5 Related Work and Discussion

In this section, we discuss the work presented in this chapter and compare it with other efforts on service modelling. We first consider the model-driven methodologies in general and how they need extensions to cover service engineering activities. Then we focus on service engineering methodologies and how our service modelling approach can be integrated in these by using SoaML as a means for service specification.

2.5.1 Model-Driven Methodologies

There are many general purpose model-driven methodologies such as the Rational Unified Process (RUP) [11] and KobrA [3]. These methodologies have differences and similarities but they all emphasize on the systematic use of models as primary software artefacts throughout the software engineering life-cycle.

However, service engineering needs additional artefacts and activities which are not found in development paradigms such as object-oriented analysis and design (OOAD) where MDE is commonly applied. There are especially two characteristics of service engineering that should be addressed by a model-driven service engineering methodology:

- Core concepts of SOA such as service, services architecture and service contracts should be covered and there should be specific activities in the methodology that lead to the specification and modelling of these core concepts.
- Service orientation essentially means focusing on service functionality and services architecture, and how services fulfil business goals. This requires modelling services in a platform independent way. Implementation details on the other hand are covered by transforming the PIMs to the selected platforms and should be hidden at the service modelling stage.

Thus existing general methodologies with focus on objects and components need higher level abstraction level including services which is the contribution of this work.

2.5.2 Service Engineering Methodologies

There are numerous methods for technologies related to service-based system engineering where [4] provides a comprehensive overview. SOAD (Service Oriented Analysis and Design) [18] developed by IBM is one of the first systematic approaches to service engineering. The idea was to combine object-oriented analysis and design, enterprise architecture and business process modelling in a hybrid approach in order to support SOA deployment. This idea was further developed in SOMA (Service Oriented Modeling and Architecture) [2], where services, flows and components realizing services are identified. The methodology describes a business-driven top-down approach, combined with and IT-based bottom-up approach (where existing services can be reused). Our approach is therefore close to the process of SOMA in starting from business models and aligning services to business goals. Another methodology that have influenced our work was developed in the FP6 EU project SIMS[5] [8] which defined a top-down approach for specifying mobile services, starting from a high level specification of the system and modelling composite collaboration representing the services and refining these to fine grained specification of components, interfaces and data.

Our contribution to service engineering methodologies is introducing SoaML as the modelling language to be used in the specification and modelling of services. SoaML standardization is in the final phase and it is already supported by several modelling tools. Thus SOA methodologies will benefit from using the language in their life cycle models and include activities proposed in this chapter in order to take advantage of the standard. Other phases of development such as deployment, monitoring and management are out of the scope of this work.

2.5.3 Discussion

Any project that adopts SOA should cover the phases of service identification and specification, in addition to the phases of composition, realization, monitoring and management of services. This paper proposes a methodology that starts from higher-level models such as goal models, requirement models or business process models down to the modelling of services and their realization by software components. We have covered key concepts, activities, and models pertaining to a service engineering life-cycle method. The methodology takes advantage of SoaML as the modelling language and is therefore complementary to existing service engineering methods that are either silent about the language or take advantage of non-standard solutions for the purpose of service modelling. Another contribution of the work is proposing relations between business processes and goals and service constructs that may be basis for transformations or validation activities.

Many of the service-oriented methods analysed are mostly dedicated to a specific technology and define static procedures that can hardly be combined into a comprehensive methodology for integrated engineering frameworks. Because of the fact that engineering situations vary considerably from one application system development project to another, the traditional systems development methods are often not well suitable. Even though they claim to be universal and propose a large number of models and views for system analysis and specification, they cannot foresee all possible development situations. To overcome this, our approach follows the idea of Situational Method Engineering (see [10] and [6]) where reusable method chunks are assembled into customized engineering methods for particular application scenarios. Most of them use assembly techniques based on the reuse of existing method parts in the construction of new methods or in the enhancement of existing ones.

---

[5] Semantic Interfaces for Mobile Services (SIMS), http://www.ist-sims.org/

We have chosen the Eclipse Process Framework (EPF)[6] as the technical infrastructure for implementing our methodology. EPF is an open-source project for defining customizable software engineering processes, providing a specification framework for methods and processes along with editing and content management facilities. Recent approaches aim at providing a generic infrastructure for customizable software engineering methodologies. Most notably, OpenUP provides an open-source implementation of the Unified Process – a generic framework for iterative software engineering processes [9] – within EPF, and the IBM Rational Method Composer (RMC)[7] provides a commercial tool with IBM's own SoaML-based Service-Oriented Modeling and Architecture (SOMA) methodology [1]. Thus EPF provides the possibility to integrate the steps proposed in our methodology with other processes that cover other activities of software development.

2.6 Concluding Remarks and Future Work

In this chapter we have presented an overview of our MDSE methodology and in particular how the SoaML modelling language has been applied in a top-down manner to model a subset of the telecommunication use case. By following the methodology, which uses the SoaML language to represent both a business perspective and an IT perspective of SOA, better business and IT alignment can be achieved since the IT-level model can be viewed as a refinement of the business-level SOA model. Additionally, the SoaML model artefacts can be linked to business goals described in BMM to further help in the alignment process.

The MDSE methodology is currently in the finalization phase and is being revised according to user feedback and experience. Moreover, the methodology is being aligned with the latest changes in the SoaML specification which is also currently under finalization in the OMG. One aspect of the methodology that requires further work is to provide better guidelines for behavioural modelling. SoaML is quite open with regards to behavioural modelling, and explicitly states that any UML behaviour can be used. There is also a synchronization and integration to be done with the ongoing BPMN 2.0 specification [15], which introduces some service concepts that overlaps with the SoaML specification.

The MDSE methodology is implemented in the Eclipse Process Framework (EPF) to allow extensibility and open access. The core methodology presented focuses on the computational independent and platform independent abstractions levels according to the OMG MDA approach. The methodology has also been extended to support various platform technologies, in particular Web services, multi-agent platforms and Semantic Web Services. These correspond to PIMs for different architectural styles. Flexibility of the solution lies in being independent of various platforms in service design while it is extensible, generalization lies in standardizing the de-

---

[6] Eclipse Process Framework (EPF), http://www.eclipse.org/epf

[7] Rational Method Composer (RMC), http://www-01.ibm.com/software/awdtools/rmc

veloped UML profile and metamodel, the business value lies in being adaptable to various platforms, while innovation lies in combining SOA with model-driven development and taking advantage of advances in both fields.

Acknowledgements The SoaML methodology presented here has mainly been developed in the 7th Framework Programme research project SHAPE (ICT-2007-216408). The overall aim of the project is to develop the foundations for the model-driven development of service-oriented system landscapes with support for the integration of other technologies in order to increase the effectiveness and quality of modern software and system engineering.

The authors acknowledge and thank collaboration with partners within the SHAPE project for stimulating input and feedback since the start-up in 2007.

References

1. Amsden, J.: Modeling with SoaML. Technical article, IBM (7 January 2010). Online: http://www.ibm.com/developerworks/rational/library/09/ modelingwithsoaml-1/index.html
2. Arsanjani, A.: Service-Oriented Modeling and Architecture - How to identify, specify and realize services for your SOA. Technical article, SOA and Web Services Center of Excellence, IBM, Software Group (9 November 2004). Online: http://www.ibm.com/ developerworks/webservices/library/ws-soa-design1/
3. Atkinson, C., Bayer, J., Bunse, C., Kamsties, E., Laitenberger, O., Laqua, R., Muthig, D., Paech, B., Wust, J., Zettel, J.: Component-based Product Line Engineering with UML. Addison Wesley (2002)
4. Bastida, L., Berre, A.J., Elvesæter, B., Hahn, C., Johnsen, S.G., Kamper, S., Kerrigan, M., Larrucea, X., Limyr, A., Muth, M., Nilsen, G., Roman, D., Rubina, J.M., Stollberg, M.: Model-driven Methodology and Architecture Specification. Deliverable D2.1, SHAPE Project (2009)
5. Blum, B.I.: A taxonomy of software development methods. Commununications of the ACM **37**(11), 82–94 (1994)
6. Brinkkemper S. Saeki, M., Harmsen, F.: Assembly Techniques for Method Engineering. In: 10th Conference on Advanced Information Systems Engineering, CAiSE'98, LNCS 1413, pp. 381–400. Springer (1998)
7. Estefan, J.A.: Survey of model-based systems engineering (MBSE) methodologies. Incose MBSE Focus Group (2007)
8. Floch, J., Carrez, C., Cieślak, P., Rój, M., Sanders, R.T., Shiaa, M.M.: A comprehensive engineering framework for guaranteeing component compatibility (2010). Journal of Systems and Software, to appear
9. Kroll, P., MacIsaac, B.: Agility and Discipline Made Easy: Practices from OpenUP and RUP. Addison-Wesley (2006)
10. Kumar, K., Welke, R.: Method Engineering: A Proposal for Situation-specific Methodology Construction. In: Cotterman, Senn (eds.) In Systems Analysis and Design : A Research Agenda, pp. 257–268. Wiley (1992)
11. Kurchten, P.: The Rational Unified Process: An Introduction. Addison Wesley (2003)
12. MDA Guide Version 1.0.1. Object Management Group, Document omg/03-06-01 (2003)
13. Business Motivation Model (BMM), Version 1.0. Object Management Group, Document formal/08-08-02 (2008). Online: http://www.omg.org/spec/BMM/
14. Business Process Model and Notation (BPMN), Version 1.2. Object Management Group, Document formal/2009-01-03 (2009). Online: http://www.omg.org/spec/BPMN/1. 2/
15. Business Process Model and Notation (BPMN), Version 2.0 - Beta 1. Object Management Group, Document dtc/2009-08-14 (2009). Online: http://www.omg.org/spec/BPMN/ 2.0/

16. Service oriented architecture Modeling Language (SoaML), Version 1.0 - Beta 2. Object Management Group, Document ptc/2009-12-10 (2009). Online: http://www.omg.org/spec/SoaML/

17. Unified Modeling Language (UML), Infrastructure, Version 2.2. Object Management Group, Document formal/2009-02-04 (2009). Online: http://www.omg.org/spec/UML/2.2/

18. Zimmermann, O., Krogdahl, P., Gee, C.: Elements of Service-Oriented Analysis and Design - An interdisciplinary modeling approach for SOA projects. Technical article, IBM (2 June 2004). Online: http://www-128.ibm.com/developerworks/webservices/library/ws-soad1/

Chapter 3
Modelling Service Requirements Variability: The DiVA Way

Phil Greenwood, Ruzanna Chitchyan, Dhouha Ayed, Vincent Girard-Reydet, Franck Fleurey, Vegard Dehlen and Arnor Solberg

Abstract This chapter tackles the challenges of variability identification, modelling and implementation for service-based systems. The DiVA methodology is applied to the Mobile Phone Service Portability case-study to demonstrate its solutions to these challenges. The DiVA methodology utilises concepts of Aspect-Oriented Software Development to encapsulate service variants in distinct modules and uses Model-Driven Development techniques to analyse and transform conceptual designs into executable services. The DiVA approach provides a tool-supported methodology for managing dynamic variability in adaptive systems and taming system complexity.

3.1 Introduction

Service engineering has changed the way in which software systems are developed and delivered to the end-user. They provide a development model that empowers organisations and individuals by allowing them to use third-party services to fulfil

Phil Greenwood
Lancaster University, Lancaster, UK, e-mail: greenwop@comp.lancs.ac.uk

Ruzanna Chitchyan
Lancaster University, Lancaster, UK e-mail: rouza@comp.lancs.ac.uk

Dhouha Ayed
Thales Theresis, Paris, France e-mail: dhouha.ayed@thalesgroup.com

Vincent Girard-Reydet
Thales Theresis, Paris, France e-mail: vincent.girardreydet@thalesgroup.com

Franck Fleurey
SINTEF, Oslo, Norway e-mail: franck.fleurey@sintef.no

Vegard Dehlen
SINTEF, Oslo, Norway e-mail: vegard.dehlen@sintef.no

Arnor Solberg
SINTEF, Oslo, Norway e-mail: arnor.solberg@sintef.no

their goals. A variety of service engineering techniques have been proposed that allow these services to be delivered to the users in an efficient manner (e.g., BPEL [3], WSDL [7], etc.). Service-engineering techniques provide an open-ended development model that allows users/developers to compose heterogenous services together to create different results with the desired emergent properties. However, they do not address extreme diversity and variability that modern systems must be able to cope with.

Moreover, service consumers are growing to expect services to be continuously available and customisable which, in turn, requires support for dynamic variability during service execution (e.g., if a consumers' preferences change). Although the open-endedness and loosely coupled nature of service engineering allows service implementations to be replaced, and so customise the service, this can be a largely inefficient due to:

- Compromises made during design to support adaptation and the overhead of service replacement at run-time;
- Complexities related to variability management arise when attempting to maintain complete service implementations for each possible combination of service variations. This creates high-levels of redundancy and duplication of code, causing difficulties when performing maintenance activities.

This chapter presents the DiVA approach which provides a tool-supported methodology for managing dynamic variability in adaptive systems and taming system complexity. DiVA considers an adaptive system as a Dynamic Software Product Line (DSPL) [14] and focuses on the variability of the system, rather than on the whole set of its possible configurations. This involves the identification and modelling of variation points in the system and the subsequent system refinement into elements of variability and commonality. DiVA consolidates each variation into a separate module to ease the management and subsequent application of variants. Furthermore, the DiVA approach also considers the specific context to which each variation is applicable, as well as how each service variant affects the rest of the system and its properties.

The remainder of this chapter show how the DiVA tools and methodology are applicable to service engineering problems. We use the Mobile Phone Service Portability (MPSP) case-study to show the DiVA approach and how it can be applied to manage the variability in this study, extract the context associated with this variability, and analyse the properties that these variants affect.

3.2 DiVA Overview

The DiVA methodology uses Model-Driven Engineering (MDE) techniques to model the various elements of the variability. This is complimented by Aspect-Oriented Software Development (AOSD) [10] to aid the encapsulation of the variants identified. Variable service properties typically tend to cut across several service implementations and also affect other co-existing and co-dependent services. AOSD techniques encapsulate crosscutting concerns in dedicated modules. Implementing variations using an AO methodology improves the overall design by removing the need to incorporate variations within the core service implementation. This promotes reuse as service implementations no longer have to consider potential variations. Furthermore, due to the loose coupling offered by AOSD techniques, the variations themselves can be reused in different systems and applied dynamically. To complement this, Aspect-Oriented Modelling (AOM) provides a means to identify, model and evaluate the potential effects of such dynamic variations in separate aspects. MDE allows developers to operate at higher levels of abstraction which simplifies and standardises the activities of the software life-cycle, thus, making automation possible. This combination of MDE and AOM for management of the evolving dynamic variability will provide the ability to model, analyse, validate and compose the volatile configurations of adaptive systems throughout their life-cycle. The DiVA methodology is outlined in Figure 3.1.

The first step of the DiVA life-cycle (Requirements Model) is to elicit the requirements of a system that relate to variability and dynamic adaptation. This step involves applying a series of tools to the requirement documentation in order to identify the high-level features that are candidates for classical services, as well as the potential variation and adaptation points within them. In addition, any relevant context and constraints are also extracted to ensure that all adaptations can be correctly dynamically applied without causing any run-time conflicts. This information is ex-

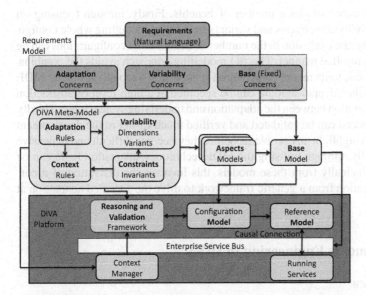

Fig. 3.1: The DiVA methodology

tracted semi-automatically from the text of the requirement documents using a series of Natural Language Processing techniques [27, 29].

The second step of the DiVA methodology (DiVA Meta-Model) involves constructing an operational model of the adaptive behaviour identified from the first step. An operational model is a representation of the underlying reality in the form of a model, including behavioural aspects that are described using operational semantics. This involves modelling the adaptation rules, elements of variability, context and constraints related to services. Subsequently, simulation and model-checking capabilities are used to validate the adaptation model.

The third and fourth steps of the DiVA methodology involves validating the models created and translating the adaptation models into models that can be executed. The models are validated with respect to the different operational profiles that represent different elements of the application and platform behaviour.

At run-time, the aspect models are used as architecture fragments that can be composed into a base model (that contains non-variable fragments). To select the configuration (composition of aspects) that adapts to the context, a reasoning framework collects context information from sensors and processes the adaptation model. The reasoning framework selects the best fit configuration that matches the adaptation rules. The complete model of the corresponding configuration can be built at runtime using the composition of aspect models. A causal link established between the models and services causes automatic reconfiguration of running services when the adaptations are applied at the model level. Due to the validation framework, the transition from one configuration to another is safe.

The DiVA approach provides a number of benefits. Firstly, through focusing on modelling variability dimensions and variants rather than modelling whole configurations variability, the explosion in the number of contexts and configurations can be managed in a controlled manner. The AO modelling approach avoids the combinatorial explosion due to its model composition capabilities. Secondly, using an MDE based approach the adaptation logic can be specified at a high-level of abstraction and allows a separation between the adaptation and underlying system logic. Thirdly, the models produced can be validated and verified much earlier in the development life-cycle and so highlight any problems before they become difficult and expensive to resolve. Finally, through utilising the MDE techniques, adaptation logic can be generated automatically from these models, this involves the derivation of a concrete implementation from a generic framework to drive the specified adaptation at run-time.

3.3 Requirements Engineering in DiVA

3.3.1 Overview

The DiVA requirements engineering (RE) approach focuses on answering the question: What (requirements, services, and context) to model? The inputs for the DiVA

RE approach are textual documents related to the system to be implemented. These documents do not need to be pre-structured in any particular way, as the input text is processed by a set of Natural Language Processing (NLP) tools [27, 29]. To create appropriate RE models the DiVA RE approach:

- Constructs a feature tree from the input requirements text, thus identifying specific requirements that need to be modelled, and refining this tree with variations and adaptation points. The feature tree is constructed by a tool called Arbor-Craft that uses Latent Semantic Analysis (LSA) techniques [32]. ArborCraft breaks the requirement text into specified-size chunks (e.g., one paragraph per chunk, one sentence per chunk, or multiple sentences per chunk, etc.) and then groups the chunks in accordance to their semantic similarity. The grouping is a bottom-up process, with most similar leaf nodes being grouped together, each subsequent higher level is formed by grouping less similar lower level nodes.

- Recovers the generic services (functionality) from the feature tree. The initial generated feature tree is reviewed by an analyst where they assign descriptive names to the features and aggregate, split, or restructure the features to create a model that better fits the domain and the analyst's mental model of it. Additionally, a complementary tool called EA-Miner [29] is used to elicit the relevant non-functional properties for the quality of service, as well as to refine the generated trees with variability, adaptation, and context information [6].

- Analyses the tree to extract the relevant context and variability/adaptation related constraints, which restricts the set of potential service configurations [2, 6].

3.3.2 Case-Study Requirements Engineering

The MPSP case-study contains several documents. We have chosen documents discussing the system goals and use-cases to illustrate the DiVA RE approach.

3.3.2.1 Automatic Generation of the Initial Feature Tree

The relevant requirement documents are saved as plain text files and passed to the ArborCraft tool [32]. ArborCraft carries out a set of NLP actions, constructing a feature tree , in a layered step-wise fashion aggregating into nodes the parts of the input text that have a similar meaning. The lower the nodes of the tree the more similar their contents are. A portion of the feature tree initially generated for the case-study input text is shown in Figure 3.2. At this point the nodes of the tree have no meaningful names, and also lack any refined detail. The tree contains a set of nodes with chunks of text, each addressing similar functionality and topics.

3.3.2.2 Feature Tree Naming and Refinement

The feature tree initially generated is then revised and refined in a number of ways:

1. Each leaf level node is provided with a suitable name. The name assigned should reflect the functions discussed in the nodes. For instance, Feature 6 presented in Figure 3.2 is named "Billing", Feature 7 is named "Reporting", etc.

2. The higher-level (non-leaf) nodes are then named in accordance with their child nodes. For instance, Feature 11 in Figure 3.2 is renamed "Manage Number Portability" in Figure 3.3, as it contains the "File Porting Request", "Evaluate Porting Request", "Choose Contract" and "Execute Porting Request" subfeatures. For this naming process the analyst applies his/her domain knowledge, and, if needed, may also request input/confirmation from the domain experts.

3. Whilst naming the features, the analyst may also merge, spilt or re-structure some nodes in accordance with the domain model and/or his/her personal knowledge. For instance, in the initial model in Figure 3.2 the tool had grouped Feature 0 (named Transparency in Figure 3.3) with the Feature 11 "Manage Number Porting". However, during the naming and reviewing of the model, the analyst decided that Transparency is a more general concern related to the quality of the whole system and moved it out of the Feature 11 structure. The analyst will choose to stop node aggregation at the point where he/she considers further aggregation unnecessary.

4. The tree refinement is further complemented via use of lexicons for nonfunctional properties (identifying words, such as "assess" and "login" for Security, "bandwidth" and "throughput" for Performance, etc.) variability/commonality (identifying words such as: "and", "or", "another", "different", etc.), and adaptation (identifying words such as, "change", "adapt", "update", etc.). When the lexicon entries are detected in the text, the respective elements are considered for refinement. Thus, for instance, the term "bound" in the present case-study was found to be relevant to the Security non-functional soft goal. However, in this case the analyst decided not to model this element in this instance as Security was not considered within the scope of the current study. Alternatively, the terms for the variability/commonality (e.g., "number is activated and bound") were used to refine the leaf features of Figure 3.2 into smaller sub-features in Figure 3.3. Additionally, the semantics of variability/commonality lexicon entries were used to define if the refined features are optional (e.g.,

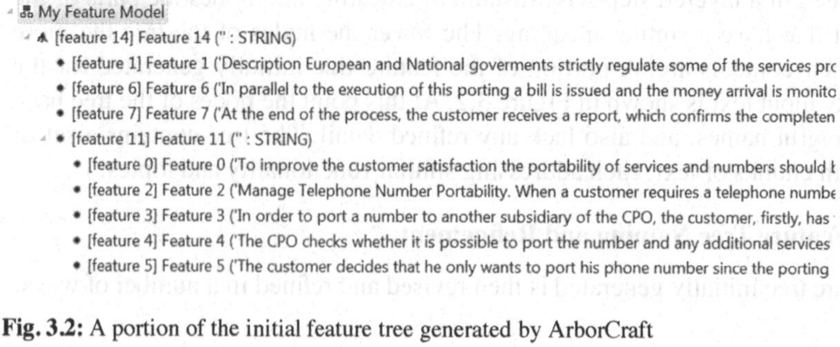

⊿ 🏛 My Feature Model
  ⊿ ⚛ [feature 14] Feature 14 (" : STRING)
    • [feature 1] Feature 1 ('Description European and National goverments strictly regulate some of the services prc
    • [feature 6] Feature 6 ('In parallel to the execution of this porting a bill is issued and the money arrival is monito
    • [feature 7] Feature 7 ('At the end of the process, the customer receives a report, which confirms the completen
  ⊿ • [feature 11] Feature 11 (" : STRING)
    • [feature 0] Feature 0 ('To improve the customer satisfaction the portability of services and numbers should t
    • [feature 2] Feature 2 ('Manage Telephone Number Portability. When a customer requires a telephone numbe
    • [feature 3] Feature 3 ('In order to port a number to another subsidiary of the CPO, the customer, firstly, has
    • [feature 4] Feature 4 ('The CPO checks whether it is possible to port the number and any additional services
    • [feature 5] Feature 5 ('The customer decides that he only wants to port his phone number since the porting

Fig. 3.2: A portion of the initial feature tree generated by ArborCraft

when used with "or", "another") or mandatory (e.g., when used with and in "activated and bound").

The higher level features produced via the DiVA RE process (such as Billing, Reporting, Mange Number Porting etc. from Figure 3.3) will normally correspond to distinct services. This is expected, as both the ArborCraft tool and the analyst would have worked on aggregating requirements that address similar and closely related topics into higher level nodes. At the same time, the leaf nodes will reflect the variability in the activities available for the service provision. Thus, for instance, the Billing feature constitutes a distinct self-contained service, which has three sub-activities: Issue Bill (mandatory), Monitor Money Arrival (mandatory), and Issue Bill Overdue Reminder (optional). The last sub-activity, in turn can be carried out in three alternative ways: via Post, Email, or SMS.

3.3.2.3 Context and Constraint Analysis

Having constructed and refined the services/feature tree as per the above discussion, the DiVA approach then considers the context and constraints for each variant.

For instance, Figure 3.4 shows an extract of constraint specification for the services/feature model of the MPSP case-study presented in Figure 3.3. The very first constraint in Figure 3.4 states that the number porting cost feature must always be

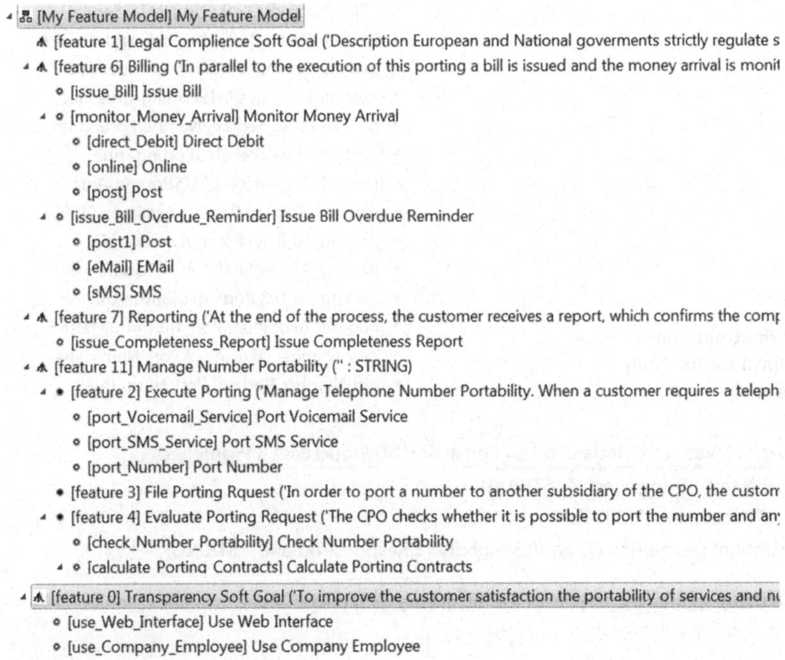

⊿ 🔠 [My Feature Model] My Feature Model
    ⋏ [feature 1] Legal Complience Soft Goal ('Description European and National goverments strictly regulate s
  ⊿ ⋏ [feature 6] Billing ('In parallel to the execution of this porting a bill is issued and the money arrival is monit
     ○ [issue_Bill] Issue Bill
  ⊿ ○ [monitor_Money_Arrival] Monitor Money Arrival
     ○ [direct_Debit] Direct Debit
     ○ [online] Online
     ○ [post] Post
  ⊿ ○ [issue_Bill_Overdue_Reminder] Issue Bill Overdue Reminder
     ○ [post1] Post
     ○ [eMail] EMail
     ○ [sMS] SMS
  ⊿ ⋏ [feature 7] Reporting ('At the end of the process, the customer receives a report, which confirms the comp
     ○ [issue_Completeness_Report] Issue Completeness Report
  ⊿ ⋏ [feature 11] Manage Number Portability (" : STRING)
  ⊿ ● [feature 2] Execute Porting ('Manage Telephone Number Portability. When a customer requires a teleph
     ○ [port_Voicemail_Service] Port Voicemail Service
     ○ [port_SMS_Service] Port SMS Service
     ○ [port_Number] Port Number
    ● [feature 3] File Porting Rquest ('In order to port a number to another subsidiary of the CPO, the custom
  ⊿ ● [feature 4] Evaluate Porting Request ('The CPO checks whether it is possible to port the number and an;
     ○ [check_Number_Portability] Check Number Portability
  ⊿ ○ [calculate Porting Contracts] Calculate Porting Contracts
⊿ ⋏ [feature 0] Transparency Soft Goal ('To improve the customer satisfaction the portability of services and n
    ○ [use_Web_Interface] Use Web Interface
    ○ [use_Company_Employee] Use Company Employee

Fig. 3.3: Refined feature model

selected when port number service feature is selected. In addition, these constraints are used to define mutual feature exclusion (if set to "=false"), dependence between a feature and a set of other features (e.g., portingLocation=IT, UK, BL), etc.

Finally, the DiVA RE model allows modelling of the significant properties for service quality. During the feature/service tree analysis a set of relevant soft-goals will be identified either directly via automated tree generation process (e.g., the Legal Compliance soft-goals in Figure 3.3), or via the lexicon-based analysis (e.g., the Security soft-goal). For each of these soft-goals a set of properties, relevant for satisfying these goals, is defined. For instance, as shown in Figure 3.5, the Transparency soft-goal is considered to be satisfied when the cost is minimised (denoted by Cost =0 at the lower part in Figure 3.5), Simplicity is maximised (denoted by Simplicity=1), and Response Time minimised (denotes as Response Time=0). Such properties are provided as a result of soft-goal analysis consideration.

In summary, the DiVA RE approach provides a semi-automated methodology for identifying: services from the textual requirements documents, the core and variable set of such services necessary for a particular system, and specifying constraints and properties that will define the expected quality of the selected services.

⊿ ⌶ Additional Constraints

- [number_Porting_Cost] port_Number_Service
- [sMS_Porting_Cost] port_SMS_Service
- [uTMS_Porting_Cost] port_UMTS_Service
- [execute_Porting] NumberPorting=true,false
- [execute_Porting] SMSPorting=true,false
- [execute_Porting] UMTSPorting=true,false
- [port_Number_Service] NumberPorting=true
- [port_SMS_Service] SMSPorting=true
- [port_UMTS_Service] UMTSPorting=true
- [manage_Porting] PortingLocation=IT,UK,BL
- [porting_To_Italy] PortingLocation=IT
- [porting_To_Belgium] PortingLocation=BL
- [porting_To_UK] PortingLocation=UK
- [number_Allocation] Port_Num=true,false
- [new_Number_Allocation] Port_Num=false
- [old_Number_Porting] Port_Num=true

Fig. 3.4 ArborCraft constraints defined for the Number Porting study

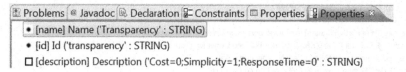

| 🗊 Problems | @ Javadoc | 🗎 Declaration | 🗗 Constraints | 🖿 Properties | 🗗 Properties ✕ |

- [name] Name ('Transparency' : STRING)
- [id] Id ('transparency' : STRING)
- ☐ [description] Description ('Cost=0;Simplicity=1;ResponseTime=0' : STRING)

Fig. 3.5: Defining significant properties for the quality of service

3.4 Variability Modelling in DiVA

3.4.1 Overview

The DiVA methodology provides a conceptual framework for modelling the adaptations and variability elements of a system . Figure 3.6 illustrates the DiVA metamodel. The purpose of this model is to capture and formalise how and when the target system should adapt. This includes an adaptation model that drives the specification, validation and execution of the adaptive system. It captures the dynamic variability information, i.e. which implementation should be used depending on the context. To achieve this, the adaptation model needs to capture the variability in the system, the environment of the system and the link between the two. The objective of the proposed approach is to model the adaptations and validate the adaptation logic earlier in the development cycle. This is supported via dedicated tools. At runtime, the model is processed by a runtime adaptation framework which is connected to the running application [23].

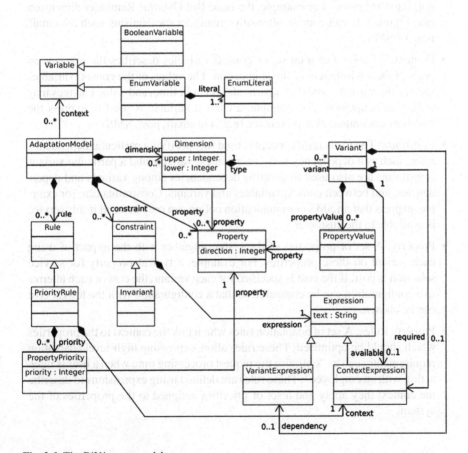

Fig. 3.6: The DiVA meta-model

In DiVA, the adaptation meta-model is the central pillar of the methodology. This meta-model acts as a canvas to which the results of the DiVA requirements analysis activity are mapped and used to model adaptation in the early design phases of an adaptive system. This model can be semi-automatically constructed from the services/feature models created via DiVA's requirement engineering approach described in Section 3.3. A mapping (shown in Table 3.1) has been created between the DiVA RE and adaptation meta-model. This mapping describes how the elements from the requirements can be translated into DiVA model elements. The adaptations designed using this meta-model are then used as a direct input into the DiVA runtime development. The meta-model, shown in Figure 3.6, has an AdaptationModel as its root container, this adaptation model contains five different elements to model different properties of an adaptive system:

- Dimension/Variant: A Dimension corresponds to a variation point in the application and is associated with one or more alternative variants which can be used at this variation point. A variant is a piece of functionality that can be included (or not) into the system. For example, the Issue Bill Overdue Reminder dimension (see Figure 3.3) can contain alternative reminder mechanisms such as: email, post, or SMS.

- Context Variable: The total set of context variables describes the relevant aspects of the environment of the application. The values of the context variables specify the current context at a particular point in time, and value changes may trigger an adaptation. For example, a context variable is used to express the customer communication preference (e.g., via email, post, SMS).

- Constraint: The Constraint concept is used for specifying particular dependency rules, such as a dependency between a context variable and a particular variant. Constraints are also used to describe dependencies among variants and dependencies, and between context variables and variants. Constraints can, for example, express that an SMS communication option can only be used if this service is available to the customer.

- Property: A set of properties of the system together with the impact of using each variant on these properties. For example, a typical property for service selection is cost. If the cost is specified for each variant, the cost of each alternative configuration can be compared so that a configuration with the lowest cost can be chosen.

- Property Rules: A set of adaptation rules which link the context to the properties which should be optimised. These rules allow expressing high-level adaptation requirements such as "optimise the request processing time when a user is interacting with an employee". These rules are defined using expressions to describe the context they apply and a set of priorities assigned to the properties of the system.

3.4.2 Requirements Mapping

Modern systems are typically very large and broad, covering a wide variety of functionality. This generally translates to requirement documents that are very large, unstructured and heterogeneous. Documents of this nature are difficult to read and understand; variability and adaptation related properties are particularly difficult to manually extract due to their typically scattered and implicit nature. This in turn makes it difficult to manually create a DiVA model and define the various elements that make up a DiVA model (i.e., dimension/variant, context variable, constraints, etc.). By utilising a semi-automated approach the developer can gain initial insights on the domain and system to create an initial model that can be refined and improved upon in subsequent iterations. Table 3.1 provides a summary of the DiVA RE services/feature model to DiVA adaptation meta-model mapping.

When DiVA RE models are converted to DiVA adaptation models the tools automatically suggest relevant conversion options. The developer can then impart his/her knowledge of the domain and system by making additions, changes, and corrections to the derived DiVA model.

Table 3.1: Summary of feature model to DiVA meta-model mappings

Feature Tree Element	DiVA Meta-Model Element
Child features	Candidate variants
Parent features	Candidate dimensions
Mandatory features	Base model of the metamodel
Context information attached to any features as a constraint	Enumvariable if the constraint has multiple values a BooleanVariable if the constraint has only a single variable.
Constraints on the feature model which relate to Context information. Intra-feature constraints are needed when multiple contexts are specified within a single feature. Inter-feature constraints are constructed by analysing the relationship between siblings and the parent feature.	Candidate Rules in the Metamodel.
Constraints on the feature models which relate to variants of non-context features (constraints specified in terms other that Context information)	Candidate Constraints in the Metamodel.
Properties added to any feature in the feature tree where the name of the property is the same as the name of the feature.	Property
Values of the Property artefacts (where the property equals the name of the feature).	Property Value.

The above mapping can be applied flexibly. For instance, when used literally, it may cause duplicates with the same feature being suggested as both a variant and dimension. This issue can be avoided through a more restrictive policy and by taking into account other semantic information contained within the feature model. For example, features with an OR or XOR relationship should be considered as being variants as these relationship types explicitly indicate alternative implementations. Similarly, restrictions can be imposed regarding the position of features to derive dimensions/variants (e.g., only leaf-nodes and the parents of the leaf-nodes can be considered).

For a complete adaptive system to be constructed it is important that the base system (i.e., the core of the system that does not adapt but to which adaptations are applied) is also modelled. This can also be extracted from the feature model by filtering those services/features that are mandatory. If a service/feature is mandatory it must be included in all system variants and at all times.

A variety of properties and constraints can be attached to the feature models generated from DiVA's requirements engineering technique to describe when features should be included or omitted. Some of this information can be translated to dynamic information and used to construct the DiVA model. For example, context information can be extracted from requirement documents that describe when a feature is needed. This involves not only identifying the context that can change but also the different values that the context can take. This information is mapped to context variables of the DiVA meta-model to indicate when certain adaptations should be triggered. There are two different types of context variables in the DiVA meta-model: enumeration and boolean. When the context can take on multiple values (i.e., more than two) the context is mapped to an enumeration variable, whereas when the context can only take two values a Boolean variable is used instead.

Analysing features individually allows the extraction of different context related information and the values this context information can take. However, in order to define correct triggers it is necessary to examine the context information across all features in the feature model and combine them in a representative manner. This involves analysing the relationship between the siblings and the parents of each feature and combining the specified context information to create adaptation rules. For example, child features relating to how bill reminders should be sent (e.g., via e-mail) are attached to the customer's communication preference. However, bill reminders are only needed when the customer's bill is unpaid (determined by the parent's context). The context of the parent also applies to all of its children. Therefore, these two pieces should be combined to create a rule that states the e-mail bill reminder should only be sent when the bill is unpaid and the customer's communication preference is e-mail.

Feature models are used to define the relationship between features and are implicitly specified by its structure. Often relationships exist between features across the feature model that need to be defined explicitly as they cannot be implicitly defined via the structure. These relationships typically relate to constraints between features. Such relationships are also relevant in a dynamic context and are represented as candidate Constraints in the DiVA meta-model. They are used to determine whether the target system is in a correct state for a variant to be applied.

Similar to features being relevant only in certain contexts, certain features may affect different properties in different ways. For example, the inclusion of a feature that relies on communicating via post will have slower processing time than a feature that relies on SMS. Expressing this information can be critical for deciding which features should be included and those that should be omitted if certain characteristics need to be fulfilled. Such affects can be expressed in services/feature models by adding properties to the relevant services/features. These can then be translated and mapped to properties and property values in the DiVA meta-model so that the effects of adaptations can be properly evaluated.

Finally, the priorities associated with these Properties need to be determined so that an accurate trade-off analysis can be performed. This analysis involves determining the effects of including each feature in a configuration whilst taking into account the priority of fulfilling these properties to ensure the configuration created fulfils the user's needs. The feature models produced by the DiVA requirements engineering approach is extended to support this information and allow these priorities to be transferred to the DiVA models.

3.4.3 Case-Study DiVA Model

From analysing and processing the MPSP case-study, a number of services were extracted. Furthermore, a number of alternative implementations of these services were identified. These alternative implementations are candidates for dynamic adaptation and variability. However, in order to determine the scenarios which these various implementations should be applied we also need to extract the context associated to these services. All of this information is extracted via the DiVA requirement engineering technique. For this information to be useful in terms of assessing the validity of different configurations and creating an adaptive service implementation, it has to be converted to a DiVA model representation. Here we describe the DiVA model representation created from the requirements engineering process described in Section 3.3.

3.4.3.1 Dimensions and Variants

The first set of DiVA model elements that require extracting are the dimensions and variants associated to the MPSP example. These dimensions and variants were automatically derived from the services/feature models produced via the requirements engineering approach described in Section 3.3 by applying the mappings shown in Table 3.1.

A number of dimensions and variants for the MPSP system are shown in Figure 3.7. Recall that a dimension (Element 1 in Figure 3.7) relates to a variation point in the application and the variants (Element 2 in Figure 3.7) of the dimensions represent alternative implementations of those variations. Both dimensions and variants are given descriptive names (Element 3 in Figure 3.7) and unique IDs (Element 4 in Figure 3.7) so that they can be referred to elsewhere in the model. The leaf nodes of a feature model generally relate to low-level implementation details and the relationships between these leaf-nodes allow alternatives to be identified. For the MPSP case-study, leaf-nodes are interpreted as being variants and the parents of these nodes as dimensions.

Each of these relate to the alternative services that are available to the customer (e.g., what elements of their phone service they wish to port) and how they wish to achieve this porting (e.g., how they wish to pay, how they want to interact with the phone company).

These variants represent each of the alternative implementations of services that can be selected to customise the MPSP system for each particular customer. For example, if the customer only requires their phone number to be ported (SMS and UMTS porting are not needed) then only the Port Number Service will be included. Similarly, the customer's choice regarding how they interact with the phone company can be customised (via a web interface or via a company employee) or how they pay for their services (using direct debit, online payment or payment by post). The DiVA model does not impose any restrictions regarding how the actual services and the variations should be implemented. For example, the relevant services could be composed via some process orchestration technique, such as BPEL, for execution. To adapt and administrate the running system, a casually connected model and relevant run-time scripts need to be created for the target platform.

3.4.3.2 Context Model

In order to determine when each of these variants is applicable, a context model needs to be created. This context model consists of a series of context variables that

	Name	ID
Dimension	NumberAllocation	NA
Variant	NewNumberAllocation	NNA
Variant	OldNumberPorting	ONP
Dimension	Calculate Porting Costs	CPC
Variant	Number Porting Cost	NPC
Variant	SMS Porting Cost	SMSPC
Variant	UMTS Porting Cost	VPC
Dimension	NumberPortabilityRequest	TRA
Variant	Web Interface	WI
Variant	Company Employee	CE
Dimension	Execute Porting	EP
Variant	Port Number Service	PNS
Variant	Port SMS Service	PSMSS
Variant	Port UMTS Service	PVS
Dimension	ManagePorting	MP
Variant	PortingToItaly	PIT
Variant	PortingToBelgium	PBE
Variant	PortingToEngland	PUK
Dimension	Monitor Money Arrival	MMA
Variant	Direct Debit	DD
Variant	Online	ONL
Variant	Post	POS
Dimension	Issue Bill Overdue Reminder	IBOR
Variant	E-Mail	EM
Variant	SMS	SMS
Variant	Post	POS1

Fig. 3.7 Identified dimensions and variants

correspond to different stimuli of the system that can affect the variants identified. The context variables can then be used to drive the run-time adaptation of the target system with different variants selected when the context variables change.

Figure 3.8 illustrates the context model created for the MPSP system. This consists of a number of context variables that can vary in value depending on the customer's preferences and how they interact with the system. For example, they can select to interact Directly or Indirectly with the system. This has purposefully been left ambiguous to remain independent to future implementation. Currently, to interact Directly the customer uses a Web-Interface, and to interact indirectly, the customer contacts a Company Employee. This context variable can change at run-time if the customer chooses to change how they interact, changing this value should be reflected in the service (re)configuration. To implement this, a run-time probe is needed to determine the values of these variables; again at this stage the precise implementation of these probes is unimportant.

Two different types of variables are used in this Context Model: boolean (Element 1 in Figure 3.8) and enumeration (Element 2 in Figure 3.8) variables. The enumeration variables are used when the context which they represent can take one of a possible number of values (Element 3 in Figure 3.8). For example, the customers should select just one way which they prefer the phone company to communicate with

	Name	ID	Values
① Boolean	NumberPortabilityPreference	PORTPREF	-
◢ ≣ Enum	PortingLocationPreference	PORTLOC	{IT, EN, BL}
▬ Literal	ItalianDepartment	IT	-
▬ Literal	EnglishDepartment	EN	-
▬ Literal	BelgianDepartment	BL	-
⊞ Boolean	CustomerPreferenceSMSPorting	④ SMSPORT	-
⊞ Boolean	CustomerPreferenceTemporaryNumberPorting	TEMPNBRPORT	-
⊞ Boolean	CustomerPreferenceUMTSPorting	UMTSPORT	-
② Enum	Interaction	INT	{DIR, IND}
▬ Literal	Direct	DIR	-
③ ▬ Literal	Indirect	IND	-
◢ ≣ Enum	PaymentMethod	PAY	{DD, ONL, POS}
▬ Literal	Direct Debit	DD	-
▬ Literal	Online	ONL	-
▬ Literal	Post	POS	-
⊞ Boolean	BillPaid	PAID	-
◢ ≣ Enum	CustomerCommunicationPreference	COMPREF	{EMAIL, SMS, POST}
▬ Literal	E-mail	EMAIL	-
▬ Literal	SMS	SMS	-
▬ Literal	Post	POST	-

Fig. 3.8: Context variables

them (i.e., e-mail, SMS, or post). Boolean values can either be set to true or false to represent whether that particular context is activated or not. Again, unique IDs are assigned to the variables and values so that they can be referenced throughout the model (Element 4 in Figure 3.8). Boolean variables have been used to represent the services that the customer has selected to port. A boolean variable is created for each service that is available to be ported, these variables should be set to true if the service they represent should be ported. This design was selected rather than using a single enumeration variable to represent the service to be ported as it is likely that multiple services will have to be ported simultaneously. As these variables can only take a single value it would be impossible for them to represent the porting of multiple services without using a more convoluted design. Therefore, these multiple boolean variables can be simply used to indicate the services to be ported.

3.4.3.3 Adaptation Constraints

Currently, we have only presented the context and variability separately. In order for adaptations to be correctly and consistently applied the context and variants need to be modelled together. The DiVA methodology allows a series of constraints to be defined that link context variables to specific variants. Furthermore, a series of adaptation rules can be created that are based on certain properties that need to be optimised.

	Name	ID	Lower	Upper	dependency	available	required
▲ Dimension	NumberAllocation	NA	1	1	-	-	-
Variant	NewNumberAllocation	NNA	-	-			not PORTPREF
Variant	OldNumberPorting	ONP	-	-			PORTPREF
▲ Dimension	Calculate Porting Costs	CPC	0	-1	-	-	-
Variant	Number Porting Cost	NPC	-	-	PNS	TEMPNBRPORT	TEMPNBRPORT
Variant	SMS Porting Cost	SMSPC	-	-	PSMSS	SMSPORT	SMSPORT
Variant	UMTS Porting Cost	VPC	-	-	PVS	UMTSPORT	UMTSPORT
▲ Dimension	NumberPortabilityRequest	TRA	1	1	-	-	-
Variant	Web Interface	WI	-	-			INT=DIR
Variant	Company Employee	CE	-	-			INT=IND
▲ Dimension	Execute Porting	EP	0	-1	-	-	-
Variant	Port Number Service	PNS	-	-		TEMPNBRPORT	
Variant	Port SMS Service	PSMSS	-	-		SMSPORT	
Variant	Port UMTS Service	PVS	-	-		UMTSPORT	
▲ Dimension	ManagePorting	MP	1	1	-	-	-
Variant	PortingToItaly	PIT	-	-			PORTLOC=IT
Variant	PortingToBelgium	PBE	-	-			PORTLOC=BL
Variant	PortingToEngland	PUK	-	-			PORTLOC=EN
▲ Dimension	Monitor Money Arrival	MMA	1	1	-	-	-
Variant	Direct Debit	DD	-	-		PAY=DD	
Variant	Online	ONL	-	-		PAY=ONL	
Variant	Post	POS	-	-		PAY=POS	
▲ Dimension	Issue Bill Overdue Reminder	IBOR	1	-1	-	-	-
Variant	E-Mail	EM	-	-		not PAID and COMPREF=EMAIL	
Variant	SMS	SMS	-	-	PSMSS	not PAID and COMPREF=SMS	
Variant	Post	POS1	-	-	POS	not PAID and COMPREF=POST	

Fig. 3.9: Adaptation constraints

Figure 3.9 reveals the adaptation constraints that have been defined for the MPSP case-study and the applicable variants. The distinction between available (Element 4 in Figure 3.9) and required (Element 5 in Figure 3.9) elements relates to contexts in which the variant can or must be used. For example, the Port Number Service is available only when the customer requests it, represented by the TEMP_NBR_PORT being true.

Combining multiple context variables can create more complex constraints. For example, the Issue Bill Overdue Reminder dimension has a number of possible variants that are only applicable when a number of conditions are met (Element 4 in Figure 3.9). The associated variants relate to the mechanism used to issue the bill reminders (e.g., E-Mail, SMS and Post). The customers communication preference (represented by the COMPREF context variable) is taken into account when selecting the variant. However, these service variants are only applicable when the customer's bill is unpaid (represented by the PAID boolean context variable). Therefore, a complex constraint is needed that combines these two context variables. This complex constraint specifies that an E-Mail reminder should be sent when the bill is not paid (not PAID) and the customer communication preferences is e-mail (COMPREF=EMAIL).

This constraints view also allow dependencies between variants to be modelled and specified (Element 3 in Figure 3.9). These constraints allow relationships between variants to be created that define those variants that need to be present for another to operate correctly. In the MPSP case-study a number of these relationships exist. For example, the variants that relate to calculating cost depend on which Execute Porting variants are present. For example, the Number Porting Cost service is only needed when the Port Number Service (PNS) is present. These dependencies were established so that only relevant Calculate Porting Costs are included in the final service configuration.

Finally, the multiplicity of each dimension is modelled. This multiplicity relates to the minimum (Element 1 in Figure 3.9) and maximum (Element 2 in Figure 3.9) number of variants that need to be present to fulfil that dimension. For example, to fulfil the Monitor Money Arrival dimension, both the lower and upper value is 1. This indicates that only one variant should be selected to fulfil this dimension. In contrast, the Executing Porting dimension specifies that its variants have a lower multiplicity of 0 and an upper multiplicity of -1. This indicates that any number of porting services can be included, including none or several.

3.4.3.4 Quality of Service

Although the constraints described above go someway towards modelling the necessary adaptations, they do not help with selecting the configuration that is best suited to a particular context . In order to support this decision, a number of properties have been identified that should be optimised within the MPSP case-study. These properties are shown in Figure 3.10.

Four properties have been identified in the case-study, each having a descriptive name (Element 1 in Figure 3.10) and unique ID (Element 2 in Figure 3.10): Cost, Simplicity, Portability Process Time and Bill Payment Interval. The direction (Element 3 in Figure 3.10) associated to each of these properties relates to whether it is desirable to maximise (1) or minimise (0) a property. For example, it is desirable to minimise cost but to maximise the simplicity of the system. To facilitate the decisions surrounding the adaptations it is necessary to link the properties to both the variants and the context. This will allow the impact that each variant has on each of the properties to be modelled and also identify the properties that should be optimised for each context.

Figure 3.11 illustrates the interface for defining the impact that dimensions and variants have on each of the identified properties. Each row relates to either a dimension (Element 1 in Figure 3.11) or variant (Element 2 in Figure 3.11) originally shown in Figure 3.7. The columns (Element 3 in Figure 3.11) represent each of the properties identified in Figure 3.10. For each dimension a field exists (Element 4 in Figure 3.11) that can be set to true or false to indicate whether that dimension affects the property in question. For each variant, values (Element 5 in Figure 3.11) can be provided to indicate the degree of impact the variant has on the property. These values can be Very Low, Low, Medium, High or Very High. This model plays a critical role when optimising the adaptations as it will allow a trade-off analysis to be performed for the current context.

Related to this, Figure 3.12 presents the adaptation rules for MPSP system. The purpose of these rules is to capture what properties are most important for each of the contexts that have been identified. This involves specifying each relevant context (Element 1 in Figure 3.12) and identifying the properties that the context affects (Element 2 in Figure 3.12). The importance of the property for each context can then be set (Element 3 in Figure 3.12). For example, when the user is paying by post it is important that the Bill Payment Interval is kept low to prevent the user having to constantly mail their payments to the phone company. Similarly, when the user is interacting with a company employee the response time in terms of feedback of porting success should be kept to a minimum to maximise the efficiency of company employees.

3.4.4 Simulation for Configuration Selection

Before using an adaptation model to dictate changes in the system run-time, the model needs to be properly validated. The DiVA approach supports such validation.

Fig. 3.10 Properties of the Service and Phone Number Porting case-study

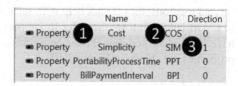

For a given context, processing the adaptation model has to yield the best suited configuration for the system in that context. The simulation feature of the DiVA tools allow us to validate both the constraints (Figure 3.9) and the priority rules (Figure 3.12) of the adaptation model. This process is split into two parts; resolving the hard constraints and ranking the configurations.

As the total number of contexts for an adaptive application is huge, in general it cannot be exhaustedly simulated but it can be tested with representative context evolution scenarios. Consequently, the developer has to set up different context situations to simulate. This is done in the following way; for each context situation, we have to specify a value for each context variable, thus creating different context combinations; then, for each of these context combinations we specify our expected partial configuration. In other words, we specify a set of variants that we expect to be included in the best configurations for the given context. This is set in the oracle column, and is illustrated in Figure 3.13.

	Cost	Simplicity	PortabilityProcessTime	BillPaymentInterval
NumberAllocation (NA)	false	false	false	false
NewNumberAllocation (NNA)	-	-	-	-
OldNumberPorting (ONP)	-	-	-	-
Calculate Porting Costs (CPC)	true	false	false	false
Number Porting Cost (NPC)	High	-	-	-
SMS Porting Cost (SMSPC)	Medium	-	-	-
UMTS Porting Cost (VPC)	Low	-	-	-
NumberPortabilityRequest (TRA)	false	true	true	false
Web Interface (WI)	-	Low	High	-
Company Employee (CE)	-	High	Low	-
Execute Porting (EP)	true	false	false	false
Port Number Service (PNS)	High	-	-	-
Port SMS Service (PSMSS)	Medium	-	-	-
Port UMTS Service (PVS)	Low	-	-	-
ManagePorting (MP)	true	false	false	false
PortingToItaly (PIT)	-	-	-	-
PortingToBelgium (PBE)	-	-	-	-
PortingToEngland (PUK)	-	-	-	-
Monitor Money Arrival (MMA)	false	false	true	true
Direct Debit (DD)	-	-	High	High
Online (ONL)	-	-	Very High	Very High
Post (POS)	-	-	Low	Low
Issue Bill Overdue Reminder (IBOR)	false	true	true	true
E-Mail (EM)	-	High	High	High
SMS (SMS)	-	Medium	Very High	Very High
Post (POS1)	-	Low	Low	Low

Fig. 3.11: Variant impact on properties

Figure 3.13 shows a list of 6 context situation to simulate for the MPSP system. Each column in the table corresponds to a context variable[1]. Each row corresponds to a context, i.e. a set of values for the context variables. The simulation model groups a set of context definitions in a scenario and each context is composed by a set of values for the context variables of the system (defined in the context model). The oracle column allows to specify expected properties on the system in this particular context. For example, the context number 3 (C3) correspond to a situation where preferences are to port the number to the English department with SMS and temporary number but without UMTS. This interaction is direct, the payment method is debit, the bill has not been paid and the preferred communication channel is Email. Once a set of contexts and expected partial configurations are defined, the model can be simulated in order to compute what configuration it will yield in these various contexts.

Figure 3.14 shows the results for context number 3 (C3), which is calculated according to the description above. There is a four-level hierarchy for the rows:

- Scenario: The grouping of context definitions.

- Context: A context is given a value for each of the properties, and these values are calculated based on the priority rules (Figure 3.12). If a context row is green, it means that at least one of the found configurations matches the oracle expression in the simulation definition, and that at least one of these are ranked first.

	Name	ID	context		Cost	Simplicity	PortabilityProcessTime	BillPaymentInterval
Rule	Service		SMSPORT		Medium	-	-	-
Rule	Service		TEMPNBRPORT		Low	-	-	-
Rule	Service		UMTSPORT		High	-	-	-
Rule	Payment		PAY=DD		Low	-	-	High
Rule	Payment		PAY=ONL		Low	-	-	Medium
Rule	Payment		PAY=POS		High	-	-	Low
Rule	Interaction		INT=IND		High	High	-	-
Rule	Interaction		INT=DIR		Low	Medium	-	-

Fig. 3.12: Properties and context rules

	Name	Nu...	PortingLocationP...	Cust...	Cust...	Cust...	Intera...	PaymentM...	BillP...	Custo...	oracle
Scenario	SCN	-	-	-	-	-	-	-	-	-	-
Context	C1	true	ItalianDepartment	true	true	true	Direct	Direct Debit	true	E-mail	ONP
Context	C2	false	ItalianDepartment	false	true	false	Indirect	Online	true	Post	NNA
Context	C3	true	EnglishDepartment	true	true	false	Direct	Direct Debit	false	E-mail	ONP
Context	C4	false	ItalianDepartment	false	false	false	Direct	Online	true	SMS	NNA
Context	C5	true	BelgianDepartment	true	false	true	Indirect	Direct Debit	false	E-mail	ONP
Context	C6	true	ItalianDepartment	false	false	true	Indirect	Post	false	E-mail	ONP

Fig. 3.13: Part of the simulation model for the MPSP system

---

[1] Column names collapsed to fit in the figure.

- Configuration: The set of configurations and contained variants identified for each context is decided by the hard constraints. The order of the configurations is computed through the priority rules. Within one context, we can see that each configuration is scored against the properties defined for the system, which is a summarisation of the variant scores.

- Variant: These are given scores for each property based on the priority rules.

As can be seen from the figure, there are two possible configurations for this context. The configuration are green since the expected property specified in the simulation input is verified for both. If properties were to be violated by some configuration, they would appear as red to highlight an error which might come either from the model constraints, rules or simply from the simulation input. The two possible configurations for context C4 can be used in that context but one has been ranked higher than the other based on the priority rules defined in the adaptation models. In practice the simulation is an important feature of the DiVA tool and methodology since it allows incrementally developing and checking the adaptation models. Further details on the adaptation modelling language and simulation can be found in [12].

3.5 Adaptive Service Implementation and Integration

This section demonstrates the last step of the DiVA methodology that consists of translating the variability models to executable models, generating the code of the components that implement the variable services, and integrating the variable services . Here only a brief overview the DiVA implementation methodology is demonstrated in relation to the case-study. More details of this can be found in [21, 22].

The adaptation model designed during variability modelling is used with other classical business analysis views, such as BPMN diagrams or UML activity diagrams, use case and sequence diagrams, to refine the functional view of the system into a technical view. The DiVA analysis can be complemented with other service engineering approaches such as SOAML to design a set of technical services that realise the system. By identifying the variable parts of the system and how they interact with the other components early, the variable technical services can be isolated earlier in the design process and special attention can be paid to integration issues that may arise due to their volatile nature.

The adaptation model is then translated to a model that can be executed [21]. Each service variant is thus refined into an aspect model that includes the specification of the components that actually implement the service. The aspect models are then used as architecture fragments that can be composed into a core model containing the architectural elements that are always present in the system. The composition of aspects is performed on-demand at run-time by an Aspect-Oriented weaver to build the actual configuration of components corresponding to the required service variants. By focusing on variability dimensions and variants rather than focusing on whole configurations, the aspect-oriented modelling approach allows us to avoid the combinatorial explosion of configurations and adaptation rules.

Figure 3.15 shows two examples of translating variants into aspect models. The first aspect model encapsulates the components that implement the SMSPortingCost variant of the Calculate "Porting Costs" variability dimension and the second aspect model encapsulates the components that implement the PortingToItaly variant of the Manage Porting variability dimension. The components depicted in the right-hand part of the figure will be added to the system and bound as represented by the dashed-red lines. The left-hand part of the figure shows where the components will be woven and against which components the running system will be matched before weaving. We can see that by encouraging thinking in terms of components straight from the early stages of technical modelling, the DiVA methodology allows to take into account the integration of optional pieces of logic early in the design phases and avoid later problems. Also, the methodology does not impose any particular aspect language and weaver, which allows to trade off easily between the overhead

	COS	SIM	PPT	BPI	Total
◢ ✦ Scenario SCN	-	-	-	-	-
› ✦ Context C1	High	Medium	Lowest	High	-
› ✦ Context C2	High	High	Lowest	Medium	-
◢ ✦ Context C3	High	Medium	Lowest	High	-
◢ ✦ Configuration (-616)	-224	16	-8	-64	-616
✦ OldNumberPorting (0)	0	0	0	0	0
✦ Number Porting Cost (-128)	-64	0	0	0	-128
✦ SMS Porting Cost (-96)	-48	0	0	0	-96
✦ Web Interface (36)	0	16	-4	0	36
✦ Port Number Service (-128)	-64	0	0	0	-128
✦ Port SMS Service (-96)	-48	0	0	0	-96
✦ PortingToEngland (0)	0	0	0	0	0
✦ Direct Debit (-204)	0	0	-4	-64	-204
› ✦ Configuration (-724)	-224	48	-12	-128	-724
◢ ✦ Context C4	High	Medium	Lowest	Medium	-
› ✦ Configuration (-99)	0	16	-9	-40	-99
◢ ✦ Context C5	High	High	Lowest	High	-
› ✦ Configuration (-498)	-160	64	-6	-64	-498
› ✦ Configuration (-510)	-160	128	-10	-128	-510
› ✦ Context C6	High	High	Lowest	Low	-

Fig. 3.14: Simulation output for the MPSP system

of the run-time weaving process and the complexity of the pointcut expressions to be expressed in the aspect models.

The final step is to implement the components modelled in the aspects. The DiVA Studio assists this task by providing code-generating transformation that generates the factories, the interfaces and a base class for these components.

Figure 3.16 shows how are the variable services (such as PortingManagement or PortingCostsCalculation services) are integrated within the whole system and how they are deployed on top of already deployed telephony, billing and contact management services offered by each Cell Phone Operator (CPO). Each operator has their own set of service APIs that potentially differ and must be integrated. Also, there can be discrepancies between the departments of a single CPO, due for example to external growth strategies. Thus, an ESB (see Figure 3.16) is used to provide the necessary mediation, transformation, routing and orchestration facilities that smooth the integration of services between departments and between CPOs. The components of the case study are deployed inside the ESB as new services or extensions of service providers.

The underlying OSS platform supporting the component model is OSGi , because it offers the introspection APIs that support the manipulation of the architecture of a running system, and it integrates natively the notion of service dynamicity. The

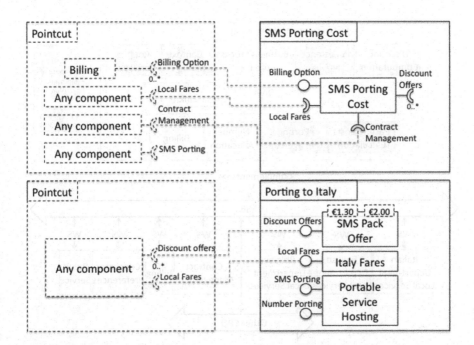

Fig. 3.15: Example aspect models

generic component model [23] used to model aspects is thus deployed and maintained by a OSGi-based causal link that implements components as bundles.

During the experimentations, the business services were developed before generating the DiVA wrapper classes. Little effort was required to port the components to the DiVA model. As the binding logic was already designed using OSGi due to the early choice of the OSS platform, only the dependencies managed by DiVA had to be changed. The major change is that dependencies managed by SpringDM are instead injected by the DiVA causal link. By using DiVA components on top of OSGi we thus realise a dynamic, model-driven ESB with little code overhead.

3.6 Related Work

This chapter has covered a number of different techniques to tackle the challenges of variability identification, modelling and maintenance for service-based systems. This section will examine other work which is also related to these challenges to offer a comparison between our approach and alternatives. The structure of this section will reflect the earlier part of the chapter where we first consider work related to requirements engineering, then variability modelling and finally service implementation.

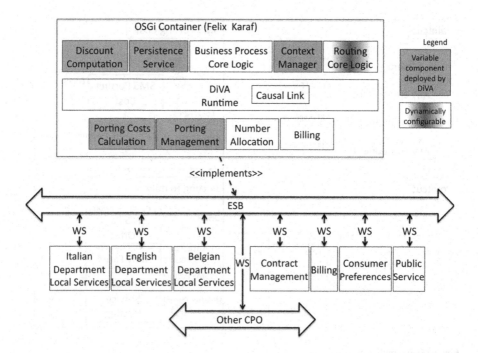

Fig. 3.16: Case study architecture

3.6.1 Variability Requirements Engineering

Addressing dynamic change in requirements is a new research area for Requirements Engineering . Consequently, there is only a small body of work directly addressing this problem [5, 18, 19, 33, 34].

Berry [5] provides a reflective view on requirements engineering for adaptive systems. They suggest that there are four levels of RE associated with an adaptive system that allows increasing levels of detail to be extracted from analysing the domain and system to identify adaptation elements. This process requires a large degree of manual effort and analysis of the running system to accurately determine these adaptation elements. In [33] the RELAX language is presented which aims to support requirements adaptation. It is based on the idea of capturing uncertainty declaratively with modal, temporal, ordinal operators and formalising the natural-language uncertainty semantics via fuzzy branching temporal logic. Additionally, [24] proposes a technique to allow requirements reflection whereby requirements are promoted to first-class run-time entities. This allows adaptive systems to reason about, understand, explain and modify requirements at runtime.

Alternatively, Lapouchnian [18, 19] suggest that in order to develop better autonomous systems, i.e., systems that handle their own configuration, healing, optimisation and protection at run-time, one needs to use a development process that extracts the alternative ways a system achieves its primary functionality and designs these alternatives as available options for system execution. To fulfil this aim the authors suggest the use of goal-based requirements models as the basis for such a development process. These models can be constructed using goal decomposition graphs to represent the alternatives necessary. These models can be subsequently furnished with goal dependencies and sequences via the insertion of additional notations such as AND and OR relationships. This approach proposed by Lapouchnian has subsequently been extended [34] where the goal based models are transformed into a set of feature models, state-charts and component-connector models. This enables the various variability elements to be modelled and represent stakeholder-motivated alternative solutions. Our approach builds upon this in an automated fashion, whereby requirements are processed to identify points of variability with the requirements text using Latent Semantic Analysis (LSA). This process allows different features of the system to be identified and structured according to the specified variability relationships.

In [25] Niu and Easterbrook describe an approach for supporting variability/commonality identification for functional requirement profiles. These profiles work with "primitive requirements" which are verb-direct object pairs (e.g., mark assignment) captured from the textual requirements. These primitive requirements are then qualified with a set of relevant lexical units (single words or phrases, such as, mark late/on-time assignment) which appear closely in the text with the verb-direct object. Each cluster is formed by grouping the primitive requirements with the most similar elements. Our approach differs from this as we do not require preliminary selection of primitive requirements or their attributes; instead we use LSA to automate clustering based on the full content of the textual requirements.

3.6.2 Variability Modelling

A variety of work has examined the area of adaptive application modelling and execution [20, 28, 31]. While these general approaches for adaptive system development and execution are contextually relevant to the DiVA modelling approach, we narrow the scope in this related work section and compare our work with existing techniques for expression of adaptation policies. This is appropriate since the DiVA model described in Section 3.4 is not a complete environment for adaptive system construction and execution, instead our model could be an alternative for modelling the adaptation logic in these broader scoped approaches. In general there are two families of approaches that have been defined for capturing adaptation policies: i) approaches based on explicit event-condition-action (ECA) rules and ii) approaches based on the definition of utility functions to be optimised. The DiVA modelling approach combines the strengths of these two approaches with respect to efficiency, scalability and verification capabilities.

The main strengths of ECA, such as [9, 15, 16], approaches are twofold; i) the readability and elegance of each individual rules, and ii) the efficiency with which the rules can be processed. At run-time, rules are matched and applied to adapt the system configuration. On the other hand, the main limitations of these techniques are related to scalability and validation. Managing a large set of possibly interacting adaptation rules rapidly becomes difficult. Validation becomes a major issue: how to ensure that the set of rules will yield the best possible configuration for every possible context of the application.

The alternative to the ECA approach is to view adaptations as an optimisation problem. The adaptation policies are expressed as high-level goals to achieve, and at run-time the configuration of the system is optimised with respect to these goals. The benefit of optimisation-based approaches, such as [1, 13, 16], is the abstraction they provide to express much simpler adaptation rules. In addition, utility functions are an efficient way to determine how well suited a configuration is, depending on the context. However, specifying these functions may not be easy for designers and may require several iterations in order to adjust. Also, while the approach does not explicitly describe all the possible configurations of the system a priori, the runtime reasoning has to calculate utility values for all of them, thus encountering scalability and efficiency issues.

The approach used by DiVA is a compromise between rule-based approaches like [11] and optimisation-based approaches like [13] which enable for design-time validation techniques such as defined in [35]. This makes the proposed approach a good trade-off for large-scale dynamic adaptive system by mastering the combinatorial explosion of the number of contexts and configurations.

3.6.3 Adaptive Service Implementation

Using a high-level representation of the running system (models at run-time) and an aspect model weaver, we are able to construct configurations on demand, by selecting and weaving a set of aspects (dynamic features) well adapted to the current context. David [8] presents the SAFRAN aspect-oriented approach for implementing self-adaptive behaviour on top-of the Fractal execution platform. This separates adaptation logic from the business logic and is similar to the DiVA approach. Batista [4] proposes a similar kind of approach but for the OpenCOM execution platform. These approaches do not provide an explicit representation of the target configurations, making it difficult to both visualise and also validate the proposed adaptations before being applied.

Ensuring software correctness is an important issue when considering dynamic adaptation. A number of approaches have been proposed to address configuration in a static manner within the software product line community. This issue has been addressed [26, 30] in terms of identifying defects and incompatibilities in a particular configuration. However, testing systems with many potential configurations can cause an explosion in the number of tests performed. Techniques have been proposed [17], based on model-checking, to control this explosion. For the DiVA approach, the main difference is that verifications can be done at run-time. This allows new aspects (adaptations) to be added/removed at run-time when unanticipated evolution occurs. The DiVA approach allows such unanticipated evolution to be validated. Through utilising MDE techniques, the DiVA approach allows aspects to be applied to an abstraction the run-time system to check its correctness.

3.7 Conclusions

This chapter has tackled the challenges of variability identification, modelling and maintenance for service-based systems. The DiVA approach provides solutions to these challenges. For instance, by providing separate models and treating each variant as distinct entities no compromises have to be made during the design and the core services do not have to take into account the variants that may be applied. Furthermore, the use of AO techniques removes the need to replace entire services at run-time. The problem of modelling exponential number of possible configurations is circumvented by treating the system as a product line and analysing configurations in terms of aspect (or alternative feature dimension) weaving at the model level. The problem of exponential configurations that must be analysed at run-time for the best configuration selection is reduced by selecting an adequate configuration that maintains the specified model level constraints.

We have described how the DiVA tools and methodology can be applied to a typical service engineering case-study to identify the various adaptation and variability points that it contains. We have presented a comprehensive tool chain that implements a very clear approach and provides a well integrated set of components helping developers to model and run complex adaptive systems. This tool chain provides support to developers from the requirements engineering stage, whereby core services and variability points can be semi-automatically identified. Support is offered through the design stage which allows an adaptation model to be created and trade-off analysis performed. Finally, implementation support is provided through code generators that allow the models to be converted into executable services and causal connections establish to allow dynamic adaptations to be applied.

To demonstrate the use of the DiVA methodology in the context of service-engineering we have applied it to the Mobile Phone Service Portability case-study. A number of non-trivial variants were identified, such as the customer's communication preference, and ways of interacting with Cell Phone Operators. These were subsequently modelled with context information added to describe under what circumstances these variants would be needed and so drive the adaptation at run-time. The DiVA simulator was then applied to these adaptation models to analyse the trade-offs and compatibility between variants to determine which configuration is most appropriate for a particular context. Finally, the process of how these models can be translated into execution entities and aspects to implement the variants was described.

Acknowledgements This work was funded by the DiVA project (EU FP7 STREP, contract 215412, http://www.ict-diva.eu/)

References

1. Using product line techniques to build adaptive systems (2006). DOI 10.1109/SPLINE.2006. 1691586. URL http://dx.doi.org/10.1109/SPLINE.2006.1691586
2. Ali, R., Chitchyan, R., Giorgini, P.: Context for goal-level product line derivation. 3rd International Workshop on Dynamic Software Product Lines (DSPL09) (2009)
3. Alves, A., Arkin, A., Askary, S., Bloch, B., Curbera, F., Goland, Y., Kartha, N., Sterling, König, D., Mehta, V., Thatte, S., van der Rijn, D., Yendluri, P., Yiu, A.: Web services business process execution language version 2.0. OASIS Committee Draft (2006)
4. Batista, T., Joolia, A., Coulson, G.: Managing dynamic reconfiguration in component-based systems. pp. 1–17 (2005). DOI 10.1007/11494713_1. URL http://dx.doi.org/10. 1007/11494713_1
5. Berry, D.M., Cheng, B.H.C., Zhang, J.: The four levels of requirements engineering for and in dynamic adaptive systems. In: In 11th International Workshop on Requirements Engineering Foundation for Software Quality (REFSQ, p. 05 (2005)
6. Chitchyan, R., Greenwood, P.: Framework for identifying and modelling of dynamic variability in requirements. DiVA Project, Deliverable D1.2 (2009)
7. Christensen, E., Curbera, F., Meredith, G., Weerawarana, S.: Web service definition language (wsdl). Tech. rep. (2001). URL http://www.w3.org/TR/wsdl
8. David, P.C., Ledoux, T.: An aspect-oriented approach for developing self-adaptive fractal components. In: W. Löwe, M. Südholt (eds.) Software Composition, *Lecture Notes in Computer Science*, vol. 4089, pp. 82–97. Springer (2006)
9. David, P.C., Ledoux, T.: Safe dynamic reconfigurations of Fractal architectures with FScript. In: Proc. Fractal CBSE Workshop, ECOOP'06. Nantes, France (2006). URL http://www. lina.sciences.univ-nantes.fr/Publications/2006/DL06
10. Filman, R.E., Elrad, T., Clarke, S., Akşit, M. (eds.): Aspect-Oriented Software Development. Addison-Wesley, Boston (2005)

11. Fleurey, F., Dehlen, V., Bencomo, N., Morin, B., Jézéquel, J.M.: Modeling and validating dynamic adaptation pp. 97–108 (2009). DOI http://dx.doi.org/10.1007/978-3-642-01648-6_11

12. Fleurey, F., Solberg, A.: A domain specific modeling language supporting specification, simulation and execution of dynamic adaptive systems. In: A. Schürr, B. Selic (eds.) MoDELS, *Lecture Notes in Computer Science*, vol. 5795, pp. 606–621. Springer (2009)

13. Floch, J., Hallsteinsen, S., Stav, E., Eliassen, F., Lund, K., Gjorven, E.: Using architecture models for runtime adaptability. IEEE Software **23**, 62–70 (2006). DOI http://doi.ieeecomputersociety.org/10.1109/MS.2006.61

14. Hallsteinsen, S., Hinchey, M., Park, S., Schmid, K.: Dynamic software product lines. Computer **41**(4), 93–95 (2008). DOI 10.1109/MC.2008.123

15. Keeney, J., Cahill, V.: Chisel: A policy-driven, context-aware, dynamic adaptation framework. Policies for Distributed Systems and Networks, IEEE International Workshop on **0**, 3 (2003). DOI http://doi.ieeecomputersociety.org/10.1109/POLICY.2003.1206953

16. Kephart, J.O., Das, R.: Achieving self-management via utility functions. IEEE Internet Computing **11**, 40–48 (2007). DOI http://doi.ieeecomputersociety.org/10.1109/MIC.2007.2

17. Kishi, T., Noda, N., Katayama, T.: Design verification for product line development. In: J.H. Obbink, K. Pohl (eds.) SPLC, *Lecture Notes in Computer Science*, vol. 3714, pp. 150–161. Springer (2005)

18. Lapouchnian, A., Liaskos, S., Mylopoulos, J., Yu, Y.: Towards requirements-driven autonomic systems design. ACM SIGSOFT Software Engineering Notes **30**(4), 1–7 (2005). URL http://dblp.uni-trier.de/db/journals/sigsoft/sigsoft30.html#LapouchnianLMY05

19. Lapouchnian, A., Yu, Y., Liaskos, S., Mylopoulos, J.: Requirements-driven design of autonomic application software. In: CASCON '06: Proceedings of the 2006 conference of the Center for Advanced Studies on Collaborative research, p. 7. ACM, New York, NY, USA (2006). DOI http://doi.acm.org/10.1145/1188966.1188976

20. Morin, B.: Survey and evaluation of approaches for runtime variability management. DiVA Project, Deliverable D3.1 (2009)

21. Morin, B.: Diva run-time reference architecture. DiVA Project, Deliverable D3.2 (2010)

22. Morin, B., Barais, O., Nain, G., Jézéquel, J.M.: Taming dynamically adaptive systems using models and aspects. In: ICSE, pp. 122–132. IEEE (2009)

23. Morin, B., Fleurey, F., Bencomo, N., Jézéquel, J.M., Solberg, A., Dehlen, V., Blair, G.: An aspect-oriented and model-driven approach for managing dynamic variability. In: MoDELS '08: Proceedings of the 11th international conference on Model Driven Engineering Languages and Systems, pp. 782–796. Springer-Verlag, Berlin, Heidelberg (2008). DOI http://dx.doi.org/10.1007/978-3-540-87875-9_54

24. Nelly Bencomo Jon Whittle, P.S.A.F., Letier, E.: Requirements reflection: Requirements as runtime entities. ACM/IEE 32nd International Conference on Software Engineering (2010)

25. Niu, N., Easterbrook, S.: Extracting and modeling product line functional requirements. In: RE '08: Proceedings of the 16th International Requirements Engineering Conference (2008)

26. Pohl, K., Metzger, A.: Software product line testing. Commun. ACM **49**(12), 78–81 (2006). DOI http://doi.acm.org/10.1145/1183236.1183271

27. Rayson, P.: Wmatrix: A web-based corpus processing environment. Tech. rep., Computing Department, Lancaster University (2008)

28. Rouvoy, R.: Requirements of mechanisms and planning algorithms for self-adaptation. MUSIC FP6 Integrated Project D1.1 (2007)

29. Sampaio, A., Rashid, A., Chitchyan, R., Rayson, P.: Ea-miner: Towards automation in aspect-oriented requirements engineering. Transactions on Aspect-Oriented Software Development **3**(4), 4–39 (2007)

30. Svahnberg, M., Bosch, J.: Issues concerning variability in software product lines. In: IW-SAPF-3: Proceedings of the International Workshop on Software Architectures for Product Families, pp. 146–157. Springer-Verlag, London, UK (2000)

31. Tolchinsky, P.: State of the art. ALIVE FP7 Project D2.1 (2008)

32. Weston, N., Chitchyan, R., Rashid, A.: A framework for constructing semantically compos-
    able feature models from natural language requirements. In: SPLC'09: Proceedings of the
    13th International Software Product Line Conference (2009)
33. Whittle, J., Sawyer, P., Bencomo, N., Cheng, B.H., Bruel, J.M.: Relax: Incorporating uncer-
    tainty into the specification of self-adaptive systems. Requirements Engineering, IEEE Inter-
    national Conference on **0**, 79–88 (2009). DOI http://doi.ieeecomputersociety.org/10.1109/RE.
    2009.36
34. Yu, Y., Lapouchnian, A., Liaskos, S., Mylopoulos, J., Leite, J.: From goals to high-variability
    software design. pp. 1–16 (2008). DOI 10.1007/978-3-540-68123-6_1. URL http://dx.
    doi.org/10.1007/978-3-540-68123-6_1
35. Zhang, J., Cheng, B.H.C.: Specifying adaptation semantics. In: WADS '05: Proceedings of
    the 2005 workshop on Architecting dependable systems, pp. 1–7. ACM, New York, NY, USA
    (2005). DOI http://doi.acm.org/10.1145/1083217.1083220

Chapter 4

Coordination, Organisation and Model-driven Approaches for Dynamic, Flexible, Robust Software and Services Engineering

Juan Carlos Nieves, Julian Padget, Wamberto Vasconcelos, Athanasios Staikopoulos, Owen Cliffe, Frank Dignum, Javier Vázquez-Salceda, Siobhán Clarke, and Chris Reed

Abstract Enterprise systems are increasingly composed of (and even functioning as) components in a dynamic, digital ecosystem. On the one hand, this new situation requires flexible, spontaneous and opportunistic collaboration activities to be identified and established among (electronic) business parties. On the other, it demands engineering methods that are able to integrate new functionalities and behaviours into running systems composed by active, distributed, interdependent processes. Here we present a multi-level architecture that combines organisational and coordination theories with model driven development, for the implementation, deployment and management of dynamic, flexible and robust service-oriented business applications, combined with a service layer that accommodates semantic service description, fine-grained semantic service discovery and the dynamic adaptation of services to meet changing circumstances.

Juan Carlos Nieves · Javier Vázquez-Salceda
Software Department, Universitat Politècnica de Catalunya, Barcelona, Spain, e-mail: jcnieves@lsi.upc.edu, e-mail: jvazquez@lsi.upc.edu

Julian Padget · Owen Cliffe
Department of Computer Science, University of Bath, Bath, BA2 7AY, United Kingdom. e-mail: jap@cs.bath.ac.uk, e-mail: occ@cs.bath.ac.uk

Wamberto Vasconcelos
Department of Computing Science, The University of Aberdeen, AB24 3UE, United Kingdom, e-mail: wvasconcelos@acm.org

Athanasios Staikopoulos · Siobhán Clarke
Department of Computer Science, Trinity College Dublin, Dublin, Ireland. e-mail: Siobhan.Clarke@cs.tcd.ie, e-mail: Athanasios.Staikopoulos@cs.tcd.ie

Frank Dignum
Department of Informatics, University of Utrecht, Utrecht, The Netherlands, e-mail: dignum@cs.uu.nl

Chris Reed
Calico Jack Ltd., DD1 1QP, United Kingdom. e-mail: chris@calicojack.co.uk

4.1 Introduction

Visions about the future World Wide Web (referred to by some as the Future Internet or the Web 3.0) describe the need of networked applications that can be dynamically deployed, adjusted and composed. This new generation of networked service applications should be able to: communicate and reconfigure at run-time, adapt to their environment dynamically and combine sets of building block services into new applications. These (emerging) requirements have the capacity to change profoundly the way in which software systems are designed, deployed and managed, replacing existing "design in isolation" engineering with new approaches able to integrate new functionalities and behaviours into running systems and active, distributed, interdependent processes.

Technical progress in the area of service-oriented architectures (SOAs) in recent years has been impressive, with new models, tools and standards emerging to cover a wide range of core and related functions. Furthermore, advances have come from a variety of sources, including: enterprise interoperability, Grid computing, software engineering, database and knowledge-base theory, artificial intelligence, object-oriented systems and logic.

This rapid progress has, for the first time, raised the realistic possibility of deploying large numbers of services in intranets and extranets of companies and public organisations, as well as in the public Internet, in order to create communities of services that are always connected, frequently changing, open or semi-open, and form the baseline environment for distributed software applications. However, this shift brings about not only potential benefits, but also serious challenges for how such systems and applications should be designed, managed and deployed. Existing approaches in some important areas (such as security, transactions and federation) tend to cover only technology issues such as, for example, how to secure a protocol or connect federated directories, without considering the paradigm shift that occurs when large numbers of services are deployed and managed over time. In particular, existing approaches do not offer satisfactory answers to these questions:

- How to manage work-flows in non-trivial environments, where not all services are owned by the same organisation? Since we cannot assume that all parties are either benevolent or that they will deliver results unless explicit obligations are defined and enforced, should work-flows be agreed upon by all parties before they can be executed?
- How to align the configurations and settings needed by a service to operate with those of the operational environment?
- How is service execution affected by issues of trust, rights, obligations and prohibitions?
- What if critical applications simply cease to function if services provisioned from third parties disappear or malfunction?
- How to deal with knowledge representation when connecting or binding together two or more actual entities or services using different ontologies?

These issues point to the need for a "social layer" as part of the service interaction context. From an engineering perspective, new approaches are needed that take an holistic view of service environments, and take into account not only the properties of individual applications, but also the objectives, structure and dynamics of the system as a whole. In recent years, research in fields as diverse as social science, management science, economics, biology, distributed systems and multi-agent systems, has analysed, modelled and explained a wide range of social phenomena often seen in human and animal societies and tried to apply those results to computational systems. In particular, techniques have been developed, that:

- Make it possible to characterise and model the organisational structures commonly used by humans to organise themselves in societies with particular needs;
- Capture coordination patterns that are often used between humans to solve common problems (e.g., to sell goods or achieve specific goals);
- Characterise autonomous actors in an environment and model their potential, rational behaviour (in order to predict, for example, how individuals will act in the context of a given set of "rules").

This chapter will present an approach, that we call ALIVE, for combining Coordination Technology and Organizational Theory with technologies for Model Driven Engineering to create a framework for software and services engineering addressing the new reality of "live", open systems of active services. The approach is inspired by the belief that many of the strategies used today to organise the vastly complex interdependencies found in human social and economic behaviour will be essential to structuring future service-based software systems. We aim to achieve this by providing flexible, high-level means to model the structure of inter-actions between services in the environment and by the provision of automated transformations from models on to multiple target platforms.

The ALIVE approach extends current trends in engineering by defining three levels for the design and management of distributed systems:

- The *organisational level*, which provides context for the other levels, supporting an explicit representation of the organisational structure (composed by patterns and rules) of the system, and effectively allowing a structural adaptation of distributed systems over time;
- The *coordination level*, which provides the means to specify, at a high level, the patterns of interaction among services, transforming the organisational representation (including information flows, constraints, tasks and agents) coming from Organisational Level into coordination plans; and
- The *service level*, which allows the semantic description of services and the selection of the most appropriate services for a given task (based on the semantic information contained in the service description), effectively supporting high-level, dynamic service composition.

The rest of the paper is organized as follows. We start in Section 6.3 by describing an extended version of one of the scenarios common to this book, namely the portability of the services associated with a mobile phone, as the device moves between different domains. We then introduce the ALIVE approach in Section 4.3, where we set out the three layers of organization, coordination and service and the connections between them that characterise our project, using the mobile telephony scenario to illustrate notable aspects. Section 8.5 offers some reflection on the process outlined and its advantages and disadvantages. We follow this in Section 4.5 with a survey of related work in service oriented architectures from the multiple perspectives of whole systems, key components and software engineering methodologies. Finally in the last section, we present our conclusions.

4.2 Motivating Scenario

We explore a scenario to highlight the challenges involved in providing portability of services to which a customer has subscribed; in such scenarios, customers, depending on their context, dynamically request new communication services, as well as change and cancel some of their currently contracted services. More specifically, let us assume that a large cell phone operator would like to extend their communication services to on-line social networks and virtual communities such as SecondLife[1] (SL) or Bebo[2].

These services should support communication through a number of distinct types of media channels such as mobile telephony, plain old telephony services (POTS), video, SMS, e-mail, and instant messaging[3] (IM). We notice that when connecting such disparate channels, our aim is to bring them together to offer users the experience of a seamless cross-channel communication service. Crucially though, it is not realistic to pursue naïve unifications of the underlying technologies: our aim is to produce a virtual communication device—not an IM client glued on to a mobile phone glued on to an e-mail client. The goal should be to allow *the dynamic reconfiguration of communication pathways* based, on the one hand, *on the availability of services* (Does the user have a phone? Is the user currently registered to receive voice-mail messages in Bebo? Is the user currently signed up for a VoIP provider?) and on the other hand, *on the availability of the user*.

Social context, once formally captured, provides knowledge that can be exploited in routing and configuring calls. Players of SL have a social context represented within SL, such as groups, tribes, friends, and so on, but those players also have

---

[1] Second Life (http://secondlife.com/) is an Internet-accessible virtual world launched in 2003; it enables its users to interact with one another through avatars, allowing them to explore, meet other residents, socialise, participate in individual and group activities, and create and trade virtual property and services with one another, or travel throughout the world.

[2] Bebo (http://www.bebo.com/), an acronym for "Blog Early, Blog Often", is a social networking website, founded in 2005.

[3] Instant messaging puts together various technologies to allow real-time text-based communication between two or more participants over the Internet or some form of internal network/intranet.

identities on Facebook[4], Bebo, Orkut[5] and so on. By connecting these identities (through mechanisms such as OpenID[6]) social context can be used to reconfigure the services required to effect communication on-the-fly. These social structures involve normative relationships: if A and B are friends on Facebook, they can write on each others' "walls", but that does not mean that, say, they have rights to view each other's data on LinkedIn[7]. However, it might mean that if A wants to communicate with B, A has permission to use a Facebook wall as a medium.

In addition to the technological and social constraints above, software solutions to such scenarios must factor in any regulations governing communication over electronic media. We argue that regulations are more naturally captured via an explicit specification of norms (namely, permissions, prohibitions and obligations on components of the solution) that, together with the social context, should define the design space of software solutions.

We call the system under study a "Service Communication Router" (SCR). The main business goals the SCR has to achieve are:

- To satisfy national and European regulations;
- To make portability and customisation of services as transparent as possible to the customer; and
- To provide new added-value services.

The details of these business goals are presented elsewhere in this volume (respectively in tables 3, 4 and 5, of Chapter 1).

4.2.1 A More Concrete Example

Within the broad class of scenarios sketched above, we want to make the discussion more concrete and detail a more concrete example. Let us suppose that Bob is in a band, the AliveA5Os. They have decided to preview their new track in SL. Bob uses his SL communicator to send a message to all of his friends. He types in: "Hi all! Come hear AliveA5Os' new song, Hawaiian Mussels, at 1900CET at Alive Island". The following sequence of events unfolds:

---

[4] Facebook (http://www.facebook.com/) is a social networking Web site in which users create a profile and then add friends to this profile, being able to send these friends messages; users are able to update their personal profiles and notify friends about themselves. Users can also join networks organised by city, workplace, school, and region.

[5] Orkut (http://www.orkut.com) is a free-access social networking service owned and operated by Google (http://www.google.com). Orkut is designed to help users meet new friends and maintain existing relationships.

[6] OpenID (http://openid.net/) is an open standard for authenticating users which can be used for access control, allowing users to log on to different services with the same digital identity where these services trust the authentication body. OpenID replaces the common login process that uses a login-name and a password, by allowing a user to log in once and gain access to the resources of multiple software systems.The term OpenID can also refer to an ID used in the standard.

[7] LinkedIn (http://www.linkedin.com/) is a business-oriented social networking site launched in 2003, mainly used for professional networking.

1. Alice is in Bob's tribe on SL. She's tinkering in SL and receives a message through her SL IM client.
2. Henry is a friend of Bob on facebook, and also in Bob's IM friends list. He's working at home and receives the message through his MSN client.
3. Hirta and Max are on holiday. They're friends of Bob on Bebo: when they next check in to an internet cafe, they notice the message waiting for them on Bebo.
4. Verig is the A&R man at Irish Beach records, and is in Bob's LinkedIn network. He's on the move, and receives a call to his mobile; an automated voice reads out the message.
5. Estragon is a close friend of Henry; they're friends on Facebook and in SL. Estragon is in a meeting at work. When he gets out, he has an email in his inbox containing the message.
6. Pandora is using Facebook. Her wall is updated with the message from Bob, and she's impressed and forwards it to her network of friends. They each receive the message in the channel, and on the device most appropriate to them, including Vladimir, who's playing SL and receives a voice call on his SL communicator reading him the message forwarded via Pandora.

4.2.2 Components of the Scenario

In this section we outline the various components of our scenario. Initially, we list its various stakeholders: we refer to these in a generic fashion, using the *roles* they play. The roles we have chosen to represent in our scenario are:

- *customers* – initiate and receive messages/calls.
- *managers* – represent interfaces to static or dynamic information repositories
- *subscription managers* – responsible for subscription look-up
- *context managers* – responsible for interfacing with the emergent presence determination service
- *profile managers* – responsible for handling user preferences

The following data are available from customers:

- a set of *subscribed communication services*, each element of which is a tag corresponding to a particular application (*e.g.*, Facebook, SL, etc.)
- a set of *preferences*, comprising a specification of mappings from contexts to channels
- a *context* that can be determined by accessing the emergent presence engine; a context is resolved as a set of tags corresponding to contextual states (*e.g.*, "*in a meeting*", "*at work*", etc.)

The channels are the following communication media:

- *IM* is text-based instant messaging communicated (typically) over XMPP
- *SL-Text* is text-based communications coming from bespoke subsystems in SecondLife
- *POTS* is traditional voice telephony
- *VoIP* is packet-switched voice over IP infrastructure

- *SMS* is standard mobile text messaging

To deal with messages coming into and going out of the SCR we have various handlers. For the incoming material we have *handle_im* for IM, *handle_pots* for voice calls over POTS, *handle_sms* for text messages and *handle_SL_text* for chat from SecondLife. For outgoing material we provide delivery components, namely, *deliver_sms* to deliver text messages, *deliver_pots* to deliver voice calls and *deliver_email* to deliver email. We also consider transformations that are responsible for performing transcoding tasks. We have *perform_asr* for automated speech recognition and *perform_tts* for text to speech transformation.

When selecting which channel to use, the SCR makes use of functionality *determine_possible* that identifies possible communication channels for a participant and *determine_appropriate*, that identifies appropriate communication channels for a participant (based on the participant's profile and preferences). The SCR accesses a reasoning service *calculate_possible* that supports *determine_possible* and *calculate_appropriate* that supports *determine_appropriate*. The SCR uses functionalities to access other sources of information, namely, *get_preferences*, that accesses the customers' profile data, *get_context*, that accesses emergent presence data, and *get_subscription*, that accesses subscription data.

4.3 The ALIVE Approach

4.3.1 ALIVE Architecture

The ALIVE architecture combines *model driven development* (MDD) [24] with coordination and organisational mechanisms, providing support for *live*—that is, highly dynamic—and *open* systems of services. The ALIVE approach extends current trends in engineering by defining three levels (see Fig. 4.1 and below) for the design and management of distributed systems, namely: services, coordination and organisation.

The *Service Level* extends existing service models to make them aware of their social context and of the rules of engagement with other services. This is achieved via semantic Web technologies, that are particularly useful when highly dynamic and frequently-changing services are present, as the semantic meta-information in each service description helps in finding substitutes when a given service is not available or performing properly.

The *Coordination Level* provides the means to specify, at a high level, patterns of service interaction. Current service oriented systems specify the coordination between services using choreography and orchestration languages, that assume coordination patterns are designed off-line and the whole work-flow is predetermined. This only works for applications where no adjustments to the work-flow are needed during execution, but fails when it has to be changed due to the circumstances (e.g. unavailability of services). In ALIVE we use a variety of powerful coordination techniques from recent research in the area [10, 18], based on agent technology. These tech-

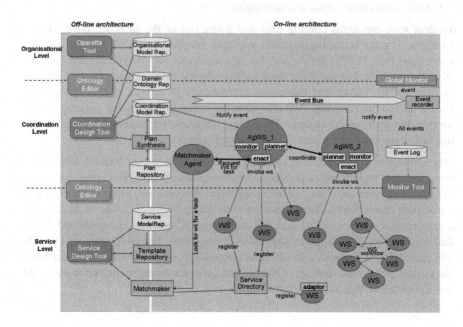

Fig. 4.1: ALIVE multi-Level architecture

niques include *agentified services* (AgWS) that are organisation-aware (aware of the system objectives) and manage task allocation as well as work-flow construction and agreement. Thus, work-flows can be adapted *while* the system is running.

The *Organisational Level* resides above coordination, providing a social context for the Coordination and the Service levels. This level specifies the rules that govern interaction. Many facets are described only in an abstract way so as to allow for more than one implementation and/or changes in implementation (different services, work-flows, interaction patterns) over time, making the organisational level the most stable of the three. This level defines the system on the basis of goals and results, abstracting away from the specific actions used to accomplish them. Hence, the organisational level defines the playground within whose boundaries the coordination and service levels can adjust, securing some overall stability of the system and guaranteeing global results. Although the organisational level is the most static, we also use recent developments in organisational dynamics [31] to allow the structural adaptation of the global system over time.

The ALIVE architecture provides a service-oriented middleware supporting the combination, reorganisation and adaptation of services at both design- and run-time. These activities follow organisational patterns and adopt coordination techniques. The MDD paradigm integrated in the architecture provides semi-automated transformations between models at the three levels and capacity for multiple target platforms and representation languages. Finally, there are graphical tools to support system administrators in the management of the system. The *Monitor Tool* allows inspecting the status of a system's execution, keeping track of the events generated at execution time and how the system handles them. The *Service Set-up Tool* can be used to check and modify the setup of the running environment. Finally the *Service Matchmaking Tool* (also available off-line) allows for manual searching for services that match a given task description, which helps when the system is not able to cope with a particular issue or the administrator wants to change manually an automatically selected service.

In the succeeding sections, a more detailed description of the architecture is provided. Complementary theoretical aspects are described in [4] and related methodological aspects are described in [3].

4.3.2 Modelling the Scenario

The Service Communication Router (SCR) from our extension of the telecommunications scenario places demands on each of ALIVE's three levels:

- At the organisational level, the SCR requires expressions of roles and access permissions for communication channels (allowing in-game friends access to in-game VoIP and IM, and real-world email, for example; allowing Facebook friends access to in-game IM, etc.).
- At the coordination level, the SCR requires reasoning to determine service selection in specific situations. This reasoning may introduce external resources, such as a representation of the user's diary.
- At the service level, the SCR requires specification of communication channels, including both in-game and real-world, and redundancy (*e.g*,. using multiple SMS delivery services, using VoIP vs. POTS, using IM over XMPP, IM over SIP).

To make the relationships between the levels clearer, let us consider the following example. At the organisational level, a user allows in-game friends to communicate with them via in-game VoIP and real-world email. At the coordination level, a communication request from Bob is routed to the user's VoIP device mapping from the in-game user-id through to an agentive representation where normative rules are applied, then back to the in-game user-id for delivery. At the service level, finding VoIP engaged, dynamic reconfiguration is required to re-route through an automatic speech recognition (ASR) service, and then to the user's email.

Turning our attention to the more concrete example of Section 4.2.1, Bob is in a meeting and has both wi-fi and mobile phone access, while Alice, his boss, is at the office, tinkering with some new gadget she's acquired in SecondLife. Suddenly she remembers the deadline for the marketing report she's supposed to compile: she needs to get hold of her report writing staff, namely, Bob and Charlie. She fires off a message from her SecondLife IM client (SL-IM). Her preferences are for voice messages whilst working, but for calls to be routed to his email if she has a meeting arranged in his diary. Charlie, on the other hand, is at work but surreptitiously playing SecondLife. His preference is for work material to be routed to his voice-mail. In the first part of the story, Alice's message is delivered via email to Bob and transcoded to audio and then delivered to Charlie's voice-mail. In the second part of the story, Alice notices she's not had a response, and resends her message with a high priority. This priority results in the norm of allowing recipients' preferences to be overridden. Hence, the delivery channels used are the same (or as close as possible) to the sender's. In this case, the SL-IM message is delivered as SL-IM to Charlie and as SMS to Bob. Finally, in a re-run, there are two examples of fail-ure recovery. In the first example, the first SMS delivery service fails (that is, it is switched off). The service level uses an alternative service. In the second example, the sole voice-mail service is unavailable. The coordination level replans and sends the audio to Charlie's email.

4.3.3 The Organisational Level

As said before, the organisational level is meant to create a number of fixed points that are used by the coordination and service level to aim at during their planning and adaptation processes. The objectives of the organisation and the division of them over the different roles in an organisation indicate which interactions should take place and what the desired result of these interactions are. In the use case, Alice is the boss and thus is responsible for the marketing reports. As such she has to interact with Bob and Charlie who work for her and create parts of these reports. The goal of this interaction is thus for Alice (as boss) knowing the status of the marketing reports in time. This is independent from the way the interaction takes place, but the interaction should be done in a way that Alice gets the information in time. At the organisational level we can also specify that the boss has the right to request status updates and thus answers should always be given quick and accurately. This means that the agents and services performing the actions should be implemented in a way that giving an answer to these requests get priority over other work if the deadline is close. Thus the specification of the organisation restricts (or fixes) some of the implementation choices in a consistent way such that overall objectives of the system are fulfilled.

For modelling the organisational level of the system, we use the *OperettA Tool* (see Fig. 4.1). The tool is based on the framework for Agent Organizations (OperA) [7], which is a general framework to specify the organizational context of multi-agent systems. OperA views an organisation as a set of entities (the stakeholders) and their interactions, which are regulated by mechanisms of social order. The organisational models built by this tool abstract away from the low-level details of the services that may be invoked. The OperettA Tool supports ALIVE's model-driven approach us-ing a meta-model defined to capture these entities and interactions. In later sections, we will see how relevant scenario elements at the organisational level map to the ele-ments in the other layers. The organisational model at this level is specified in terms of four structures: (i) *social*, (ii) *interaction* (iii) *normative* and (iv) *communicative*. These aspects are briefly explained in following sub-sections.

4.3.3.1 Social Structure

The social structure of an organization describes the objectives of the society, its roles and what kind of model governs coordination. Roles are abstractions that provide away to ascribe stereotypical behaviours (i.e. whoever takes up a role is expected to behave in a particular way) [7]. Roles identify activities necessary to achieve organisational objectives and abstract from the specific actors and/or services that will eventually perform them. Roles are described in terms of objectives (what an actor of the role is expected to achieve) and norms (how an actor is expected to behave) and also specify the rights associated with the role. Actors of institutional roles are fixed and controlled by the society and are designed to enforce the social behaviour of other actors assuring the global activity of the society. External roles can be enacted by any actor, according to the access rules specified by the society (e.g. services that are not under direct control of the organization are modelled at the organisational level as external roles). The notion of role is closely related to cooperation and coordination. Societies establish dependencies and power relations between roles. These relationships describe how actors can interact and contribute to the realisation of the objectives of each other (i.e. one role is dependent on another role for the realisation of its objectives). Each role dependency gives rise to an interaction pattern in which the actors fulfilling the roles delegate tasks and report on their activities.

4.3.3.2 Interaction Structure

The interaction structure describes a partial ordering of a number of *scenes* in which the roles interact, defining a very abstract work-flow of the whole system. Following paths through the different scenes should lead to fulfilling the overall objectives of the organisation. Each of the scenes specifies which roles interact, its intermediate states of interaction (interaction patterns) its desired results (scene results) and the norms regulating the interaction (scene norms). The specification of the expected interaction in scenes is based on the concept of landmark patterns, which induce a partial ordering by describing temporal relationships between landmarks. Landmark patterns describe the states that must be part of any protocol that will eventually be used by actors to achieve the scene results providing an abstract and flexible way to describe expected interactions. A scene typically relates to the achievement of an objective or set of objectives. Usually all role objectives should be related to scene results. Scene results are declarative state expressions that describe the desired final states for the scene, that is, the states in which the scene ends and actors can leave it successfully.

4.3.3.3 Normative Structure

The normative structure is the part of the Organisational Model that represents the collection of norms and rights related to the social and interaction structures. Norms define the obligations, permissions and prohibitions of the actors in the organisation, related to the roles they play, or to a particular area of activity. We distinguish regulative and constitutive norms [11]. Regulative norms regulate the behaviour of agents enacting roles and are expressed via deontic declarative expressions. Constitutive norms regulate the creation of institutional facts and are part of the ontological specification of the system in the form of "counts-as" statements. The regulative norms are spread over role norms, scene norms, and transition norms:

- Role norms specify the rules of behaviour for actors performing that role, irrespective of the interaction scene.
- Scene norms describe the expected behaviour of actors in a scene.
- Transition norms: impose additional limitations on actors attempting to follow a transition between two scenes. These are typically used if a result in one scene limits the subsequently accessible scenes.

Role rights indicate the capabilities that actors of the role receive when enacting the role. These are capabilities that an agent usually does not possess but which are inherent to the role, and will receive when it enacts the role.

4.3.3.4 Communicative Structure

The communication structure specifies the ontologies for describing the domain concepts (an ontology that defines the concepts used in the messages) and communication illocutions (the message types that can be used).

4.3.3.5 Scenario's Social/Organisational Component

Both senders and receivers enact the *Participant* role. A single scene which forms the core of the use case, the *communication scene*, involves the *Participant*, who performs a number of information seeking actions with resources under the control of other roles. For subscription information, this is the *Subscription_Manager* (accessed via *Retrieve_Receiver_Subscription*); for context, *i.e.*, emergent presence data, this is the *Context_Manager* (accessed via *Retrieve_Receiver_Context*); and for preference information, this is the *Profile_Manager* (accessed via *Retrieve_Receiver_Profile*). We show in Figure 4.2 the graphic representation of the social/organisational component of the scenario.

4.3.4 The Coordination Level

As the sequence of events of our concrete example of Section 4.2.1 unfolds, the components must coordinate their activities. For instance, when Bob sends a message to his friends, alternative means must be in place to reach those who cannot be directly contacted by instant messaging (IM, the quickest channel). If Alice's IM client is not available, then a composition of other channels, with adequate transformations, could be used instead, thus allowing Bob to reach her, somehow. In our concrete example, the text aimed at the IM client could be transformed, using speech synthesis techniques, onto speech, which could then be delivered either via

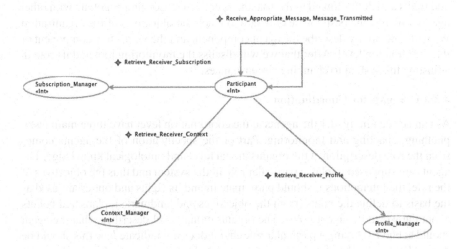

Fig. 4.2: Social/organisational component of scenario

POTS or VoIP channels. These options should be weighed against costs and users' preferences (that is, both the preferences of the user sending the message and the preferences of the user receiving the message). The coordination layer allows such alternatives to be automatically explored: software agents create plans which will fulfil goals represented at the organisational (social) level, making use of services and their composition.

Very importantly, unlike the organisational level, the coordination and service levels of the system are supposed to adapt to the current situation. Therefore they have an off-line, design aspect and an on-line aspect that is used while the system is running.

The *Coordination Design Tool* is used to create and manage the coordination model. The coordination level connects the high level, abstract objectives of the organisation to work-flows that invoke services that can actually achieve those objectives. To achieve this connection the level defines the agents and the work-flows (or plans). This tool assists the user in the definition of actors and tasks, the generation of the agents that will perform the actual coordination tasks and the inspection of predefined and generated plans. As before, the model-driven approach is supported by ensuring the elements defined by the user conform to an ALIVE meta-model, which provides us with the means to provide automated transformations between the layers. For example, at this level, the agents map to the roles defined at the organisation level, in that roles describe what agents should achieve. We use agents at this level because we want to be able to create these work-flows on the fly (e.g. from existing plan libraries) and adjust them when circumstances require so. In order to do this we need agents that can fulfil organisational roles and thus "know" about the organisational objectives for that role and the boundaries within which that role has to act. By using knowledge about the purpose of a work-flow, planning knowledge and rights and duties linked to the role the agent can reason and negotiate with other agents which is the best course of action to reach the objectives of the organisation. We will now briefly describe the agent component and the work-flow component of the coordination level. After that we will discuss the monitoring tool and its role in adjusting the system to changing circumstances.

4.3.4.1 Agents for Coordination

As can be seen in fig. 4.1 the agents at the coordination level have three main tasks: planning, enacting and monitoring. Part of the specification of the agents comes from the role description at the organisational level and ontological knowledge. The agents are supposed to play a particular role in the system and thus the objectives of the role, the interactions it should participate in and its rights and duties are used as the basis to define the goals (from the objectives and landmarks), plans and beliefs about the world the agent holds. The organisational level describes what the agent should achieve (playing a particular role) but it does not indicate *how* this should be done. That is why the planning component is designed at the coordination level. Of course, the model-driven approach in ALIVE allows the Operetta Tool to generate an initial agent specification as input to the coordination level tools.

The actions of the agents can be more abstract than the actual services on the service level, but they also can directly use available services. Therefore we see agents as *agentified services* that are organisation-aware and able to coordinate with others according to a given organisation and coordination model. They are able to:

- Incorporate the description of an organisation role, including its objectives, rights, obligations and prohibitions;
- Build, at run-time, local plans to fulfil the role's objectives;
- Coordinate its activities with other agentified services, thus building a partial global plan [17].

Agentified services can interact with normal Web services by means of standard SOAP and REST interfaces. Furthermore agentified services communicate coordination-related issues to other agentified services using protocol-based conversations expressed in a coordination language. The exchanged plans are abstract work-flows possibly with tasks referring to abstract services rather than to concrete ones. When a plan is agreed upon, an agentified service will look (via the matchmaker component) for services that can fulfil the abstract tasks, binding them together.

The matchmaker agent is a special agent that forms a gateway for the agents to the service level matchmaker component. Using a matchmaker agent avoids each agent having to incorporate the protocols to communicate with the service level matchmaker, they just communicate with the matchmaker agent and make requests for abstract services using the same language and protocols they use as for communicating with the other agentified services.

Finally, the agents at the coordination level also monitor the execution of the services (work-flows) they invoke. One or more *Monitoring Components* will then ag-

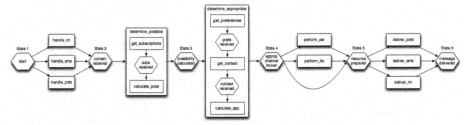

Fig. 4.3: Communication scene for scenario

gregate and analyse events related to the execution of services, the fulfilment of coordination plans and the achievements of role and/or organisational objectives. During the on-line execution, events are generated whenever deviations, exceptions or failures are detected. In such situations, when such events cannot be handled by the agentified service itself or the existing coordination plan in place, the current organisational model is evaluated and then either (i) the objectives affected by the detected issue may be re-evaluated (their priority may be lowered or they may even be dropped completely), or (ii) more significant changes in the organisation model may be required (for instance, changing the rights of a role). In case (i) the agent's coordination modules will create a new plan based on the updated organisational objectives. In case (ii) the updated model is sent to the Agent Generator component to (re)generate the agentified services that populate the system. Depending on the set-up preferences of the administrator, the monitoring component may be a separate component used by several agentified services or may be a federation of several components inside the agentified services themselves.

4.3.4.2 Coordination Models and Work-flows

The coordination level supports the definition, composition and importation of actions (descriptions) to be used by the agents. A distinctive trait of the coordination models created by this tool (in comparison with other orchestration and choreography technologies [12, 14, 33, 39]) is that the coordination models abstract away from the low-level details of the services that may be invoked. Actions are specified using an identifier (name) and their pre- and post-conditions. This specification allows the use of (simple) planning systems to create work-flows from actions to achieve certain goals. The designer is thus able to design the whole coordination level of a distributed system by means of *actors*, *tasks*, *plans* and *plan coordination mechanisms*. The Agentified Services are the ones that connect, at execution time, the abstract tasks with the actual services that are invoked. Apart from the dynamism this solution brings at execution time, this also allows end users to inspect and better comprehend coordination models.

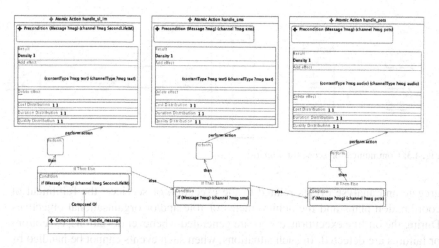

Fig. 4.4: Actions to handle message

4.3.4.3 Scenario Interaction Component

The *Participant* role is responsible for moving from the initial Start landmark through a knowledge-seeking phase, during which the recipients' subscriptions are checked to determine which communication channels are at least possible (someone without a Facebook account cannot be contacted via Facebook, for example). This is the *Know_Possible_Channels* landmark. From there, the next landmark, *Know_Appropriate_Channel* is to combine further information seeking (to determine context and preferences) with reasoning (to find out how those preferences can be combined in the current context) to determine an appropriate channel for communicating with a message recipient. From there, actioning message delivery and its successful transmission moves to the *Communication_Finished* landmark, and from there to the End. These landmarks form a part of the Communication scene, for which a sample plan graph (with actions as boxes and states as hexagons) is given in Figure 4.3; we note that the nested boxes in the diagram correspond to bodies of compound actions, with links between them indicating ordering constraints.

4.3.4.4 Scenario Modelling of Actions

The actions in the scenario are divided into several sets. First are those which handle incoming communication requests over various channels. Then there are those that are responsible for transcoding from one format to another (text-to-speech and automated-speech-recognition are the canonical examples for transcoding from one medium to another). Next are the actions that effect outgoing communication on a given channel. Finally, there are the actions responsible for acquiring information on the fly, to determine subscription data, contextual status and preference orderings. We show in Figure 4.4 the actions to handle a message, in a graphic format.

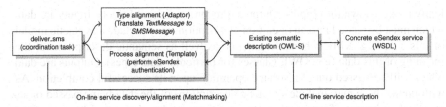

On-line service discovery/alignment (Matchmaking)   Off-line service description

Fig. 4.5: Link between coordination task (left) and service implementation (right)

4.3.5 The Service Level

The service layer connects existing, real-world services to the coordination and organisational layers of the ALIVE framework. Each task in the work-flow is resolved at run-time to a given concrete service implementation through a process of matchmaking (see Section 4.3.5.2), and, in order for a given work-flow to be enacted successfully each coordination tasks which is scheduled must be linked to one or more services. Some services may be scenario-specific, (e.g. managing users' subscriptions and preferences: *get_subscriptions* and *get_preferences* respectively, and decision-making services: *calculate_poss* and *calculate_appropriate* in the scenario), in this case new services must be defined and implemented to fulfil these specific tasks, these services will typically be implemented through the coordination agents themselves. The remaining tasks are expected to be resolved via existing service implementations such as those mentioned in Section 4.3.5.4.

In order to interact with these external services in the ALIVE framework we must have a description of their functional semantics (e.g. in OWL-S) which is semantically aligned (in the sense that it refers to concepts in the same terms) with the task descriptions in the coordination layer. Where no semantic description is present, these can be constructed using service description tools described in Section 4.3.5.1. Where a semantic description is present but not aligned with required tasks, or where an external service requires additional supporting interactions to be invoked (e.g. authentication and/or registration), adaptations and templates may be defined to align external service descriptions with a given task. Figure 4.5 shows the linkages between the *deliver_sms* service task and the eSendex SMS service (which we assume has an existing, unaligned semantic interface description).

4.3.5.1 Services

The central entities on this level are the services. The *Service Design Tool* is used by designers and system administrators to generate or inspect service descriptions, edit service templates and register them in the *service directory*. In order to discover or invoke a particular service we use externalised descriptions of the services properties and its semantics. These descriptions provide the necessary information about service interfaces and service operations and may be functional (related to the actual operation and semantics of the invocation of service operations) or non-functional. Functional descriptions are given for each operation of a given service and are typically broken down into Inputs, Outputs, Preconditions and Effects. Inputs are data which must be passed into an operation, descriptions may include a syntactic model of this data (e.g. XML schema fragments) as well as semantic descriptions of the meaning of this data (e.g. OWL Classes for particular data types). Outputs are data which will be passed out of a service operation upon its successful completion. As with inputs these may include syntactic descriptions of the data being passed or semantic descriptions of its meaning. Preconditions are descriptions of the state of the world which must be satisfied at the point of invocation in order for a particular service operation to execute successfully. Preconditions may describe restrictions on the types of inputs accepted by the service operation or external properties (such as constraints on the state of the service itself) which must be held to be true. Finally, Effects are descriptions of the new state of the world which will be reached upon the successful invocation of a given service operation. As with preconditions these may relate to the outputs of the service or to internal state of the service (or the world). Effects may be conditional on the inputs to the service such that invoking the service with one type of input might yield one effect while invoking it with another would yield a different effect.

These descriptions may be incorporated into the services themselves, or may be provided externally and may already be defined for existing services or may need to be defined separately in order to incorporate existing services into an ALIVE organisation. Typically Service descriptions are broken down into "syntactic" descriptions which describe the interfaces, operations, operation type parameters and interaction patterns of particular services, and "semantic" descriptions which extend these underlying descriptions with higher-level information describing the semantics of operations and their parameters in such a way that services may be invoked by (semi-)automatically by intelligent agents or components.

Service operation descriptions are collected into a single service interface description which defines the operations available for a single service interface. In addition to defining the service operations, service interface descriptions also define how those operations are bound to particular protocols, (e.g. SOAP) and in some cases include the service endpoint address of the service interface. Service interface descriptions are represented using the Web Services Description Language (WSDL). Each service will have exactly one service interface description. On top of the service description the service process model gives a high-level (semantically grounded) interpretation of a given call of a service interface description, with each parameter (input or output) corresponding to an ontological type in OWL (as opposed to a simple XML type in WSDL).

The service process model is part of the service profile. The service profile describes the properties of a service which may be used during service discovery in the context of semantic web services. In the context of OWL-S a service profile includes the simple process model for a given service operation (top-level inputs, outputs preconditions and effects (IOPE)), a taxonomic description of the service which allows services to be selected by category, and other non-functional properties. Once a given service is selected only the process model and service grounding are required to invoke the service. Each service has an associated service profile. For services which do not have a pre-existing service description it contains only the process model which can be inferred from an existing service interface description.

When a given task is to be executed a process model will be selected using the matchmaking process and a service grounding will be used to substitute appropriate input parameters into the actual service invocation and to extract the relevant output parameters from any return values.

As indicated before, services can also be *External Services*. That is, existing, third-party services that have not been designed following the ALIVE methodology. These external services can also be invoked at execution time according to their service description. Usually, however, external services are not consumed directly; instead, this is done via service adaptors. *Service adaptors* allow external services to be utilised for suitable organisational tasks. Typical examples of adaptation are type translation services to adapt a service interface to the entities and data types used by a given organisation.

4.3.5.2 Matchmaking

In order for an ALIVE organisation to be constructed and enacted, appropriate services must be selected for each functional unit of work within the organisation. The process of discovering such services is generally referred to as service discovery and matchmaking and may be conducted automatically based on published service descriptions or with human assistance using the *Service Matchmaking Tool* (a human interface to the matchmaker component), allowing designers to search for services matching a given task description or satisfying a given service template and registering it in the *service directory*.

The *Matchmaker* is responsible for the discovery of appropriate services that fulfils the requirements of a given task. Depending on the level of abstraction of the task to be fulfilled, a matchmaker may query a service directory directly or by the use of *service templates*, which are intermediary descriptions linking higher-level goals or tasks with specific service interactions. A template includes a parametrised process model for a class of services in terms of pre- and post-conditions. Such description may include an abstract work-flow fragment indicating required sub-steps in the process. Parameters in a template are specified as abstract types linked to the variables or parameters in the process model. The parameters are dynamically bound at execution time into concrete ontology instances and/or concrete service process models when the template is selected by a matchmaker. Service template definitions are stored in a *Template Repository*.

The *Service Directory* is a repository for service interface descriptions, service process models and service profiles. It supports several query mechanisms for the discovery of specific services based on their syntactic and/or semantic descriptions. When a work-flow is being constructed the coordination layer may query service directories to determine if a given service description can be satisfied. When a specific service is being bound to a give service process model in the execution phase a service execution framework will search and query one or more service directories in order to list potential matches for a given service description which will in turn be filtered and ordered by one or more service matchmakers.

The matchmaking process operates in two phases: (i) identification of a candidate set of services, based on IOPE, using a *subsumes* type matcher [16] (ii) computing a preference order based on criteria supplied by the client, which is in effect a partial-order over the subsumes requirement, through which we can construct either *exact* or *plugin* matches since these are both subsets of subsumes.

We have chosen to adopt the currently leading technology of OWL-S as the basis for service description and matching. An OWL-S matchmaker is a service registry that supports service querying based on the service semantics, captured in corresponding OWL-S descriptions.

Here we provide a broad description of how the matchmaker handles a matching query. At the very least, the query must describe the signature of the desired service, that is the classes of the input and output parameters. Essentially such a signature expresses two facts: (i) That the input parameter classes represent what the client promises to be able to supply to a matched service in order to invoke it. Thus, with the input parameter classes the client claims that it can fulfil any of these classes, that is it has, for any of these classes, an (indirect) instance of it. (ii) That the output parameter classes represent what output is required (and can be handled by) the client. In other words, the user wants the service to produce, for any of these classes, some value that belongs to it.

The matchmaker then computes and returns the maximal set of services such that: (i) Their input parameters can be fulfilled by the client, assuming only its advertised capabilities. That is, if the client would be able to supply arguments to the exact service signature it requested, then it can provably invoke the matched service. Note that a service may have more relaxed constraints on the inputs it requires, for example it may declare inputs that are super-classes of what the client can supply, thus they can by definition be fulfilled by a value that would fulfil the subclass, or it may declare fewer inputs, and (ii) Their outputs (assuming the service is not abnormally terminated or unavailable) are guaranteed to supply a value for any output classes the client requested. Note that the service outputs may be more specific (that is, sub-classes) than the client requested, or it may produce more outputs, which could, of course, be ignored. The above matching criteria coincide with OWLS-MX *subsumes* matching level [16].

4.3.5.3 Service Execution and Monitoring

Each service has one or more service end points that allow communication with service consumers. In the case that a provider of a service is internal to the organisation, each of these end points will be associated with a service execution environment and a corresponding agent which manages service invocations for that provider. For a given service interface, there may be more than one service provider. A service endpoint is a deployed service interface, which may be invoked by a service consumer, either within or outside the organisation. Each service end point has a Service location (URI), Service interface description (e.g. WSDL description) and optionally a semantic description (process model) of the services functionality and semantic description of the services non-functional properties (service profile). Service end points will be discovered (through the service discovery and matchmaking process) in order to achieve specific goals within the organisation. These endpoints will be invoked by agents within the organisation as part of the process of those agents achieving specific organisational goals.

A service execution framework may offer and/or consume web services. Each service execution framework may be responsible for exposing multiple services. Internally deployed services are expected to follow specific work flows: if decisions must be made within these work-flows they can be delegated to a software agent. Service execution frameworks are used within the service layer to deploy the services which will be offered by the organisation and manage the direct execution of the work-flows associated with those services. Service execution frameworks receive plans from the coordination level as abstract work-flows which will be deployed within the framework. As work-flows are executed the service execution framework will pass service execution events to the service monitoring framework which account for significant events in the service execution process. Service matchmakers are used in order to determine appropriate services for specific abstract work-flow tasks, in addition where matches require service adaptors those adaptors will be deployed within the execution framework.

The execution of the services is monitored by the service monitoring framework which provides means for aggregating and analysing events related to the deployment and execution of services. Each execution framework will be associated with a given monitoring framework which will receive messages relating to the underlying service execution. The monitoring framework will store these messages and allow historic interactions to be queried.

4.3.5.4 Scenario's Web Services Component

The web services that the SCR employs are of several types. Firstly, we have those services responsible for message handling, such as, SMS receipt, for example, for which we have two providers, csoft[8] and eSendex[9]. Secondly, we have those services responsible for message dispatch, namely, POTS through a local Asterisk[10] server, IM through Windows Live Alerts[11], and email via Yahoo!Mail[12]. Third, there are services that perform transcoding, namely, text-to-speech from NeoSpeech[13] and a bespoke automatic speech recognition (ASR) server. Finally,

---

[8] http://www.csoft.co.uk/

[9] http://www.esendex.co.uk/

[10] http://www.asterisk.org/

[11] http://alerts.live.com/

[12] http://www.yahoo.com/

[13] http://www.neospeech.com/

there is a set of services that access bespoke data resources such as the emergent presence server and the subscriptions database. For some services, existing WSDL definitions are available. For others, we worked from informal descriptions in natural language.

4.3.6 The Model-Driven Approach in ALIVE

Within a model-driven approach, models become primary elements of the development process. In the previous sections we have seen how a number of models are used to capture for example the organisation and action models of our case study. Various transformations are also defined and applied to allow the automatic generation of code from model abstractions, such as the automatic creation of plans/workflows from actions.

In particular in ALIVE our approach specifies a number of meta-models, each one reflecting particular concepts such as for organisation, coordination and service architecture. These meta-models are integrated together into a cohesive service specification, having syntax, semantics, organisation and coordination. We apply both model-to-model and model-to-text transformations from the models to generate inputs for tools as well as implementation code and artifacts for services. Automation and interoperability between different tools and formalisms are enabled via the use of meta-models and transformations.

An ALIVE architect may "start" at any of the layers and evolve the design across the layers in any order. Where possible, the tools will provide semi-automated transformations from the layer under construction to artifacts of the other layers, and validation rules will be employed to ensure the consistency and well-formedness of the models. For example, in this scenario, there was initial awareness of the rich set of Web Services that were available to the application for message handling, message dispatch and transcoding. From there, the social and organisational model of a participant was defined, followed by the communication model and message handling actions required for coordination. In our experience, the layer for which the most initial information is available to the architect is domain-specific, and is likely to influence the layer at which modelling will start.

4.4 Critical Review

The ALIVE approach and framework makes several notable contributions to the development of dynamic and robust service-oriented systems. In addition, our approach and methodology are supported by a dedicated tool-set that facilitates the development of such systems. The desirable properties conferred on systems developed through this approach are key, and perhaps critical, to any service-oriented system. They are outlined as follows, (i) raising the level of abstraction (ii) enabling integration/interoperability of components and technologies (iii) facilitating automated creation of artifacts (iv) tool support (v) promotion of autonomy and flexibility (vi) robustness, and (vii) formalisation and analysis. More specifically:

Abstraction: The model-driven aspect of the ALIVE approach allows us to develop service-oriented applications at a higher level of abstraction, based on models. In software engineering, abstraction is seen as an important property, facilitating understandability and coping with complexity, by focusing on the important qualities of our system/application. In our example agents undertake organisation roles and fulfil certain objectives. In this case, the actual agent technological details remain transparent to the end users and they are implemented automatically by a configured transformation (e.g., select agent platform).

Integration: The model-driven nature of our approach also allow us to replace components and integrate easily with different technologies. This advantage became apparent when we experimented with different planning and scheduling components—these are required for service composition—and the model-driven style made it easy to use/integrate off-the-shelf components.

Automation: Automatic creation of code and artifacts is enabled by the specification of transformations. So, plans/work-flows and agent implementations are automatically created from action descriptions and agent-role allocations.

Tool support: The whole ALIVE approach is supported with a framework and toolset that enables the smooth design of service oriented applications based on organisational and coordination concepts, their integration with standard technologies and external tools as well as their (semi)automated creation from model abstractions.

Robustness: We also observe that systems engineered with our approach have distinctively autonomic and robustness features, in that the system looks after itself. Malfunctions at the service level trigger adjustments/changes at the coordination level (namely, re-planning), and, in more extreme cases, changes at the organisation level. Our approach accommodates humans-in-the-loop but this is not essential. Autonomic features are desirable in SOA if we expect scalability and robustness. In that way, the autonomic property allows our system to dynamically adapt and recover from errors.

Autonomy: The use of software agents provides a number of advantages for the ALIVE architectural design and methodology, mainly by raising the level of flexibility and autonomy of the service-oriented system. In principle, agents facilitate elaborate decision making, recovering from errors and deadlocks, by creating and maintaining their own plans according to their obligations and goals. In turn this leads to dynamically participating on work-flows and invoking services.

Formalisation: In addition, ALIVE applications are well formalised both at design and run time. At design time, models are checked against consistency and conformance rules that are specified at (meta) model level and applied upon the models. Once problems or inconsistencies are identified, they are reported back to the designers. Similarly, rules, norms and constraints are applied among specified entities, such as services and agents. In principle, they form a domain knowledge which is shared across all layers of the system. At run time, these formalisations are evaluated and enforced by the system's monitoring component. Moreover, due to the dynamic and autonomous nature of the ALIVE applications, formalisation enables us to perform run-time analysis and reporting about specific properties of the executing system such as liveness and deadlocks.

As a result, we can conclude that the synergy of all these features and capabilities is what it makes the ALIVE approach distinctive, in developing dynamic and flexible service-oriented applications.

The actual evaluation of the ALIVE approach is in progress. The method is primarily based on questionnaires and feedback from the ALIVE users. The core criteria for evaluation are the distinctive properties of the ALIVE approach set out in Section 8.1. In addition, we will assess our approach in respect of (i) the effort required for a user to learn and adopt our methodology, (ii) usability – usefulness and effectiveness of our tools from a user's perspective, (iii) development life-cycle coverage – from analysis to implementation and deployment for an ALIVE application and (iv) maintainability – ease of accommodation of changes to existing requirements, models, standards and tools.

4.5 Limitations in Existing Approaches

An exhaustive literature survey would be out of place in an article of this size, so we tackle the issue of laying out the context to which ALIVE is contributing from three perspectives: (i) top-down: the overall problem space of service-oriented architectures, the state of the art, some projects and their goals, (ii) bottom-up: examining the state of the art of various key component technologies and (iii) methodological: how to engineer SOAs.

We reiterate our characterisation of the SOA problem space as follows:

1. In any non-trivial environment it must be assumed that not all services are owned by the same organisation (or at least by the same department).
2. Many of the configurations and settings needed by a service to operate must be aligned to and fit with its operational environment.
3. Issues of trust, rights, obligations and permission immediately arise—and may significantly affect service executions.
4. Work-flows must be agreed on by all parties before they can be executed, since it can no longer be assumed that all parties are either benevolent or will deliver results unless explicit obligations are recorded and met.
5. Critical applications may simply cease to function when services provisioned by third parties disappear or malfunction.

The *"social layer"* that is an essential—and novel—aspect of ALIVE is realised through: (i) organizational models that capture governance specifications for the entities—both human and software—that interact within the organizational framework, and (ii) coordination models that construct and enact work-flows that observe the organizational norms and at the same time are able to adapt to changing circumstances, but still keep within their governing regulations.

4.5.1 Service-Oriented Architecture

The Service-Oriented Architecture (SOA) framework is becoming a mainstream approach for distributed systems, as it clearly caters for the requirements of current computerised systems: solutions must be heterogeneous, open, scalable, and distributed. Industry has provided (and is currently improving) technologies and standards to support the realisation of SOA. Existing frameworks such as OASIS [21] or W3C WSA [1] and their extensions define how distributed services should be defined and composed, mostly focusing on interoperability issues. SOA concepts and architectures have become widely accepted in recent years, for example, ebXML [14] allows the modelling of complex organisational structures, however it does not clearly support dynamic evolution of these structures over time. Jini [19] is a network architecture that seeks to simplify the connection and sharing of devices. With this technology it is intended to be possible to create distributed systems, where capabilities are shared between machines on a common network.

In each of these approaches, the main common features revolve around the idea of encapsulating key functionality in remotely accessible and composable services that are able to discover one another, communicate and operate together to offer combined functionality. However, in general little attention has been given to the creation of methodological and technical solutions to support the engineering of collections of Web services—with the notable exceptions of [6] and [20].

There are a number of current and recent projects that have positioned themselves to address significant areas of this "big picture". However, rather than repeat material that appears elsewhere in this volume, we cite those projects that we consider the most closely related or having some overlap with ALIVE, namely: SLA@SOI[14], SOA4ALL[15], MOST[16], SeCSE[17], GREDIA[18], COMPAS[19], SHAPE[20] and S-CUBE[21].

4.5.2 Service-Oriented Components

The organizational aspect seems to be unique to ALIVE and does not appear to feature in any current work on SOA apart from appearing in the objectives of

---

[14] http://www.sla-at-soi.eu/

[15] http://www.soa4all.eu/

[16] http://www.most-project.eu/

[17] http://www.secse-project.eu

[18] http://www.gredia.eu/

[19] http://www.compas-ict.eu/

[20] http://www.shape-project.eu/

[21] http://www.s-cube-network.eu/

SOA4ALL, but there appear to be no publications on the subject to date. Consequently we defer discussion of organizational modelling until section 4.3, and in
considering component technologies, we focus on those issues that look to be common, namely how business processes are defined, constructed—that is which services are used to realize them—and enacted, then drilling down further, how services are described and discovered.

Process definition Work-flow descriptions tend to be technology specific and hard
to follow by domain experts who are not familiar with the work-flow formalism used.
There are some initiatives such as the Taverna project [22], that proposes more abstract work-flow languages and supporting tools to facilitate easy use of work-flow
and distributed compute technology within the eScience community. The interface
being developed in ALIVE presents tools via the widely-used Eclipse IDE where
each of the layers has a corresponding formal model.

Process enactment Current models for orchestration and choreography tend to be
static (in the sense that they are built once and remain the same during the lifetime of the system). An exception is WSMX[22] (Web Service Modelling eXecution
environment), an execution environment for business application integration where
semantics web services are integrated for various business applications. The aim is
to increase business processes automation in a very flexible manner while providing scalable integration solutions, which has much in common with all the projects
cited earlier. However, this does not address the lack of methodological guidelines
on how to coordinate services and service work-flows, how to evaluate their performance and how to feed that back into the design. For instance, it would be useful
to keep a log of important events during the operation of Web services which can
then be fed output from the deployment stage back into the design stage. The log
of events could be used to *animate* re-runs connecting events with the high-level
specification—this can help engineers isolate the parts of their high-level specification that contributed to problems. We believe this intention to connect the execution
of a very large, highly distributed (and hence asynchronous) software system with
its higher-level specification, is entirely novel to ALIVE.

Service description WSDL is the W3C recommended language for describing the
service interface [37] to conventional web services. It provides a simple and extensible way for service providers to describe the basic format of requests to their systems
regardless of the underlying protocol (such as SOAP or XML) or encoding (such as
Multipurpose Internet Messaging Extensions). Semantic service descriptions complement WSDL and allow more flexible service reuse and discovery. In particular,
OWL-S [36] builds on the W3C standard ontology language OWL [32] and prior
work on DAML-S and adopts a model for describing service semantics in terms
of: (i) their functional properties (the process model) in terms of Inputs, Outputs,
Preconditions and Effects (IOPEs), (ii) discoverable features and non-functional
properties of the service (the service profile) and (iii) how the high-level seman-

---

[22] http://www.wsmx.org/

tics of the service are linked to the underlying service implementation (the service grounding). Over time OWL-S has evolved into a useful standard with a number of supporting tools and experimental frameworks. A recent alternative is the Web Service Modeling Ontology (WSMO) [40] that provides an framework and a formal language for semantically describing relevant aspects of Web services with a focus on composition and interoperability between services and service ontologies. Although potentially very relevant, WSMO is currently an emerging standard with limited tool support and little validation outside the developers of the underlying concepts, making it an unsuitable choice for the delivery of functional demonstrators at this time.

It is clear that the problem of how best to describe service description is difficult to solve, with different application areas having differing and sometimes conflicting requirements. Both WSMO and OWL-S are conceptually complicated for service authors, and both require a level of compliance (in terms of descriptions) and reasoning capability (in terms of tools) to be used effectively. Consequently, languages such as WSDL-S and SAWSDL [34, 35] have been proposed which offer a more pragmatic approach to service descriptions, by extending WSDL in an ontology-agnostic way.

Service discovery Matchmaking between service advertisements and requests remains an open problem in the context of semantic web services. Typically, several features may be chosen to characterise services in order to rank them by suitability against a given service request. Approaches to date have focused on pre-defined combinations of two or more of these features in order to improve the quality of service matches. Lack of space precludes a detailed survey, but details can be found in the ALIVE State of the Art document [2]; however, here we highlight the work of Sycara et al. [27, 28], Paolucci et al. [26], Jaeger et al. [13], Klusch and Fries [16] and Kiefer and Bernstein [15].

In response to the short-comings identified in the above, we have developed an extensible matching algorithm that generalises over existing approaches by offering a framework to which more matchers may be added and thus more ways by which services may be matched *without* rewriting the matching algorithm. We have also developed a preference algebra that allows the client to express and evaluate arbitrary combinations of qualitative preferences over service ranking, instead of being restricted to a few predefined matching degrees and scoring functions. Consequently, selection is determined on a *per-client-request* basis, providing the means for much more accurate identification of services at the point of need.

Service adaptation Independently of the specific language chosen for service description, currently there is a gap between abstract specifications of Web services (e.g., [6] and [20]) and their implementation or prototyping. This gap tends to be bridged manually: an error-prone practice that becomes worse with the complexity of the system. The work of [30] proposes means to synthesise individual components from a representation of global aspects of a collection of software agents. The adaptation and extension of this technique to synthesise Web service components and an orchestration infra-structure is a promising starting point. Another interesting work is [29], that describes technology for the synthesis of services to translate data from one format to another (semantically) compatible format automatically and to publish semantic descriptions for subsequent service discovery.

4.5.3 Engineering of SOAs

Software engineering for SOAs has become a major focus of activity in recent years. As with the earlier discussion of related projects, an in-depth is not appropriate or feasible in the space available (but see the ALIVE State of the Art report [2] for a more analysis of selected approaches). Thus, we here highlight the following: (i) Service-Oriented Modelling and Architecture (SOMA) [38] (ii) Service-Oriented Modeling Framework (SOMF) [5] (iii) Service Component Architecture (SCA) [25] now supported directly in Eclipse through the SOA Tools Platform [8] (iv) Service Oriented Architecture Reference Model (SOA-RM) by OASIS [21] (v) Service oriented architecture Modeling Language (SoaML) [23] (vi) Web Service Modeling Framework (WSMF) [9]

In comparison to the above, we contend that the ALIVE approach offers a more balanced design methodology approach, providing flexibility and autonomy of service invocations, a service-oriented infrastructure consisting of organisation, coordination and service layers, semantic capabilities and reasoning based on standard ontology specifications, an adaptive and monitoring framework, and a methodology supported by meta-model specifications, model-driven automations and tools.

4.6 Conclusion

This chapter describes an approach to combining Coordination Technology and Organizational Theory with Technologies for Model Driven Engineering in order to support the design and development of distributed systems suitable for highly dynamic environments. The ALIVE approach is based on three interconnected levels: service, coordination and organisation.

The crucial distinction between the ALIVE approach and existing ones is that it provides an organisational context (such as, for instance, objectives, structures and regulations) that can be used to select, compose and invoke services dynamically. ALIVE also provides a notion of organisational awareness to some components (such as the agentified services at the Coordination Level or the matchmaker component at the Service Level) that can direct system execution in order to achieve higher-level organisational objectives. One of the effects is that the ALIVE approach enables managing of exceptions at multiple levels either substituting services (service level) looking for alternative work-flows to connect two landmarks (coordination level) or even looking to achieve alternative landmarks among the same scene (organisational level). The agentified services at Coordination Level enable this medium and high-level exception handling which are not commonly seen in other SOA approaches.

Furthermore, organisational and coordination models are defined at a level of abstraction that allows non-expert end-users to better support the design and maintenance of the system.

The first version of the ALIVE tool suite is now under development and will become available through the project's Sourceforge site: `http://sourceforge.net/projects/ict-alive/`.

Acknowledgements This research has been carried out within the context of the ALIVE project (FP7-215890), funded by the European Commission.

References

1. 11, W.W.G.N.: Web Services Architecture. `http://www.w3.org/TR/wsarch/`, retrieved 20100104. (2004)
2. ALIVE-project: Alive state of the art. `http://www.ist-alive.eu/` (2008)
3. ALIVE-project: ALIVE Methodology Document. `http://www.ist-alive.eu/` (2009)
4. ALIVE-project: Alive theoretical framework. `http://www.ist-alive.eu/` (2009)
5. Bell, M.: Service-Oriented Modeling (SOA): Service Analysis, Design, and Architecture. Wiley & Sons (2008). DOI 978-0-470-14111-3. 978-0-470-14111-3
6. Deutsch, A., Sui, L., Vianu, V.: Specification and Verification of Data-driven Web Services. In: Proceedings of 23rd Symposium on Principles of Database System (PODS '04), pp. 71–82. ACM Press (2004)
7. Dignum, V.: A model for organizational interaction: based on agents, founded in logic. Ph.D. thesis, University of Utrecht (2004)
8. Eclipse: SOA Tools Platform Project. `http://www.eclipse.org/stp/`, retrieved 20091230. (2007)
9. Fensel, D., Bussler, C.: The Web Service Modeling Framework WSMF. Electronic Commerce Research and Applications 1(2), 113–137 (2002). DOI 10.1016/S1567-4223(02)00015-7
10. Ghijsen, M., Jansweijer, W., Wielinga, B.: Towards a Framework for Agent Coordination and Reorganization, AgentCoRe. In: Coordination, Organizations, Institutions, and Norms in Agent Systems III, *LNCS*, vol. 4870, pp. 1–14. Springer, Heidelberg (2008)
11. Grossi, D.: Designing Invisible Hand cuffs. Formal Investigations in Institutions and Organizations for Multi-Agent Systems. Ph.D. thesis, University of Utrecht (2007)
12. IBM: Business process execution language for web services version 1.1, july 2003. `http://www.ibm.com/developerworks/library/specification/ws-bpel/` (Retrieved 20091120)
13. Jaeger, M., Goldmann, G.R., Liebetruth, C., Mühl, G., Geihs, K.: Ranked Matching for Service Descriptions Using OWL-S. Kommunikation in Verteilten Systemen (KiVS) pp. 91–102 (2005). DOI \url{http://doi.acm.org/10.1007/b138861}
14. ebXML Joint Committee, O.: The Framework for eBusiness. `http://www.oasisopen.org/committees/download.php/17817/ebxmljcWhitePaperwdr02en.pdf`, retrieved 20091230. (2006). See also: ebXML Web Site at `http://www.ebxml.org/`
15. Kiefer, C., Bernstein, A.: The Creation and Evaluation of iSPARQL Strategies for Matchmaking. In: 5th European Semantic Web Conference (ESWC2008), pp. 463–477 (2008). URL \url{http://data.semanticweb.org/conference/eswc/2008/paper/133}
16. Klusch, M., Fries, B.: Hybrid owl-s service retrieval with owls-mx: Benefits and pitfalls. In: T.D. Noia, R. Lara, A. Polleres, I. Toma, T. Kawamura, M. Klusch, A. Bernstein, M. Paolucci, A. Leger, D.L. Martin (eds.) SMRR, *CEUR Workshop Proceedings*, vol. 243. CEUR-WS.org (2007). URL \url{http://dblp.uni-trier.de/db/conf/semweb/smrr2007.html\#KluschF07}

17. Lesser, V., Decker, K., Wagner, T., Carver, N., Garvey, A., Horling, B., Neiman, D., Podor-ozhny, R., Prasad, M.N., Raja, A., Vincent, R., Xuan, P., Zhang, X.: Evolution of the GPGP/TAEMS Domain-Independent Coordination Framework. Autonomous Agents and Multi-Agent Systems **9**(1), 87–143 (2004). URL \url{http://mas.cs.umass.edu/paper/268}

18. Matskin, M.: Enabling Web Services Composition with Software Agents. In: Proc. of the Conference on Internet and Multimedia Systems, and Applications (2005)

19. Microsystems, S.: Jini Architectural Overview. Technical White Paper. http://www.sun.com/software/jini/whitepapers/architecture.html, retrieved 20091230. (1999)

20. Narayanan, S., McIlraith, S.: Verification and Automated Composition of Web Services. In: Proceedings of 11th International Conference on World Wide Web (WWW'02), pp. 77–88. ACM Press (2002)

21. OASIS, C.S.: Reference Model for Service-oriented Architecture 1.0. http://www.oasisopen.org/committees/download.php/19679/soarmcs.pdf, retrieved 20091230. (2006)

22. Oinn, T., Addis, M., Ferris, J., Marvin, D., Senger, M., Greenwood, M., Carver, T., Glover, K., Pocock, M., Wipat, A., Li, P.: Taverna: a tool for the composition and enactment of bioinformatics workflows. Bioinformatics **20**(17), 3045–3054 (2004). DOI 10.1093/bioinformatics/bth361

23. OMG: Service oriented architecture Modeling Language (SoaML). OMG Adopted Beta Specification, ptc/2009-04-01 (2009). URL \url{http://www.omg.org/spec/SoaML/}

24. OMG: Model Driven Architecture. http://www.omg.org/mda/ (Retrieved 20091120)

25. Open-SOA: Service Component Architecture (SCA). version 1.00 (2007). URL \url{http://www.osoa.org/display/Main/Service+Component+Architecture+Specifications}

26. Paolucci, M., Kawamura, T., Payne, T.R., Sycara, K.P.: Semantic Matching of Web Services Capabilities. In: International Semantic Web Conference, pp. 333–347 (2002)

27. Sycara, K., Klusch, M., Widoff, S., Lu, J.: Dynamic service matchmaking among agents in open information environments. SIGMOD Rec. **28**(1), 47–53 (1999). DOI \url{http://doi.acm.org/10.1145/309844.309895}

28. Sycara, K., Widoff, S., Klusch, M., Lu, J.: Larks: Dynamic Matchmaking Among Heterogeneous Software Agents in Cyberspace. Autonomous Agents and Multi-Agent Systems **6**, 173–203 (2002)

29. Szomszor, M., Payne, T., Moreau, L.: Automated Syntactic Mediation for Web Service Integration. In: Proceedings of IEEE International Conference on Web Services (ICWS 2006) (2006)

30. Vasconcelos, W., Robertson, D., Sierra, C., Esteva, M., Sabater, J., Wooldridge.M.: Rapid Prototyping of Large Multi-Agent Systems through Logic Programming. Annals of Mathematics and Artificial Intelligence **41**, 135–169 (2004)

31. van der Vecht, B., Dignum, F., Meyer, J.J.C., Dignum, V.: Organizations and Autonomous Agents: Bottom-up Dynamics of Coordination Mechanisms. In: In: 5th Workshop on Coordination, Organizations, Institutions, and Norms in Agent Systems (Estoril 2008)

32. W3C: OWL – Web Ontology Language. http://www.w3.org/TR/2004/REC-owl-features-20040210/ (2004). Retrieved 20091120

33. W3C: Web Service Choreography Description Language (WS-CDL). http://www.w3.org/TR/ws-cdl-10/ (2005). Retrieved 20091120

34. W3C: Web Service Semantics – WSDL-S. http://www.w3.org/Submission/WSDL-S/ (2005)

35. W3C: Semantic Annotations for WSDL (SAWSDL). http://www.w3.org/2002/ws/sawsdl/ (2007)

36. W3C: OWL-S - Semantic Markup for Web Services, 2004. http://www.w3.org/Submission/OWL-S/ (Retrieved 20091120)

37. (W3C), W.W.W.C.: Web Services Description Language (WSDL) 1.1. http://www.w3.org/TR/wsdl/, retrieved 20091230. (2001)

38. Wahli, U., Ackerman, L., Di Bari, A., Hodgkinson, G., Kesterton, A., Olson, L., Portier, B.: Building SOA Solutions Using the Rational SDP. IBM Redbooks. Vervante (2007)
39. WfMC: XML Process Definition Language (XPDL). Document Number WFMC-TC-1025: Version 1.14 Document Status - Final (2005)
40. WSMO: WSMO working group: Web Service Modeling Ontology, ESSI cluster. http://www.wsmo.org/ (Retrieved 20091120)

Chapter 5
Model-aware Monitoring of SOAs for Compliance

Ta'id Holmes, Emmanuel Mulo, Uwe Zdun, and Schahram Dustdar

Abstract Business processes today are supported by process-driven service oriented architectures. Due to the increasing importance of compliance of an organization with regulatory requirements and internal policies, there is a need for appropriate techniques to monitor organizational information systems as they execute business processes. Event-based monitoring of processes is one of the ways to provide runtime process-state information. This type of monitoring, however, has limitations mostly related to the type and amount of information available in events and process engines. We propose a novel approach – model-aware monitoring of business processes – to address these limitations. Emitted events contain unique identifiers of models that can be retrieved dynamically during runtime from a model-aware repository and service environment (MORSE). The size of the events is kept small and patterns of events that signify interesting occurrences are identified through complex event processing and are signaled to interesting components such as a business intelligence. To illustrate our approach we present an industry case study where we have applied this generic infrastructure for the compliance monitoring of business processes.

5.1 Introduction

Business compliance, i.e., the conformance of an organization's business activities and practices with existing laws (cf. [16, 19, 34, 42]), regulations (cf. [4, 26, 27]) and its own internal policies, is a major concern of today's business community. However, these compliance concerns frequently change, making it hard to systematically and quickly accommodate new compliance requirements. The COMPAS project [15] aims to design and implement novel models, languages, and an architec-

Ta'id Holmes · Emmanuel Mulo · Uwe Zdun · Schahram Dustdar
Distributed Systems Group, Institute of Information Systems, Vienna University of Technology, Vienna, Austria, e-mail: \{tholmes,e.mulo,zdun,dustdar\}@infosys.tuwien.ac.at

117

tural framework to ensure dynamic and on-going compliance of software services to business regulations and stated user service-requirements. In this chapter we present part of the results from this project related to runtime monitoring of compliance in process-oriented systems.

Business processes are today supported by process-driven service oriented architectures (SOA). A business process comprises a collection of related, structured activities within or across organizations, that produce a specific service or product for a particular customer. Process-driven SOAs aim to increase productivity, efficiency, and flexibility of an organization, by aligning high-level business processes with applications supported by information technology. Such architectures constitute a process (or workflow) engine that orchestrates services to realize activities in a business process [24]. In an enterprise scale process-driven SOA, moreover, there exist multiple business processes and process instances that are interacting with different external entities at runtime (e.g., services, databases).

While business processes are primarily aimed at creating an output for a specified consumer, one of the other objectives that they realize is providing an auditable asset with which an organization can demonstrate its fulfillment of compliance regulations [23]. Monitoring process-driven SOAs (process instances) at runtime enables a diagnosis of process states, and therefore, provides the necessary information regarding the fulfillment of compliance requirements in the business processes. Please note that in the context of this work such compliance requirements are specified in terms of models (cf. [6]). Also the processes are generated from models. Thus, for the development of process-driven SOAs with compliance concerns model-driven engineering is used.

A typical monitoring solution consists of an external component to which events are sent – these events are recorded in audit logs (files) that can later be analyzed to identify anomalies in system behavior [29, 30, 33, 35]. Monitoring solutions that leverage complex event processing (CEP) techniques, perform an online analysis of streams of events as they happen [21, 31, 38]. These CEP-based solutions are able to deduce high-level events, i.e., events that represent certain semantics in a special domain, through analyzing patterns and properties of the events emitted by monitored components.

In the context of monitoring business processes with such event-based monitoring solutions, some limitations need to be addressed:

- When designing such solutions, it is hard to foresee all kinds of monitoring information needed during process execution. An event captures the state of the process execution at a *point* in time, whereas for monitoring purposes we are interested in the *entire* process, i.e., a wider perspective. Moreover, due to changes of requirements, the monitoring components need to consider additional information that is not transmitted with the events.

- Event-based monitoring solutions usually receive very large amounts of events. Due to the amounts of system resources consumed with this type of monitoring, it is usually only feasible to process a limited number of events together. Moreover, it is often not feasible to embed large amounts of data in an event message, such as a model together with all its related models.

We propose a novel approach, model-aware, event-based monitoring of business processes at runtime. The monitoring is *model-aware* in the sense, that it can access and reflect on process models at runtime. High-level events (that correspond to business events), containing references to the process models, are recognized from low-level process events using complex event processing techniques. The model references enable runtime retrieval and reflection on the original process models. As a consequence, the size of the events is kept small, and (new) models and model elements can be considered during monitoring. We apply our approach in the context of monitoring for compliance of business processes. We demonstrate this through a mobile number portability case study.

The rest of this paper is structured as follows: Section 5.2 presents a motivating scenario to highlight the issues that arise during monitoring for compliance and how our approach aims to address them. Section 5.3 gives an overview of our approach and presents the details on the architecture we use to realize this approach. Section 5.4 presents an industry case study to evaluate our approach, Section 5.5, discussions, Section 5.6, related work, and finally, conclusions in Section 11.5.

5.2 Motivating Scenario

In this section, we present a scenario to illustrate issues that arise while monitoring for compliance in an organization's business processes. The scenario is based on *mobile number portability* (MNP) in mobile telecommunication companies.

Mobile telecommunication companies, usually referred to as Cell Phone Operators (CPOs), provide voice and data services to their subscribers. A CPO may operate in a single country or have branches in several countries. Inhouse services are offered by the CPO to manage all the subscribers and their stipulated contracts. Moreover each subscriber is usually able to view private information regarding their contract, or public information regarding services offered by the CPO. Not all CPOs have their own telecom infrastructure – some of them rent the network services from big telecom companies and provide a service to subscribers. Such a CPO is referred to as a Virtual Operator (VOs).

In an MNP scenario, a subscriber has the right to keep their mobile telephone number when switching between CPOs [9]. According to various National and European Union (EU) regulations (cf. [18]), MNP is one of the mandatory services a CPO must provide to its subscribers. The MNP procedure is regulated with the aim of allowing the subscribers to freely select the best CPO according to their requirements, without having to change their contact number. Therefore, one of the primary compliance concerns for a CPO as they are implementing MNP procedures is to satisfy national and EU rules and regulations.

There are essentially two steps in the MNP process. The subscriber wishing to port his number contacts the so-called recipient network, i.e., the CPO who shall be their new provider. The recipient network then executes the porting. This step of executing the porting involves a number of sub-activities, including contacting the donor network (i.e., the subscriber's current CPO), performing the porting, possibly charging the subscriber, and making a payment to the donor network. A number of issues are regulated in this process. Table 5.1 shows examples of MNP regulations in Austria [9].

Table 5.1: MNP regulations in austria [9]

Compliance/Regulatory Issue	Example of Implementation
Porting Charges	Donor network allowed to charge maximum €19 porting fees. Recipient network allowed to charge subscriber €4 – €15.
Speed of Porting	Porting should take maximum 3 days.
Porting Initiator	Porting initiated by recipient network.

In order to monitor compliance in this scenario, an event-based monitoring solution would transmit a number of events that together reflect occurrence of activities like `Request Number Porting` and `Execute Number Porting`. These events may, additionally, contain information to identify details like the subscriber number, the subscriber's geographical location, and the donor network. In this scenario we can illustrate some of the limitations we attempt to address in this work.

- We are not able to embed all information in individual events, for example, which compliance regulation may have been violated. In our scenario, a compliance violation may occur due to the `Execute Number Porting` activity, whereby the porting of the number took longer than the three (3) days permitted by regulations. This activity is detected by correlating a number of low-level events through CEP techniques. Even then, the complex event processing engine only correlates the events. We would need another source for more detailed information concerning the compliance regulations.

- Such business processes are considered long-running and may take many hours or days for completion. For event-based monitoring solutions, maintaining a history of the entire process execution state for *every* process instance could consume a large amount of resources. Therefore, the monitoring of events would be performed within limited time windows to save on resources. In this case, we would need an external source to deduce information concerning the entire process.

- Some activities within the business processes, for example `Charge Customer`, may occur in other business processes and contexts. When we present monitoring information, however, we would like to know in exactly which of the processes and context this violation occurred.

With our proposed solution, we address some of the limitations stated here. More details of this scenario and how we apply our approach are given in the case study section (Section 5.4). First, we give details of the approach in Section 5.3.

5.3 Model-Aware Event-Based Monitoring

In this section, we present our approach for model-aware, runtime monitoring of business processes in a process-driven SOA. It is based on monitoring and processing of events, coupled with runtime access to business process models and annotating models. We first present an overview of the approach and then elaborate on this overview in subsequent sections.

5.3.1 Approach Overview

Before we present some parts of the architecture in more detail, we first provide an overview of our approach. For model-aware monitoring, we propose our Model-Aware Repository and Service Environment (MORSE) [25] and an event monitoring and processing infrastructure. Our approach comprises the following steps:

- For the design and development of processes we apply *model-driven development* (MDD). We use a view-based modeling framework [43] to design process models and generate WS-BPEL [37] (BPEL) code. We propose to store these process models in a model repository, and require that each model and model element is uniquely identifiable.

- During code generation we embed *traceability information* into the BPEL processes for relating the code with original models that we make identifiable by unique identifiers, i.e., UUIDs [28].

- The BPEL process, instrumented with traceability information, contains a BPEL extension for transmitting *low-level events*, e.g., for process invocation, containing traceability information.

- The low-level events are processed by a complex event processing engine. *Business events* are recognized and raised.

- An interested component consumes the business events and provides for *adaptation*, *compensation*, or *synchronization*.

We illustrate our approach in Figure 5.1. Business processes, represented as process models, are at the center of our approach. We propose to store these process models (1) in a model repository that can be queried (7a and 8a). Each process model and element in the repository is identifiable by a Universally Unique Identifier (UUID) [28]. The model repository manages and versionizes models and model instances. Additional information about related models or models in other versions can be discovered by querying the repository.

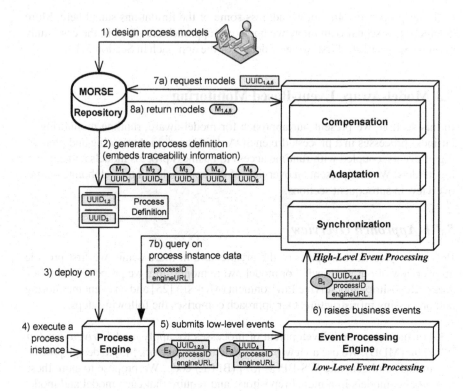

Fig. 5.1: Overview of the approach

In a generation step (2), traceability information is embedded into the process definition. That is, the process and the process elements are linked in the code via UUIDs to the models. After this model-to-code transformation an executable form of a business process, such as BPEL [37], is provided to a process engine (3). Each process execution essentially orchestrates different business activities to realize the entire process. In order to monitor a process execution (4), we monitor the progress of each process instance through events that are emitted by the process engine (5). Within these events, we embed the UUIDs of the instance's process model. Events emitted by the process engine are considered low-level events. In order to detect events at a business level, complex event processing techniques are applied (6). Business events containing, among other things, the relevant UUIDs are passed on to a component, say business intelligence (BI) component, that can perform subsequent retrieval and reflection on the process models (7a and 8a). For accessing instance data, we assume the process engine also exposes an interface for querying (7b).

In the following sections we present the details of our model-aware, event-based monitoring approach.

5.3.2 Model-Aware Repository and Service Environment

In our approach we aim at addressing the problem of monitoring and analyzing business processes to identify compliance violations through MORSE[1]. For the processes and the compliance concerns we use dedicated models. These models are used in the model-driven development (MDD) process and related to during runtime. Thus, information on a process such as stored in control-, orchestration-, or information-view models [43] and annotating compliance models is stored in and managed by MORSE that allows for the *storage* and *retrieval* of MORSE objects such as models, model elements, model instances, and other MDD artifacts. It offers read and write access to all artifacts at runtime and design time. Moreover, it stores relationships among the MDD artifacts, e.g., model-relationships such as instance, inheritance, and annotation relations. Moreover, the MORSE repository provides *versioning* capabilities not only to MDD artifacts, but also to their relationships. This way, models can be manipulated at runtime of the client system with minimal problems regarding maintenance and consistency. New versions and old versions of the models can be maintained in parallel, so that old model versions can be used until all their model instances are either deleted or migrated to the new model version.

Figure 5.2 shows the internal architecture of MORSE. The model repository exposes all its functionality as Web services which ease the integration of MORSE into service-oriented environments. The services can be consumed by various clients, e.g., design tools, administrative clients, monitoring services, or services that provide for adaptation. Thus, MORSE supports the development of models during design-time and allows for the retrieval of models at runtime.

5.3.2.1 Model-Traceability for Process-Driven SOAs

With MORSE we follow a model-driven approach. That is, we apply model-to-code transformation for the generation of process code, deployment artifacts, and monitoring directives. For this the process models and annotating models such as a compliance metadata model are processed by a transformation template. During this step we embed traceability information into the generated code so that the original model(s) can be related to during runtime. As MDD artifacts in MORSE repositories are identifiable by UUIDs, the traceability information uses these UUIDs as well. Thus, the generator automatically weaves references into the generated source code or configuration instructions, so that the corresponding models can be identified and accessed from the running system.

For the traceability of models in process-driven SOAs we propose an extension for BPEL. Figure 5.3 shows an excerpt of a BPEL process[2] with a BPEL extension

---

[1] http://www.infosys.tuwien.ac.at/prototype/morse

[2] For simplicity reasons most XML namespaces have been omitted.

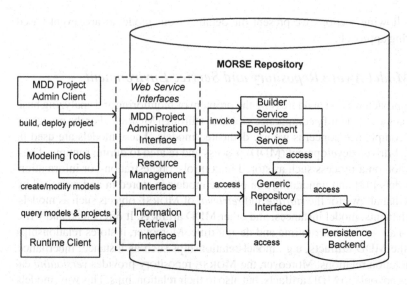

Fig. 5.2: MORSE architecture

for mapping code elements of the BPEL process to MORSE object identifiers. The `traceability` element, that indicates the UUID of the `build` as an attribute, is a sequence of `rows` that maps BPEL elements to the `uuids` of corresponding MORSE objects. The XML Path Query Language (XPath) [5] is chosen as the default query language for selecting the XML elements of the BPEL code. For extensibility, an optional `queryLanguage` attribute, that has the same semantics as in BPEL (cf. Section 8.2 of [37]), can specify an alternative query language or XPath version.

Note that this traceability information can annotate any XML based target code and can often be supplied as an inline extension[3]. It can also be supplied exogenously within a separate file. As a consequence, our approach is not limited to BPEL but can applied to other process languages as well.

5.3.3 Event Monitoring and Processing

In MORSE each model and model-element is identifiable by a UUID. These are embedded as traceability-links in the process definition as discussed in the previous section. During process execution, events are emitted by the process engine, for example, an activity starts, a database is accessed, etc. Whereas the events emitted by the process engine are considered low-level events, we are interested in business related events. Business events cannot be observed directly – rather, they are derived by observing and aggregating patterns of low-level events, through certain processing rules. Therefore, in addition to monitoring, events are processed to iden-

---

[3] Supposed that such extensibility is provided with an any element in the XML schema.

```
<process name="NumberPortabilityProcess">
  <extensions>
    <extension mustUnderstand="yes"
        namespace="http://xml.vitalab.tuwien.ac.at/ns/morse/traceability.xsd"/>
  </extensions>
  <import importType="http://www.w3.org/2001/XMLSchema"
      namespace="http://xml.vitalab.tuwien.ac.at/ns/morse/traceability.xsd"
      location="http://xml.vitalab.tuwien.ac.at/ns/morse/traceability.xsd"/>
  <morse:traceability build="ec46dcdc-3f81-4dec-b437-8da5269ad334">
    <row query="/process[1]"
        queryLanguage="urn:oasis:names:tc:wsbpel:2.0:sublang:xpath1.0">
      <uuid>65130c63-dda7-4193-9bac-fe7eda9f38b9</uuid>
      <uuid>2e3261fc-452c-4b55-8c77-fc4aaac29ddf</uuid>
      <uuid>9a7f6681-2616-4797-9510-0c5cd126b24c</uuid>
      <uuid>11194fb5-3b9f-4507-a3a0-6b3f7e8e146a</uuid>
    </row>
    <row query="/process[1]/sequence[1]/receive[1]">
      <uuid>0e4bc6b8-8f28-4e0d-a8f7-ebf99bf95b62</uuid>
    </row>
    <row query="/process[1]/sequence[1]/invoke[2]">
      <uuid>8b62c1ef-2c12-41f3-a660-dae82c6168dc</uuid>
    </row>
  </morse:traceability>
  <sequence>
    <!-- ... //-->
  </sequence>
</process>
```

Fig. 5.3: BPEL process with an extension for MORSE traceability

tify high-level events that have significance from the business perspective, e.g., a low-level event indicating database access might not be so interesting, however, a combination of events that indicate completion of a specific business activity is of more interest to business actors.

As a business process is executed, events are emitted that represent the state in the progress of the business process. In a large scale SOA, multiple instances of different business processes execute concurrently, resulting in the emission of an interwoven sequence of events. The event processing engine has a sequential view of these events as they arrive at its interface. In order to process these events, the event processing engine is configured with queries based on a number of factors like the type of event, the data contained within the event, or the expected patterns of events. Typically queries for configuring the engine are defined in an Event Processing Language (EPL). These EPL statements are similar to Structured Query Languages (SQL) for database querying. The statements instruct the engine on which events, event data, or patterns of events to search for in an event stream. For example, the query shown in the inset of Figure 5.4 enables the engine to identify a business activity D from a stream of events.

The queries enable the correlation of events and identification of a particular group of business events within a specific process instance. In Figure 5.4, we see the pattern of events 8-9-10 matches activity D of a process instance. Further filtering of

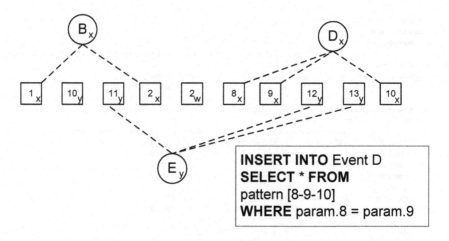

Fig. 5.4: EPL query

events is performed through comparison of their parameters. In the example, we use the subscript x as a parameter to indicate that these events belong to the same process instance. The WHERE clause performs a more fine-grained selection of events based on related parameters, for example, the process instance. Within the same stream, there are other events that belong to different process instances. Therefore, using such filtering mechanisms we are able to separate events into different business activities in their distinct process instances. Finally, these business-events are passed on to a BI component to make the necessary compliance checks and decisions on actions to take.

Combining the low-level and high-level events with runtime access to a model repository, we provide information to enable compliance detection tasks. Business events represent the execution progress of a process instance and, in addition, provide a UUID to its process model. The UUIDs enable querying of the model repository, for retrieval of additional information that is not directly accessible to the event processing engine, but is required for compliance detection.

5.4 Case Study

In this section we present details of the case study introduced in Section 5.2 that deals with monitoring for compliance in the mobile number portability (MNP) process. We demonstrate how we use our approach to achieve a model-aware, event-based monitoring solution, that checks for compliance at runtime. In the first step, we need to annotate the process models with compliance data. We do not present details concerning the MDD environment, however, it is important to note that when the executable processes are generated from the process models, UUIDs are incorporated into them to allow for unique identification of the models. Following this we define relevant EPLs that enable filtering of the low-level events to high-level, business events. We consider one of the compliance requirements that relates to the quality of service (QoS) regarding the MNP process, i.e., the portability needs to be performed within three (3) days (cf. Table 5.1).

5.4.1 Annotating Business Process Models with Compliance Concerns

Figure 5.5 illustrates an excerpt of a compliance model with concepts from the compliance domain. In this domain compliance experts derive Compliance Requirements from Compliance Sources. Such sources refer to national, European, or international regulations and laws or internal policies. For realizing the compliance to requirements, Controls are employed together with Compliance Rules. The latter formalize the requirements for a control in a way suitable for the BI to check the compliance of a system. Using Controls, Compliance Targets such as Business Processes, activities (BP Activities), and external Web Services can be annotated.

In our work we use name-based matching for such annotations. That is, model elements from different models that contain the same name are matched. Thus, a process P with the name MNP in a model M_1 can be annotated exogenously by a compliance model M_2. In this model a control C references a named element with the same name MNP. Please note, that our approach is not limited to name-based matching. Any form of annotation or direct relation from compliance controls to compliance targets is possible in order to specify compliance concerns for business processes.

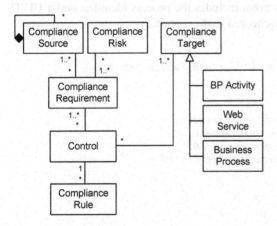

Fig. 5.5: Excerpt of a compliance model

For the generation of process definitions, instances of the process and compliance models are taken as inputs. The MORSE builder service realizes this generation step of the model-driven development process by weaving traceability information into the code. This traceability information is stored as a traceability matrix that relates code elements to the UUIDs of the model(-element)s.

The traceability matrix was realized as a BPEL extension (see also Section 5.3.2.1)[4]. We modified the Apache ODE [41] BPEL process engine so that events from the engine contain the UUIDs as specified in the BPEL extension. That is, if a BPEL event for an activity is raised by the engine it would contain the correlating UUIDs for the activity as specified in the traceability matrix.

5.4.2 Event Processing

In order to detect business events of interest, a CEP engine is configured automatically with EPL rules or statements that specify event types, event data, and patterns of events to detect at runtime. The CEP engine observes a stream of low-level events emitted by the process execution engine and deduces that a particular business event has occurred.

In our MNP process, a number of low-level events are emitted by the Apache ODE process engine in response to the execution of the different process steps. The events contain, among other things, the process engine's internal identifier of the process instance (processID), a URL of the process engine, and UUIDs of the models and model-elements that relate to the process and process elements. Using the low-level events, we monitor that the Execute Number Porting activity occurred before we can alert of the need to check for compliance. We have the simple EPL statements illustrated in Figure 5.6, that show how such an event combination can be monitored with CEP. The EPL statement emits a business event corresponding to the Execute Number Porting activity. This event includes the process identifier and a UUID indicating the target model to be checked in the repository.

```
INSERT INTO ExecuteNumberPortEvent(pid, sUUID, eUUID)
SELECT StartEvent.pid,
       StartEvent.UUID,
       EndEvent.UUID
FROM ActivityExecStartEvent as StartEvent,
     ActivityExecEndEvent as EndEvent
WHERE StartEvent.pid = EndEvent.pid AND
      StartEvent(id = 'executeNumberPort')
```

Fig. 5.6: Number portability EPL

---

[4] Following a model-driven approach we profit from the abstraction and platform independent models. That is, although we realized support for the generation of BPEL code, our approach is not limited to this technology but support for other process languages can be developed.

Since the UUIDs of the business process models and model elements are embedded in the events, we send them to the BI component that uses them to query the MORSE repository in order to look up more information concerning the process. We present the types of tasks that would be expected from such a BI component in the next section.

5.4.3 Compliance Checking

The compliance checks are performed by a BI component that receives business events from the CEP engine. The BI component uses the event type and UUID data in order to determine what compliance concerns have to be checked, and in case of compliance violations consequently what actions to invoke. As the Execute Number Porting activity executes, the process execution engine emits low-level events to the CEP engine, e.g., when a process activity is started. However, when the combination of two process engine events ActivityExecStartEvent and ActivityExecEndEvent, have occurred, the CEP engine recognizes this as a business event Execute Number Portability, and alerts the BI component the occurrence of this business event.

For realization of the compliance checking, we assume that the process engine exposes an API for querying process instance data, e.g., variables of a process instance. The BI component consumes the business event, looks up the compliance metadata model from the repository and requests process-instance data, i.e., the time, the activities have been performed, from the process engine. With this information, i.e., by reflecting on the compliance model and process instance data, a violation of the compliance requirement as stated in Table 5.1 can be determined. Finally, if a violation was detected, a compensation action can be initiated. For example, the Cell Phone Operator may account free credits to the customer as a compensation to the tardy number porting.

5.5 Discussion

In this section we motivate some advantages and limitations of our model-aware, event-based monitoring approach.

First of all, with the MORSE approach we expand the usage of models and propagate them from the design time to the runtime. That is, models are not only used for describing business processes and specifying compliance concerns during design time but they are related to during runtime, using automatically embedded traceability information, and used for the compliance checks. Coupled with an event-based (CEP) approach, a business intelligence profits from accessing and reflecting on the models. That is, having defined abstraction levels, the conceptual models are suitable for the required reflections.

Upon the detection of a compliance violation, the user typically wants to understand which process has caused the violation and why. With MORSE the user can access the process model that has caused the violation. However, the process model in general is not the only relevant information or not the root cause of the violation. Other models such as a compliance model that annotates the process model might carry the answer to the violation; hence, they are accessed, too. Examples are the model specifying the compliance rule that has been violated or the models of the processes that have invoked the process leading to the violation. Finally, once the root cause has been identified, it is likely that the user will fix the affected models. Then, the corrected models should from then on be used for new instances of the business processes. Here, a transparent versioning support as realized by MORSE is crucial, as it is typically not possible to automatically migrate running process instances from one model to another. Old model versions are supported as long as instances of them are running, unless the execution of such instances is halted.

Event-based (CEP) monitoring solutions usually receive large volumes of events. Typically, these solutions do not persist long-running information about process executions. This limits the size of the window of events, over which these solutions are able to store and process data regarding process executions – processing a large window size would require lots of computing resources. In our approach, we embed traceability information, i.e. identifiers to models and model-elements, in the process events. In this way, the CEP engine is still able to identify interesting business events, and in a further step, relevant information concerning the entire process model and process instance data can be retrieved by a business intelligence (BI) component. For instance, the BI can lookup process and annotating compliance models such as compliance requirements and rules at MORSE as well as process-instance data from the process engine. Additionally, we believe that size of events is kept to a minimum when we use traceability information that allows later querying.

Because compliance rules are looked up by the BI, they may dynamically change during runtime without the need to adapt the CEP. For example, the BI may want to consider the latest requirements when determining the compliance. In other circumstances processes only need to comply to the set of requirements as effective during instantiation. Both scenarios are supported with MORSE, that realizes a transparent versioning of models.

There is a clear separation of the CEP engine, that task is to identify interesting events, and the BI, that reasons about the compliant execution. Thus, the CEP does not need to comprise the logic from the BI but its configuration is kept simple and therefore is manageable. In contrast, the BI unit focuses on determining the compliant execution. It does so by, first, retrieving all relevant information and, second, reason about it.

One of the main limitations we view with our approach at the moment, is that for some scenarios it is not readily applicable to support long-running monitoring at the process instance level – this would require access to process instance variables. We currently assume existence of a query interface on the process engine, which provides access to this information.

Our approach assumes that model-driven engineering is used for the development of the system. That is, the business process definitions (BPEL code) and the traceability matrix (BPEL extension for the MORSE traceability) are generated from models. It is possible to introduce our approach into a non-model-driven project (e.g., as a first step into model-driven development). For that, existing business process definitions would be manually extended and related to compliance models. In this case the traceability matrix would only relate elements from the process definition to compliance models but not process models. This would limit the business intelligence in case the latter models are needed as well.

Finally, our approach introduces some complexity to the system. That is, in addition to the process engine we employ a MORSE repository, a CEP engine, and a business intelligence.

5.6 Related Work

Some of the work related to integrated event-based monitoring solutions are now presented. In addition we relate to work in the field of requirements monitoring. Finally, we mention on various model repositories and compare to MORSE.

5.6.1 Related Work on Event-based Monitoring

Event-based support of process executions has been previously researched [12, 22]. Casati and Discenza [12] proposes extending workflow models with the capability to specify points at which events can be raised during the workflow execution. This is a similar idea to the events raised by the process engine in our approach, except that in our case, the engine would emit a fixed set of events (process started, process end); in their approach, the user has greater control over the types of events emitted and when an event should be emitted. Their approach also proposes an event service that can filter and correlate events to dispatch them to other workflow models. The main difference in our approach is the use of the model repository to provide extra information concerning process models. Hagen and Alonso [22] use events for direct communication between processes. A process instance exchanges an event with another process instance, to make decisions on how to proceed with the execution.

In the MOSES approach and framework [11], process models (e.g., BPEL) are fed into the system – these models are required to fulfill certain criteria. The system builds a behavioral model which is used in optimization calculations. Monitoring at runtime observes the system and the optimization calculations to decide on adaptation. The monitoring, however, is not based on events, and the process models fed into the system are from external entities, hence necessitating model verification. On the other hand the approach provides adaptation based on *per instance* variables. A similar idea to the MOSES approach is proposed by Cappiello et al. [10], where quality attributes are monitored to determine adaptation. The difference is that this approach proposes predictive adaptation.

5.6.2 Related Work on Requirements Monitoring

While particular monitoring infrastructures can be integrated with MORSE and used for the compliance checking, our work particularly focuses on relating to models, the monitored systems have been generated from. Thus, our work makes such models accessible at runtime. Note, that not only, e.g., process models but also compliance concern models are managed by MORSE. This allows for the novel and direct linkage and correlation of model-driven system and requirements models. In this section we refer and relate to work in the areas of runtime requirements-monitoring.

Feather et al. [20] discuss an architecture and a development process for monitoring system requirements at runtime. It builds on work on goal-driven requirements engineering [17] and runtime requirements monitoring [14].

Skene and Emmerich [39] apply MDD technologies for producing runtime requirements monitoring systems. This is, required behavior is modeled and code is generated for, e.g., the eventing infrastructure. Finally, a metadata repository collects system data and runs consistency checks to discover violations. While in our work we also showcase the generation of code for the eventing infrastructure (see Section 5.3.2), our approach assumes an existent monitoring infrastructure. In case of a violation the MORSE approach not only allows us to relate to requirement models but also to the models of the monitored system.

Chowdhary et al. [13] present a MDD framework and methodology for creating Business Performance Management (BPM) solutions. This is, a guideline is described for implementing complex BPM solutions using an MDD approach. Also, with inter alia the specification of BPM requirements and goals the framework provides runtime support for (generating) the eventing infrastructure, data warehouse, and dashboard. The presented approach allows for the monitoring and analysis of business processes in respect of their performance. Thus, similarly to our approach, compliance concerns such as quality of service concerns as found in service level agreements can be specified and monitored by the framework. Besides the monitoring of business processes and service-based systems in general, our approach particularly focuses on also relating to conceptual models of the systems from the runtime, not only their requirements. As a consequence, the system and end-users can directly relate to the MDD artifacts of a system in case of a violation. This allows for the subsequent reflection, adaptation, and evolution of the system. In contrast, the BPM solution supports compensation, i.e., the execution of business actions according to a decision map.

Another model-based design for the runtime monitoring of quality of service aspects is presented by Ahluwalia et al. [1]. Particularly, an interaction domain model and an infrastructure for the monitoring of deadlines are illustrated. In this approach, system functions are abstracted from interacting components. While a model-driven approach is applied for code generation, the presented model of system services is only related to these in a sense that it reflects them. This is, it is not a source model for the model-driven development of the services. In contrast, MORSE manages and is aware of the real models, systems are generated from. This allows for root cause analysis and evolution of as demonstrated in the presented case study.

5.6.3 Related Work on Model Repositories

Besides the monitoring of runtime requirements in form of compliance concern models, the MORSE approach particularly focuses on the management of models of service-based systems and their accessibility during runtime. Particularly, it targets at integration with services and – as presented in this work – facilitates model-aware monitoring. For this reason, a model repository with versioning capabilities is deployed (see Section 5.3.2). It abstracts from modeling technologies and its UUID-based implementation allows for a straightforward identification of models and model elements.

Other model repositories primarily aim at model-based tool integration. Model-Bus [40], e.g., addresses the heterogeneity and distribution of model tools and realizes transparent model update. Designed as an open environment, ModelBus focuses on integrating functionality such as model verification, transformation, or testing into a service bus.

Odyssey-VCS 2 [36] is an EMF based model repository after initially relying on the NetBeans Metadata Repository [32]. Odyssey-VCS 2 [36] and AMOR [2, 7] particularly have a focus on the versioning aspect of model management (see also [3]), e.g., for the conflict resolution in collaborative development (cf. [8]).

These works mainly focus on the design time. MORSE, in contrast, focuses on runtime services and processes and their integration, e.g., through monitoring, with the repository and builds on the simple identification for making models accessible at runtime. Instead of aiming at reconciling a multitude of modeling tools' languages and the integration of arbitrary (legacy) tools, MORSE also concentrates on some selective concepts such as relations between models. The MORSE repository abstracts from technologies, focuses on MDD projects, and targets at integration with services.

5.7 Conclusion

We propose a model-aware approach for runtime monitoring of business compliance in process-driven SOAs. Our approach leverages a model repository and event-based monitoring. Business process models are stored in a model repository that can be queried. The process models are uniquely identifiable, and relations between process models can also be discovered. During execution a process engine emits low-level events, embedded with a reference to the process models. These low-level events are correlated into high-level business events that trigger compliance checking actions. Any additional information required for compliance checks is retrievable through the query interface of our MORSE repository.

With the model-aware monitoring for SOAs we have presented a novel and generic approach of how to relate system models and system requirements models. In the context of compliance monitoring for example and by relating processes and process activities to compliance models a business intelligence has reacher means of analyzing the runtime process execution as dynamic reflection on the models and related models becomes possible.

Our approach supports compliance checking by combining the power of CEP techniques, which work best in a limited processing window, and the model querying capabilities from a model repository to provide a wider context of information from the models. At the moment, for context information regarding a process model, we provide MORSE. However, at the process instance level, we assume the possibility to query an event processing engine. Our future work shall look into how such a querying interface can be provided for an engine, to manage queries at process instance level.

Acknowledgements For realizing support for the BPEL extension for the MORSE traceability at the Apache ODE engine the authors would like to thank Petra Bierleutgeb as well as the Institute of Architecture of Application Systems from the University of Stuttgart for their work.

This work was supported by the European Union FP7 project COMPAS, grant no. 215175.

References

1. Ahluwalia, J., Krüger, I.H., Phillips, W., Meisinger, M.: Model-based run-time monitoring of end-to-end deadlines. In: W. Wolf (ed.) EMSOFT, pp. 100–109. ACM (2005)
2. Altmanninger, K., Kappel, G., Kusel, A., Retschitzegger, W., Seidl, M., Schwinger, W., Wimmer, M.: AMOR – towards adaptable model versioning. In: 1st International Workshop on Model Co-Evolution and Consistency Management, in conjunction with MODELS '08 (2008)
3. Altmanninger, K., Seidl, M., Wimmer, M.: A survey on model versioning approaches. IJWIS 5(3), 271–304 (2009)
4. Bank for International Settlements: Basel II: International Convergence of Capital Measurement and Capital Standards: A Revised Framework - Comprehensive Version. http://www.bis.org/publ/bcbsca.htm (2006). [accessed in June 2010]
5. Berglund, A., Boag, S., Chamberlin, D., Fernández, M.F., Kay, M., Robie, J., Siméon, J.: XML path language (XPath) 2.0. W3C recommendation, W3C (2007). [accessed in July 2009]
6. Bézivin, J.: On the unification power of models. Software and System Modeling 4(2), 171–188 (2005)
7. Brosch, P., Langer, P., Seidl, M., Wimmer, M.: Towards end-user adaptable model versioning: The by-example operation recorder. In: CVSM '09: Proceedings of the 2009 ICSE Workshop on Comparison and Versioning of Software Models, pp. 55–60. IEEE Computer Society, Washington, DC, USA (2009). DOI http://dx.doi.org/10.1109/CVSM.2009.5071723
8. Brosch, P., Seidl, M., Wieland, K., Wimmer, M., Langer, P.: We can work it out: Collaborative conflict resolution in model versioning. In: ECSCW 2009: Proceedings of the 11th European Conference on Computer Supported Cooperative Work, pp. 207–214. Springer (2009). URL http://dx.doi.org/10.1007/978-1-84882-854-4_12
9. Buehler, S., Dewenter, R., Haucap, J.: Mobile number portability in europe. Telecommunications Policy 30(7), 385 – 399 (2006). DOI DOI:10.1016/j.telpol.2006.04.001. URL http://www.sciencedirect.com/science/article/B6VCC-4K5JBY0-1/2/e83f338b89f16a55cb0fb8d852473840. Mobile Futures

10. Cappiello, C., Kritikos, K., Metzger, A., Parking, M., Pernici, B., Plebani, P., Treiber, M.:
    A quality model for service monitoring and adaptation. In: First Workshop on Monitoring,
    Adaptation and Beyond in conjunction with ICSOC-ServiceWave Conference, pp. 183–195
    (2008)
11. Cardellini, V., Casalicchio, E., Grassi, V., Lo Presti, F., Mirandola, R.: Qos-driven run-
    time adaptation of service oriented architectures. In: Proceedings of the 7th joint meet-
    ing of the European software engineering conference and the ACM SIGSOFT symposium
    on The foundations of software engineering on European software engineering conference
    and foundations of software engineering symposium, pp. 131–140. ACM (2009). DOI
    http://doi.acm.org/10.1145/1595696.1595718
12. Casati, F., Discenza, A.: Supporting workflow cooperation within and across organizations. In:
    Proceedings of the 2000 ACM symposium on Applied computing, pp. 196–202. ACM (2000).
    DOI http://doi.acm.org/10.1145/335603.335742
13. Chowdhary, P., Bhaskaran, K., Caswell, N.S., Chang, H., Chao, T., Chen, S.K., Dikun, M.J.,
    Lei, H., Jeng, J.J., Kapoor, S., Lang, C.A., Mihaila, G.A., Stanoi, I., Zeng, L.: Model driven
    development for business performance management. IBM Systems Journal **45**(3), 587–606
    (2006)
14. Cohen, D., Feather, M.S., Narayanaswamy, K., Fickas, S.S.: Automatic monitoring of software
    requirements. In: ICSE '97: Proceedings of the 19th international conference on Software
    engineering, pp. 602–603. ACM, New York, NY, USA (1997). DOI http://doi.acm.org/10.
    1145/253228.253493
15. COMPAS Consortium: Compliance-driven Models, Languages, and Architectures for Ser-
    vices. http://compas-ict.eu (2007). [accessed in June 2010]
16. Congress of the United States: Public Company Accounting Reform and Investor Protec-
    tion Act (Sarbanes-Oxley Act), Pub.L. 107-204, 116 Stat. 745. http://www.gpo.gov/
    fdsys/pkg/PLAW-107publ204/content-detail.html (2002). [accessed in June
    2010]
17. Dardenne, A., van Lamsweerde, A., Fickas, S.: Goal-directed requirements acquisition. Sci.
    Comput. Program. **20**(1-2), 3–50 (1993)
18. European Parliament and Council: Directive 2002/22/EC of the European Parliament
    and of the Council of 7 March 2002 on universal service and users' rights re-
    lating to electronic communications networks and services (Universal Service Di-
    rective).   http://eur-lex.europa.eu/LexUriServ/LexUriServ.do?uri=
    CELEX:32002L0022:EN:NOT (2002). [accessed in June 2010]
19. European Parliament and Council: Directive 2004/39/EC on markets in financial in-
    struments. http://eur-lex.europa.eu/LexUriServ/LexUriServ.do?uri=
    CELEX:02004L0039-20060428:EN:NOT (2004). [accessed in June 2010]
20. Feather, M., Fickas, S., van Lamsweerde, A., Ponsard, C.: Reconciling system requirements
    and runtime behavior. In: Software Specification and Design, 1998. Proceedings. Ninth Inter-
    national Workshop on, pp. 50–59 (1998). DOI 10.1109/IWSSD.1998.667919
21. Greiner, T., Düster, W., Pouatcha, F., von Ammon, R., Brandl, H.M., Guschakowski, D.: Busi-
    ness activity monitoring of norisbank taking the example of the application easycredit and the
    future adoption of complex event processing (CEP). In: Proceedings of the 4th international
    symposium on Principles and practice of programming in Java, pp. 237–242. ACM (2006)
22. Hagen, C., Alonso, G.: Beyond the black box: event-based inter-process communication in
    process support systems. In: 19th IEEE International Conference on Distributed Computing
    Systems, pp. 450–457 (1999). DOI 10.1109/ICDCS.1999.776547
23. Havey, M.: Essential Business Process Modeling. O'Reilly Media, Inc. (2005)
24. Hentrich, C., Zdun, U.: Patterns for process-oriented integration in service-oriented architec-
    tures. In: Proceedings of 11th European Conference on Pattern Languages of Programs (2006)
25. Holmes, T., Zdun, U., Dustdar, S.: MORSE: A Model-Aware Service Environment. In:
    M. Kirchberg, P.C.K. Hung, B. Carminati, C.H. Chi, R. Kanagasabai, E.D. Valle, K.C. Lan,
    L.J. Chen (eds.) Proceedings of the 4th IEEE Asia-Pacific Services Computing Conference
    (APSCC), pp. 470–477. IEEE (2009). DOI 10.1109/APSCC.2009.5394083

26. Information Systems Audit and Control Association: Control Objectives for Information and Related Technology (CobiT). http://www.isaca.org/cobit (1996). [accessed in June 2010]
27. International Accounting Standards Committee (IASC) Foundation: International Financial Reporting Standards. http://www.iasb.org/IFRSs/IFRS.htm. [accessed in June 2010]
28. International Telecommunication Union: ISO/IEC 9834-8 Information technology – Open Systems Interconnection – Procedures for the operation of OSI Registration Authorities: Generation and registration of Universally Unique Identifiers (UUIDs) and their use as ASN.1 object identifier components (2004)
29. Kang, J.G., Han, K.H.: A business activity monitoring system supporting real-time business performance management. In: Third International Conference on Convergence and Hybrid Information Technology, vol. 1, pp. 473–478 (2008)
30. Kung, P., Hagen, C., Rodel, M., Seifert, S.: Business process monitoring & measurement in a large bank: challenges and selected approaches. In: Sixteenth International Workshop on Database and Expert Systems Applications, pp. 955–961 (2005)
31. Luckham, D.C.: The Power of Events: An Introduction to Complex Event Processing in Distributed Enterprise Systems. Addison-Wesley (2002)
32. Matula, M.: NetBeans metadata repository. http://mdr.netbeans.org. [accessed in July 2009]
33. McGregor, C., Kumaran, S.: Business process monitoring using web services in B2B e-commerce. In: Parallel and Distributed Processing Symposium., Proceedings International, pp. 219–226 (2002)
34. Ministre de l'économie, des finances et de l'industrie: loi de sécurité financière. http://www.senat.fr/leg/pjl02-166.html (2003). [accessed in June 2010]
35. zur Muehlen, M., Rosemann, M.: Workflow-based process monitoring and controlling-technical and organizational issues. In: Proceedings of the 33rd Annual Hawaii International Conference on System Sciences, p. 10 pp. vol.2 (2000)
36. Murta, L., Corrêa, C., Jo a.G.P., Werner, C.: Towards Odyssey-VCS 2: Improvements over a UML-based version control system. In: CVSM '08: Proceedings of the 2008 international workshop on Comparison and versioning of software models, pp. 25–30. ACM, New York, NY, USA (2008). DOI http://doi.acm.org/10.1145/1370152.1370159
37. Organization for the Advancement of Structured Information Standards: Web service business process execution language version 2.0. OASIS Standard, OASIS Web Services Business Process Execution Language (WSBPEL) TC (2007). [accessed in February 2010]
38. Rozsnyai, S., Vecera, R., Schiefer, J., Schatten, A.: Event cloud - searching for correlated business events. In: The 9th IEEE International Conference on E-Commerce Technology and the 4th IEEE International Conference on Enterprise Computing, E-Commerce, and E-Services, pp. 409–420 (2007)
39. Skene, J., Emmerich, W.: Engineering runtime requirements-monitoring systems using mda technologies. In: R.D. Nicola, D. Sangiorgi (eds.) TGC, Lecture Notes in Computer Science, vol. 3705, pp. 319–333. Springer (2005)
40. Sriplakich, P., Blanc, X., Gervais, M.P.: Supporting transparent model update in distributed case tool integration. In: H. Haddad (ed.) SAC, pp. 1759–1766. ACM (2006)
41. The Apache Software Foundation: Apache ODE (Orchestration Director Engine). http://ode.apache.org. [accessed in June 2010]
42. The Netherlands Corporate Governance Committee: The Dutch corporate governance code. http://www.commissiecorporategovernance.nl/page/downloads/CODEDEFENGELSCOMPLEETII.pdf (2003). [accessed in June 2010]
43. Tran, H., Zdun, U., Dustdar, S.: View-based and model-driven approach for reducing the development complexity in process-driven SOA. In: Intl. Working Conf. on Business Process and Services Computing (BPSC'07), Lecture Notes in Informatics, vol. 116, pp. 105–124 (2007)

Chapter 6

Integrating Perfective and Corrective Adaptation of Service-based Applications

Andreas Gehlert, Andreas Metzger, Dimka Karastoyanova, Raman Kazhamiakin, Klaus Pohl, Frank Leymann and Marco Pistore

Abstract Service-based Applications (SBAs) can be dynamically adapted to address various goals, which include (1) aiming to better achieve the users' requirements (perfective adaptation), and (2) repairing and preventing failures (corrective adaptation). When building applications which aim at addressing more than of such goals, it is important to understand the interplay of these different adaptation goals. Otherwise this can lead to conflicting adaptations. This chapter introduces a framework to integrate and align perfective and corrective adaptations, while addressing the problems that are due to the interactions between these two kinds of adaptation. The framework uses requirements engineering techniques to trigger perfective adaptation and online testing techniques to trigger corrective adaptations. Based on the above techniques, this chapter investigates the interplay and interaction between the two types of adaptation. We demonstrate how perfective and corrective techniques can be integrated in a meaningful way to support the overall adaptation requirements of the service-based applications, while avoiding the above problems. As a solution, we propose exploiting an enterprise service registry, which restricts the ways in which a service-based application can be adapted.

Andreas Gehlert, Andreas Metzger, Klaus Pohl
Paluno (The Ruhr Institute for Software Technology), University of Duisburg-Essen, Gerlingstr. 16, 45127 Essen, Germany, e-mail: andreas.gehlert@sse.uni-due.de, andreas.metzger@sse.uni-due.de, klaus.pohl@sse.uni-due.de

Dimka Karastoyanova, Frank Leymann
IAAS, University of Stuttgart, Universitaetsstr. 38, 70569 Stuttgart, Germany, e-mail: dimka.karastoyanova@iaas.uni-stuttgart.de, frank.leymann@iaas.uni-stuttgart.de

Raman Kazhamiakin, Marco Pistore
FBK-IRST, Via Sommarive 18, 38100 Trento, Italy, e-mail: raman.kazhamiakin@fbk.eu, marco.pistore@fbk.eu

6.1 Introduction and Overview

6.1.1 Motivation and Problem Statement

Organizations increasingly rely on the flexibility offered by service-based applications (SBAs). This flexibility allows those applications to operate in a highly dynamic world, in which the level and quality of service provisioning, (legal) regulations, as well as requirements keep changing and evolving. To respond to those changes, service-based applications need to modify their functionality and quality dynamically depending on the usage situation, context, and deployment platform. In addition, those applications will need to react to failures of the constituent services to ensure that they maintain their expected functionality and quality. In such a dynamic setting, evolution and adaptation methods and tools become key to enable SBAs to respond to changing conditions.

Following the terminology defined by the S-Cube Network of Excellence [35], we refer to evolution as the more traditional modification of a system's requirements, specification, models and so forth during design time ("maintenance"), while we understand adaptation to refer to the modification of a specific instance of a system during run-time. In this chapter, we focus on adaptation of service-based applications and thus address *adaptive service-based applications*.

The adaptation of an SBA can address various goals, such as (1) correcting faults contained in the SBA (corrective adaptation [25, p. 43]), and (2) adapting the SBA to new and yet unknown requirements (perfective adaptation) [47, p. 493].

When building adaptive SBAs that address two or more such goals, precautions must be taken to ensure that the interplay and the interactions between the different types of adaptations are considered, as otherwise this can lead to conflicting adaptations, which need to be avoided. As an example, to address the goal of corrective adaptation, the service-based application might aim at replacing a failed service A with a service B, while at the same time the SBA, in order to address the aim of perfective adaptation, aims to replace service A with a service C, which promises to provide a better quality of service than service A. In fact, coordinating various adaptation goals is considered one of the key challenges in self-adaptive software [43].

In this chapter we present innovative solutions from the S-Cube Network of Excellence (http://www.s-cube-network.eu/) that specifically focus on understanding how the need for the corrective adaptation of a SBA must be aligned and synchronized with the opportunity for the perfective adaptation of a SBA.

6.1.2 Solution Idea

To demonstrate how conflicts between adaptation goals can be avoided, we focus on the two adaptation goals introduced above: corrective and perfective adaptation. More specifically, we exploit the following techniques to determine the demand for an adaptation of the SBA (i.e., to determine an adaptation trigger [43]):

Corrective adaptation based on online testing: Online tests of services are performed during run-time (operation) of the SBA to determine possible failures of the SBA's constituent services. A failure of such a test constitutes a corrective adaptation trigger, which could possibly be satisfied by replacing the failed service with an alternative service.[1]

Perfective adaptation based on requirements engineering (RE): Typically, enterprises have contract relationships with other business partners. This fact is reflected in the set of services that may be used in SBAs. These partner services usually meet the requirements specified by the requirements engineers in the enterprise. In some cases however, due to the dynamic nature of the service provision, new relationships are established with other (previously unknown) business partners. If the newly introduced service is better and/or more appropriate (e. g. cheaper or faster), the requirements engineer could recommend the use of this new service and thereby issue a perfective adaptation trigger. In addition, these new services may bring additional and/or enhanced functionalities, which may anticipate new requirements.

Both of the above techniques share the characteristic that they are pro-active in nature, i. e., both techniques lead to "predictive" adaptation triggers. In the case of online testing, the failure of a service could point to a problem of the SBA (which involves this service) in the future. In the case of recommendations from RE, this provides the possibility to improve the SBAs and to anticipate future requirements. Thereby, both of those adaptation drivers, which are the core building blocks of our proposed solution, share a fundamental commonality. This simplifies addressing the problem of synchronizing the two adaptation goals.

In addition, to exploiting this commonality, a further key idea of our approach is to use a central enterprise service registry. This registry contains references to in-house services, e. g. those services provided by the enterprise itself, and to external services, e. g., those services, that are provided by external service providers. Only these services are allowed to be used in the enterprise's service-based applications. Each reference to one of the services is accompanied by a service description (cf. Section 6.4 for more details). Since the enterprise service registry is a private registry, it can be administrated solely by the enterprise. On the one hand, this enterprise service registry constrains possible adaptations and, thereby, reduces the flexibility of the SBA. On the other hand, it enables the use of techniques (such as testing techniques) that require a certain level of stability (cf. Figure 6.1).

---

[1] Online testing does not replace normal testing activities, which need to be carried out before the SBA is put into operation. However, due to the fact that the service provider may change the service without any prior notice, it is important to regularly test the services in order to ensure the overall quality of the SBA. Since these testing activities are carried out during the normal usage of the SBA—thus the term online testing.

6.1.3 Focus and Assumptions

In order to focus our chapter, we restrict ourselves to service-based applications built from service compositions that use the workflow-approach, i.e., we assume that a service composition is described in terms of a control flow (sequence of tasks), data flow (data exchange between tasks), exception handling and services, which realise the functionality of the tasks. Therefore, service composition descriptions are organized in two dimensions—control logic and functionality.

To further constrain the scope of the chapter, we consider the exchange of individual services as the only mechanism for performing adaptations of SBAs. This means that we only adapt SBAs by changing the bindings of services (or end points) to the workflow. The modification of the control or data flow structure is not addressed here and will be part of the future work in the S-Cube project.

6.1.4 Outline of the Approach

Figure 6.1 provides an overview of our approach. Below, we briefly illustrate how the two adaptation goals—perfective and corrective adaptation—are addressed in this book chapter, and how we envision to avoid conflicting adaptations. The remainder of this chapter will provide more details on the individual techniques and their synchronisation:

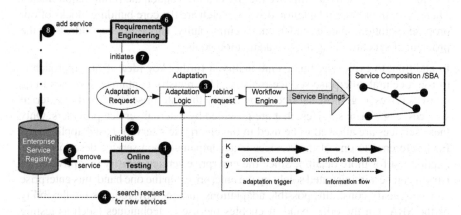

Fig. 6.1: Overall approach

Corrective Adaptation: Assume that online testing uncovers a failure of one of the SBA's services (①in Figure 6.1). In this case, the online testing activity issues an adaptation trigger ② Based on this adaptation trigger, the actual adaptation component of the SBA ③needs to determine how to adapt the SBA, in our case this means it needs to find an alternative service (e. g., by searching the service registry). The adaptation component then has to notify the workflow engine to bind this alternative service to the service composition in place of the failed service ④. To avoid using the failed service in other SBAs of the enterprise, the online testing activity removes it from the enterprise service registry ⑤.

Perfective Adaptation: Assume that a new service was discovered during requirements engineering and that this service is cheaper or better than the previously used one ⑥. If the requirements engineer decides to use this service in the SBA, s/he needs to add it to the enterprise service registry ⑧ and to trigger an adaptation ⑦. This adaptation trigger will eventually notify the workflow engine ③ and, similar to above, the workflow engine rebinds the new service to the service composition instead of the old one ④.

For the purpose of this chapter, we assume that an SBA is already running and, therefore, uses services from the enterprise service registry. During this run-time phase, the online testing activity continuously tests the SBA's services for failures and if a failure is observed, the respective service is removed from the enterprise service registry. The requirements engineering activity continuously searches for new and innovative services and if such a service is found, it is added to the enterprise service registry. Since our approach requires that every service-based application in the enterprise uses services from the enterprise service registry, this registry together with the workflow adaptability serve as tools to synchronize the activities of requirements engineering and online testing. For instance, it is not possible in our scenario that online testing and requirements engineering concurrently replace services in the workflow. Since there is only the possibility to add or remove services to/from the registry, the state of the workflow cannot become inconsistent (cf. Section 6.7.3 for a detailed discussion).

6.1.5 Structure of Chapter

Following the structure of Figure 6.1, the remainder of this chapter is organized as follows: In Section 6.2 we present the relevant state of the art on requirements engineering, monitoring, adaptation and testing on which our research is built. In Section 6.3 we introduce the scenario, which we use in the text to illustrate our results. Subsequently we describe the requirements engineering (Section 6.4) and online testing techniques (Section 6.5), which may trigger adaptation. In Section 6.6 we explain how the two techniques interact with each other, which is demonstrated with the help of an example. Section 6.7 contains a critical discussion of our results. The conclusions are summarized in Section 7.8.

6.2 Related Work

The state of the art discussion in this section is structured as follows: In Section 6.2.1 we first discuss related work that addresses the problem of synchronizing adaptations in the presence of more than one adaptation goal. Section 6.2.2 describes the related work on requirements engineering, which is relevant for Section 6.4 of this chapter. Sections 6.2.3 and 6.2.4 summarize the related work on monitoring and online testing respectively, which is relevant for Section 6.5 of this chapter.

6.2.1 Related Work on Multi-Goal Adaptation

In [43] Salehie and Tahvildari stress that "coordinating [...] goals at different levels of granularity is one of the significant challenges in self-adaptive software." As a result of the literature survey carried out in that paper, the authors reach the conclusion that only very few approaches address more than one goal of adaptation (or, self-* property). In addition, they observe that most approaches that address more than one goal do not systematically coordinate those goals. One concrete, architecture-based approach that addresses multiple goals is introduced by Cheng et al. in [14]. However, rather than addressing high-level goals, such as perfective and corrective adaptation, which are addressed in our approach, the authors address conflicting situations between more fine-grained objectives, such as performance and other quality of service characteristics.

6.2.2 Related Work on Requirements Engineering

Requirements engineering aims at eliciting, documenting and agreeing upon the goals, assumptions and requirements of the software system to be built [39]. In the context of RE, goals provide an intentional description of the requirements towards the software system. In our chapter, we chose a goal-driven approach for RE, as reasoning techniques for goal models are available, which allows analysing the effect of the satisfaction of a single goal on the whole goal model. This facilitates the analysis of the impact of a single service on the entire SBA and thereby can support perfective adaptation.

Tropos was one of the first goal modeling techniques, which were successfully applied to the service domain (for an introduction see Section 6.4). Aiello and Giorgini for instance explore quality of service aspects using Tropos actor models [2]. The authors use Tropos' formal reasoning techniques in [19] to calculate the fulfilment of a goal structure according to a given set of services. As the approach by Aiello and Giorgini does not cover the adaptation of a SBA, our approach is an extension to [2]. In another approach Penserini et al. explore how Tropos can be used to develop SBAs. However, the authors do not focus on adaptation. Another application of Tropos was put forward by Pistore et al. in [38]. The authors explain how SBAs can be developed by step-wise refining plans and complementing these plans with a formal workflow definition. Since the focus of Pistore et al. is on deriving service compositions, the authors do not cover adaptation issues. The introduction to Tropos in [12] also contains a comparison of goal models to chose the architecture of the software system [12, p. 373]. This comparison is limited only to choosing so called architectural styles and, thus, does not explain adaptation.

A similar approach to ours was put forward by Herold et al. in [21]. The authors relate existing components to goal models. This relation is established by so called generic architectural drivers. These drivers enable the selection of existing components, which fit with the goals and soft-goals of the goal model. Herold et al.'s approach focuses on finding appropriate components and refining the initial goal model with the help of these components. However, the approach does not address adaptation.

Another RE approach, which is similar to ours, was put forward in the Service Centric Systems Engineering (SeCSE) project [28]. In SeCSE initial requirements are formulated as goal models [28, pp. 21] or use cases [23, 52–54], which are than translated into services queries [28, p. 31]. These services queries are sent to a registry. The resulting services are used to refine the initial set of requirements. However, in SeCSE the focus was on changing the requirements according to the current service provision but not on adapting existing SBAs.

6.2.3 Related Work on Monitoring for Adaptation

In order to detect events and situations that necessitate an adaptation of a service-based application, the majority of adaptation approaches from the service-oriented computing field resorts to exploiting *monitoring* techniques. Monitoring provides a way to collect and report relevant information about the execution and evolution of a service-based application. Depending on the goal of a particular adaptation approach, different kinds of events are monitored and different techniques are used for this purpose.

In many approaches (e. g., [6, 7, 18, 33]) the events that trigger the adaptation are failures. These failures include typical problems such as application exceptions, network problems and service unavailability [6, 33], as well as the violation of expected properties and requirements. In the former case fault monitoring is provided by the underlying platform, while in the latter case specific facilities and tools are necessary. In [7] Baresi et al. define the expected properties in the form of assertions (pre-conditions, post-conditions, and invariants), which define constraints on the functional and quality of service (QoS) parameters of the service composition and its context. In [45] Spanoudakis et al. use properties in the form of complex behavioral requirements expressed in event calculus. In [18] Erradi at al. express expected properties as policies on the QoS parameters in the form of event-condition-action (ECA) rules. When a deviation from the expected QoS parameters is detected, the adaptation is initiated and the application is modified. In such a case, adaptation actions may include re-execution of a particular activity or a fragment of a composition, binding/replacement of a service, applying an alternative process, as well as re-discovering and re-composing services. In [44] Siljee et al. use monitoring to track and collect the information regarding a set of predefined QoS parameters (response time, failure rates, availability) infrastructure characteristics (load, bandwidth) and even context. The collected information is checked against expected values defined as functions of the above parameters, and in case of a deviation, the reconfiguration of the application is triggered.

Summarizing, all these works follow the reactive approach to adaptation, i. e., the modification of the application takes place *after* the critical event happened or a problem occurred.

The situation with reactive adaptation is even more critical for approaches that rely on post-mortem analysis of the application execution. A typical monitoring tool used in such approaches is the analysis of workflow logs [1, 20, 34]. Using the information about histories of application executions, it is possible to identify problems and non-optimalities of the current business process model and to find ways for improvement by adapting the service-based application. However, once this adaptation happens, many workflow instances might have already been executed in a "wrong" mode.

6.2.4 Related Work on Online Testing and Regression Testing

The goal of testing is to systematically execute services or service-based applications (service compositions) in order to uncover failures, i. e., deviations of the actual functionality or quality of service from the expected one.

Existing approaches for testing service-based applications mostly focus on testing during design time, which is similar to testing of traditional software systems. There are a few approaches that point to the importance of online testing of service-based applications. In [49] Wang et al. stress the importance of online testing of web-based applications. The authors, furthermore, see monitoring information as a basis for online testing. Deussen et al. propose an online validation platform with an online testing component [15]. In [13] metamorphic online testing is proposed by Chan et al., which uses oracles created during offline testing for online testing. Bai et al. propose adaptive testing in [3, 5], where tests are executed during the operation of the service-based application and can be adapted to changes of the application's environment or of the application itself. Finally, the role of monitoring and testing for validating service-based applications is examined in [11], where the authors propose to use both strategies in combination. However, all these approaches do not exploit testing results for (self-)adaptation.

An approach related to online testing is regression testing. Regression testing aims at checking whether changes of (parts of) a system negatively affect the existing functionality of that system. The typical process is to re-run previously executed test cases. Ruth et al. [41, 42] as well as Di Penta et al. [16] propose regression test techniques for Web services. However, none of the techniques addresses how to use test results for the adaptation of service-based applications.

Summarizing, in spite of a number of approaches for online testing and regression testing, none of these approaches targets the problem of proactive adaptation.

6.3 Illustrative Scenario

In this section we provide a concrete scenario based on the overall application domain, which in turn will be used to demonstrate the application and usefulness of our approach (see Section 6.6.2). Specifically, our scenarios support the business goals "Provide mobile phone number portability" (TELCO_BG_01) and "Provide mobile services portability" (TELCO_BG_02) and refines the scenario "Manage Telephone Number Portability" (TELCO_S_01) as introduced in Chapter 1.

The abstract workflow of this scenario is depicted in Figure 6.2 using the Unified Modeling Language (UML) activity diagram syntax. Annotations are used to model how concrete services are assigned to tasks in the workflow.

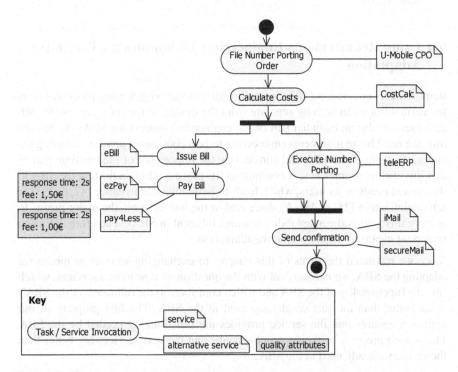

Fig. 6.2: Number porting scenario (modeled using the UML activity diagram syntax)

The scenario we use in the following can be described as follows: "Mrs. P is a regular user of her mobile phone. She uses it for making phone calls, writing short messages and surfing in the internet. Currently, she has a contract with her preferred Cell Phone Operator (CPO) in Germany. Because she plans to study in England for one year, she is interested in switching to an English CPO to avoid high expenses for the phone services she uses. Mrs. P found out that her current CPO also operates in England and she decided to contact the English partner." As she wants to keep her telephone number, she has to follow the rules given by her German CPO below:

1. Each customer has to file a "Number Porting Order" to start the number porting workflow.

2. Based on this order, the CPO calculates the costs for this order using the "Cost-Calc" service.

3. In parallel to the execution of the number porting (using the service "teleERP" from the CPO's Enterprise Ressource Planning (ERP) system), the bill is issued (using the "eBill" service) and the payment of that bill is initiated (using either the "ezPay" or the "pay4Less" service).

4. After the completion of the two parallel workflow branches, a confirmation is sent to the customer. This task is supported either by the "iMail" or the "secure-Mail" service.

6.4 Using Requirements Engineering Techniques for Perfective Adaptation

Requirements engineering (RE) in traditional software engineering processes is often carried out as an activity separate from the design of the software system. RE activities are also an essential part of the engineering process for SBAs. In this setting, the need for requirements engineering to be a continuous process, covering the entire life cycle of the SBA and considering the importance of the run-time part of that life-cycle, becomes key. A continuous RE process allows adjusting the SBA to the current needs of its users, which leads to perfective maintenance [47, p. 493] or self-optimization [25, p. 43]. As discussed in the introduction, the major means to achieve this goal is the adaptability features inherent in SBAs. Therefore, RE is an important means to trigger perfective adaptation.

Since we restricted the focus of this chapter to exchanging services as means for adapting the SBA, we need to deal with the question on how to find services, which "fit" the functionality of the SBA and which contribute to the fulfilment of the SBA's goals better than the service already used in the SBA. The first property of our approach ensures that the service provides the functionality needed by the SBA. The second property of the approach ensures that the new services are better than the services already used in the SBA.

To achieve those properties, we chose a goal-driven approach (also see Section 6.2.2). First, we compare the goal model of the SBA and the goal model of the new service. The service is only useable if it "fits" in the goal model of the SBA. Second, to find out whether the service provides higher satisfaction ratios for the SBA's goal model, we use the goal reasoning mechanism provided in [19]. We argue, that an adaptation of an initial SBA is advisable if all goals are at least as satisfied as in the initial situation but one goal has a higher satisfaction rate (pareto principle). In case that the new services satisfies some goals better and some goals worse, the requirements engineer may decide on the usage of this service. Lastly, an adaptation may also be advisable when the new service provides additional functionally.[2]

This chapter relies on the Tropos approach [10, 12]. The rationale for using Tropos is threefold: First, Tropos is a comprehensive approach to develop software systems from early requirements to its implementation. We are here particularly interested in the early RE activities, which are well covered by Tropos. Second, Tropos has already been applied to the service discipline, e. g., it has already been shown to be applicable to SBAs [2, 26, 32, 36, 38]. Third, Tropos has a formalisation which allows to reason about goal satisfaction in a goal model [19].

6.4.1 Goal Modelling in Tropos

Tropos rests on the agent oriented paradigm and uses goal modelling techniques known from i* [51] for analysing early and late requirements. These early requirements are documented as actor and goal models. Actor models include actors, their goals and their dependencies. The actor diagram is complemented by a goal model for each actor. This goal model shows the decomposition of the actor's goals into sub-goals and plans (tasks in i*; cf. Figure 6.3 for an example).

Since we are interested in SBAs rather than in their interaction with other actors, we only use the goal models of Tropos. The main concepts of Tropos goal models are actors, goals, resources and plans. These elements are connected with decomposition, contribution and means-end links. An actor represents an organisational unit, a position or a role. The Actor's strategic interests are represented by goals. Goals are further divided into hard-goals and soft-goals. While hard-goals have clear cut measurement criteria to specify its fulfilment, soft-goals do not have such criteria. In this chapter we use hard-goals to model functional and soft-goals to model quality requirements. Goals can be decomposed using And/Or decomposition links. A plan is an activity which may contribute to a goal. A plan may contribute positively or negatively to soft-goals. Means-end links are used to represent which plan or goal (means) is used to fulfil a goal (end, [10, pp. 206]).

In a SBA each plan describes a service, which realises this plan [2, p. 21]. To implement a SBA, it is therefore necessary to find services, whose descriptions fit the plan. Consequently, a SBA in the Tropos early RE perspective is a set of services fitting a set of plans.

6.4.2 Using Goal-Models to Trigger Adaptation

To define the fitness relation between a plan and a service we need to define what a plan and a service is. A plan in Tropos is defined by its name and its relations to goals and soft-goals via a set of means-end links M and via a set of contribution

---

[2] The satisfaction rates are part of the goal modelling process and are, thus, subject of an agreement between the requirements engineer and the end-user of the SBA. Deciding about and agreeing on these satisfaction rates are outside the scope of this book chapter.

links C. Since we later use a satisfaction propagation mechanism to describe the dependencies between different goals, it is sufficient to include only directly connected means-end and contribution links in the definition of a plan. Thus, we can define a plan as a tuple of sets of means-end and contribution links: $plan = <M,C>$.

To compare plans and services we assume:

(A1) Services are described by Tropos goal models. These goal models are registered together with the service in a service registry.

(A2) Each service's goal model contains only the name of the service as plan and only goals and soft-goals connected by means-end and contribution links. Consequently, the service goal model is structurally equivalent to the plan's goal model.

Assumption (A1) is critical insofar as service providers need to append their services with a goal model. A detailed discussion of this assumption is postponed to Section 6.7.1. Assumption (A2) is not critical as we describe below an algorithm, which produces this sub-model from any Tropos goal model.

According to assumption (A2) services and plans are described by the same elements. Consequently a service is also a tuple of sets of means end and contribution links: $service = <M,C>$. A means-end link $m \in M$ is a connection between one Tropos model element e and a goal g. Each contribution link $c \in C$ is a connection between one Tropos model element e and a soft-goal s. It is attributed with a quantitative number to express the strength $\prod$ of the contribution to this soft-goal: $c = <e,s,\prod>$.

As we concentrate on requirements engineering for adapting a SBA, we assume that a SBA is already running and that its initial set of requirements are expressed as Tropos goal model. In addition, each service in this SBA fits to one plan in the requirements specification.

After the initial SBA is operating, the service provisioning is monitored, e.g., by regularly querying public service registries. When new services are available, a RE cycle is triggered. The first activity in this cycle extracts a goal model for each plan. These goal models are in turn compared to goal model of the service found when querying service registries. After this comparison, the goal achievement for the Tropos goal model is calculated based on formal reasoning techniques. These results are then used to decide whether the new service should be used. In the positive case the service is added to the enterprise service registry and an adaptation is triggered. After this decision the RE process starts again.

The underlying assumption of this RE process can be formulated as follows:

(A3) New services may become available over time.

This assumption is fair because the flexibility of SBAs, in parts, relies on new services becoming available over time.

At first we need to describe how the goal model for each plan can be extracted from the entire Tropos model. Extracting a goal model for each plan is necessary since we want to delegate the execution of each plan to a service and since the Tropos model represents the entire SBA and not only one individual service. Intuitively the goal model for each plan contains all its contribution and means-end links and all the connected elements. Both link types are important because we want to know how the service for each plan influences the goal achievement of the entire SBA. In sum, the plan's goal models contains: the plan, all connected goals via contributions links and all connected goals via means-end links (cf. Figure 6.3).

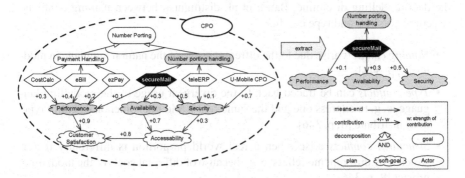

Fig. 6.3: Extracting the sub-model for the plan "secureMail Service"

Figure 6.3 provides an example of a goal model for the number porting service-based application described in Section 6.3. The main goal of this number porting system is to transfer the mobile phone number and its associated services to another country. This goal can be decomposed into the handling of the payments and into the number porting handling itself. Plans, which correspond to services in Figure 6.2, are assigned to those goals using means-end links. The goal "Payment Handling" is supported by the plans, which calculate the costs ("CostCalc"), issue the bill ("eBill") and handle the payment ("ezPay"). The goal "Number Porting Handling" is supported by the plans to handle number porting orders ("U-Mobile CPO"), execute the number porting itself ("teleERP") and sends a confirmation via mail ("secure-Mail"). Each of the before-mentioned plans influence one or more soft-goals. For instance, the "secureMail" plans influences the softgoal "Security" positively with a strength of $+0.5$.

At the beginning of the continuous RE process, the goal model of this service is identical to the extracted goal model of the plan (see above). The goal model for the plan "secureMail", for instance, contains the hard-goal "Number Porting Handling" and the soft-goals "Performance", "Availability" and "Security" as well as the respective means-end and contribution links (Figure 6.3, right).

6.4.2.1 Comparing the Service and the Plan Goal Models

After the specification of the initial requirements and the extraction of the goal model for each plan, we need to monitor the service provision in the registry. If the service provision changed we want to find out whether the newly available services "fit" the existing plans better than the initial set of services. In this section we define this fitness relation. This fitness relation is based on the comparison of the plan's goal model and the service's goal model in accordance with assumptions (A1) and (A2).

The systematic analysis of model comparison conflicts was initially developed in the data modelling discipline. Batini et al. distinguish between naming conflicts, structural conflicts and type conflicts:

- *Naming conflicts* arise due to the different usage of the natural language in models [8, p. 344].

- *Type conflicts* can be traced back to the divergent usage of the modelling language, e. g. to express one and the same real world phenomenon as entity type or as at-tribute [8, p. 346].

- *Structural conflicts* arise when a real world proportion is differently reconstructed by different modellers, e. g., because of different goals of the modelling project [8, p. 346].

A model comparison rests on the identification of conflicts and aims to resolve naming and type conflicts. Structural conflicts cannot be resolved and represent the differences in the compared models. As the resolution of naming conflicts was already discussed in the literature [40, p. 344], we assume that these naming conflicts were already resolved:

(A4) The service's goal model and the plan's goal model use a shared ontology, i. e. two goals with the same name are identical and two goals with different names are different.

As the naming conflicts are already resolved, model comparison can be reduced to resolving type conflicts and to analyse structural conflicts. Resolving type conflicts means to define a similarity relation between equivalent or similar model structures. Our models contain only hard-goals, soft-goals, contribution links and means-end links (cf. assumption (A2)). In addition, hard-goals describe functional requirements and soft-goals represent quality requirements. As functional requirements in the service domain are often described by the web service description language (WSDL) and non-functional requirements are often described by means of service level agreements (SLA), it follows that hard-goals and soft-goals are mutually exclusive and cannot be resolved in the type conflict analysis. The remaining elements are means-end and contribution links. Means-end links are used whenever plans and soft-goals provide a means to achieve a goal [10, p. 208]. Consequently, the means fully satisfies the goal or soft-goal, which is identical to a contribution link with a degree of $+1.0$.

To define the fitness relation between a plan and a service we introduce the function $name()$, which returns the name of a goal model element and $type()$, which returns the type of a model element. Based on this analysis of type conflicts we can now define when a plan p fits a service description s:

$$p \xrightarrow{fits} s \Leftrightarrow$$
$$\forall m_P \in M_P : (\exists m_s \in M_S : (name(g_P) = name(g_S) \wedge (type(g_P) = type(g_S)))) \vee$$
$$\exists c_s \in M_s : (name(g_p) = name(s_S) \wedge type(g_P) = \text{``soft} - goal\text{''} \wedge d_S = 1))$$
$$\wedge$$
$$\forall c_P \in C_P : (\exists c_S \in C_S : (name(s_P) = name(s_S)) \vee$$
$$\exists m_S \in M_S : (name(s_P) = name(g_S) \wedge type(g_S) = \text{``soft} - goal\text{''}))$$

This fitness relation holds if:

1. Each means-end m_P link in the plan's goal model exists also in the service's goal model (m_S) and the connected goals have identical names and types. As a means end link can also be represented as contribution link, it follows: Each means end link m_P of the plan's goal model exists in the service's goal model as contribution link with the strength $d_S = 1$ and the connected goals have the same name and the plan's goal is a soft-goal.

2. It must additionally hold that for each contribution link in the plan's goal model c_P there is either a contribution link c_S in the services goal model and the connected goals have identical names. The contribution link c_P may also be represented as means end link m_S in the service's goal model. In this case both connected goals must have the same name and the service's goal must be a soft-goal.

6.4.2.2 Decision Support for Adapting a SBA

An adaptation of the SBA is only feasible if the relation $p \xrightarrow{fits} s$ holds—otherwise the service does not provide the required functionality needed by the SBA. When a new service is registered in a registry (assumption (A3)) and the fitness relation holds for this service for one plan, we can distinguish three cases:

1. *Equal Goal Satisfaction Rates*: The goal model of the new service is identical with the plan's goal model. In this case the new service can be used to substitute an existing service, e. g., when the existing service fails (cf. Section 6.5).

2. *Different Goal Satisfaction Rates*: The new service may contribute differently to existing soft-goals by assigning different strengths to contribution links. These

different strengths are further propagated in the goal model and may lead to different satisfaction ratios of goals and soft-goals. The adaptation decision is based on these new goal satisfaction ratios.

3. *Goal Extension*: The new service may provide additional functionality not used in the initial SBA. This new functionality will be expressed as additional hard-goals in the service goal model. These new hard goals do not correspond to any goal in the plan goal model (structural conflict). The SBA may be adapted accordingly to exploit the additional functionality of the new service. Using this new functionality, however, may require a major adaptation of the SBA and, consequently, may require considerable human intervention.

In the following we demonstrate the calculation of the goal satisfaction values in accordance to the newly available service. We use the quantitative reasoning techniques in Tropos goal models presented in [19, p. 10]. The algorithm presupposes that each goal has two predicates $Sat(G)$ and $Den(G)$ describing the satisfiability and deniability of the goal. These variable are computed according to the strength $\varPi$, which is annotated to contribution links. This strength describes the im-pact of one goal on another goal. Due to space limitations, we restrict ourselves to goal satisfyability.

For each contribution link $G_2 \overset{\varPi+s}{\rightarrow} G_1$ with the strength $\varPi$ Giorgini et al. define the following propagation axiom: $G_2 \overset{\varPi+s}{\rightarrow} G_1 : Sat(G_2) \geq x \rightarrow Sat(G_1) \geq (x \otimes \varPi)$ [19, p. 12]. The operator $\otimes$ is defined as $p_1 \otimes p_2 =_d ef p_1 \times p_2$. In addition, we assume that means-end links can be treated like contribution links with $\varPi = 1$. We can now use the axiom to calculate for each goal of the goal model. This goal propagation assumes the following:

(A5) The strengths $\varPi$ of all service's goal models are comparable, e. g., they are measured objectively.

This assumption is necessary to actually compare the satisfaction ratios of the soft-goals among the different service. We discuss this assumption in Section 6.7.1.

The result of the label propagation can be presented as bar chart. The y-axis is labelled with the different goals and soft-goals, the x-axis is labelled with the degree of satisfaction and the bars show the degree of satisfaction of the different goals. The bar chart representation of the goal model in Figure 6.3 is depicted in Figure 6.4 (black bars).

Assume that new services were registered in a service registry. To use these new services we require, that their goal models are structurally identical to the plan's goal model. Three goal models of new services, which fulfil this requirement are depicted in Figure 6.4.

In comparison to the goal model in Figure 6.3, the contribution links of the "iMail₁" service in ①in Figure 6.4 to Security and to Availability have an increased strength (0.8 instead of 0.5 and 1.0 instead of 0.3). Using the "iMail₁" service means to

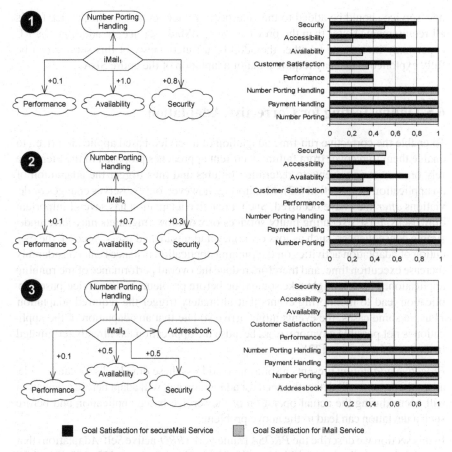

Fig. 6.4: Services with the same functionality but different qualities

achieve higher fulfilment rates for all soft-goals. Consequently, using service ① is beneficial from the RE perspective for the SBA (case 2) and it should be added to the enterprise service registry.

The "iMail₂" Service ② in Figure 6.4 has a reduced strength for the contribution link to Security (0.3 instead of 0.5) but an increased strength for the contribution link to Availability (0.7 instead of 0.3). The goals Accessibility, Availability and Customer Satisfaction have now a higher satisfiability. However, the satisfiability of the goal Security dropped. A RE expert has to decide about the usage of that service in the SBA. In this case the "iMail₂" service may be valuable because the goal Consumer Satisfaction increased slightly. The RE expert has to balance this advantage with the disadvantage of a lower satisfiability of the goal Reliability.

"iMail₃" service ③ in Figure 6.4 provides more functionality (expressed as additional goal Addressbook) and a higher satisfiability for the soft-goal Availability (0.5 instead of 0.3). "iMail₃" service ③ combines cases 2 and 3. Consequently, the new service should be added to the enterprise service registry as the service fulfils all requirements better than the previous "secureMail" service. In addition, the RE expert may investigate whether the additional functionality of this service can be fully exploited. This may require a major adaptation of the entire SBA.

6.5 Online Testing for Corrective Adaptation

To enable the corrective run-time adaptation of a service-based application (i.e., to enable them to recover from failures), current approaches proposed in the literature rely on monitoring events to determine failures and thus trigger the adaptation of an application (see Section 6.2). Monitoring, however, only observes changes or deviations *after* they have occurred. Such a reactive adaptation has several important drawbacks. First, executing faulty services or workflow fragments may have undesirable consequences, such as loss of money and unsatisfied users. Second, the execution of adaptation activities on the running application instances can considerably increase execution time, and therefore reduce the overall performance of the running application. Third, it might take some time before problems in the service-based application lead to monitoring events that ultimately trigger the required adaptation. Thus, in some cases, the events might arrive so late that an adaptation of the application is not possible anymore, e.g., because the application has already terminated in an inconsistent state [22].

Proactive adaptation presents a solution to address these drawbacks, because – ideally – the system will detect the need for adaptation and will adapt before a deviation will occur during the actual operation of the service-based application and before such a deviation can lead to the above problems.

In this section we describe the *PROSA* framework (*PRO*-active *S*elf-*A*daptation) that introduces a novel way of achieving corrective adaptation (see [22, 30]. Based on the framework, a prototype based on existing Web Service technologies is currently being implemented.

PROSA exploits online testing solutions to pro-actively trigger adaptations. Online testing means that testing activities are performed during the operation (run-time) phase of service-based applications. This means in addition to testing the service-based application during design-time, dedicated testing activities are performed on the 'production system' during run-time (cf. [9]). Obviously, an online test can fail; e.g., because a faulty service has been invoked during the test. This point to a potential problem that the service-based application might face in the future of its operation; e.g., when the application invokes the faulty service. In such a case, PROSA will proactively trigger an adaptation to prevent undesired consequences.

The remainder of this section is structured as follows: In Section 6.5.1 we present an overview of the PROSA framework by describing its key elements and by discussing how those elements could be implemented by utilizing or extending existing testing and adaptation techniques. The alignment of this framework with perfective adaptation is explained and illustrated in Section 6.6.

6.5.1 PROSA: Proactive Self-Adaptation Through Online Testing

As introduced above, the novel contribution of the PROSA framework is to exploit online testing for proactive adaptation. Therefore, the PROSA framework prescribes the required online testing activities to determine whether to adapt the application. Figure 6.5 provides an overview of the PROSA framework and how the proactive adaptation enabled by PROSA relates to "traditional" reactive adaptation which is enabled by monitoring.

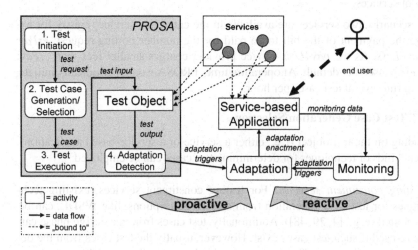

Fig. 6.5: The PROSA framework

The PROSA framework prescribes the following four major activities, which are discussed in more detail the remainder of this section and which will be illustrated by means of the scenario from Section 6.3:

1. *Test initiation*: The first activity in PROSA is to determine the need to initiate online tests during the operation of the service-based application.

2. *Test case generation/selection*: Once online testing has been initiated by activity 1, this second activity determines the test cases to be executed during online testing. This can require creating new test cases or selecting from already existing ones.

3. *Test execution*: The test cases from activity 2 are executed (see Section 6.5.1.3).

4. *Adaptation detection*: Finally, an analysis of the test results provides information on whether to adapt the service-based application, i. e., whether to produce adaptation triggers.

It should be noted that—as depicted in Figure 6.5—online testing performs tests of the constituent parts of the service-based application (e. g., individual services or service compositions) in parallel to the applications ('production system') in operation.

6.5.1.1 Test initiation

The initiation of the actual online testing activities (i.e., PROSA's activities 2 and 3) depends on the kinds of changes or deviations that should *proactively* be addressed (see [22] for a comprehensive discussion). As an example, the online testing activities can be triggered periodically (or randomly) to uncover failures or the unavailability of services.

In our scenario, two services are available in the enterprise service registry for executing the payment of the bill to be paid for the number porting request: *ezPay* and *pay4Less*. As the *pay4Less* service provider charges smaller fees than *ezPay*, *pay4Less* is used per default. At operation time, PROSA would periodically initiate step 2 to run several test cases per hour.

6.5.1.2 Test Case Generation/Selection

Depending on the test object (i.e., either a service or a service-based application), different kinds of techniques for determining test cases can be employed:

- *Testing constituent services:* For testing constituent services, existing techniques for test case generation from service descriptions, like WSDL, can be exploited (e.g., [4, 29, 48]). Additionally, test cases from the design phase can be re-used if such test cases exist. However, usually the test cases from the design phase will not suffice, because typically at that time not all services are known due to the adaptation of a service-based application that can happen during run-time.

- *Testing service-based applications:* For testing service compositions of a SBA, test cases can be generated from composition specifications, like BPEL (Business Process Execution Language, e.g., [17, 27]). If a set of test cases for testing service compositions already exists, online testing has to determine which of those test cases to execute again (i.e., test cases have to be selected). This is similar to regression testing, which has been discussed in Section 6.2.4. Consequently, existing techniques for regression testing of services (like [16, 41, 42]) can be utilized.

A more detailed survey on existing test case generation and selection techniques for service-based applications can be found in [37].

In the scenario, test cases would have to be derived for testing the individual services, i.e., the *ezPay* and *pay4Less* services. As an example, a test case could involve issuing a payment for some representative amounts (typical ones as returned by the *Calculate Costs* activity, see Figure 6.2) and some dummy payment information (such as a special credit card number used for test purposes). In addition, a response time of at most 2 seconds could be provided as an expected outcome of the test.

6.5.1.3 Test Execution

The responsibility of activity 3 in the PROSA framework is to execute the test cases that have been determined by activity 2. This means that the test object (which is either a service or a service composition) is fed with concrete inputs (as defined in the test cases) and the produced outputs are observed.

The test execution can be implemented by resorting to existing test execution environments, e. g., the ones presented in [16, 29]. It is important to note that invoking services can lead to certain "side effects" which should not occur when invoking the service for testing purposes only (this problem is also discussed in [27]). As an example, when invoking the service of an online book seller for testing purposes, one would not like to have the "ordered" books actually delivered. Thus, it is necessary to provide certain services with a dedicated test mode. As an example, one could follow the approaches suggested for testing software components, where components are provided with interfaces that allow the execution of the component in "normal mode" or in "test mode" (see [46]).

In our scenario, the online testing component would periodically run several of the test cases (determined in the previous step). To address the number of parallel users and thus consider the higher impact of failures, let's say that the component executes four test cases per hour during the day and one test case per hour during the night. Let us now assume that one of those tests uncovers that *pay4Less* does not respond within the given 2 seconds (see above).

6.5.1.4 Adaptation Detection

The final activity 4 of PROSA determines the actual adaptation triggers, that represent the need for a modification of the service-based application. An adaptation should be triggered when the observed output of a test deviates from the expected output, i. e., whenever a test case fails. This includes deviations from the expected functionality as well as from the expected quality of service.

In the scenario, one test case has observed that *ezPay* has not satisfied its expectations. Thus, PROSA provides the adaptation component with this information. As an example, the alternative service *ezPay* could then be chosen instead of *pay4Less*.

6.6 Integrating Perfective and Corrective Adaptation

In order to define the integration and synchronization of the perfective adaptation triggers (from requirements engineering) with the corrective adaptation triggers (from online testing), we describe how those adaptation triggers will be used to modify the service composition (Section 6.6.1) and how the enterprise service registry allows coordinating the two kinds of adaptation triggers (Section 6.6.1.1).

6.6.1 Introduction to Workflow Adaptation

Adaptations in service compositions can be carried out during design time or during run-time. During design time the workflow model, which describes control and data flow can be modified in any possible way, including the assignment of services to tasks (i. e., activities) or the modification of the control and data flow of the workflow definition.

During run-time the workflow model may be altered so as to assign new services to workflow tasks [24] or to modify the control and data flow completely. After these modifications it must be decided whether all running instances should benefit from these modifications (instance migration), whether some of the running instances should benefit from these modifications or whether future instances should use the modifications only. If the modifications target some instances of a workflow model only, these ad-hoc changes are not reflected in the workflow model. As mentioned in Section 6.1.3, in this chapter we focus on modifying the assignment of services to workflow tasks during run-time.

Such an assignment is based on so called binding strategies. According to [50] and [24, p. 536] we can distinguish between two major binding strategies: First, the static binding strategy requires that the services are assigned to the activities during design or deployment time. Second, the dynamic binding strategy requires a declarative description of the requirements of the service at design or deployment time. The actual services are then discovered by the workflow engine (or service middleware) during run-time based on the declaratively specified criteria.

The dynamic binding strategy is the most flexible approach for service binding because it enables the discovery of services during run-time based on requirements for the service selection specified declaratively prior to the workflow execution. In case of a services failure, the middleware is then able to discover alternative services according to the specified requirements. The functional part of the requirements is often defined by the service composition (e. g., by means of operations and port types) and the non-functional requirements are often defined in separate artefacts associated with that composition (e. g., using web-service -Policy). It is important to note that these requirements for service selection are specified at the latest during the deployment phase of SBA development. This means, that the selection criteria— even in the most flexible strategy for service binding—are fixed during run-time.

6.6.1.1 The Enterprise Service Registry

As motivated in Section 6.1.2, a central enterprise service registry is used to synchronise the requirements engineering, online testing and workflow adaptation activities. The main idea is that, the enterprise service registry is a collection of references to all services used by service-based applications within the enterprise.[3] This registry provides the required stability necessary for testing techniques while allowing

---

[3] There may also be services listed in the enterprise service registry, which are currently not used by any service composition.

a certain degree of freedom (adding and/or removing services) to apply adaptation techniques to SBAs.

In the static binding strategy, all tasks in the workflow must be assigned with services from the enterprise service registry at design time. Before a service can be removed from the registry, each task in all workflows must be inspected. If a task binds the service, which is to be removed, the service binding must be updated and the new workflow model must be re-deployed. If there are already running workflow instances, these instances must be adapted (ad-hoc adaptation). Similarly, if the requirements engineer adds a service to the enterprise service registry, the workflow models and all running workflow instances should be updated to benefit from the qualities of the new service.

In the dynamic binding scenario, the workflow engine discovers the required services at run-time from the enterprise service registry so that it automatically makes use of new services added by the requirements engineer. In addition, the workflow engine will not use services, which are removed from that registry. Assume a new service A' is added to the registry, to replace the existing service A. Once the workflow reaches the task, which binds the service A, the workflow engine looks it up in the enterprise service registry (late binding). Since the new service A' was added, it will use this service instead and will immediately benefit from the enhanced qualities of the new service. In a similar manner, if online testing would remove service A' from the registry (because it turned out to be faulty), the workflow engine would bind the "old" service A instead. In case the removal of A' was done when the service A' was already bound to a task, the execution of the task can still be completed because the registry contains only references to services, not the services themselves.

The comparison of the static and dynamic binding strategies shows clearly that the dynamic binding strategy should be preferred due to the reduced amount of manual activities.

6.6.2 Validation Scenario

In this section we illustrate the integration and synchronization of the two kinds of adaptation goals (and thus adaptation triggers) as explained above. We will use the example workflow introduced in section 6.3 to this end. Figure 6.6 depicts the steps and artifacts of our approach in terms of the elements from the example scenario. The figure also shows the available services that are assigned to the tasks either by static or dynamic binding—e. g. the "eBill" service is statically bound to the "Issue Bill" task while "ezPay" and "pay4Less" are two different payment services, the binding of which can be determined during run-time to support the "Pay Bill" task.

The workflow is executed by a workflow engine which relies on a service middleware. The middleware supports among others the discovery and invocation of services that the workflow composes (infrastructure services). If the binding strategy for a task is static, the middleware can only invoke the service defined in the workflow definition; the middleware receives the input data for the service and its

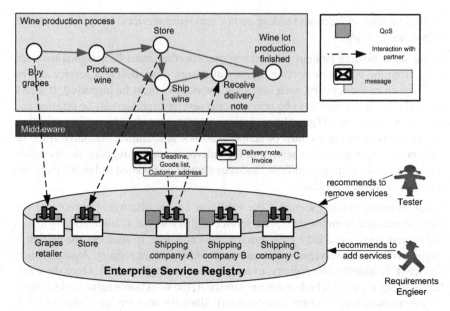

Fig. 6.6: Example of the number porting scenario

endpoint reference. After the invocation of the service, the middleware returns the result from the service invocation to the workflow engine and hence to the workflow instance. The middleware performs an additional step if the binding strategy is dynamic. Before a service invocation can be carried out, a discovery of a set of services compliant with the requirements (provided in the workflow definition), is triggered and the most appropriate service is selected.

In the remainder of this section we present possible adaptation approaches initiated by the different kinds of adaptation triggers.

6.6.2.1 Adaptation Triggered by the Requirements Engineer

As new services become available outside the enterprise service registry, the requirements engineer needs to decide whether the newly available service should be used. This decision is made according to the mechanism described in Section 6.4. Once a decision to use the new service is made, the requirements engineer has two choices to make use of the service in the service composition: Using the static binding strategy, the requirements engineer may exchange the static service reference of one or more tasks directly in the workflow model and to either migrate all instances, selected instances or no instances to this new workflow model. If the dynamic binding strategy is used, it is sufficient to register the new service in the service registry. Due to the enhanced service characteristics, the new service will be given preference by the middleware's service discovery component.

Assume that a new E-Mail service "iMail" become available and the requirements engineer decides to use it for the above service composition. In a static binding scenario the requirements engineer initiates the exchange of the static reference for the task "Send Confirmation" from the E-Mail service "secureMail" to the E-Mail service "iMail". In a dynamic binding scenario, the "iMail" service is registered in the enterprise service registry and the middleware will automatically prefer it over the "secureMail" service because of its better suitability to the requirements.

6.6.2.2 Adaptation Triggered by Online Testing

As described above, online testing may uncover failures, which require an adaptation. The adaptation action required depends on the binding strategy. If the binding strategy prescribes static binding, the faulty service must be replaced in the workflow model (usually in the deployment information). After this replacement the workflow model must be re-deployed and it must be decided whether all running instances (instance migration), selected running instances or all new instances should be migrated to the new workflow model.

Assume that the payment service "ezPay" should be tested in our example above. The tester generates test cases with costs, account number and customer data as input. Then the output is checked against the expected output. In our scenario, the expected output is an invoice. If the "ezPay" service cannot deliver the invoice, this failure is reported and an adaptation is triggered. The "ezPay" service is then removed from the workflow model (static binding) or from the registry (dynamic binding) and replaced by the "pay4Less' service.

6.7 Discussion

In this section we discuss our approach critically and aim at providing future research directions. The section is divided into three subsections: In Sections 6.7.1 and 6.7.2 we discuss the requirements engineering and online testing approaches individually. Finally, in Section 6.7.3 we discuss their integration with respect to the two binding strategies in workflows and the role of the enterprise service registry.

6.7.1 Discussion of the Requirements Engineering Technique

The proposed RE process is constrained by assumptions (A1)–(A5) (see Section 6.4). In particular it relies on the assumption that new services become available over time (A3). This assumption is fair because changing environments lead to new solutions in the past and will lead to new services in the future.

Assumption (A2) is based on assumption (A1) and requires that each provider provides a goal model as description of his/her service (A1) and that this goal model consists only of one plan representing the service as well as goals and soft-goals directly connected to the plan with means-end and contribution links. This assumption is also less critical since we explained how such a reduced goal model can be extracted from a larger model.

Assumption (A4) requires that service providers and service consumers use a shared vocabulary. Although this assumption is not realistic, it can be eliminated by linguistic approaches, which resolve homonyms and synonyms, or by employinig semantic technologies. For instance, WordNet [31] was successfully used to resolve homonyms and synonyms in the SeCSE approach to requirements engineering [23].

The most critical assumptions are (A1) and (A5). They require that service providers provide a goal model for each service (A1) and that the strengths of the contribution links are objectively comparable between different services. Both assumptions seem unrealistic. However, instead of forcing service providers to describe their services with goal models, these goal models could be generated from existing information. The central plan element can be generated according to the service's name. The functional requirements of this service are described in a WSDL document. Consequently, the hard-goals are represented by the methods contained in this WSDL document. In addition, a SLA describes the quality requirements for a service and it may be used to generate soft-goals. These SLA documents could be used to quantify the strengths of the contribution links.

6.7.2 Discussion of the Online Testing Technique

Although exploiting only testing for proactive adaptation provides many benefits, we acknowledge at this stage that further work is required in order to demonstrate the applicability of the PROSA idea (see Section 6.5) in practice. One aspect that, for example, has to be investigated, is the possible impact of the execution of test cases on the performance of the application. Thus, key issues that we will target in our future work are to create a proof-of-concept prototype based on existing techniques and tools (as discussed in the chapter) and to apply these prototypes to realistic cases.

It should be noted that when taking pro-active adaptation decisions it is key that, based on an observed deviation, one can predict with high confidence that this deviation will also occur in the future. In other words, pro-active adaptations should not be initiated based on sporadic failures. Especially, in the case where a service-based application is built from third party (external) services and thus those constituent services are not under the control of the service composer, the observed quality of service and functionality of those constituent services can vary between different service invocations. As an example, a failure observed at one point in time can disappear at a later point in time, as for instance, a service provider could have repaired the service in the mean-time. This means that even if an online test fails, it might well be the case that the test would have passed when invoked at a later point in time. Thus, if the sporadic failure were used as a basis adaptation decisions, this would lead to an unnecessary adaptation of the SBA. Such an unnecessary adaptation can have severe shortcomings: Firstly, an unnecessary adaptation is costly—even in the pro-active case—as it can require the execution of additional activities (such as SLA negotiation for the alternative services). Secondly, the unnecessary adaptation could be faulty, leading to severe problems as a consequence. Thus, unnecessary adaptations should be avoided as far as possible [30].

Finally, proactive and reactive adaptation may work together in an integrated dynamic adaptation framework. In such a framework, online testing and monitoring could mutually benefit from each other, thereby improving the overall quality and efficiency of adaptation. As an example, the results of monitoring may be used to identify "better" test cases for online testing.

Our current research activities in the S-Cube Network of Excellence[4] are devoted to addressing the above issues. More specifically, we are defining new techniques that augment monitoring with online testing and statistical techniques to predict future failures with high confidence.

6.7.3 Discussion of the Integrated Approach

As discussed in Section 6.6, there are two binding strategies for services in workflows: static and dynamic binding. Although dynamic binding seems to be the most flexible approach, static binding strategies may especially be used for reliable and stable workflows, e. g., to prevent adaptation. The handling of the adaptation triggers by requirements engineering and online testing activities is different for the two binding strategies and is described in the following:

- *Static Binding Strategy*: In order to integrate requirements engineering, online testing and workflow adaptation techniques, we need to ensure that the services, which are statically bound to the workflow are contained in the enterprise service registry. This constraint can only be fulfilled if, first, all services are contained in the service registry once the workflow is designed and the initial static assignment is being made. Second, if requirements engineering or online testing triggers adaptation, each workflow using static binding must be analyzed and, if needed, the reference to the relevant service must be updated. Afterwards, this update should be propagated to all running and all future instances of the workflow, e. g., we need to update the workflow model (for future instances) and to apply ad-hoc adaptation to the running instances.

- *Dynamic Binding Strategy*: Using the dynamic binding strategy, the workflow engine and its middleware discover services automatically, which comply with the given declarative service description. Under the condition that the workflow engine searches the enterprise service registry only, there is no need to explicitly trigger an adaptation and all workflow instances can benefit from the current status of the services in this registry immediately.

However, there are a number of potential problems, which may arise in our integration setting, which are discussed in the following:

---

[4] http://www.s-cube-network.eu

- *Removal of service in use:* When online testing uncovers a failure of a service, the online tester might decide to remove the failed service from the enterprise service registry. In this case, the service may still be in use (bound) in a workflow. Since this binding is done at design time (static binding strategy) or right before the service invocation (dynamic binding strategy), the removal of the service does not mean that its invocation fails once the service is in use (intended effect). Once the service is removed and all service invocations are finished and applying the dynamic binding strategy, this service will not be longer used in the workflow (intended effect). Once the service is removed and applying the static binding strategy, an ad-hoc adaptation must be initiated. Without this ad-hoc adaptation, the workflow would continue using a service, which is not part of the enterprise service registry (uninteded effect).

- *Removal of problematic services*: Once the online tester detects a failure in one of the services, s/he should remove the service from the enterprise service registry to avoid future problems in the workflow. However, this option is only valid if there is an alternative service, which could be used instead. If such a service does not exist, the workflow blocks. Therefore, before removing the service, the online tester needs to make sure that an alternative service exists in the enterprise service registry. This step requires checking whether all tasks of all workflows can still be executed once the problematic service is removed.

- *Insertion of a new service by the requirements engineer*: Once a new service is inserted into the enterprise service registry by the requirements engineer, the old service should be replaced in the workflow by the new one. Given the static binding strategy, this exchange has to be initiated manually otherwise the workflow uses a inferior service (unintended effect). In case of the dynamic binding strategy, the workflow engine is only capable of binding the new service, if the service description language is consistent with the language used for requirements engineering (intended effect). If this consistency is not achieved, the workflow engine may still prefer the old and inferior service (unintended effect). Future work is needed to achieve this consistency.

Another possibility to avoid this problem would be to remove the inferior service from the enterprise service registry once a new service is found. This alternative should not be considered for two reasons: First, once an enterprise has more than one workflow running, it may well be that the new service fulfils the requirements of workflow *A* better and at the same time is inferior for workflow *B*. In this case, removing the old service would lead to a better fulfilment of the requirements for workflow *A* but for a worse fulfilment of the requirements of workflow *B*. Second, once the new service is added to the enterprise service registry, it becomes subject of online testing. In this case, the online tester may find—at a certain time in the future—that the service does not work correctly any more. In this case, the online tester can only remove the service from the service registry, if there is an alternative service, which could be used (see above). This alternative services, however, is only in the enterprise service registry, if it was not removed in the first place.

• *Interaction between requirements engineering and online testing*: Once the online tester has removed a service from the enterprise service registry, the requirements engineer has the freedom to add the service to this registry, thereby creating an unnecessary insertion/removal loop (unintended effect). Therefore, the activities of the requirements engineer and the online tester need further alignment, which is subject to future research.

6.8 Conclusions and Perspectives

In this chapter we have shown how perfective adaptation (as enabled by requirements engineering) could be integrated and synchronized with corrective adaptation (as enabled by online testing) in a meaningful way. Thereby, this chapter has demonstrated a possible solution to the problem of how to handle multiple adaptation goals in service-based applications, which has been identified in the literature as one of the key challenges of adaptive software systems. Our solution has relied on state-of-the-art adaptation mechanisms for service compositions as well on the use of an enterprise service registry as a mechanism for achieving the synchronization.

The discussion in this chapter has also lead to the conclusion that the dynamic binding strategy driven by pre-described service requirements is beneficial over the static binding strategy. The dynamic binding strategy automatically respects the decisions of the requirements engineer to add new services and of the online tester to remove faulty services without human intervention. The static binding strategy, however, requires a modification of the workflow model, its re-deployment and ad-hoc adaptations for already running workflows. Since the services are restricted by the enterprise service registry, static binding does not prevent any unintended adaptation (its initial purpose) and should, therefore, not be used in this scenario.

Related to the contribution of this chapter, we see the following, potential future research directions:

• *Integration of requirements engineering and workflow adaptability*: Using the dynamic binding strategy requires that the languages used for describing services in the requirements engineering and workflow design disciplines are compatible, as otherwise the insertion of a new service into the enterprise service registry may not have an effect (cf. Section 6.7.3). Consequently, research is need to define mappings between requirements engineering and workflow design languages.

• *Integration of online testing and workflow adaptability*: Once a failure in a service is detected, it should be removed from the enterprise service registry. This removal should only be done if an alternative service exists in the enterprise service registry otherwise the workflow will block. Thus, the online tester must have the ability to check for all tasks in all workflows in the enterprise whether the faulty service has actually an alternative in the enterprise service registry. This check needs to be applicable to static and dynamic binding strategies.

- *Integration of requirements engineering and online testing*: Once the online tester removed a service from the enterprise service registry, the requirements engineer may add this service again and, therewith creates an unnecessary insertion/removal loop. Therefore, the activities of the requirements engineer and the online tester should become more integrated.

- *Integrating corrective and perfective adaptation*: Instead of merely synchronizing the two adaptation goals, corrective adaptation could also be used to support perfective adaptation. In our setting, online testing could be used to determine the best possible alternative for an adaptation decision before the adaptation is executed. This means whenever an adaptation decision is imminent and different alternatives exist, those alternatives could be "pre-tested" and the best one (e. g., the one that does not fail) could be chosen.

- *Extension to other adaptation goals:* In addition to perfective and corrective adaptation, the adaptation of an SBA can follow other goals such as protection or configuration (see [43]).

Acknowledgements The research leading to these results has received funding from the European Community's Seventh Framework Programme FP7/2007-2013 under grant agreement 215483 (S-Cube).

References

1. van der Aalst, W.M.P., Pesic, M.: Specifying and Monitoring Service Flows: Making Web Services Process-Aware. In: L. Baresi, E. Di Nitto (eds.) Test and Analysis of Web Services, pp. 11–55. Springer (2007)
2. Aiello, M., Giorgini, P.: Applying the tropos methodology for analysing web services requirements and reasoning about qualities. UPGRADE: The European Journal for the Informatics Professional 5(4), 20–26 (2004)
3. Bai, X., Chen, Y., Shao, Z.: Adaptive web services testing. In: 31st Annual International Computer Software and Applications Conference (COMPSAC), pp. 233–236 (2007)
4. Bai, X., Dong, W., Tsai, W.T., Chen, Y.: WSDL-Based Automatic Test Case Generation for Web Services Testing. In: Proceedings of the IEEE International Workshop on Service-Oriented System Engineering (SOSE), pp. 215 – 220. IEEE Computer Society (2005)
5. Bai, X., Xu, D., Dai, G., Tsai, W., Chen, Y.: Dynamic reconfigurable testing of service-oriented architecture. In: Proceedings of the 31st Annual International Computer Software and Applications Conference (COMPSAC), pp. 368–375 (2007)
6. Baresi, L., Ghezzi, C., Guinea, S.: Towards Self-healing Service Compositions. In: First Conference on the PRInciples of Software Engineering (PRISE'04), pp. 11–20 (2004)
7. Baresi, L., Guinea, S., Pasquale, L.: Self-healing BPEL processes with Dynamo and the JBoss rule engine. In: ESSPE '07: International workshop on Engineering of software services for pervasive environments, pp. 11–20 (2007)
8. Batini, C., Lenzerini, M., Navathe, S.B.: A comparative analysis of methodologies for database schema integration. ACM Computing Surveys (CSUR) 18(4), 323–364 (1986)
9. Bianculli, D., Ghezzi, C., Pautasso, C.: Embedding continuous lifelong verification in service life cycles. In: Proceedings of Principles of Engineering Service Oriented Systems (PESOS 2009), co-located with ICSE 2009, Vancouver, Canada. IEEE Computer Society Press (2009)
10. Bresciani, P., Perini, A., Giorgini, P., Giunchiglia, F., Mylopoulos, J.: Tropos: An agent-oriented software development methodology. Autonomous Agents and Multi-Agent Systems 8(3), 203–236 (2004)

11. Canfora, G., di Penta, M.: SOA: Testing and Self-checking. In: Proceedings of International Workshop on Web Services - Modeling and Testing - WS-MaTE, pp. 3 – 12 (2006)
12. Castro, J., Kolp, M., Mylopoulos, J.: Towards requirements-driven information systems engineering: The tropos project. Information Systems 27(6), 365–389 (2002)
13. Chan, W., Cheung, S., Leung, K.: A metamorphic testing approach for online testing of service-oriented software applications. International Journal of Web Services Research 4(2), 61–81 (2007)
14. Cheng, S.W., Garlan, D., Schmerl, B.: Architecture-based self-adaptation in the presence of multiple objectives. In: SEAMS '06: Proceedings of the 2006 international workshop on Self-adaptation and self-managing systems, pp. 2–8. ACM, New York, NY, USA (2006)
15. Deussen, P., Din, G., Schieferdecker, I.: A TTCN-3 based online test and validation platform for Internet services. In: Proceedings of the 6th International Symposium on Autonomous Decentralized Systems (ISADS), pp. 177–184 (2003)
16. Di Penta, M., Bruno, M., Esposito, G., et al.: Web Services Regression Testing. In: L. Baresi, E. Di Nitto (eds.) Test and Analysis of Web Services, pp. 205 – 234. Springer (2007)
17. Dong, W.L., Yu, H., Zhang, Y.B.: Testing BPEL-based Web Service Composition Using High-level Petri Nets. In: EDOC '06: Proceedings of the 10th IEEE International Enterprise Distributed Object Computing Conference, pp. 441–444. IEEE Computer Society (2006)
18. Erradi, A., Maheshwari, P., Tosic, V.: Policy-Driven Middleware for Self-adaptation of Web Services Compositions. In: ACM/IFIP/USENIX 7th International Middleware Conference, pp. 62–80 (2006)
19. Giorgini, P., Mylopoulos, J., Nicchiarelli, E., Sebastiani, R.: Formal reasoning techniques for goal models. In: Journal on Data Semantics, Lecture Notes in Computer Science, pp. 1–20. Springer, Berlin, Heidelberg (2003)
20. Günther, C.W., van der Aalst, W.M.P.: Fuzzy Mining - Adaptive Process Simplification Based on Multi-perspective Metrics. In: Business Process Management, 5th International Conference, BPM, pp. 328–343 (2007)
21. Herold, S., Metzger, A., Rausch, A., Stallbaum, H.: Towards bridging the gap between goal-oriented requirements engineering and compositional architecture development. In: Proceedings of the 2nd Workshop on SHAring and Reusing architectural Knowledge Architecture, Rationale, and Design Intent (SHARK-ADI 2007), May 19–20, 2007, Minneapolis, USA (2007)
22. Hielscher, J., Kazhamiakin, R., Metzger, A., Pistore, M.: A framework for proactive self-adaptation of service-based applications based on online testing (2008)
23. Jones, S.V., Maiden, N.A.M., Zachos, K., Zhu, X.: How serivce-centric systems change the requirements process. In: E. Kamsties, V. Gervasi, P. Sawyer (eds.) Proceedings of the 11th International Workshop on Requirements Engineering: Foundation for Software Quality (REFSQ 2005), June 13–14 2005, Porto, Portugal, Essener Informatik Beitr?ge, vol. 10, pp. 105–119. Universit?t Duisburg-Essen, Essen (2005)
24. Karastoyanova, D., Houspanossian, A., Cilia, M., Leymann, F., Buchmann, A.: Extending BPEL for run time adaptability. In: Proceedings Ninth IEEE International EDOC Enterprise Computing Conference, pp. 15–26 (2005)
25. Kephart, J.O., Chess, D.M.: The vision of autonomic computing. IEEE Computer 36(1), 41–50 (2003)
26. Lau, D., Mylopoulos, J.: Designing web services with tropos (2004)
27. Lübke, D.: Unit Testing BPEL Compositions. In: L. Baresi, E. Di Nitto (eds.) Test and Analysis of Web Services, pp. 149 – 171. Springer (2007)
28. Maiden, N.: Service centric system engineering: A2.d5 SeCSE requirements process v2.0. Deliverable R004/CIT/V0.3, City University London (2006)
29. Martin, E., Basu, S., Xie, T.: Automated Testing and Response Analysis of Web Services. In: IEEE International Conference on Web Services (ICWS), pp. 647 – 654 (2007)
30. Metzger, A., Sammodi, O., Pohl, K., Rzepka, M.: Towards pro-active adaptation with confidence: Augmenting service monitoring with online testing. In: Proceedings of the ICSE 2010 Workshop on Software Engineering for Adaptive and Self-managing Systems (SEAMS '10). Cape Town, South Africa (2010)

31. Miller, G.A.: Wordnet - princeton university cognitive science laboratory, http://wordnet.princeton.edu/ (2006)
32. Misra, S.C., Misra, S., Woungang, I., Mahanti, P.: Using tropos to model quality of service for designing distributed systems (2006)
33. Modafferi, S., Mussi, E., Pernici, B.: SH-BPEL: a self-healing plug-in for Ws-BPEL engines. In: 1st workshop on Middleware for Service Oriented Computing, pp. 48–53 (2006)
34. Nezhad, H.R.M., Saint-Paul, R., Benatallah, B., Casati, F.: Deriving Protocol Models from Imperfect Service Conversation Logs. IEEE Transactions on Knowledge and Data Engineering (TKDE) (2008). To appear
35. Nitto, E.D., Ghezzi, C., Metzger, A., Papazoglou, M., Pohl, K.: A journey to highly dynamic, self-adaptive service-based applications. Automated Software Engineering pp. 257–402 (2008)
36. Penserini, L., Perini, A., Susi, A., Mylopoulos, J.: From stakeholder needs to service requirements. In: Proceedings Service-Oriented Computing: Consequences for Engineering Requirements, SOCCER'06 Workshop, pp. 8–17 (2006)
37. Pernici, B., Metzger, A.: Survey of quality related aspects relevant for service-based applications. Deliverable PO-JRA-1.3.1, S-Cube Consortium (2008). URL http://www.s-cube-network.eu/results/. The following institutions contributed to this deliverable: Université Claude Bernard Lyon, Vienna University of Technology, Universidad Politécnica de Madrid, Politecnico di Milano, The French National Institute for Research in Computer Science and Control, University of Duisburg-Essen, Center for Scientific and Technological Research, MTA SZTAKI ? Computer and Automation Research Institute, University of Crete, Consiglio Nazionale delle Ricerche, and University of Stuttgart
38. Pistore, M., Roveri, M., Busetta, P.: Requirements-driven verification of web services. Electronic Notes in Theoretical Computer Science 105, 95–108 (2004)
39. Pohl, K.: Requirements Engineering. Springer (2010)
40. Rahm, E., Bernstein, P.A.: A survey of approaches to automatic schema matching. VLDB Journal 10(4), 334–350 (2001)
41. Ruth, M., Oh, S., Loup, A., Horton, B., Gallet, O., Mata, M., Tu, S.: Towards automatic regression test selection for web services. In: Proceedings of the 31st Annual International Computer Software and Applications Conference (COMPSAC), pp. 729–734 (2007)
42. Ruth, M., Tu, S.: A safe regression test selection technique for Web services. In: Second International Conference on Internet and Web Applications and Services (ICIW) (2007)
43. Salehie, M., Tahvildari, L.: Self-adaptive software: Landscape and research challenges. ACM Transactions on Autonomous and Adaptive Systems 4(2), 14:1 – 14:42 (2009)
44. Siljee, J., Bosloper, I., Nijhuis, J., Hammer, D.: DySOA: Making Service Systems Self-adaptive. In: 3rd International Conference Service-Oriented Computing - ICSOC 2005, pp. 255–268 (2005)
45. Spanoudakis, G., Zisman, A., Kozlenkov, A.: A Service Discovery Framework for Service Centric Systems. In: SCC '05: Proceedings of the 2005 IEEE International Conference on Services Computing, pp. 251–259 (2005)
46. Suliman, D., Paech, B., Borner, L., Atkinson, C., Brenner, D., Merdes, M., Malaka, R.: The MORABIT approach to runtime component testing. In: Proceedings of the 30th Annual Int'l Computer Software and Applications Conference (COMPSAC), pp. 171–176 (2006)
47. Swanson, E.B.: The dimensions of maintenance. In: Proceedings of the 2nd international conference on Software engineering, pp. 492–497. IEEE Computer Society Press (1976)
48. Tarhini, A., Fouchal, H., Mansour, N.: A simple approach for testing Web service based applications. In: 5th International Workshop on Innovative Internet Community Systems, Lecture Notes in Computer Science Vol.3908, pp. 134–146 (2006)
49. Wang, Q., Quan, L., Ying, F.: Online testing of Web-based applications. In: Proceedings of the 28th Annual International Computer Software and Applications Conference (COMPSAC), pp. 166–169 (2004)
50. Weer-Awarana, S., Curbera, F., Leymann, F., Ferguson, D.F., Storey, T.: Web Services Platform Architecture: Soap, WSDL, WS-Policy, WS-Addressing, WS-BPEL, WS-Reliable Messaging and More. Prentice Hall (2005)

51. Yu, E.: An organisational modelling framework for multiperspective information system design. Tech. rep., Department of Computer Science, University of Toronto, Toronto (1993)
52. Zachos, K., Maiden, N., Howells-Morris, R.: Web services to improve requirements specifications: Does it help? In: Proceedings of the 14th International Workshop on Requirements Engineering: Foundation for Software Quality (REFSQ 2008), June 16–17 2008, Montpellier, France, *Lecture Notes in Computer Science*, vol. 5025, pp. 168–182. Springer, Berlin, Heidelberg (2008)
53. Zachos, K., Maiden, N.A.M., Zhu, X., Jones, S.: Discovering web services to specify more complete system requirements. In: J. Krogstie, A.L. Opdahl, G. Sindre (eds.) Proceedings of the 19th International Conference on Advanced Information Systems Engineering (CAiSE 2007), June 11–15, 2007, Trondheim, Norway, *Lecture Notes in Computer Science*, vol. 4495, pp. 142–157. Springer (2007)
54. Zachos, K., Zhu, X., Maiden, N., Jones, S.: Seamlessly integrating service discovery into UML requirements processes. In: Proceedings of the 2006 International Workshop on Service-Oriented Software Engineering (SOSE 2006), May 27–28, 2006, Shanghai, China, pp. 60–66 (2006)

Chapter 7
Combining Domain-driven Design and Mashups for Service Development

Carlos A. Iglesias, José I. Fernández-Villamor, David del Pozo, Luca Garulli and Boni García

Abstract This chapter presents the Romulus project approach to Service Development using Java-based web technologies. Romulus aims at improving productivity of service development by providing a tool-supported model to conceive Java-based web applications. This model follows a Domain Driven Design approach, which states that the primary focus of software projects should be the core domain and domain logic. Romulus proposes a tool-supported model, *Roma Metaframework*, that provides an abstraction layer on top of existing web frameworks and automates the application generation from the domain model. This metaframework follows an object centric approach, and complements Domain Driven Design by identifying the most common cross-cutting concerns (security, service, view, ...) of web applications. The metaframework uses annotations for enriching the domain model with these cross-cutting concerns, so-called aspects. In addition, the chapter presents the usage of mashup technology in the metaframework for service composition, using the web mashup editor *MyCocktail*. This approach is applied to a scenario of the Mobile Phone Service Portability case study for the development of a new service.

Carlos A. Iglesias
Informática Gesfor, Av. Manoteras, 32 - 28040 Madrid (Spain), e-mail: `cif@germinus.com`

José Ignacio Fernández-Villamor
Universidad Politécnica de Madrid, ETSI Telecomunicación, Ciudad Universitaria s/n - 28050 Madrid (Spain), e-mail: `jifv@gsi.dit.upm.es`

David del Pozo
Informática Gesfor, Av. Manoteras, 32 - 28040 Madrid (Spain), e-mail: `dpozo@grupogesfor.com`

Luca Garulli
AssetData S.r.l., Via Rhodesia, 34 - 00144 Rome (Italy), e-mail: `luca.garulli@assetdata.it`

Boni García
Universidad Politécnica de Madrid, ETSI Telecomunicación, Ciudad Universitaria s/n - 28050 Madrid (Spain), e-mail: `bgarcia@dit.upm.es`

7.1 Introduction

Web software development is one of the most active areas and fastest growing industries in software and services development in Europe. Furthermore, Java Enterprise Edition is the mainstream European technology option for one million European developers. Since web development is not still a mature area, the proliferation of frameworks and components has both increased the required skills of web engineers, and has affected considerably their productivity. For that reason, the evolution of existing Java based web applications and services is a very hard and time-consuming task.

Currently, the wide range of technologies and frameworks available for Java Web Development gives it a wide range of attributes when compared to other solutions that have emerged, such as Ruby on Rails. Nevertheless, this is also one of its main shortcomings, as developers spend a substantial amount of time learning new technologies and frameworks and new versions of these frameworks, which in turn decreases productivity. In addition, simple tasks require too much coding. New solutions such as Ruby on Rails have shown that web development can be easier, based on important concepts, such as (1) convention over configuration, (2) providing a framework that automates up to 80 percent of the most common tasks and (3) a simple and modular MVC model for developing applications. Romulus project aims to learn from the lessons of Ruby on Rails and provide a productive solution based on Java. Romulus is pushing to improve Java Web Development in several directions such as improving the productivity with the provision of a Domain Driven Design (DDD) Roma Metaframework and IDE integration, and involving soft goals in the development process such as providing web and security testing facilities; and research on how mashup technology can improve web development.

This chapter presents the DDD Roma Metaframework for improving productivity in service development. Roma Metaframework follows an object centric approach for conceiving services and applications. Then, the chapter presents how services and mashups have been modeled in Roma Metaframework, with the purpose of composing or customizing existing services, or developing new ones.

The chapter is structured as follows. First, Sect. 7.2 presents the Mobile Phone Service Portability (MPSP) case study. In particular we focus on the *invitation service*, which is used throughout the chapter to show how Romulus addresses service development. Next, Sect. 7.3 outlines the main steps to develop a service in Romulus. Sect. 7.4 overviews the main DDD principles and their application, while Sect. 7.5 describes the design and model of Roma Metaframework. Sect. 7.6 details how Roma has taken advantage of mashup technology for service composition to provide a uniform view for Enterprise and Web mashups. Finally, Sect. 11.4 and 7.8 conclude with a comparison with existing related work and the main conclusions of the chapter.

7.2 Case Study

One of the most common complaints from business development and marketing units is that engineering units fail to provide a suitable "time-to-market" solution when developing new services. The MPSP case study includes two scenarios, TELCO_BG_O5 and TELCO_S_03 that deal with this topic: how can we speed up service development?

The scenario described in TELCO_S_03 is detailed in this section.

Case Study: New Service for Promotions

The innovation department of a telecom company decides to launch a new service which offers their customers a promotion to see free pay-per view movies. Customers can send up to 10 invitations to their friends from a social network to watch one free movie per invitation. Customers should select both the friends and the movies, and can add a message to the invitation. Friends can accept the invitation, which includes providing some marketing info. Once a friend accepts the invitation, the customer is also allowed to see the movie. The service will provide a set of reports about the success of the promotion based on the collected marketing data.

In order to analyze this scenario in detail, a use case diagram is shown in Fig. 7.1, which collects the usage scenarios as well as the actors identified, which are specified in Table 7.1.

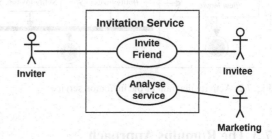

Fig. 7.1 Use case diagram of the invitation service

For the purpose of this chapter, we are going to develop in detail just one of these use cases: the use case *Invite Friend*, which is described in Table 7.2 and Fig. 7.2.

Table 7.1: Actors dictionary

Field	Description
Inviter:	Customer of the Telco company who participates in the Invitation Service.
Invitee:	An *Inviter*'s friend, who receives the invitation to participate in the service. Although it is not explicitly stated in the service description, it is assumed that the Invitees are not customers of the telco company yet.
Marketing:	Staff from the telco company responsible for launching the service and analyzing its impact.

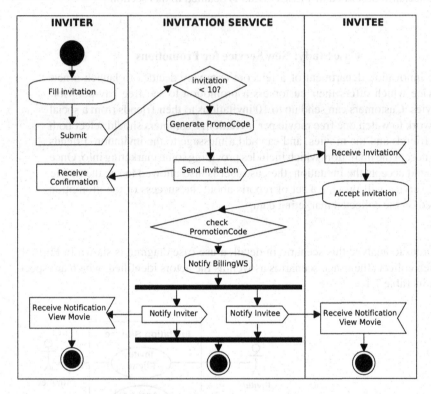

Fig. 7.2: Activity diagram of the invitation service

7.3 The Romulus Approach

Romulus (*Domain Driven Design and Mashup Oriented Development based on Open Source Java Metaframework for Pragmatic, Reliable and Secure Web Development*) [44] is a European R&D project whose aim is improving productivity, reliability and security of Java Web Applications. With this purpose, the Romulus consortium has combined industrial partners, such as Informática Gesfor (Spain), Asset Data (Italy), IMola Informatica (Italy) and Liferay (Germany), as well as academic partners such as Universidad Politécnica de Madrid (Spain), NUIG-DERI (Ireland) and ICI (Romania).

Table 7.2: Use case invite friend

Field	Description
Unique ID:	UC_IS_01
Use Case Name:	Invite Friend
Related to:	TELCO_S_03
Summary:	A user invites her friends from a social network to watch a movie for free in case friends accept a marketing promotion.
Actors:	Inviter, Invitee
Preconditions:	The Inviter is a customer of the telco company.
Triggers:	The telco sends a message presenting the promotion and giving access to the Inviter application.
Steps:	1. Inviter receives the promotional message from the telco company. 2. In case Inviter is interested in the promotion, Inviter accesses to a web application where he can select his friends and movies to send the invitation. 3. The system checks the invitation and recipient info, the maximum invitations allowed in the promotion, and if the email of invitee is correct. 4. In case any Invitee confirms the invitation, the inviter receives a free access to a movie.
Alternatives:	1. If Inviter is not interested in the promotion, after receiving the promotion, the service does not start. 2. If the recipient address is wrong, the system notifies Inviter. 3. If Inviter sends more than 10 invitations, he receives a message pointing out that he has reached the allowed limit. 4. It can be assumed that the promotion code expires after some period. If an invitee accepts the invitation after the expiration deadline, the service will notify inviter and invitee about this issue, without contacting the Billing web service.
Postconditions:	If the use case succeeds, the following postconditions are met: 1. Inviter has free access to as many movies as invitees have accepted the promotion. 2. Invitees accepting the promotion have free access to the movie selected by the Inviter. 3. Telco company has collected marketing data from Invitees.
Additional material:	See Fig. 7.2.

This chapter presents Roma Metaframework (Sect. 7.5) and MyCocktail, the Romulus Mashup Builder tool 7.6.2, developed within the project Romulus.

Romulus is focused on the definition of a tool-supported lightweight process that simplifies Java web development. The process for developing applications and services is outlined in Fig. 7.3.

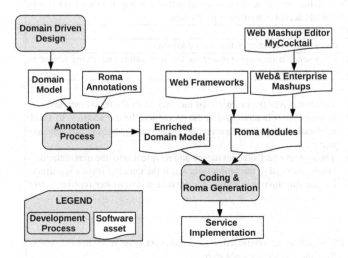

Fig. 7.3: Romulus approach to service development

The first step in Romulus is the definition of a domain model, which is built by following DDD principles. Before building the domain model, the bounded context of the model is identified using service oriented principles. The overall service landscape is determined and scoped. Then, the domain model is created to identify and document the key entities and the common domain vocabulary, shared among all the domain stakeholders.

The second step consists of annotating the domain model using attribute oriented programming. This step is supported by Roma Metaframework, which provides an abstraction layer for integrating cross-cutting concerns (aspects). This allows to isolate the domain model from the cross-cutting concerns. An additional advantage of the metaframework is that it provides a generic interface to some of the most popular web frameworks, which also isolates the application from a particular technology.

The third step involves coding, adding Roma modules that implement the Roma aspects, and execute and test the application. This step may include the development of services using Enterprise Mashup or Web Mashup facilities.

The main benefit of this approach is that Roma provides a uniform, consistent and stable environment to the developer, reducing the technological complexity. In this way, the developer can focus on modeling and understanding complex domains. In addition, the concept of metaframework reduces the risk of technological selections, since applications and services can evolve to other technologies without modifying the original application, and only a module for that new technology should be developed or used in case it is already available.

7.4 Domain Driven Design

7.4.1 Overview

The term *Domain Driven Design* (DDD) was coined by Eric Evans in his homonymous book [16]. The basic idea of DDD is that engineers should focus not in the technology they use, but in the understanding of the application model. Understanding the system to be developed is the main problem for succeeding in software projects. Traditional software engineering has put emphasis on analysis models based on UML notation, while Agile methodologies have focused on the code itself. DDD proposes a trade-off solution: its model driven approach is based on agreeing on a common language which describes the model and can be assisted by graphical notations. In addition, this model should be maintained very close to its implementation. Its main characteristics are:

- An *ubiquitous language* [16] should be used throughout the development. An *ubiquitous language* is a language that is shared between technicians and domain experts. DDD encourages the usage of this common vocabulary and terminology for building the domain model, which can be extended and understood by technicians and domain experts without extra-translations, resulting in richer semantic models. Although graphical models with notations such as UML can help in the communication, the primary description of the model should be explicit with natural language using the *ubiquitous language*.
- The model should be a *rich semantic model*, where objects have behavior and enforced rules, instead of just a database schema. The purpose is that domain experts should be able to feed the model with their deep knowledge of the business.
- The model should be *bound to its implementation*. Instead of maintaining an analysis model disconnected from its code, DDD proposes to describe the model in a way that the mapping with the code is straightforward. In order to maintain this close mapping, DDD organizes the application in a layered architecture, which offers the building blocks of the domain. In addition, DDD promotes the usage of design patterns (value objects, repositories, etc.) and refactoring techniques.

Romulus follows a DDD approach to applications and service development.

Context Identification

The goal of this preliminary task is the identification of the bounded context of the domain model, in order to define explicitly the context in which the model is applicable as well as the relationships of the domain model with external systems. With this purpose, a service oriented approach is followed, and the service landscape is determined. A Service Engineering Methodology such as the one by Bayer [6] can be used with this end. Nevertheless, the lack of a rich domain model can lead to a *Fat Service Layer* [41] or an *Anemic Domain Model* [18,41], with duplicated objects and business logic distributed among multiple objects.

The need of including domain modeling in service modeling has also been pointed out previously. Boroumand [7] declares *"service-orientation and object-orientation are not the same. Each is distinct with its own goals and approaches. However, by understanding that one has roots in the other, we can leverage established practices and techniques and incorporate them"*. Her proposal extends MSOAM (Mainstream SOA Methodology) [1] with RUP (Rational Unified Process) [29].

Domain Model Design

The purpose of this activity is the design of the domain model, using a common vocabulary (*ubiquitous language*) which facilitates the communication among technical and business stakeholders.

The activity starts with the development of an initial design based on users' indications. This initial class diagram should include all the elements required to develop the task in progress.

Then, the initial design is refactored through the application of DDD patterns and best practices, and keeping the original functionality. Next, a set of steps are exposed in order to refactor the initial domain model.

1. *Analyzing associations:* An association establishes a relationship among two or more objects. The model has to be as simple as possible and avoiding complicate associations is a good mechanism to achieve this. Some ideas to simplify associations are: imposing a direction; adding a qualifier, reducing multiplicity; and eliminating non-essential associations.

2. *Entities, value objects and services:* The model must be clear, distinguishing between entities and value objects. An entity is a fundamental concept: it requires an unique attribute to identify it because its state can change during software execution. Meanwhile, a value object only describes a characteristic of the domain. A value object has no identity and can be shared. In some cases, making it immutable improves implementation features.

   Finally, in a domain model there are services. These represent processes that are not responsible of any entity or value object in particular. But sometimes services are overused and functions that correspond to the business logic of an object are implemented as a service. A good practice to avoid this situation is to use a verb to name the service.

3. *Using aggregations:* An aggregation is made up of a set of associated objects, but only one of those (the root) can be referenced by objects that are outside the

aggregation. The objects involved in an aggregation acts as a unit, facilitating the management of complex associations between objects.

4. *Selecting repositories:* Another pattern to get a good domain model is the use of repositories. A repository manages the storage of a concrete type of objects. It implies the implementation of typical operations over a database like adding, editing and removing elements and querying facilities. Repositories are domain objects associated with an aggregate that manage the data storage and retrieval, abstracting persistence mechanisms required to perform these operations.

5. *Using factories to create objects:* Another issue to consider is the object creation and the possibility of using factories for this purpose. A factory defines the creation process of an object. Using a factory is useful only when the object to create is complex. In the rest of cases its use can complicate the process and it is better to use a simple constructor.

   A factory for a value object is not the same thing as a factory for an entity. In the first case, the factory has to completely define the process of creation, because value objects are immutable and they need to be fully described since their creation. Meanwhile, the state of an entity can change during software execution, and its factory only has to define some characteristics of it. Especially, we cannot forget its identifying attributes.

6. *Validating the model:* At this point, using several scenarios to confirm that the model fits the requirements is a good practice to go ahead with security. We must ensure that tasks to develop in this iteration can be implemented.

7. *Dividing the model into modules:* In the development of an enterprise application, the collaboration of many people that work in parallel is required, being necessary to divide the domain model into a set of modules. In order to maintain the integrity of the system, each module has to be defined with a *bounded context*. There has to be a continuous integration and it is also advisable to represent the relationships among the models involved in the system in a map context.

7.4.2 Case Study

The case study involves the interaction of several external services, including a movie renting facility, a social network, a billing service and a SMS messaging service. Based on Fig. 7.2, several services can be identified that interact with the envisioned Invitation service, as shown in Fig. 7.4.

The invitation service should provide two different user interfaces, one for the Inviter and another one for the Invitees. The interactions of the Invitation Service with the services identified are shown in Fig. 7.5.

Once the service landscape for the considered bounded context has been analyzed, the next step is the domain design of the service. In this step, domain elements of the service model are identified (therefore creating an ubiquitous language) and modeled. This will produce the domain model of the bounded context.

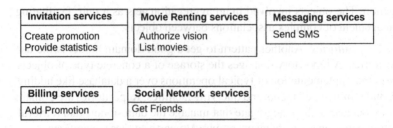

Fig. 7.4: Service landscape of the invitation service

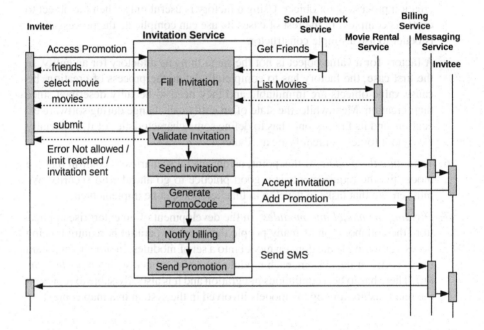

Fig. 7.5: Interaction diagram for the inviter application

The service model that can be seen in Fig. 7.4 involves several concepts that comprise the ubiquitous language of the domain model:

- *Promotion*. This is a promotion set by the telco company. It is associated with a set of invitations. Initially, one invitation is sent to a user, who can create more invitations up to a maximum number that is set in the promotion.

- *Invitation*. This is the invitation that a user receives from another user. It is associated with a movie. It also has a creation date, which determines expiration, and a state, that represents if the invitation has been rejected or accepted.

- *Movie*. This represents the movie that can be watched by invitees.

- *SMS*. This represents the messages that are sent to each user and which contain the invitations. They are sent by a user to another user.

- *User*. A user is the Invitation Service user that can potentially send and receive invitations.

- *Statistics*. These are the statistics that can be retrieved from the Invitation Service, and which are thus associated with a promotion.

The next step is identifying entities and value objects. On the one hand, *entities* are objects that have an identity, and therefore require an internal ID to identify them. On the other hand, *value objects* are identified by the value of their attributes. In our domain model, movies, invitations, users, and promotions are entities, which require an identifier in order to differentiate them. Therefore, two different movies might have the same title, as well as two users could have the same name, while being different objects. Statistics are value objects, since it is not necessary to track the particular object with an identifier. Similarly, SMSs are value objects, as they act only as temporary objects that are built in order to interact with the Messaging Service.

Services were already identified previously, and typically consist of cross-cutting operations that cannot be included in any particular class. The entities' lifecycle determines the domain model as well. The Invitation Service covers the promotions' lifecycle, the Social Network Service covers the users' lifecycle, and the Movie Renting Service covers movies' lifecycle. Invitations' lifecycle needs to be managed as well, so an InvitationFactory and an InvitationRepository should be defined, which would allow creating and storing invitations. However, this is not necessary in the Romulus Framework, as persistent objects are managed through a Persistence Aspect, which abstracts these common operations. Finally, SMSs and statistics are value objects and therefore do not require factories or repositories to manage their lifecycle.

After creating an ubiquitous language, identifying entities and value objects, and defining services, factories and repositories, the resulting domain model can be seen in Fig. 7.6.

7.5 Roma Metaframework

7.5.1 Roma Overview

Romulus proposes that developers should be focused on understanding and developing a domain model as presented in the previous section. Then, thanks to the usage of Roma Metaframework, services and applications can be developed in a straightforward way.

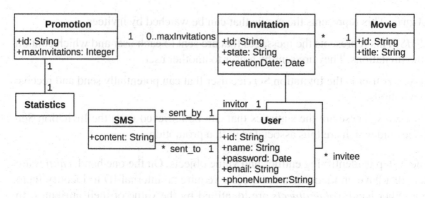

Fig. 7.6: Domain model for the invitation service

Roma Metaframework [46, 54] is the main result of the project Romulus, and is available as an open source project. Roma provides a full approach to Java Web based development. It is based on three design decisions: (1) POJO orientation, (2) metaframework notion and (3) Attribute Oriented Programming for enriching the domain.

First of all, Roma follows a full POJO (*Plain Old Java Object*) orientation. PO-JOs [17, 48] are just simple Java objects which encapsulate the business logic. In Roma, everything is programmed as a POJO. For example, at the interface level, each screen is modeled as a POJO, and each component (menu, button, area, ...) in the screen is also modeled as a POJO. At the service level, invoking a web services is done by calling a method or exposing a web service is done by annotating a method. The main benefits of this approach are [48]:

- *Reduction of complexity*, thanks to the separation of concerns, the developer can focus only on implementing the domain model with POJOs, without worrying about other aspects such as persistence, transactions, or web flow.

- *Improvement in productivity*. The developer can develop and test the service as traditional objects.

- *Better portability*, since the domain implementation is not tied to a specific implementation technology, such as EJB (Enterprise Java Beans).

Second, Roma is based on the notion of a *metaframework*. POJOs are simple and good for testing, but they do not provide support for many of the common needs when developing a service, such as registering services, invoking other services, presenting a user interface, administering users, persisting or maintaining the session through the service lifetime. Web frameworks such as Struts [22], Struts2 [9], Spring [58] or Hibernate [61] come in for solving these needs. Nevertheless, web languages and frameworks [27] lack consolidation, since the current generation of web languages and frameworks reflects the frenetic pace of technological development in the area. The main undesired consequences of this constant evolution are the

(i) increasing complexity of of web applications combining different web technologies [10]; (ii) the need to migrate between framework versions [51] with impacts directly on the application reusability and (iii) the high required skills to develop a full web application using several web frameworks. The Roma metaframework concept tries to overcome these problems by providing an abstraction layer on top of the most popular web frameworks. The metaframework has identified the most common aspects of the existing web frameworks, and has defined interfaces for these aspects. Then, frameworks can be used by implementing adaptors to these metaframework interfaces, following the *plugin* design pattern [47].

Finally, Roma separates application's business logic from the infrastructure specific concerns through the usage of *annotations*. *Attribute Oriented Programming (A@P)* [50, 52, 57] is a code-level marking technique. Developers can mark code elements (e.g. classes, methods, fields) using *annotations* to indicate that they have application specific or domain specific semantics. This approach has been followed in several languages, such as Java [19] or C# [25]. For example, a developer may mark a method with a *logging* annotation to indicate that the associated calls to this method should be logged. These annotations are preprocessed by an annotation processor that generates the final detailed code. In this example, the generator may insert logging code in the methods annotated with the *logging* annotation.

In order to combine these approaches, Roma proposes to implement the domain model using POJOs. Since "cross-cutting concerns" are not present in the domain model, they are modeled through metaframework *aspects*. Aspects represent independent views of the application that affect different logical or domain units. Roma uses annotations to associate aspects with POJOs. Then, the metaframework provides *modules* which implement one or more aspects, or provide some common functionality. In this way, applications are defined in a technologically independent way according to the different aspects. Then, different modules can be plugged in or out later on. The metaframework will allow that the implementation of the application remains untouched.

To sum up, in a Roma application the domain concepts are defined through POJOs. Annotations are included in these POJOs to define aspect details. Finally, modules are selected to implement these aspects.

Roma brings a number of benefits. First, it provides a a stable framework based on automatic code generation techniques. Second, the manual migration process between frameworks can be avoided thanks to the metaframework notion. Thus, company investments are preserved. Finally, Roma reduces considerably the need to master different web frameworks and their evolution.

7.5.2 Roma Metaframework Model

The domain model is the center of Roma Metaframework Model. Roma Metaframework has identified and implemented defines a set of cross-cutting concerns (aspects) that can be needed for developing a web application. Other aspects can be easily integrated thanks to its pluggable architecture.

The main elements of Roma metaframework model are (Fig. 7.7):

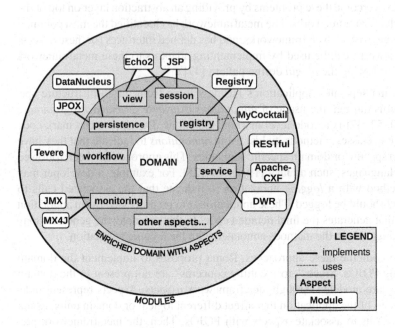

Fig. 7.7: Simplified roma metaframework model

- *Domain Model*. The domain model, as presented before, follows a DDD approach and is implemented with POJOs.

- *Aspects*. Each aspect of the metaframework defines a common functionality needed for developing an enterprise application. Each aspect defines a set of interfaces and has a set of associated annotations. An *enriched domain model* is an annotated domain model with annotation aspects, which can use aspect interfaces for its business method implementation. Annotations can be defined using standard Java annotations [19] or Roma XML Annotations. Roma XML annotations have been defined in order to allow to keep the domain model separated from the infrastructure's needs, and improving reusability. In any case, both annotation mechanisms can be used.

- *Modules*. Modules may implement or use one or more aspect interfaces, providing an implementation of some functionality. Each aspect can have more than one module that implements or uses it.

Next, a summary of the main aspects defined in Roma Metaframework is presented, in order to provide a better understanding of its applicability.

View aspect. This aspect is the basis for the automatic generation of a graphical interface for an application, based on an abstract interface layer, which can be mapped on different interface technologies (frameworks). This aspect defines several annotations in order to define the layout (*ViewClass*, *ViewField* and *ViewAction*) of the POJO components. Based on this specification or additional configuration, Roma selects a graphical renderer for each POJO and its fields and methods. Roma provides modules for rendering with Java Server Pages technology [5] and the Echo2 [15] framework. This is one example of the benefits of the metaframework concept. The interface of the application can be changed without modifying the application code, just changing the module it uses.

Validation aspect. It provides validation facilities for POJOs fields. Roma provides the annotation *ValidationField* which provides attributes for defining if the field is mandatory (attribute *required*), allowed length (attributes *min* and *max*) or required string patterns (attribute *match*).

Internationalization aspect. This aspect enables to present the application in different languages, according to the current location. *I18N Aspect* is implemented as a part of the core module and is based on Java resource bundles.

Authentication aspect. Authentication is the process of verifying that someone is who claims to be. Therefore, this aspect is useful to control users access to some application functionalities that require a security access. Authentication aspect is based on the *users module*, that provides user management and profiling facilities. There are three modules for implementing this aspect using token, LDAP or password authentication methods.

Security aspect. This aspect allows the developer to define the users' permissions on POJOs at class, field or action level. It provides annotations with this purpose (*SecurityClass*, *SecurityField* and *SecurityAction*). Developers can restrict these permissions (read, write and execution) based on user roles or access control lists.

Flow aspect. The flow aspect is used to define the execution flow of the application. Implementation of this aspect is based on core module which presents a Java annotation, called *FlowAction*, that allows developers to define next classes to be executed and another class in case of error.

Session aspect. This aspect collects all the business logic for managing user session, and is used by the modules that implement the View Aspect.

Workflow aspect. This aspect provides a generic interface to a workflow engine. Roma provides their own web-based workflow engine, so called *Tevere*, which has been developed using Roma Metaframework.

Logging aspect. This aspect facilitates the use of logs to control the execution of the application and defines the *LoggingAction* annotation. The logging aspect is implemented by the *admin module*.

Monitoring aspect. With this aspect, business objects can be monitored externally, being accessible outside the application. The annotations *MonitoringClass*, *MonitoringField* and *MonitoringAction* are used to define classes, fields and actions to be monitored. Monitoring aspect can be implemented with JMX [42] or MX4J [36] modules.

Persistence aspect. This aspect is used to store Java objects and retrieve them from a database. Roma provides modules based on the frameworks JPOX [28] and Datanucleus [13] technology. The persistence aspect is based on JDO (*Java Data Objects*) [56]. and provides interfaces for the most common persistence tasks, such as creation, updating, query or deletion of objects.

Reporting aspect. This aspect automates the generation of reports from the POJOs annotations. View annotations are used to generate a template that can be customized in order to obtain the desired result. This aspect is implemented by *Reporting-JR module*, which is based on JasperReports library [26].

Service aspect. The purpose of the service aspect is to facilitate the usage of services from a POJO. The Service aspect provides facilities for exposing a POJO as a web service and creating a client for a web service, The aspects provides an annotation (*ServiceClass*) for exposing an interface as a service as well as interfaces for service invocation. There are three modules implementing this aspect, in order to provide support to Web Services standards (*Apache CXF* module) [4], REST services (RESTful module) and integration with JavaScript client-side services based on DWR [14].

Registry aspect. The registry aspect provides a registry interface and annotation (*RegistryClass*) for WSDL [12] services and REST services described with WADL [20]. There is a module implementation based on WSO2 registry [60].

Enterprise Aspect. The enterprise aspect exposes Roma Services in an Enterprise Service Bus (ESB). The aspect provides two annotations: *EnterpriseClass* and *BPELClass*. The *EnterpriseClass* annotation exposes a service in an ESB previously annotated with the service aspect. The *BPELClass* indicates that the service should be exposed in the ESB through a BPEL [2] delegation process. The current module implementation is based on OpenESB [38].

Scripting aspect. This aspects adds server-side scripting capabilities to Roma applications, which leverages the facility to develop and modify functionalities with scripting languages, such as JavaScript.

Semantic aspect. This aspect provides facilities for taking advantage of semantic web facilities. The aspect defines annotations (*SemanticClass*, *SemanticField*) for exposing a POJO as RDF. A Jena [34] based module provides an implementation of this aspect.

These aspects provide a uniform modeling paradigm to the developers, who do not need to integrate, understand, and evolve each of the frameworks that provide the needed facilities.

Further details of these aspects and the usage of the Roma Metaframework can be found in the Roma Handbook [54].

7.5.3 Case Study

The implementation phase takes advantage of Romulus' DDD-based approach to software development by providing a simple mapping between design and implementation elements. Domain classes and design aspects have their corresponding Java classes or annotations that implement the model that was defined in the design phase.

In Romulus, each element in the domain model is implemented as a POJO, while cross-cutting aspects are implemented through the use of Java annotations. A set of annotations are defined for each of the available aspects considered in Romulus. The resulting annotated POJO is an enriched model of the domain model that was defined in the design phase.

Therefore, by following our case study, the following Java classes should be defined: Promotion, Statistics, Invitation, SMS, User, and Movie. Each of these Java classes are POJOs that include the different private attributes and public accessors, which can be seen in Fig. 7.6. Also, methods that implement the business logic of each POJO need to be implemented.

Java annotations are added to this basic POJO structure, and enrich the model by defining secondary aspects. The Java classes that were mentioned previously might require configuration for the different aspects, so a set of annotations need to be added to each POJO. Romulus will set sensitive defaults for each aspect, but further configuration is often needed. Namely, we should expect to include annotations regarding the view aspect. Most times, not all the defined fields have to be shown to the users. For each field that defaults do not apply, a *ViewField* annotation should be set. Similarly, methods' visibility can be customized by including a *ViewAction* annotation. The annotation *ViewField* of the method *getMovies()* shows how the result of a web service can be integrated in a combo box of the interface using only annotations.

We will focus on implementing the business logic and user interface of the invitations, thus illustrating the usage of Romulus' view aspect (for user interface implementation) and validation aspect (for the definition of model constraints). The Invitation class is shown in Fig. 7.8.

In that code fragment, attributes are defined for the Invitation class according to the model defined in the design phase. Notice that *creationDate* is automatically assigned with the current date whenever an invitation is created. Additionally, methods are defined for each business logic action. For instance, the *getMovies* method queries an external service to obtain the movies that are available in the system.

Also, annotations for Roma Validation and View aspects have been set:

- The *ViewField* annotation is employed to hide fields that should not be visible when showing an invitation object on the presentation layer.

- *ValidationField* annotations are used to indicate that the value for the state field is constrained to a couple of values, as long as invitations can only be pending

```
public class Invitation {
  @ViewField(visible=false)
  @ValidationField(required=true)
  private String id;

  @ViewField(visible=false)
  @ValidationField(match="(pending|accepted)")
  private String state = "pending";

  @ViewField(visible=false)
  private Date creationDate = new Date();

  @ViewField(visible=false)
  @ValidationField(required=true)
  private User inviter;

  @ValidationField(required=true)
  private User invitee;

  @ViewField(visible=false)
  @ValidationField(required=true)
  private Promotion promotion;

  @ValidationField(required=true)
  private Movie movie;

  @ViewField(render = ViewConstants.RENDER_TEXTAREA)
  private String invitationText;

  @ViewField(selectionField = "entity.movie", render = "select",
             description = "Select movie")
  public Movie[] getMovies() {
     Map<String,Object> paramMovie = new HashMap<String,Object>();
     paramMovie.put(InvokeServiceCommand.SERVICE_URL, "http://www.movies.com/");
     paramMovie.put(InvokeServiceCommand.OPERATION_NAME, "getMovies");
     InvokeServiceCommand isc = new InvokeServiceCommand();
     return (Movie[]) isc.execute(new CommandContext(paramMovie));
  }
  @ViewField(selectionField = "entity.invitee",
             render = "select", description = "Select friend")
  public User[] getInvitees() {
      // Invoke Social network Web Service as in getMovies()
  }
@ViewAction(visible = false)
  public void validate() throws ValidationException {
      if (!Promotion.availableInvitations(inviter)) {
          throw new ValidationException(this, "inviter",
                             "No invitations left", null);
      }
  }
  @ViewAction(visible = false)
  public void generatePromoCode() {
      // Generate Discount Coupon
  }
  @ViewAction(visible = false)
  public void notifyBilling() {
      // Invoke billing web service as in getMovies()
  }
  @ViewField(visible = false)
  public void sendInvitation() {
      // Invoke SMS web service as in getMovies()
  }
  /* Public getters and setters are ommitted */
}
```

Fig. 7.8: Sample implementation of invitation with Roma annotations

or accepted, and that other fields are required. Also, a *validation* method has been added to perform further checks before persisting an invitation.

In addition, note that no persistence annotations need to be set, as the Persistence Aspect (which allows storing and querying for objects in the database) abstracts all mappings between class definitions and the database schema.

This class is enough to produce the output that is shown in Fig. 7.9. The user inter-

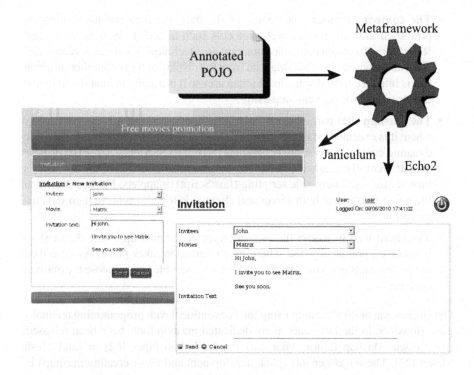

Fig. 7.9: Invitation service's user interface

face that is shown in that picture makes use of two different presentation frameworks (Janiculum and Echo2). Switching between them requires changing a configuration option, and serves as example of the flexibility of the metaframework approach. Aspects are therefore a powerful mechanism in Romulus that allow keeping a clean POJO implementation while adding important details that extend to other concerns, such as presentation, validation, persistence or security.

7.6 Mashups in Romulus

7.6.1 Overview

Mashups [63] are web applications that combine existing data sources to create new applications in order to provide a value added to these data. Mashups may play an important role in service engineering [31], since they provide a flexible and easy to use way for service composition on web.

The architecture of mashup web applications [35] is composed of three parts:

- **The content provider:** the source of the data, the data providers often expose their content through web-protocols such as REST, Web Services, and RSS/Atom. To obtain data, mashups can use a technique known as screen scraping which consists in extracting data from the display output of another program that is intended to be display to a human user so it is usually neither documented nor structured for convenient parsing.

- **The mashup site:** part where the mashup logic resides but it is not necessarily where it is executed. Mashups can be implemented using traditional server-side dynamic content generation technologies like Java Servlets, CGI, PHP or ASP and alternatively, mashed content can be generated directly within the client's browser through client-side scripting (JavaScript) or applets. Mashups can also use a combination of both server and client-side logic to achieve their data aggregation.

- **The client web browser:** the user interface of the mashup where the mashup is rendered graphically and where user interaction takes place. As described above, mashups often use client-side logic to assemble and compose the mashed content.

Developers can build a mashup using the conventional web programming technologies. However, in the last years many dedicated mashup tools have been released, like Google Mashup Editor, Microsoft Popfly, Yahoo Pipes [62] or Intel Mash Maker [23]. These tools enable quick development and allow creating mashups in an easy way, some of them even can be used by end users in order to compose their own mashups. The Romulus project provides its own mashup builder, which is called MyCocktail. is fully integrated with Roma Metaframework to retrieve the data exposed by the application through the services to build mashups.

7.6.2 MyCocktail

MyCocktail [45], the Romulus Mashup Builder, is a web application which provides a graphical user interface for building mashups easily, allowing the user to develop mashups faster and, thus, increasing productivity.

This tool allows users to combine information obtained from different services. This information can be modified with operators and later presented with a wide variety of renderers. The whole process is developed with a graphical user interface and it is as easy as to drag and drop some components and combine them. This helps to reduce considerably the time for developing a mashup.

MyCocktail allows designers and programmers to use services without dealing with the low-level details. Users only have to fill a simple form and the tool processes it and makes the requests to the different services.

MyCocktail is based on Afrous [43] and provides three kinds of components which should be combined to build a mashup:

- **Services:** Several RESTful services can be invoked: del.icio.us (tags, posts, etc.), Yahoo Web Search, Google AJAX Search, Flickr Public Photo Feed, Twitter, Amazon, etc. These are the default services but MyCocktail allows to get data from any REST service which provides a JSONP response using the JSONP operator. MyCocktail also automatically imports the REST services of the Roma Metaframework which are annotated by the developer. The integration between the Roma Metaframework and MyCocktail is made with WADL [20] as format to interchange information about the services created in the applications made with the Roma Metaframework.

- **Operators:** The information obtained can be processed with the operators. For example, it is possible to sort, filter or group the information by a given parameter.

- **Renderers:** the information can be represented in different renderers:

  - **HTML renderers:** these renderers generate HTML elements (image, link or table tags). One renderer can be displayed into others, while the output of a renderer can be used as input of another renderer.
  - **Statistic renderers:** two kinds of statics diagrams can be generated: pie chart and bar chart.
  - **Google Maps renderer:** a renderer that shows elements on a map.
  - **Timeline renderer:** a renderer that shows a time line with elements sorted by date.

MyCocktail (Fig. 7.10) provides an action panel for designing the mashup flow. Services, operators and renderers may be dragged and dropped onto this action panel for its combination while designing a mashup. All the operators, services and renderers are represented in the panel as a form with some fields. By submitting the form, the result of each operator is shown in the lower part of them. The output of one component is usually used as input of another one to combine them.

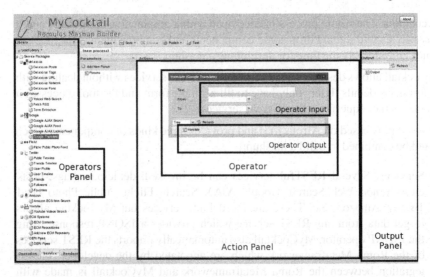

Fig. 7.10: MyCocktail mashup builder structure

7.6.3 Mashups in Roma

Once we have presented the mashup technology and the MyCocktail tool, this section presents how Roma Metaframework can benefit from using mashup technology. This section describes two scenarios.

The first scenario consists of a mashup that combines data sources, external web services, enterprise web services and Roma services (see Fig. 7.11).

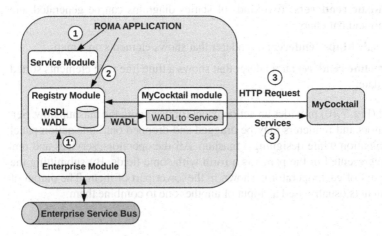

Fig. 7.11: MyCocktail module architecture

As presented before, the *Service Aspect* allows a Roma Application to expose the methods of an interface as web services, which can be registered in a Service Registry using the *Registry Aspect*. The *Registry aspect* has been extended in order to be able to register services developed with MyCocktail and described with WADL. In addition, MyCocktail has been integrated as a module in Roma using the Service and Registry aspects. The main purpose is that MyCocktail can auto discover the registered services. In this way, MyCocktail mashup facilities can be used for combining Roma Services. Furthermore, since MyCocktail registers its services in the Registry, Roma Applications can use directly the mashups developed with MyCocktail.

In addition, Roma provides an *Enterprise aspect* that exposes a service in an enterprise bus. The service can be exposed as a delegated BPEL process. The purpose of this aspect is the integration of *Enterprise Mashups* in Roma. Enterprise mashups are different from web mashups since they are server side and combine business processes. The integration between Roma and Enterprise and web mashups is shown in Fig. 7.11, First, Roma can expose services in the registry using the service and registry aspects. In addition, the *Enterprise aspect* can be used to publish a service in an ESB. Then, MyCocktail mashup builder discovers all the services of the registry.

As a conclusion, Roma applications can be easily integrated with Enterprise and Web Mashups without requiring to modify its architecture or technology. The usage of mashups can leverage the service development effort. For example, Enterprise mashups based on BPEL orchestration has been used in a project management tools developed with Roma, while the control dashboard has been developed with web mashups.

The second scenario consists of the server-side mashup execution in Roma Metaframework (Fig. 7.12).

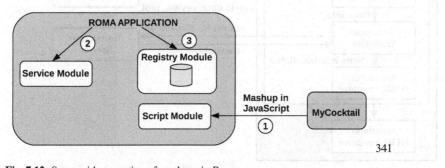

Fig. 7.12: Server side execution of mashups in Roma

Thanks to the Roma *Scripting aspect*, Roma POJOs can implement methods with scripting languages such as JavaScript. Since MyCocktail exports the mashups in JavaScript, some mashup processes can be moved to the server side. The main advantages of this approach are:

- Security reasons. The mashup can contain sensible business logic that should be hidden. In addition, this can provide secure access to other server resources, such as legacy applications, intranet services and ESB.

- The mashup can have direct access to server resources without the need to expose them. For example, the mashups can query directly the persistence layer.

7.6.4 Case Study

The selection of the movie (second step in Fig. 7.5) will be implemented through a mashup. This mashup should retrieve the movies registered in the promotion (Movie Renting Service). The information provided by this service is not too extensive, so we will obtain these data from an external service which provides the plot, reviews, runtime, etc. and mix these data with the existent information of the movie. All the information will be showed to the users translated to their preferred language to help them choosing the movie to recommend to their friends.

The steps followed for building this mashup are shown in Fig. 7.13.

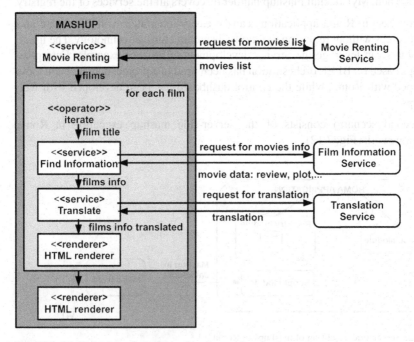

Fig. 7.13: MyCocktail mashup architecture for movie selection

The first step consists of retrieving the movie data using the aforementioned service. The service returns all the available movies offered in the promotion, and the tool shows the results in a tree-like mode.

The second step involves invoking an external service to retrieve the information of the movies. This search should be made over each recovered movie. The Iterate operator provides this functionality, and allows to design an internal flow for its application over a collection of elements. In our case, the flow applied to each element of the collection is based on a movie search operation based on their titles. Thus, the information of all the movies is retrieved as a whole.

In order to translate the movie reviews, there is an available translator operator, which can be configured with the origin and target languages. This translator operator is applied in the internal flow of the Iterator operator.

Finally, when the mashup operations are concluded, the resulting mashup can be represented with some graphical gadgets (pie chart, ...) and then exported as a Google widget, a Netvibes widget, JavaScript or HTML.

As a conclusion, mashup technology provides benefits in development and maintenance tasks. Roma provides several alternatives for its seamless integration presented in this section.

7.7 Related Work

This chapter has proposed an agile service development model based on Roma Metaframework following a DDD approach. In addition, the chapter has shown how this approach can benefit from enterprise and web mashup technologies. In this section, we review other approaches also focused on improving productivity in web development.

7.7.1 Agile Web Frameworks

Agile web frameworks started with Ruby On Rails [21, 24], which defined a new approach to web development, based on a single web framework. Most of the agile web frameworks follow a DDD approach to domain modeling. Some of the most popular agile web frameworks are Grails, Trails, Ruby on Rails and OpenXava, which are introduced below.

Grails [49] is a Java-based Rails-like development framework that was built in response to Ruby on Rails. As a result, their principles are the same and Grails is heavily Rails inspired. To provide Java integration while providing a dynamic oriented language, Grails is based on the Groovy language, a dynamic object-oriented scripting language for the Java virtual machine and with Java-like syntax.

Trails [55] is a web development framework that is inspired in Ruby on Rails and Naked Objects [32]. Its target is offering domain driven design by providing a full-stack web application framework. As a result, Trails takes advantage of the stability and maturity of a closed set of already existing frameworks. Trails enhancements to the direct use of the frameworks are tight integration and automatic code generation for common tasks.

Ruby on Rails [21] is a framework that is aimed at agile development of web applications. It was mainly developed by David Heinemeier Hansson and was extracted out of Basecamp, a production-ready commercial web application. Ruby on Rails' community argues that this extraction is the best proof of the framework's suitability for the development of web applications. Nowadays, Ruby on Rails have gain great popularity. Some of their mains characteristics are metaprogramming, migration facilities and the active records.

OpenXava [39] is an agile framework that follows a POJO orientation. It is developed by Javier Paniza and is integrated with JPA and portal technologies.

The main difference between Roma metaframework and the other agile web approaches is the notion itself of metaframework. The metaframework offers a common application programming interface to a set of pluggable Java frameworks to transparently provide persistence, presentation or internationalization services. In addition, the Roma target is POJO-based development with a minimum coupling with the underlying frameworks and, following the model driven architecture paradigm, provide framework-specific code generation for eventual fine tuning of code. Another different characteristic is the integration of mashup technology in Roma. Roma provides a server-side mashup repository and registry.

7.7.2 Mashups for Service Composition

Mashup technology is considered a promising technolgoy for closing the gap in Service-to-User interaction in Service Oriented Architecturas (SOA) [37], since mashups provide a user-centric and participative approach to service composition [53].

Regarding *service composition approaches*, BPEL [2] has shown effective for service orchestration, although it is primarily targeted at professional developers. Given its complexity, several proposals have emerged [40] for its extension for REST services. Other approaches have integrated BPEL in their mashup development environments, such as LiquidApps [30], providing a visual representation of the underlying processes. The approach followed on Romulus has been targeted at technical users, which have to develop complex applications on Java platforms. In order to reduce BPEL complexity, Romulus provides BPEL integration through the Enterprise Aspect in Roma and its integration with MyCocktail Mashup tool through the Registry Aspect.

Maximilien et al. [33] address service composition with mashups by defining a domain specific language, that is processed for generating the targetted platform. This work points out one of the challenges of mashup technology, its interoperability between mashup editors, which is still an open issue. languages and

Liu et al. [31] proposes to extend SOA with mashup concepts. The proposed architecture integrates a service component in the mashup component. MyCocktail follows a similar approach, since it integrates a service component that are registered in a REST registry using WADL. Our approach has been tested in the integration of enterprise mashups with the *Enterprise Aspect* and with Semantic DERI Pipes Mashups [59], thanks to the *Semantic Aspect*.

Model driven approaches have been used in order to automate web engineering processes. For instance, a web specific modeling language (WebML) is used for composing web services [8] or web applications [3, 11]. WebML conceives data intensive web applications with two models: data model, which describes the schema of data resources, and schema model, which describes how data resources are assembled into information units and pages. WebML is supported by a graphical environment and supported by an IDE tool. Roma follows a different approach based on a rich object model, while navigation is expressed in the Flow Aspect.

7.8 Conclusions

This chapter has presented the problems of web development that have emerged because of the frenetic evolution of web frameworks. In order to simplify maintenance and development activities, Romulus proposes to follow a DDD approach and define a rich domain model. This domain model allows the interaction throughout the project among business domain experts and engineers. In this way, business domain experts can contribute during testing activities, as well as help in the evolution of the domain model.

Roma metaframework provides a layer of abstraction on top of existing web frameworks. As shown in the article, the metaframework delivers a large set of functionalities, including semantic integration, automatic user interface generation, and integration with web and enterprise mashups. In addition, Romulus project has researched on several architectures for integrating mashup technology with Roma metaframework.

The chapter has illustrated the main concepts of the Romulus approach through the development of a case study: a promotion service showing the need to meet the time-to-market deadlines for a telco development, which has been proposed as an extension of the Mobile Phone Service Portability scenario. First, we have applied DDD techniques for modeling the domain. The modeling phase has included a first phase of service landscaping. Design patterns such as entity and value object have been applied to the refactoring of an initial domain model. Roma aspects representing cross-cutting concerns have been employed for annotating POJOs that implement the entities of the domain model. The chapter has shown some of the benefits of using a metaframework, such as seamless framework switching at user interface level. Moreover, a functionality of the case study has been developed with MyCocktail Romulus Mashup Builder. In conclusion, the chapter has illustrated how DDD and mashup technology can leverage and improve Java-based web development.

Acknowledgements Our work has partly been supported by the European Commission under Grant No. 217031, FP7/ICT-2007.1.2, project Romulus – "Domain Driven Design and Mashup

Oriented Development based on Open Source Java Metaframework for Pragmatic, Reliable and
Secure Web Development"

References

1. SOA Priciples of Service Design. Prentice Hall (2007)
2. A. Alves A. Arkin, S.A.C.B.B.B.F.C.M.F.Y.G.A.G.N.K.C.L.R.K.D.K.M.M.e.: Web services
   business process execution language (BPEL) version 2.0. Tech. rep., Committee Specification,
   OASIS (2007)
3. Acerbis, R., Bongio, A., Brambilla, M., Butti, S., Ceri, S., Fraternali, P.: Web applications design and development with webml and webratio 5.0. In: R.F. Paige, B. Meyer
   (eds.) TOOLS (46), *Lecture Notes in Business Information Processing*, vol. 11, pp. 392–411.
   Springer (2008). URL http://dblp.uni-trier.de/db/conf/tools/tools46-
   2008.html#AcerbisBBBCF08
4. Apache CXF Project: Apache CXF web site. an open source service framework. available at
   http://echo.nextapp.com/site/echo2. URL http://echo.nextapp.com/site/echo2
5. Avedal, K., Halberstadt, A., Ayers, D., Briggs, T., Burnham, C., Haynes, R., Hen, Zeiger, S.,
   Holden, M.: Professional JSP. Wrox Press Ltd., Birmingham, UK, UK (2000)
6. Bayer, J., Eisenbarth, M., Lehner, T., Petersen, K.: Service engineering methodology. In:
   Semantic Service Provisioning, chap. 8, pp. 185–201 (2008). DOI 10.1007/978-3-540-78617-
   7_8
7. Boroumand, S.: Working with SOA and RUP. SOA Magazine (XVI) (2008). URL http:
   //www.soamag.com/I16/0308-1.php
8. Brambilla, M., Ceri, S., Comai, S., Fraternali, P., Manolescu, I.: Model-driven specification
   of web services composition and integration with data-intensive web applications. IEEE Data
   Eng. Bull. **25**(4), 53–59 (2002)
9. Brown, D., Davis, C., Stanlick, S.: Struts 2 in Action (In Action). Manning Publications Co.,
   Greenwich, CT, USA (2008)
10. Cardone, R., Soroker, D., Tiwari, A.: Using xforms to simplify web programming. In: WWW
    '05: Proceedings of the 14th international conference on World Wide Web, pp. 215–224. ACM,
    New York, NY, USA (2005). DOI http://doi.acm.org/10.1145/1060745.1060780
11. Ceri, S., Fraternali, P., Matera, M.: Conceptual modeling of data-intensive web applications.
    IEEE Internet Computing **6**(4), 20–30 (2002). DOI http://dx.doi.org/10.1109/MIC.2002.
    1020321
12. Christensen, E., Curbera, F., Meredith, G., Weerawarana, S.: Web services description lan-
    guage (WSDL) 1.1. W3c note, World Wide Web Consortium (2001). URL http://www.
    w3.org/TR/wsdl
13. DataNucleus Project: DataNucleus web site. available at http://www.datanucleus.org. URL
    http://www.datanucleus.org/
14. DWR Project: DWR (Direct Web Remoting)web site. available at
    http://directwebremoting.org/dwr/index.html. URL http://directwebremoting.
    org/dwr/index.html
15. Echo2 Project: Echo2 web site. available at http://echo.nextapp.com/site/echo2. URL http:
    //echo.nextapp.com/site/echo2
16. Evans, E.: Domain-Driven Design: Tackling Complexity in the Heart of Software. Addison-
    Wesley (2004)
17. Fowler, M.: POJO (Plain Old Java Object). Martin Fowler, available at
    http://martinfowler.com/bliki/POJO.html (2000). URL http://martinfowler.
    com/bliki/POJO.html
18. Fowler, M.: Anemic domain model. Martin Fowler, available at
    http://martinfowler.com/bliki/AnemicDomainModel.html (2003). URL http:
    //martinfowler.com/bliki/AnemicDomainModel.html

19. Gosling, J., Joy, B., Steele, G.L., Bracha, G.: The Java Language Specification, 3. edn. Addison-Wesley, Upper Saddle River, NJ (2005). URL http://java.sun.com/docs/books/jls/

20. Hadley, M.J.: Web Application Description Language (WADL). Available at https://wadl.dev.java.net/wadl20090202.pdf (2009). URL Availableathttps://wadl.dev.java.net/wadl20090202.pdf

21. Holzner, S.: Beginning Ruby on Rails (Wrox Beginning Guides). Wrox Press Ltd., Birmingham, UK, UK (2006)

22. Husted, T.N., Dumoulin, C., Franciscus, G., Winterfeldt, D.: Struts in Action — Building Web Applications with the Leading Java Framework. Manning Publications (2003)

23. IBM: Intel mash maker. Available at http://mashmaker.intel.com

24. Ignacio Fernández-Villamor, J., Díaz-Casillas, L., Iglesias, C.A.: A comparison model for agile web frameworks. In: EATIS '08: Proceedings of the 2008 Euro American Conference on Telematics and Information Systems, pp. 1–8. ACM, New York, NY, USA (2008). DOI http://doi.acm.org/10.1145/1621087.1621101

25. International, E.: Standard ECMA-334 - C# Language Specification, 4 edn. (2006). URL http://www.ecma-international.org/publications/standards/Ecma-334.htm

26. JasperReports Project: JasperReports web site. available at http://jasperforge.org/projects/jasperreports. URL http://jasperforge.org/projects/jasperreports/

27. Jazayeri, M.: Some trends in web application development. In: FOSE '07: 2007 Future of Software Engineering, pp. 199–213. IEEE Computer Society, Washington, DC, USA (2007). DOI http://dx.doi.org/10.1109/FOSE.2007.26

28. JPOX Project: JPOX (java persistent objects) web site. available at http://www.jpox.org. URL http://www.jpox.org/

29. Kruchten, P.: Rational Unified Process. An Introduction. Addison-Wesley (2004)

30. LiquidApps: Liquidapps. Available at http://liquidappsworld.com

31. Liu, X., Hui, Y., Sun, W., Liang, H.: Towards service composition based on mashup. In: IEEE SCW, pp. 332–339. IEEE Computer Society (2007). URL http://dblp.uni-trier.de/db/conf/IEEEscc/scw2007.html#LiuHSL07

32. Lüfer, K.: A stroll through domain-driven development with naked objects. Computing in Science and Engineering 10, 76–83 (2008). DOI http://doi.ieeecomputersociety.org/10.1109/MCSE.2008.67

33. Maximilien, E.M., Ranabahu, A., Gomadam, K.: An online platform for web apis and service mashups. IEEE Internet Computing 12, 32–43 (2008). DOI http://doi.ieeecomputersociety.org/10.1109/MIC.2008.92

34. McBride, B.: Jena: a semantic web toolkit. IEEE Internet Computing 6(6), 55–59 (2002). DOI 10.1109/MIC.2002.1067737

35. Merrill, D.: Mashups: The new breed of Web app. Available at http://www.ibm.com/developerworks/xml/library/x-mashups.html (2006). URL Availableathttp://www.ibm.com/developerworks/xml/library/x-mashups.html

36. MX4J Project: Open source JMX for enterprise computing (MX4J) web site. available at http://mx4j.sourceforge.net/. URL http://mx4j.sourceforge.net/.

37. Nestler, T.: Towards a mashup-driven end-user programming of soa-based applications. In: iiWAS '08: Proceedings of the 10th International Conference on Information Integration and Web-based Applications & Services, pp. 551–554. ACM, New York, NY, USA (2008). DOI http://doi.acm.org/10.1145/1497308.1497408

38. OpenESB: OpenESB project, available at https://open-esb.dev.java.net/. Available at https://open-esb.dev.java.net/

39. openxava: openxava project, available at http://www.openxava.org/web/guest/home. Available at http://www.openxava.org/web/guest/home

40. Pautasso, C.: Restful web service composition with bpel for rest. Data Knowl. Eng. 68(9), 851–866 (2009). DOI http://dx.doi.org/10.1016/j.datak.2009.02.016

41. Penchikala, S.: Domain driven design and development in practice. InfoQueue (2008). URL http://www.infoq.com/articles/ddd-in-practice
42. Perry, J.S.: Java Management Extensions, 1. edn. O'Reilly, Beijing (2002)
43. Project, A.: Afrous project web site (2009). Available at ttp://www.afrous.com/
44. project, R.: Romulus web site. available at http://www.ict-romulus.eu/. URL http://www.ict-romulus.eu/
45. Project, R.: Mycocktail web site (2009). Available at http://www.ict-romulus.eu/web/mycocktail
46. project, R.M.: Romulus web site. available at http://www.romaframework.org/. URL http://www.romaframework.org/
47. Rice, D., Foemmel, M.: Plugin Design pattern, p. 499. Addison-Wesley (2002). URL http://martinfowler.com/eaaCatalog/plugin.html
48. Richardson, C.: POJOs in Action: Developing Enterprise Applications with Lightweight Frameworks. Manning Publications Co., Greenwich, CT, USA (2006)
49. Rocher, G.: The Definitive Guide to Grails (Definitive Guide). Apress, Berkely, CA, USA (2006)
50. Rouvoy, R.: Leveraging component-oriented programming with attribute-oriented programming. In: In Proccedings of WCOP 2006 (2006)
51. Schäfer, T., Jonas, J., Mezini, M.: Mining framework usage changes from instantiation code. In: ICSE '08: Proceedings of the 30th international conference on Software engineering, pp. 471–480. ACM, New York, NY, USA (2008). DOI http://doi.acm.org/10.1145/1368088.1368153
52. Schwarz, D.: Peeking inside the box: Attribute oriented programming in java. ONJava.com, O'Reilly (2004)
53. Soriano, J., Lizcano, D., Hierro, J.J., Reyes, M., Schroth, C., Janner, T.: Enhancing User-Service Interaction through a Global User-Centric Approach to SOA. IEEE (2008). DOI 10.1109/ICNS.2008.37. URL http://ieeexplore.ieee.org/xpl/freeabs_all.jsp?arnumber=4476558
54. Tagliaferri, E., Maestro, G., Garulli, L., Molino, L., Dell'Aquila, L., Stefano, M.d.: Roma MetaFramework Handbook v2.1, 2.1 edn. Romulus Project (2009)
55. Trails: Trails project, available at http://www.trailsframework.org/. Available at http://www.trailsframework.org/e
56. Tyagi, S., Vorburger, M., McCammon, K., Bobzin, H.: Core Java Data Objects. Prentice Hall PTR / Sun Microsystems Press (2004)
57. Wada, H., Takada, S.: Leveraging metamodeling and attribute-oriented programming to build a model-driven framework for domain specific languages. In: In Proc. of the 8th JSSST Conference on Systems Programming and its Applications (2005)
58. Walls, C., Breidenbach, R.: Spring in Action. Manning (2005). URL http://www.amazon.de/gp/redirect.html%3FASIN=1932394354%26tag=ws%26lcode=xm2%26cID=2025%26ccmID=165953%26location=/o/ASIN/1932394354%253FSubscriptionId=13CT5CVB80YFWJEPWS02
59. Westerski, A.: Integrated environment for visual data-level mashup development. In: 10th International Conference on Web Information Systems Engineering (WISE), pp. 481–487 (2009). URL administrator/components/com_jresearch/files/publications/esiw2009_westerski.pdf
60. WSO2: Wso2 registry, available at http://wso2.com/products/governance-registry/. Available at http://wso2.com/products/governance-registry/
61. Xue, M., Zhu, C.: Design and implementation of the hibernate persistence layer data report system based on j2ee. In: PACCS, pp. 232–235. IEEE Computer Society (2009). URL http://dblp.uni-trier.de/db/conf/paccs/paccs2009.html#XueZ09
62. Yahoo: Yahoo pipes. Available at http://pipes.yahoo.com
63. Yu, J., Benatallah, B., Casati, F., Daniel, F.: Understanding mashup development (2008). URL Availableathttp://www.floriandaniel.it/university/ops/download.php?oid=45

Chapter 8
Guidance in Business Process Modelling

Andreas Bartho, Gerd Gröner, Tirdad Rahmani, Yuting Zhao and Srdjan Zivkovic

Abstract This chapter shows how process modellers can be supported by guidance. If a telecommunication provider introduces a value-added service, this might involve the establishment of new business processes, whose specification is not trivial. A guidance engine can help a process engineer develop a new business process by stepwise refining, i.e. creating a more concrete version of the process from an abstract version. The guidance engine identifies inconsistencies and proposes possible refinement steps. The topics covered in this chapter range from theoretical foundations of business process refinement over the formalisation of refinement problems in ontologies to implementation issues. The presented solutions were developed in the MOST project.

Andreas Bartho
Technische Universität Dresden, Nöthnitzer Str. 46, 01187 Dresden (Germany), e-mail: andreas.bartho@tu-dresden.de

Gerd Gröner
University of Koblenz-Landau, Universitätsstraße 1, 56070 Koblenz (Germany), e-mail: groener@uni-koblenz.de

Tirdad Rahmani
SAP Research, Vincenz-Prießnitz-Str. 1, 76131 Karlsruhe (Germany), e-mail: tirdad.rahmani@sap.com

Yuting Zhao
University of Aberdeen, Aberdeen AB24 3UE (United Kingdom), e-mail: yuting.zhao@gmail.com

Srdjan Zivkovic
BOC AG, Wipplingerstraße 1, 1010 Vienna (Austria), e-mail: srdjan.zivkovic@boc-eu.com

8.1 Introduction

Today, there is a rapidly increasing pressure in the market forcing the industry into the transition from a fixed and isolated business structure to flexible interoperation of businesses in a chain or a grid of interdependent value-added services. Ordinarily a value-added service encapsulates a tangible set of activities together with some data and behaviour constraints between them. Value-added services are offered by a service provider, such as the telecommunication provider from the case study of this book, to a service purchaser, such as the provider's end customers, in exchange of money.

One strongly related discipline to service engineering and consequently value-added services is *Business Process Management (BPM)*. From a BPM viewpoint a value-added service can also be seen as an encapsulation of a business process. On the other hand, business processes might be necessary to back up the value-added service in an enterprise.

A prominent technique used in BPM since the 90s is *Business Process Modeling*, which is used to describe behavioural constraints of a process, or a value-added service, respectively. The modelling of business processes is a complex task which requires the expertise of several people within an organisation and can only be accomplished through collaboration. The end result of the modelling stage will be a process that incorporates all relevant business requirements in one model, hence will make it difficult to understand different parts of the model that were included successively over time.

One of the increasingly important techniques to reduce the complexity of process models is modelling on different interrelated levels of abstraction. For this purpose we will focus on *refinement* as a special way of dealing with modelling levels in one and the same modelling language like the *Business Process Modeling Notation* (BPMN). This chapter shows how ontology technology can be used to provide guidance for the stepwise refinement of a BPMN process and thus make it easier and less error-prone. The presented results are from the MOST project, which aims to Marry Ontology and Software Technology.

The chapter is structured as follows: Sect. 8.2 integrates the process refinement approach into the telecommunication case study. Sect. 8.3 presents the state of the art in process refinement along with its limitations and defines syntax and semantics of process models and process refinements. Sect. 8.4 shows in an example how guidance for process refinement may look like, using a guidance engine. Then the realisation of an ontology-based guidance engine is explained. It follows an evaluation in Sect. 8.5, and finally, Sect. 11.5 concludes the chapter.

8.2 Motivating Scenario

Due to increased competition in the field of telecommunication the telecommunication company has decided to expand their field of operations by providing value-added services. In this chapter we refer to the business goal TELCO_BG_05 of the case study, which is reproduced here for convenience:

Table 8.1: To provide new added-value services

Field	Description
Unique ID	TELCO_BG_05
Short Name	To provide new added-value services
Type	Business Goal
Description	The system shall enable CPOs to easily provide new services. Mainly regarding on the evolution of the Web and the spread of new application under the 2.0 umbrella, CPOs need to increase the number of services by considering all the users that consume this kind of applications.
Rationale	Increase the market rate.
Involved Stakeholders	CPOs and customer
Priority of accomplishment	Should have

According to market research, games are an especially fast-growing market. It has been decided to purchase a standard gaming service from a third party provider.

This gaming service offers standard features such as playing games, rate games or compare highscores. However, as more and more phones can access web content, there are plenty of free alternatives for the users, making them unlikely to pay for this service.

Therefore the gaming service has been extended by in-house developers to be capable of running contests. In a contest a challenge is posed, which involves reaching specific goals in a game. Such goals can be arbitrarily easy or complex, for example

- be the fastest person to finish a game

- have the highest score when the contest ends

- solve in-game tasks such as

    - beat every single enemy in a stage

    - find all rainbow-coloured unicorns in the hidden fairy forest and feed them a magic carrot of joy

The winner is awarded a prize. It is assumed that the competition factor and the prospect of a prize will convince many of the company's customers to sign up for the gaming service.

Running a contest involves not only technical but also organisational preparations. For instance, the contest goals and prizes have to be decided, developers have to be contacted to prepare their games accordingly and the prizes have to be sent to the winners.

Therefore the running of a contest is a business process. According to company guidelines, all business processes must be explicitly modelled. However, there are different types of contests, each of which requires a slightly different course of action. For example, there are simple contests that involve transferring prize money to the winners, but also sponsored contests which need negotiations with sponsors and packages sent to the winners. For maintainability reasons it has been decided to have a dedicated business process model for each type of contest, instead of one big model that captures all possibilities.

This is feasible because at an abstract level all contests are equal. Instead of creating a new business process model from scratch for a contest type, there will be an abstract process which can be stepwisely refined.

Appropriate tool support is vital for process refinement. On the one hand consistency is important. It must be ensured that a refined process does not contradict with a more abstract process. On the other hand the procedure of refining business process models should be supported. There are often multiple, sometimes non-obvious possibilities to continue refining. The telecommunication provider has a business process refinement guidance tool, which fulfils these requirements and guides process modellers through the act of process refinement. The tool can propose refinement actions to be taken (process guidance) and point out inconsistencies between refinement steps (consistency guidance).

8.3 Existing Approaches and Their Limitations

Business process refinement can generally be seen as a technique which allows to add more information to a business process model on a certain abstraction level while preserving the original information and constraints on a more abstract (or specific) level. This technique is especially useful when several people with different expertise and responsibilities work on the same business process.

8.3.1 State of the Art

Originally process refinement theory stems from the idea to check for a given abstract process model with a high level of nondeterministic behaviour and a process model with a more deterministic behaviour whether the possible behaviours (control flows) are consistent with each other. Interesting work in this field is done by R.L. van Glabbeek by utilising bisimulation techniques in [5]. However the problem addressed there is not general enough to handle process models with different granularity levels of interrelated activities.

By developing business processes using *Model Driven Architecture* (MDA) approaches it is often required to compare process models on different abstraction layers and with different granularity levels for consistency. One prominent discipline dealing with the scenario that we are interested in is action refinement. Action refinement was massively formally researched in the early 1990s by the process algebra community. The efforts culminated in a detailed survey by Gorrieri & Rensink [13]. Our view differs from the majority of action refinement approaches in two respects:

- Abstract and specific process and component models are not directly related, but stand for themselves. They are rather loosely connected via the refinement relation. Most notably, multiple correct refinements may exist for an abstract process, which has been widely neglected by recent works.

- Traditional action refinement discovers process equivalence notions. Relaxed forms of refinement are more appropriate for business process engineering, especially for exploiting maximal or minimal execution set semantics.

Our view of refinement is also called vertical implementation. Since 2000, action refinement in general received less attention: A subset of vertical implementation where tasks are considered atomic and cannot interfere with others in the refinement was practically applied to software testing by Bijl, Rensink, and Tretmans [2]. General action refinement has been applied to software engineering by Diertens [4]. We know of no application to business process engineering.

The most important influence for our research came from the MIT process handbook project (http://ccs.mit.edu/ph/). That research categorises all business processes for documentation purposes in a hierarchy by comparing their execution sets introduced by Wyner and Lee in [11]. Using that method, navigation from higher-level abstract processes to lower-level variants and concretely occurring process examples is possible. The main idea for our formal definition of correct refinement and grounding base on the informal notions of minimal and maximal execution set semantics in the MIT process handbook project.

One of the main obstacles for formal analysis of business processes is the lack of formal semantics of process specifications. Neither the UML activity diagram nor the business process modelling notation (BPMN) nor the event-driven process chain (EPC) definition [7] – to name a few pseudo-standards for business process modelling – come with a standard mapping to mathematics. The lack forced theoreticians to create competing semantic definitions for business process languages, for example using the abstract state machines (ASM) formalism of Börger and Thalheim [3]. Formal proofs of interesting process properties can be performed in ASM. Unfortunately, the general formalism is too complex for automatic validations. Therefore, the mapping to a more lightweight formalism is more relevant to us. Wil van der Aalst extensively studied workflow nets (WF-nets) being a subclass of Petri Nets for the purpose of business process analysis [1]. Unfortunately, process steps do not consume time in a WF-net. The potential temporal overlapping of time-consuming steps is however important for the refinement of business processes. In either case, the work of Aalst is a good starting point for our business process specifications and for its potential, later extension by more sophisticated control constructs.

Two concrete solutions have been proposed for the validation of refinement and grounding: One reduces the validation problems to description logic (DL) reasoning introduced by Ren et al. in [12], and the other to the graph analyser GReQL introduced by Schwarz, et al. in [14]. The DL approach also starts from the definition of execution sets according to the MIT process handbook project. The GReQL approach starts from a set of logic constraints that are necessary, but probably not sufficient for validating refinement. The appropriate definition of correct refinement contains a lot of tricky and interrelated challenges as the action refinement research based on process algebra has revealed. In this chapter we are focusing on DL reasoning techniques for specifying and validating process refinements.

8.3.2 Mathematic Background of Business Process Refinement

Generally in the case of business processes there are two major categories of constraints which have to be considered and preserved on any abstraction layer:

- **Behavioural Constraints:** Behavioural constraints are necessary to describe which possible execution flows are allowed in a process or will be undertaken in the default or the exceptional cases.

- **Data Constraints:** Data constraints are concerned with the compatibility of input and output formats of occurring process activities and tasks independently of whether they are automatic tasks (realisable by web service operations) or human tasks (needing human interaction).

In this book chapter all refinement techniques are primarily related to behavioural constraints, since our focus is on internal business processes for which data consistency problems are not considered a challenge.

8.3.2.1 Syntax of Process Models

All process models in this chapter are based on core modelling elements of BPMN, which is a well known and community wide accepted OMG standard in the business process management domain.

A process model – or short: process – is a non-simple directed graph $P = \langle E, V \rangle$ without multiple edges between two vertices. In our definition, vertices (V) fall into activities, gateways $(A, G \subseteq V)$, and the specific vertices start and end event $(v_0, v_{end} \in V)$. Fig. 8.1a shows a BPMN diagram which consists of two activities between the start and end events.

A gateway is either opening or closing $(G^O, G^C \subseteq G)$, and either exclusive or parallel $(G^\otimes, G^\oplus \subseteq G)$. The process models (c) and (d) in Fig. 8.1 contain exclusive and parallel gateways, respectively. We call a process *normal* if it does not contain parallel gateways $(G^\oplus = \emptyset)$ – as, for example, process model (c).

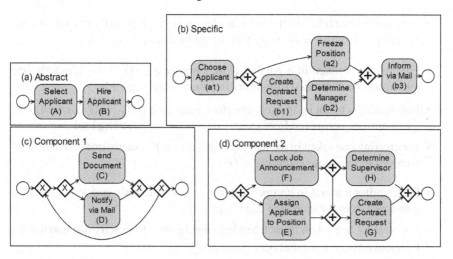

Fig. 8.1: Example process refinements

The edge set (E) is a binary relation on V. We define the predecessor and the successor functions of each $v_1 \in V$ as follows: $\mathrm{pre}(v_1) := \{v_2 \in V \mid (v_2, v_1) \in E\}$, $\mathrm{suc}(v_1) := \{v_3 \in V \mid (v_1, v_3) \in E\}$. The start (end) event has no predecessor (successor): $|\mathrm{pre}(v_0)| = |\mathrm{suc}(v_{\mathrm{end}})| = 0$ and exactly one successor (predecessor): $|\mathrm{suc}(v_0)| = |\mathrm{pre}(v_{\mathrm{end}})| = 1$. Each open gateway $o \in G^O$ (close gateway $c \in G^C$) has exactly one predecessor (successor): $|\mathrm{pre}(o)| = |\mathrm{suc}(c)| = 1$. Each activity $a \in A$ has exactly one predecessor and successor: $|\mathrm{pre}(a)| = |\mathrm{suc}(a)| = 1$. We can then construct gateway-free predecessor and successor sets as follows:

$$PS(v_1) := \{v_2 \in A \mid v_2 \in \mathrm{pre}(v_1) \text{ or } \exists u \in G \text{ s.t. } u \in \mathrm{pre}(v_1) \text{ and } v_2 \in PS(u)\}$$

$$SS(v_1) := \{v_3 \in A \mid v_3 \in \mathrm{suc}(v_1) \text{ or } \exists u \in G \text{ s.t. } u \in \mathrm{suc}(v_1) \text{ and } v_3 \in SS(u)\}$$

These two definitions make gateways "transparent" to ordering relations. For example in Fig. 8.1b, $SS(a1) = \{b1, a2\}$, in Fig. 8.1c, $PS(C) = \{C, D\}$.

8.3.2.2 Execution Set Semantics of Process Models

We define the semantics of a process model using the execution set semantics [15]. An execution is a *proper* sequence of activities $(a_i \in A)$: $[a_1 a_2 \ldots a_n]$. A proper sequence is obtained by simulating token flow through a process model. A token is associated with exactly one vertex or edge. Initially, there is exactly one token, associated with the start event. Tokens can be created and consumed following the rules below. Whenever a token is created in an activity, the activity is appended to the sequence. Exactly one of the following actions is performed at a time:

- For creating a token in an activity or in the end event $v_1 \in A \cup \{v_{\mathrm{end}}\}$, exactly one token must be consumed from the incoming edge $(v_2, v_1) \in E$.

- For creating one token in the leaving edge $(v_1, v_2) \in E$, exactly one token must be removed from an activity or from the start event $v_1 \in A \cup \{v_0\}$.

- For creating a token in a parallel close gateway $g \in (G^* \cap G^C)$, exactly one token must be consumed from every incoming edge $(v, g) \in E$.

- For creating a token in an exclusive close gateway $g \in (G^* \cap G^C)$, exactly one token must be consumed from exactly one incoming edge $(v, g) \in E$.

- For creating one token in the leaving edge $(g, v) \in E$, exactly one token must be removed from a close gateway $g \in G^C$.

- For creating a token in an open gateway $g \in G^O$, exactly one token must be consumed from the incoming edge $(v, g) \in E$.

- For creating one token in each leaving edge $(g, v) \in E$, exactly one token must be removed from a parallel open gateway $g \in (G^* \cap G^O)$.

- For creating one token in exactly one leaving edge $(g, v) \in E$, exactly one token must be removed from an exclusive open gateway $g \in (G^* \cap G^O)$.

If none of the above actions can be performed, simulation has ended. The result is a proper sequence of activities – an execution. It is to be noted that each execution is finite. However, there may be an infinite number of executions for a process model. The execution set of a process model P, denoted by ES_P, is the (possibly infinite) set of all proper sequences of the process model.

For example, ES_a for process (a) in Fig. 8.1 is $\{[AB]\}$: first A, then B (for brevity, we refer to an activity by its short name, which appears in the diagrams in parentheses). Process (b) contains parallel gateways ($\diamond$) to express that some activities can be performed in any order: $ES_b = \{[a_1 a_2 b_1 b_2 b_3], [a_1 b_1 a_2 b_2 b_3], [a_1 b_1 b_2 a_2 b_3]\}$. Exclusive gateways ($\diamond$) are used in process (c) both to choose from the two activities and to form a loop: $ES_c = \{[C], [D], [CC], [CD], [DC], [DD], \ldots\}$. Process (d) shows that gateways can also occur in a non-blockwise manner: $ES_d = \{[EFGH], [EFHG], [FHEG], [FEGH], [FEHG]\}$.

8.3.2.3 Consistent Process Refinement

For refinement validation we have to distinguish between *horizontal* and *vertical* refinement. A horizontal refinement is a transformation from an abstract to a more specific process which contains the decomposition of activities. For this reason it is also called decomposition. A vertical refinement is a transformation from a principle behaviour model of a component to a process model. For simplicity the behaviour models are also described by BPMN processes. They are called component models. The transformation of activities of concrete process models consists of the grounding of activities to activities of the component models for which a correct implementation is guaranteed by each software component. Refinement validation has to take both kinds of refinement into account.

Fig. 8.1 contains several refinement relations. The process in Fig. 8.1a might have been drawn by a line of business manager to sketch a new hiring process. The process in Fig. 8.1b is drawn by a process architect who incrementally implements the sketched process. Fig. 8.1c and d show the principle behaviour models of different components. The challenge is to verify whether the refinement, horizontal or vertical, is consistent with the more abstract processes.

For validation of horizontal refinement, the process architect has to declare which activities of Fig. 8.1b implement which activity of Fig. 8.1a: $hori(a_1) = hori(a_2) = A$, $hori(b_1) = hori(b_2) = hori(b_3) = B$. For validation of vertical refinement, the process architect needs to link activities of Fig. 8.1b to service endpoints given in Fig. 8.1c and d: $vert(a_1) = E$, $vert(a_2) = F$, $vert(b_1) = G$, $vert(b_2) = H$, $vert(b_3) = D$.

Correct horizontal refinement (Decomposition)

We say that a process Q is a correct *horizontal* refinement of a process P if $ES_Q \subseteq ES_P$ after the following transformations.

1. **Renaming.** Replace all activities in each execution of ES_Q by their originators (function $hori()$). Renaming the execution set $\{[a_1a_2b_1b_2b_3], [a_1b_1a_2b_2b_3], [a_1b_1b_2a_2b_3]\}$ of Fig. 8.1b yields $\{[AABBB], [ABABB], [ABBAB]\}$.
2. **Decomposition.** Replace all sequences of equal activities by a single activity in each execution of ES_Q. For Fig. 8.1b this yields $\{[AB], [ABAB]\}$.

As $\{[AB]\} \not\supseteq \{[AB], [ABAB]\}$, Fig. 8.1b is a wrong horizontal refinement of Fig. 8.1a. The cause is the potentially inverted order of AB by b_1a_2 or b_2a_2.

Correct vertical refinement (Grounding)

We say that a process Q is a correct *vertical* refinement of a process P if $ES_Q \subseteq ES_P$ after the following transformations.

1. **Renaming.** Replace all activities in each execution of ES_Q by their grounds (function $vert()$). Renaming the execution set $\{[a_1a_2b_1b_2b_3], [a_1b_1a_2b_2b_3], [a_1b_1b_2a_2b_3]\}$ of Fig. 8.1b yields $\{[EFGHD], [EGFHD], [EGHFD]\}$.
2. **Reduction.** Remove all activities in each execution of ES_Q that do not appear in P. For our example, reduction with respect to 8.1c yields $\{[D]\}$. Reduction with respect to 8.1d yields $\{[EFGH], [EGFH], [EGHF]\}$.

Fig. 8.1b is a correct vertical refinement of 8.1c because $\{[C], [D], [CC], [CD], [DC], [DD], \ldots\} \supseteq \{[D]\}$ and a wrong vertical refinement of 8.1d because $\{[EFGH], [EFHG], [FHEG], [FEGH], [FEHG]\} \not\supseteq \{[EFGH], [EGFH], [EGHF]\}$. The cause for

the wrong refinement is the potentially inverted execution of FG by $b_1 a_2$ in
Fig. 8.1b.

8.4 Proposed Approach

Building on the mathematical backgrounds of process refinement presented in
Sect. 8.3.2, we will now show how ontologies and DL reasoning can provide guidance. First an example process refinement is shown, then a short introduction to
ontologies is given, and finally two kinds of guidance and their integration into a
tool are presented.

8.4.1 Example Refinement

In this section we will show how the Contest process, which describes how a contest
for the Gaming service is organised, is being modelled with the help of the guidance
engine. We will cover several refinement steps, show the errors that can occur and
describe how the guidance engine reacts.

The refinement starts with a very abstract process, which we will call *Process A*,
as seen in Fig. 8.2. There have been no refinement steps so far, so there are no
inconsistencies. The process contains an activity that is neither refined nor grounded.
The possible refinement tasks are therefore **Refine** or **Ground Activity "Manage
Contest"**. The guidance engine shows these, along with the more abstract notions
Refine or **Ground Process A**. It is also always possible to disregard the process at
hand and get back to the previous refinement step. This is indicated by **Remodel
Process A**.

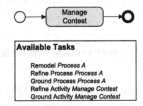

Fig. 8.2 Process A and possible refinement steps

The process modeller decides to refine activity *Manage Contest*. The result is *Process B*, a sequence of three activities as seen in Fig. 8.3. The refinement was valid
w.r.t. the rules defined in Sect. 8.3.2.3, so no inconsistencies are reported. The guidance engine shows all possible refinement steps, which are refinement or grounding
of each of the new activities or refinement or grounding of *Process B*.

The process modeller knows that the most complicated part of the final process will
be dealing with the game developer. Agreements will have to be made, contracts will
be signed, and more. He therefore decides to take care of that issue first and refines

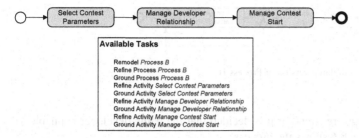

Fig. 8.3: Process B and possible refinement steps

activity **Manage Developer Relationship**, which results in *Process C* as depicted in Fig. 8.4.

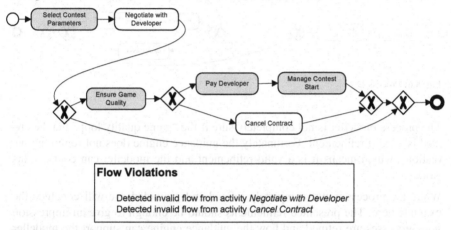

Fig. 8.4: Process C and error messages

According to the guidance engine there is something wrong with the previous refinement. Two flow violations were detected, one from activity **Negotiate with Developer** and one from activity **Cancel Contract**. The reason for the violation is that both activities are a refinement of **Manage Developer Relationship** and that they have a direct path to the end state of the process, while **Manage Developer Relationship** had not. There is a contradiction here that needs to be resolved.

Being sure that *Process C* is correct, the process modeller decides that *Process B* needs to be changed. A new path is added so that the process can be finished without executing activity **Manage Contest Start**. The result is shown in Fig. 8.5.

After these changes the guidance engine detects no more violations and proposes refinement steps as usual.

In the last step of this example the process modeller refines the activity **Ensure Game Quality**. Ensuring game quality involves testing the contest version of the game which the game developer prepared. If bugs are found the game developer is given order to fix them and deliver a new version of the game. This loop continues

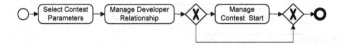

Fig. 8.5: Process B' – updated version of Process B

until no more bugs are found or it is decided that the game developer is unable to fulfil his duty. Fig. 8.6 shows the process.

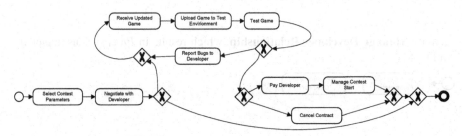

Fig. 8.6: Process D

The process modeller is not completely sure if the "game quality loop" that he created is a valid refinement. Fortunately the guidance engine does not report any violations, which means it is a valid refinement and the modeller can continue his work.

While the process is not completely refined and grounded, we will conclude the example here. The presented refinements should be enough to give an impression how processes are refined and how the guidance engine can support the modeller. The following subsections will shed light on its implementation.

8.4.2 Ontologies

The term "ontology" is often explained as an "explicit specification of a conceptualisation" [6]. Ontologies are used to describe concepts of a domain, their relationships and constraints. Using reasoners it is possible to infer knowledge that is not explicitly represented.

There are different ontology languages which differ in syntax and expressiveness. The less expressive an ontology is, the more efficient reasoning is. We will use profiles of OWL2 to implement consistency and process guidance for business process refinement.

The so-called TBox captures the terminology. It is the vocabulary of the application domain and comprises concepts (also called classes) and roles (properties). Concepts denote sets of individuals. Roles are typed binary relations which connect two concepts. Concepts and roles can be combined to build complex descriptions out of basic ones.

The ABox contains the individuals (instances). Individuals are distinguished by their name, i.e. each individual has a unique name. Individuals can belong to zero, one or many concepts.

Once TBox and ABox have been created, it is possible to reason about them. Reasoning is the process of inferring indirect knowledge from explicit knowledge. There are several typical reasoning tasks for ontologies:

- check if a TBox is satisfiable (i.e. contains no contradictions)

- check if one concept subsumes another one (i.e. whether the first concept is more general than the first one)

- check if an ABox is consistent (i.e. there are no contradictions w.r.t. to the TBox)

- check if an individual is an instance of a specific concept

Reasoning on ontologies differs from reasoning in first order logics. If in first order logics some fact is not defined (neither explicitly nor implicitly) it is assumed to be false. For example, if there is no Carl in the definition of persons, then Carl does not exist. This assumption is called Closed World Assumption (CWA).

In ontologies, however, anything that is not explicitly stated might be true or not. If Carl is not mentioned it is not known if he exists. The so-called Open World Assumption (OWA) therefore allows multiple interpretations of the knowledge base. This also means that different concepts might be equivalent, for example the concepts of Person and Vehicle. If this behaviour is not wanted, one must explicitly state that the concepts are disjoint, otherwise the reasoner might deliver undesired results.

8.4.3 Consistency Guidance

This section gives a detailed description of the Consistency Guidance service of the business process refinement guidance tool. Consistency guidance aims for pinpointing inconsistencies between process refinement steps. Given a pre- and a post-refined business process, the Consistency Guidance determines whether this refinement is valid according to the specified refinement conditions, i.e. the post-refined process does not introduce new paths that are not in the pre-refined process.

The comparison of the pre- and post-refined process is a complex and difficult task, therefore the comparison is realised by two steps, as described in Sect. 8.4.3.1. First, a reduction is performed. The reduced process representations are transformed into an ontology which is called the refinement ontology.

Sect. 8.4.3.2 shows how the process refinement is validated by using reasoning services applied to the refinement ontology. The refinement is invalid if the reasoner detects a contradiction, i.e. the refinement ontology is inconsistent.

8.4.3.1 Refinement Representation in Ontologies

This section describes the representation of the pre- and post-refined process as well as the refinement relations that are given by the hori and vert-functions in a refinement ontology.

Refinement Reduction

In order to capture horizontal and vertical refinements in a refinement ontology and validate the refinement, two kinds of refinement reductions are applied in a precomputation step.

- Parallel gateways are eliminated and replaced by exclusive gateways.
- The execution sets are reduced to finite sets of predecessors and successors.

Parallel branches describe implicitly all possible executions. The ordering of activities of different parallel branches is not explicitly defined, i.e. there are multiple allowed executions. Therefore, all parallel gateways are replaced by exclusive gateways that explicitly define all possible executions. The reduced process model of P is called the *Execution Diagram ED_P*. The execution set is built based on the execution diagram ED_P.

The second step is the reduction of the execution sets to predecessor and successor sets. If there are loops in a process model, the execution set might be infinite, whereas the predecessor and successor sets are finite.

Given a process P, the execution set ES_P is the set of all routes between the start and end activity in the reduced process model (execution diagram) (ED_P). The predecessor and successor sets are created as follows. For each activity a in ED_P, its *Predecessor Set $PS_P(a)$* is the set of all activities going to a through a direct link or a sequence containing only gateways. The *Successor Set $SS_P(a)$* is the set of all the activities going from a through a direct link or a sequence containing only gateways.

Obviously, according to the definition, for each x, y such that $x \in PS_P(a_j)$, $y \in SS_P(a_j)$, $[x, a_j, y]$ is a valid sub-path of activities in ED_P and thus $[x, a, y]$ is a valid sub-path of activities in P. Because the ED_P is finite, $PS_P(a_j)$ and $SS_P(a_j)$ are also finite for any $a_j \in P$.

By obtaining these two sets for all the activities, the relation between two execution sets can be characterised by the following property:

$$ES_Q \subseteq ES_P \; iff \; \forall a \in Q, \; PS_Q(a) \subseteq PS_P(a) \; and \; SS_Q(a) \subseteq SS_P(a). \qquad (8.1)$$

Hence, the comparison of the possibly infinite execution sets of the pre- and post-refined process (P, Q) is reduced to a comparison of the finite predecessor and successor sets of all activities.

Refinement Representation

Activities are represented as concepts, predecessor and successor relations by the roles *from* and *to*, the horizontal refinement (hori-function) by the role *compose* and the vertical refinement (vert-function) by the role *groundedTo*.

The following operators for the translation to an ontology are defined in order to validate the pre- and post-refined process in one ontology. S indicates a set of activities which is either the set of predecessors (from-operator) or the set of successors (to-operator) of an activity.

Definition 8.1. :

Pre-refinement-from operator $\mathbf{Pr}_{from}(S) = \forall from. \bigsqcup_{x \in S} x$

Pre-refinement-to operator $\mathbf{Pr}_{to}(S) = \forall to. \bigsqcup_{y \in S} y$

Post-refinement-from operator $\mathbf{Ps}_{from}(S) = \bigsqcap_{x \in S} \exists from.x$

Post-refinement-to operator $\mathbf{Ps}_{to}(S) = \bigsqcap_{y \in S} \exists to.y$

These operators are used to distinguish between the predecessor (*from*) and successor (*to*) relations of the pre- and post-refined process models that are represented in one refinement ontology. The pre-refinement operators restrict the allowed predecessors and successors which is realised by the all-quantifiers of the *to* and *from* roles in the expressions. These predecessor and successor restrictions are imposed by the pre-refined process.

The post-refinement operators describe the existing *to* and *from* relations of the post-refined process, using existential quantifiers.

Horizontal Refinement

P is the pre-refined, Q the post-refined process and z an activity in P that is refined to activities z_j in Q. For each z we define the corresponding origin $component\_z \equiv \exists compose.z$. The simultaneous refinement of multiple activities can be done in a similar manner of single refinement.

The refinement ontology $\mathcal{O}_{P \to Q}$ is defined by the following axioms:

1. for each activity a of Q and $hori(a) = z$: $a \sqsubseteq \exists compose.z$
   This axiom realises the **Renaming**, i.e. activity a is renamed to z.

2. for each $a \in Q$ and a is not refined from any z:
   $a \sqsubseteq \mathbf{Pr}_{from}(PS_P(a))[z \rightarrow component\_z]$,
   $a \sqsubseteq \mathbf{Pr}_{to}(SS_P(a))[z \rightarrow component\_z]$
   These axioms represent the predecessor and successor sets of all unrefined activities. In these sets, all activities z that are refined in the refinement from P
   to Q are replaced by $component\_z$ which represents the renaming of refined
   activities in all predecessor and successor sets of Q.

3. for each $z \in P$,
   $component\_z \sqsubseteq \mathbf{Pr}_{from}(PS_P(z) \cup \{component\_z\})[z \rightarrow component\_z]$,
   $component\_z \sqsubseteq \mathbf{Pr}_{to}(SS_P(z) \cup \{component\_z\})[z \rightarrow component\_z]$
   These axioms represent the predecessor and successor sets of all refined activities in the pre-refined process. Due to the mechanism of **Decomposing**, we
   add the corresponding $component\_z$ to their predecessor and successor sets and
   replace the activity z by the class $component\_z$.

4. for each $a \in Q, a \sqsubseteq \mathbf{Ps}_{from}(PS_Q(a))$ and $a \sqsubseteq \mathbf{Ps}_{to}(SS_Q(a))$,

   These axioms represent the predecessor and successor sets of all the activities
   in the post-refinement process.

5. for each $z \in P, Disjoint(a|a \in Q$ and $hori(a) = z)$

   These axioms represent the uniqueness of all the sibling activities refined from
   the same z.

6. *Disjoint*(all the activity in P, and all the *component_z*).

   This axiom represents the uniqueness of all the activities before refinement.

With above axioms, ontology $\mathscr{O}_{P \rightarrow Q}$ is a representation of the horizontal refinement
from P to Q by describing the predecessor and successor sets of corresponding
activities with axioms.

Vertical Refinement

Similar to the horizontal refinement, a model P is refined to a more specific process
Q. Any activity in Q can be grounded to some activity in P. Thus, after reduction,
for all activities $a \in Q$, there is an activity $b \in P$ and the activity a is grounded to
b. Therefore, for each activity $x \in P$, the axiom $grounded\_x \equiv \exists groundedTo.x$ is
defined. The refinement ontology $\mathscr{O}_{P \rightarrow Q}$ is constructed with the following axioms:

1. for each activity $a \in Q$ and $vert(a) = x, a \sqsubseteq \exists groundedTo.x$

   These axioms represent the grounding of activities by concept subsumptions,
   which realise the **Renaming** in vertical refinement.

2. for each $a \in P$

   $grounded\_a \sqsubseteq \mathbf{Pr}_{from}(PS_P(a))[x \rightarrow grounded\_x]$,

   $grounded\_a \sqsubseteq \mathbf{Pr}_{to}(SS_P(a))[x \rightarrow grounded\_x]$

   These axioms represent the predecessor and successor sets of all the activities in the pre-refinement process. Due the mechanism of **Renaming** all $x \in P$ are replaced by $grounded\_x$

3. for each $a \in Q$, $a \sqsubseteq \mathbf{Ps}_{from}(PS_Q(a))$ and $a \sqsubseteq \mathbf{Ps}_{to}(SS_Q(a))$

   These axioms represent the predecessor and successor sets of all the activities in the post-refinement process. Ungrounded activities have been removed from the process.

4. for each $x \in P$, $Disjoint(a|a \in Q$ and $vert(a) = x)$

   These axioms represent the uniqueness of all the sibling activities refined from the same activity x.

5. $Disjoint(\text{all the } grounded\_x)$.

   This axiom represents the uniqueness of all the activities before refinement.

8.4.3.2 Reasoning for Consistency Check

This section outlines the reasoning services that are applied on the refinement ontology to validate the refinements, i.e. to check whether it is a valid or an invalid refinement. The ontology is created according to the operators defined in the previous subsection. Refinement checking was already reduced to checking of subset relations between predecessor and successor sets of the pre- and post-refined process. This in turn can be reduced to an ontological satisfiability problem, as indicated by the following theorem. A proof can be found in [12].

Theorem 8.1. $PS_Q(a) \subseteq PS_P(a)$ iff
$Disjoint(x|x \in P \cup Q)$ infers that $\mathbf{Pr}_{from}(PS_P(a)) \sqcap \mathbf{Ps}_{from}(PS_Q(a))$ is satisfiable.

$SS_Q(a) \subseteq SS_P(a)$ iff
$Disjoint(x|x \in P \cup Q)$ infers that $\mathbf{Pr}_{to}(SS_P(a)) \sqcap \mathbf{Ps}_{to}(SS_Q(a))$ is satisfiable.

Based on this theorem, validation of a process refinement is reduced to satisfiability checking of the refinement ontology. The next step is to indicate invalid refined activities in an invalid refinement ontology. This is characterised by the following theorem.

Theorem 8.2. *A route that contains activity a in Q is invalid in the refinement from P to Q, iff $\mathcal{O}_{P \rightarrow Q} \models a \sqsubseteq \bot$.*

This theorem has two implications:

1. The validity of a refinement can be checked by the satisfiability of all the name concepts in an ontology;

2. The activities represented by unsatisfiable concepts in the ontology are the source of the invalid refinement.

8.4.3.3 Conclusion of Consistency Guidance

The pre- and post-refined processes are represented in a refinement ontology according to the execution set semantics. Reasoning services are applied to the refinement ontology in order to validate the refinement. The benefit of the reasoning service is twofold. First, consistency checking of the refinement ontology indicates whether it is a valid or invalid refinement (Theorem 8.1). Second, an activity that is represented by an unsatisfiable class in the refinement ontology indicates an invalid refinement of this activity from process P to process Q (Theorem 8.2).

8.4.4 Process Guidance

This section describes the Process Guidance. It presents details how to formalise and infer the knowledge about development tasks. The solution presented here can, of course, be used to guide through business process refinement, but it is general enough for other kinds of process descriptions as well. We show that the relations between modelling tasks and objects can be represented by an ontology. We also show that with such ontological representation, the tasks can be automatically inferred.

8.4.4.1 Guidance in Modelling Systems

We first introduce some important notions and knowledge assets for process guidance in general. Then we illustrate them with process modelling and refinement.

Concepts and Knowledge Assets of a Modelling Scenario

There are several important notions in modelling procedures, such as artefact, task, role, etc. Here we are mostly interested in capturing the semantics of the following notions:

1. **Tasks** of different types can be performed in a particular modelling environment, such as create a model, remodel a model, refine a model, etc.

2. **Pre- and Post- Conditions** describe the prerequisites and effects of tasks of certain types. In legacy systems, they are usually described in natural languages. For example, the post-condition of creating a model is that a model is created.

3. **Artefacts** are the various entities that can be input or output by the modelling environment.

The relations between tasks, conditions and artefacts are also interesting. Generally speaking, the status of artefacts satisfy some pre-conditions, thus enable corresponding tasks. When a task is performed, its post-conditions will result in changes of arte-facts. Although trust and security issues such as access control are also important in guidance systems, our major concern here shall be the pro-active identification of tasks.

As previously mentioned, the process guidance functionality is independent from concrete modelling scenarios. For a specific application the following knowledge assets have to be considered:

1. **Domain Meta-model** defines the syntax of the models and global constraints that are independent from concrete task types. Because in the modelling sys-tems concrete models are regarded as model instances, the meta-model actually corresponds to TBox in an ontology.

2. **Model Knowledge** is the concrete status of the models under development. In contrast to the meta-model, models correspond to the ABox of an ontology. Given the fact that models will be constantly changed during the development procedure, the ABox will also be frequently updated.

3. **Task Knowledge** characterises the pre-/post-conditions of specific task types. This knowledge is the interaction between artefacts and task types, therefore they can not be solely defined in the meta-model. The proper interpretation of task knowledge and its integration with meta-model/model is the major chal-lenge of an ontology-guided modelling system.

4. **Queries** are used to retrieve tasks and artefacts. They should be designed in a way that they are as independent from concrete domains as possible.

In the next subsection, we use process modelling and refinement as an example to introduce the above notions in detail. Our focus will be knowledge about various task types.

Process Modelling and Refinement

Processes are important types of models in software development. They are gener-alised representations of control flow, data flow, etc. The results of a development are usually produced and utilised through a process. Therefore the modelling of processes is crucial for the planning and organisation of development.

In MDSD, processes are usually designed step by step on different levels of ab-straction. This creates a refinement chain of the process models. In Sect. 8.4.3, an ontological solution for validating BPMN process refinement is presented.

The artefacts in this example include, among others, *Process*, *Activity*, *Component Behavior Model*, etc. The meta-model includes constraints such as "A process con-tains only activities (including start and end) and gateways". The task types include *Remodel Process*, *Refine Process*, *Ground Process*, etc. Knowledge about some typical tasks and their pre- and post-conditions can be described in natural language as follows:

1. **Remodel Process**: an engineer can always remodel an existing process.

   Pre-condition: a process exists.

   Post-condition: the process is remodelled.

2. **Refine Process**: when a process is neither refined nor grounded, the process needs to be refined by another process.

   Pre-condition: a process neither refined nor grounded exists.

   Post-condition: another process is created or referred to as the refinement of the current process.

3. **Ground Process**: any process that can be refined can also be grounded to a component behavior model.

   Pre-condition: a process neither refined nor grounded exists.

   Post-condition: a component behavior model is created or referred to as the grounding of the current process.

When a user is modelling processes, the system should automatically tell which task is available for which artefact. When the user performs a task and hence changes the models, task availability should also be updated accordingly.

8.4.4.2 Task Representation and Retrieval via Ontologies

Pre- and postconditions of a task described in natural language are not sufficient to provide automated guidance. A machine-readable specification is needed, which requires representation in a formal language. Here we use an ontology to represent the knowledge. Then, the challenges become:

- Formalisation of the task knowledge by ontologies
- Reduction of task retrieval to ontology reasoning problems

We will illustrate the solution with the process modelling and refinement example. Afterwards, however, we will generalise the solution to provide a generic approach and then discuss the computational aspects.

Formalising Guidance Knowledge into Ontologies

The knowledge employed for process guidance can be divided into domain knowledge and task knowledge. Both is formalised in an ontology.

Domain Ontology: Meta-model and Model

Intuitively, various artefacts can be categorised into concepts such as *Process*, *Activity*, *ComponentBehaviorModel*, etc. These concepts have a common super concept *Artefact*. The relations between these concepts are modelled as object properties. The concrete modelling entities will be instances. We call such an ontology the domain ontology. Its TBox (ABox) corresponds to the meta-model (models) of the domain. As we will show, the domain ontology has little influence on the inference mechanism of tasks, so we can regard them as separate.

Task Ontology

Various tasks can be categorised into concepts such as *RefineProcess*, *GroundProcess*, etc. These task types have a common super type *Task*. Once a task is performed, the Task ontology's ABox will be updated.

The pre-conditions of a task type can be described by axioms. For example, when a process is **NOT** refined or grounded, it should be refined or grounded. This actually implies that, **EVERY** process should be refined or grounded, to either an existing process/component behavior model, or an implicit one. The former implies that a **Refine Process** or **Ground Process** task has already been performed. The latter implies that a **Refine Process** or **Ground Process** task has to be performed. Therefore, the existence of a process actually becomes the pre-condition of a **Refine Process** or **Ground Process** task.

However, the disjunction implies that, neither **Refine Process** nor **Ground Process** is really **compulsory** for processes, but **Refine or Ground Process** is. We call these two *Alternative Tasks*. If we query for one of a set of alternative tasks, the ontology will not infer its necessity. We have to query for all of them. To solve this problem, we introduce a new task type *RefineOrGroundProcess* as the super concept of both *RefineProcess* and *GroundProcess*. Of course, *RefineOrGroundProcess* will also be a sub-concept of *Task*. We can model such semantics with an axiom in Manchester Syntax [8] as follows:

SubClassOf : Process, preconditionOf some RefineOrGroundProcess

Once a task of *RefineOrGroundProcess* is found to be needed, we shall generate two tasks *RefineProcess* and *GroundProcess* to be displayed for the user. This means *RefineOrGroundProcess* will not have direct instances. Once a *RefineProcess* or *GroundProcess* task is performed on an artefact, a *RefineOrGroundProcess* is regarded as performed because an instance of *RefineProcess* or *GroundProcess* is also an instance of *RefineOrGroundProcess*.

Regarding post-conditions, the effect of the task is the creation of another process or component behavior model. Thus, the existence of such a process or component behavior model actually becomes the post-condition of the task that is either performed or to be performed. Because *RefineOrGroundProcess* is an "abstract" task type, we only model the postcondition for *RefineProcess* and *GroundProcess*:

$$SubClassOf: \ RefineProcess, \ hasPostcondition \ some \ Process$$

$$SubClassOf: \ GroundProcess, \ hasPostcondition \ some \ ComponentBehaviorModel$$

Similarly, we will have **Remodel Process:**

$$SubClassOf: \ Process, \ preconditionOf \ some \ RemodelProcess$$

$$SubClassOf: \ RemodelProcess, \ hasPostcondition \ some \ Process$$

From these axioms, we can generalise the formalisation patterns as:

$$SubClassOf: \ [Artefact], \ preconditionOf \ some \ [Task]$$

$$SubClassOf: \ [Task], \ hasPostcondition \ some \ [Artefact]$$

where *Task* is a concrete type of task (or the super type of alternatives), *Artefact* is a concrete type of artefact. Obviously, one artefact type can be pre-condition of multiple task types. As we can see, these two patterns are independent from concrete task types, and even concrete domains. This implies that we can also design generic patterns to retrieve tasks regardless of which type or domain it is.

Retrieving Tasks by Query Answering

Once we generate the domain ontology and task ontology by the axioms presented in the previous section, we can use a reasoner to automatically retrieve the tasks. Intuitively, this can be performed by querying the artefacts on which certain task types should or could be performed. For example, if we pose the following query:

$$?x \leftarrow ?x : Artefact, (?x, ?y) : preconditionOf, ?y : RemodelProcess$$

to a query engine, it will return all artefacts $?x$ such that there exists some instance of *RemodelProcess* $?y$ of which $?x$ is the pre-condition. This literally presents all the processes that can be remodelled.

However, this query can not yet be generalised to other task types. For example, if we use the similar query for *RefineOrGroundProcess* task, the results will include the processes that have already been refined or grounded. These redundancies are due to the fact that there are actually two categories of tasks:

1. **Compulsory Task**: a task that must be performed. Once performed, it is not necessary to perform it again. Task types such as **Refine Process** and **Ground Process** belong to this category.

2. **Optional Task**: a task that could be performed. Once performed, it can still be performed again. Task types such as **Remodel Process** belong to this category.

Optional tasks can use the similar query pattern presented above. The presented compulsory tasks should only contain tasks that have not been performed yet, i.e. the **implicit** instances of tasks. They can be obtained by subtracting the performed ones from the whole set. Taking $RefineOrGroundProcess$ as an example, we pose the following two queries:

$$?x \leftarrow ?x : Artefact, (?x, ?y) : preconditionOf, ?y : RefineOrGroundProcess$$

$$?x, ?y \leftarrow ?x : Artefact, (?x, ?y) : preconditionOf, ?y : RefineOrGroundProcess$$

in which the first query returns all the processes that should be refined or grounded, the second query returns all the processes that have been refined or grounded, together with the corresponding tasks. The difference of the two will be the processes on which $RefineOrGroundProcess$ must be performed. Therefore the redundancy of compulsory tasks is resolved.

In order to distinguish the compulsory tasks and the optional tasks we introduce two concepts $CompulsoryTask$ and $OptionalConcept$ as the sub-concepts of $Task$ and super-concepts of all the compulsory tasks and optional tasks, respectively. Then the query can be generalised as follows:

1. for each direct sub-concept T of $OptionalTask$, pose query

$$?x \leftarrow ?x : Artefact, (?x, ?y) : hasOptionalTask, ?y : T$$

   The solution will be the artefacts on which task type T could be performed.

2. for each direct sub-concept T of $CompulsoryTask$, pose two queries

$$?x \leftarrow ?x : Artefact, (?x, ?y) : hasCompulsoryTask, ?y : T$$

$$?x, ?y \leftarrow ?x : Artefact, (?x, ?y) : hasCompulsoryTask, ?y : T$$

   The difference of solution $?x$ will be the artefacts on which task type T should be performed. Note that individual alternative concepts will not be tested, but their common super concept will be. Due to the introduction of common super-concepts for alternative concepts, T needs to be translated before presented to user.

Generalised Solution for Representation and Retrieval

Now we summarise the above findings to provide a generalised solution:

- Defining the domain ontology.
- For alternative tasks, introducing common super task type.
- Categorising compulsory and optional tasks.
- For each type of compulsory task, posing two queries and getting the difference to retrieve the artefacts to which such type of task is necessary.
- For each type of optional task, posing one query to retrieve the artefacts on which such type of task can be performed.
- Translating the query results to generate the task list.
- Updating the ABox with the relations of artefacts and tasks such that compulsory tasks will not be repeated.

As we can see, the above solution is independent from the concrete task types and even application scenarios, thus it can be generalised. Actually, when applied to different domains, the system only needs to load the Domain Ontology and Task Ontology, then generates queries on the available task types.

Computational Properties

We first review the language needed. There are two major types of axioms: one for pre-conditions and the other for post-conditions. They are both within the expressive power of OWL 2 EL, especially considering that disjunction of task types must be resolved.

The reasoning services requested include both TBox classification and conjunctive query answering. In order to present a generic solution for guidance, it is necessary to automatically detect all the concrete compulsory task types and optional task types instead of hard-coding them into queries. This can be easily realised by getting all the direct-subconcepts of *CompulsoryTask* and *OptionalTask*, which is a service provided by TBox classification.

When processing the queries, especially the first query of compulsory task and the query of optional task, it is important to notice that the variable $?y$ is not returned. This implies that $?y$ is a non-distinguished variable, which can be bound to either an existing individual, or an implicit individual. In terms of ontology reasoning, this arises the requirement of query answering under Open World Assumption. Query answering with non-distinguished variables is an open issue for expressive DLs. And it is even proved that query answering in arbitrary EL+ ontology is already undecidable [10]. However, we restrict the task ontology to be regular, for which a query answering algorithm and an implementation have already been developed [16]. Also, in the current example the query can be rewritten into a instance retrieval of, e.g. *preconditionOf someRemodelProcess*.

8.4.5 Integrated Guidance

In the previous subsections we introduced the ontological solutions how to perform consistency guidance and process guidance. However, for this guidance to be useful for the modellers it has to be integrated into a modelling environment. This subsection aims at providing more details on how both kinds of guidance can be combined into a single solution integrated in such an environment. First, in Sect. 8.4.5.1 an explanation is given how the consistency guidance complements the process guidance within the guidance engine. Then Sect. 8.4.5.2 summarises the design considerations regarding the ontology-based guidance support within a modelling environment.

In Sect. 8.4.4 it was stated that the principles of process guidance are general enough to be used beyond BPMN refinement. The same holds for the actual tool implementation. While we talk about process refinement in this section, the presented solutions can easily be adapted to other fields.

8.4.5.1 The Guidance Engine

The Guidance Engine is a central component which provides ontology-based guidance support for a modelling environment. The primary role of the guidance engine is to compute the tasks which need to be performed in the BPMN refinement process based on the current state of business process models and tasks that have already been performed (existing tasks). In order to achieve this objective, the guidance engine has to communicate with different information providers. On the one side, the guidance engine gathers the artefact information i.e. models and their respective metamodel from the modelling environment. On the other side, the guidance engine relies on the semantic reasoner for the consistency checking and computation and inferring of the tasks. Fig. 8.7 illustrates how the guidance engine computes the tasks by collaborating with both the modelling environment and the semantic reasoner. The focus is on the information flow that takes place during the computation of tasks within the modelling environment.

Before we explain how the guidance engine performs at run time, it is important to note that the guidance engine needs to be configured at design time for a specific development process. By configuration we mean the definition of the particular task ontology (or process-guidance ontology) together with a set of predefined queries. This specific task ontology contains knowledge about the tasks, their preconditions and postconditions and how they are related to the modelling artefacts (see Sect. 8.4.4 for an explanation of the task ontology for business process refinement).

The computation of the tasks, which happens at runtime in the guidance engine, can be divided into six major steps.

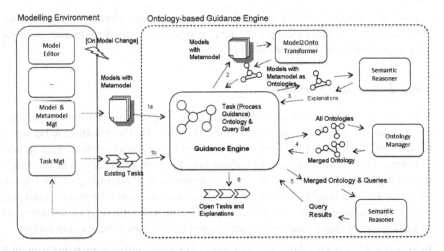

Fig. 8.7: Integrated guidance

1. **Get Current Process State**. In this step, all needed information about the current state of the development process is retrieved from the (modelling) environment. This information is crucial for building the knowledge base for further processing. This includes getting the following elements:

   - *Models*. Models represent the current state of the development process. In our case, they build up the current state of business process model refinement. The guidance engine requests from the modelling environment all models based on particular metamodels which are referenced in the guidance ontology. The corresponding metamodel is retrieved only once, since the metamodel information do not change at run time.

   - *Existing Tasks*. Existing tasks, if there are any, are retrieved from the task management component of the modelling environment, to infer the knowledge about already accomplished tasks.

2. **Convert Models to Ontologies**. The guidance engine is based on semantic technology. In order to enable reasoning, model information needs to be converted into an ontology. For that purpose, the so-called model-2-ontology transformer is used. The transformation itself is based on the two following basic rules:

   - The metamodel is transformed into the ontology TBox, thus representing the type information of the domain ontology

   - The models become the ontology ABox, thus acting as an instance data.

3. **Check Model Ontologies for Consistency**. Once the ontological representation of the models is available the consistency check can be performed. For that purpose the guidance engine relies on a dedicated semantic model validation

component (see Sect. 8.4.3). The consistency check is executed for all models. By doing so, for all valid models an additional axiom is added to the ontology stating that the particular model is a *correct model*. Contrary, for all invalid models the explanation information is collected and no axiom is created.

4. **Merge Ontologies**. In this step, the guidance engine contains all necessary information, yet spread across several ontologies. Thus, this step makes sure that the complete knowledge base is merged into a single ontology which can be given to the reasoner. The result is the unified ontology consisting of the domain ontology (model and metamodel information) which is enriched by the consistency information, and the task ontology.

5. **Compute Process Guidance Tasks**. Having the merged ontology on the one side and the predefined queries for inferring the guidance tasks on the other side, the computation can be performed. The query result retrieved from the semantic reasoner contains all possible tasks which can be done based on the current state of the models. In addition, the guidance engine needs to compute the difference between all possible tasks and the existing (already performed) tasks programmatically in order to show to the user only the current open tasks.

6. **Translate Results back to Models and Tasks**. In the final step, the guidance engine translates the results into a format that the modelling environment can deal with, so they can be displayed to the user.

8.4.5.2 Tool Support for Guidance in Modelling

The modelling of business processes and especially the modelling of process refinements is a complex step which requires the expertise of several people within an organisation and can only be accomplished through collaboration and the adequate tool support. Business process modelling tools offer solid support for modelling activities but more advanced support for consistency and process guidance during modelling is rather a rare feature. For that reason, we developed an ontology-based guidance engine as an independent component and integrated it into the prototype BPMN modelling tool developed based on the ADOxx platform.

The ADOxx is an environment which is used to develop modelling tools such as *ADONIS* [9]. It consists of the platform kernel and the extensible set of mechanisms. Whereas the kernel provides core features such as the metamodel library and the model repository, platform mechanisms represent reusable functionalities such as graphical and tabular modelling editors, model comparison, and import/export facilities, which can be combined to build an arbitrary modelling tool. Each ADOxx-based modelling tool contains a product-specific metamodel, and a set of mechanisms together with their configuration. New components can be developed and integrated into the product.

The ADOxx-based prototype BPMN modelling tool has been built as shown in Fig. 8.8. The BPMN metamodel forms the basis for storing the BPMN models in the ADOxx model repository and for editing them in the ADOxx model editors. On the business layer, the guidance engine component has been integrated into the product.

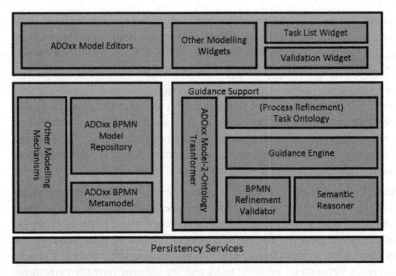

Fig. 8.8: The design of the ADOxx-based BPMN tool with guidance support

Together with the guidance engine, the semantic reasoner, model-2-ontology trans-former and the BPMN refinement library (refinement consistency checker) have been included. On the UI layer, the standard ADOxx task management widget has been included for showing the status of the tasks from the guidance engine, and the validation results widget which shows the explanations results based on consistency guidance. Fig. 8.9 shows a screenshot of the prototype of the ADOxx-based BPMN tool enriched by the guidance support.

8.5 Evaluation

The consistency guidance approach has been evaluated in terms of efficiency. This section gives a summary of the results, which were originally published in [12]. Us-ing a generator, about 200 correct and 1000 incorrect refinements have been created. With the generated scenarios a refinement analysis was performed on a laptop with a 2 GHz dual core CPU, 2 GB of RAM using Java v1.6 and Pellet 2.0.0. The analysis consisted of two parts.

1. **Transformation to OWL-DL** The refinements were transformed into an OWL-DL representation, as described in Sect. 8.4.3.1. It turned out that the size of the OWL-DL knowledge base was relatively small. For 80% of the scenarios there were less than 220 axioms, for 90% of the scenarios there were less than 400 axioms.

2. **OWL-DL reasoning** The theoretical complexity of OWL-DL reasoning is ex-ponential. However, the evaluation showed that for practical cases reasoning

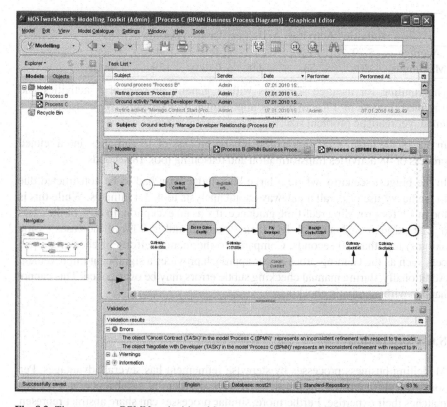

Fig. 8.9: The prototype BPMN tool with guidance support based on ADOxx

time grows less than exponentially compared to the number of axioms. Fig. 8.10 shows the reasoning times for the different scenarios, divided into valid refinements (consistent) and invalid refinements (partly inconsistent). Reasoning took most of the analysis time, about two orders of magnitude more than the transformation.

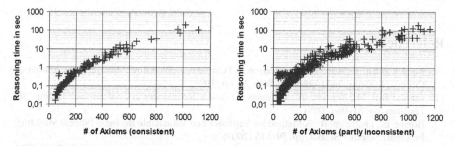

Fig. 8.10: Reasoning time for axioms on a logarithmic scale

	Generic Activities	Specific Activities	Total Activities	Trans. Time	OWL-DL Axioms	Reasoning Time
Average	5.79	17.4	23.2	4ms	154	2.8s
Maximum	30	53	69	0.4s	1159	3.4min

The runtime for average scenarios with a generic process of 6 activities and a refined process of 17 activities is approximately 3 seconds. We consider this a small, yet realistic problem size.

In one of the larger scenarios with a generic process of 15 activities and a refined process of 48 activities transformation and reasoning took 18 seconds.

In the biggest scenario, where a large knowledge base had to be constructed due to the heavy use of parallel gateways, total analysis took 3.4 minutes. While this is too much for providing real-time guidance, it was an exception. In 80% of the cases ($\leq$220 axioms) analysis took less than 1 second, and in 90% of the cases ($\leq$400 axioms) less than 10 seconds. Compared to the manual efforts of checking a process such as the Gaming process, our approach provides a significant improvement. Additionally, during manual checking subtle errors may be overlooked. This cannot happen with automatic checking.

8.6 Conclusion

Modelling business processes by stepwise refinement has several advantages. Persons with different responsibilities can work on them at an abstraction level that matches their expertise. Furthermore, similar processes can share abstract representations, which allows reuse. However, there is not one way to refine a process, there are usually many possibilities. Besides, great care has to be taken to avoid inconsistencies.

The guidance engine tackles these two problems. Embedded in a modelling tool it contains ontology driven solutions to detect inconsistencies in business process refinements and to propose refinement actions. We described the theoretical background of process refinement, explained how consistency guidance and process guidance can be implemented with ontologies and showed how both can be integrated into a modelling tool so that process modellers can easily use it.

References

1. van der Aalst, W.M.P.: The Application of Petri Nets to Workflow Management. Journal of Circuits, Systems, and Computers **8**(1), 21–66 (1998)
2. van der Bijl, M., Rensink, A., Tretmans, J.: Action Refinement in Conformance Testing. In: TestCom, pp. 81–96 (2005)
3. Börger, E., Thalheim, B.: A Method for Verifiable and Validatable Business Process Modeling. In: Lipari Summer School, pp. 59–115 (2007)
4. Diertens, B.: A Process Algebra Software Engineering Environment. CoRR **abs/0806.2730** (2008)

5. Glabbeek, R.J.v.: The Linear Time - Branching Time Spectrum II. In: CONCUR '93: Proceedings of the 4th International Conference on Concurrency Theory, pp. 66–81. Springer-Verlag (1993)

6. Gruber, T.R.: A translation approach to portable ontology specifications. Knowl. Acquis. **5**(2), 199–220 (1993). DOI http://dx.doi.org/10.1006/knac.1993.1008

7. Hommes, L.: The evaluation of business process modeling techniques. Ph.D. thesis, TU Delft (2004)

8. Horridge, M., Drummond, N., Goodwin, J., Rector, A.L., Stevens, R., Wang, H.: The Manchester OWL Syntax. In: B.C. Grau, P. Hitzler, C. Shankey, E. Wallace, B.C. Grau, P. Hitzler, C. Shankey, E. Wallace (eds.) OWLED, *CEUR Workshop Proceedings*, vol. 216. CEUR-WS.org (2006). URL http://dblp.uni-trier.de/rec/bibtex/conf/owled/HorridgeDGRSW06

9. Junginger, S., Kuehn, H., Strobl, R., Karagiannis, D.: Ein Geschäftsprozessmanagement-Werkzeug der nächsten Generation. Wirtschaftsinformatik **42**(5), 392–401 (2000)

10. Krötzsch, M., Rudolph, S., Hitzler, P.: Conjunctive Queries for a Tractable Fragment of OWL 1.1. In: ISWC/ASWC, pp. 310–323 (2007)

11. Lee, J., Wyner, G.M.: Defining specialization for dataflow diagrams. Inf. Syst. **28**(6), 651–671 (2003). DOI http://dx.doi.org/10.1016/S0306-4379(02)00044-3

12. Ren, Y., Gröner, G., Lemcke, J., Rahmani, T., Friesen, A., Zhao, Y., Pan, J.Z., Staab, S.: Validating Process Refinement with Ontologies. In: E.F. Kendall, J.Z. Pan, M. Sabbouh, L. Stojanovic, Y. Zhao (eds.) 5th International Workshop on Semantic Web Enabled Software Engineering (SWESE), *CEUR Workshop Proceedings*, vol. 524, pp. 1–15. CEUR-WS.org (2009). URL http://ceur-ws.org/Vol-524/swese2009_1.pdf

13. Rensink, A., Gorrieri, R.: Action Refinement as an Implementation Relation. In: In Bidoit & Dauchet, editors: Proceedings TAPSOFT '97: Theory and Practice of Software Development, LNCS 1214, pp. 772–786. Springer (1997)

14. Schwarz, H., Ebert, J., Lemcke, J., Rahmani, T., Zivkovic, S.: Using Expressive Traceability Relationships for Ensuring Consistent Process Model Refinement. In: Proceedings of the 15th IEEE International Conference on Engineering of Complex Computer Systems (2010). To appear

15. Wyner, G.M., Lee, J.: Defining Specialization for Process Models. In: Organizing Business Knowledge: The MIT Process Handbook, chap. 5, pp. 131–174. MIT Press (2003). URL http://ccs.mit.edu/papers/pdf/wp216.pdf

16. Zhao, Y., Pan, J.Z., Ren, Y.: Implementing and Evaluating A Rule-based Approach to Querying Regular EL+ Ontologies. In: In Proc. of the International Conference on Hybrid Intelligent Systems (HIS2009) (2009)

Chapter 9
Adaptive Service Binding with Lightweight Semantic Web Services

Carlos Pedrinaci, Dave Lambert, Maria Maleshkova, Dong Liu, John Domingue, and Reto Krummenacher

Abstract Adaptive service selection is acknowledged to provide a certain number of advantages to optimise the service provisioning process or to cater for advanced service brokering. Semantic Web Services, that is services that have been enriched with semantic annotations have often been used for providing adaptive service selection by deferring the binding of services until runtime. Thus far, however, research on Semantic Web Services has mainly been dominated by rich conceptual frameworks such as WSMO and OWL-S which require a significant effort towards the annotation of services and rely on complex reasoning for which there are no efficient solutions that can scale to the Web yet. In this chapter, inline with current trends on the Semantic Web that sacrifice expressivity in favour of performance, we present a novel approach to providing adaptive service selection that relies on simple conceptual models for services and less expressive formalisms for which there currently exist

Carlos Pedrinaci
Knowledge Media Institute, The Open University, Milton Keynes, UK
e-mail: c.pedrinaci@open.ac.uk

Dave Lambert
Knowledge Media Institute, The Open University, Milton Keynes, UK
e-mail: d.j.lambert@open.ac.uk

Maria Maleshkova
Knowledge Media Institute, The Open University, Milton Keynes, UK
e-mail: m.maleshkova@open.ac.uk

Dong Liu
Knowledge Media Institute, The Open University, Milton Keynes, UK
e-mail: d.liu.open.ac.uk

John Domingue
Knowledge Media Institute, The Open University, Milton Keynes, UK
e-mail: j.b.domingue@open.ac.uk

Reto Krummenacher
Semantic Technology Institute, University of Innsbruck, Austria
e-mail: reto.krummenacher@sti2.at

mature and performant implementations. In particular, we present a set of conceptual models defined in RDF(S) that support both Web services and Web APIs and we show how simple templates abstracting user requirements can be automatically transformed into SPARQL to enable service selection in a scalable manner.

9.1 Introduction

Web services provide means for encapsulating software functionality as remotely accessible components, independent of programming language and platform. Considerable effort has been devoted to defining architectures, developing communication middleware, and creating languages and process execution engines that can support the creation of complex distributed systems by seamlessly combining Web services. Service-oriented architectures (SOAs) advocate the development of solutions whereby service providers advertise the services they offer in a shared and publicly accessible repository. Software developers or intelligent applications can then access this repository in order to find suitable services for a given purpose and subsequently invoke them.

Web services have increasingly been used within and in some cases between enterprises. However, despite the essential advantages brought by service-oriented technologies, their use in enterprise settings is not without problems. For instance, the execution of business processes defined in this manner typically relies on rigid process models which interact with a fixed and predefined set of partner services. This rigidity impedes or at least complicates to a large extent very desirable features like the dynamic replacement of services based on their current state, the selection of those that better fit a certain context, etc. Conventional solutions to such problems are brute-force: for example, modifying the process models with somewhat artificial branches. This approach results in models that are more complex, and adapting as well as maintaining them in the light of changing conditions turns out to be a hard task [36]. These limitations are even more important in open environments like the Web, where additional difficulties appear such as the heterogeneity of data formats or the unreliability of servers. Recent trends indicate that other technologies, such as HTTP-based Web APIs, are preferred in these cases [11].

In this chapter we address the rigidity of business processes by providing adaptive service selection. This kind of technique, also known as late-binding, relies on deferring the selection and binding to the service to be executed until runtime so that up to date detailed information concerning the state of the business process and other contextual factors such as the previously monitored performance of services can help to adapt the selection to the (presumably) most optimal or appropriate solution. Adaptive service selection has often been based on exploiting semantic annotations of services. Research in this area has thus far been mainly driven by rich Semantic Web Services (SWS) conceptual models such as the Web Service Modeling Ontology (WSMO) [17] and OWL-S [29], which rely on expressive knowledge representation formalisms such as Web Service Modeling Language (WSML) [7] and OWL [35] complemented by some rule language. On the basis of these technologies, rich SWS can be defined on top of which refined service discovery algorithms and techniques can be implemented. However, creating these descriptions represents a significant knowledge acquisition bottleneck, and reasoning over them carries a considerable computational overhead that has limited the scalability of these approaches.

The issue of scalability is one that has always been central in the Semantic Web community, where recent practices, best exemplified by the linked data initiative [5], are disregarding expressivity in favour of performance and scalability. Considerable effort has gone into developing systems that can efficiently support storing, updating, and reasoning over RDFS [30] – a simple ontology representation language for the Web. Additionally, a standardised language and protocol for querying these repositories called SPARQL [38] has been devised which nowadays supports the systematic development of applications on top of large RDF(S) knowledge bases.

The work in this chapter has been conducted in the SOA4All project, an EU funded research programme which aims to harness the scalability of the Web, and to use lightweight Web technologies to begin an incremental approach to reaching its objective of 'enabling a Web of billions of services'. Based on the service portability scenario [REF Use Case Chapter] we present a novel approach to providing adaptive service selection based on lightweight semantic technologies, notably RDFS and SPARQL, so as to provide an efficient and scalable solution that can be applied on a Web scale. In particular, we provide adaptive service selection within workflows by defining processes based on service templates that specify abstract objectives rather than by directly naming concrete services. At runtime, service templates can be directly transformed into SPARQL queries that can be used to retrieve suitable services from existing repositories of service annotations informed by the current conditions and contextual knowledge which includes external information such as the location of a customer, monitoring data, and so forth.

The chapter is organised as follows. We first introduce the case study that is used to explain the technologies and methods described herein (Section 9.2). We then present background knowledge about Semantic Web Services and introduce related work in the area of service adaptability (Section 9.3). We then present our overall approach (Section 9.4) and cover each of the main technical aspects implementing it, including the formal model for describing services (Section 9.4.1), the kinds of service descriptions produced (Section 9.4.2), the service repository (Section 9.4.3), and service matchmaking techniques based on SPARQL (Section 9.4.4). Throughout, we illustrate our approach with examples based on the case study. Finally, in Section 9.5 we present our main conclusions and introduce lines for future research.

9.2 A Case Study in Added-Value Services and Service Portability

Chapter [REF Use case Chapter] defines a common use-case to be used throughout the book for illustration, clarity, and coherence purposes. The chapter identifies a number of scenarios and business goals that need to be tackled by mobile operators. In this chapter we focus on two of these business goals: the provisioning of added-value services (TELCO-BG-05), and supporting service-portability (TELCO-BG-04).

The first business goal—providing added-value services—is currently attracting more interest from telecom operators since they otherwise run the risk of becoming "dumb pipe providers" [11]. This business goal is largely aligned with current Web trends where Web APIs and RESTful services are increasingly being offered, and where an appropriate combination and integration of the data these services provide enables the provisioning of a wealth of useful low-cost added-value services. The second business goal is also related to existing trends, in this case on customers mobility, and on the fact that currently client terminals are increasingly powerful and can give access to all sorts of services offered by operators as well as openly on the Web. Both business goals come hand-in-hand as strategically important for telecom operators that aim to provide added-value services to give themselves a competitive advantage and additional revenues. Both business goals are at the core of a use-case lead by BT in SOA4All, and in general are strongly aligned with the overall goal pursued by the project which seeks to support the creation of a Web where billions of services are offered and consumed by billions of providers and customers [11].

Given that both business goals are highly generic, we use a more concrete scenario for illustration purposes. The reader should note, however, that the models, techniques and systems introduced in this chapter could be applied in a wide range of scenarios. The scenario that we have chosen is one where the Cell Phone Operator offers a simple added-value service for frequent travellers allowing them to receive timely notification of traffic reports, or delays in flights and trains so that they can rearrange their trip if necessary. This information is made available via subscription through SMS messages, or on demand using a Web-based interface.

Let us imagine a frequent traveller that has to spend a few days in Vienna to attend a meeting, and then returns to London. While in Vienna, she wants to be aware of the local traffic, so as to reach her various meetings across the city on time. The traffic reports are naturally location specific, so it is necessary to know the desired location for obtaining the reports which in turn determines which of the publicly available services is to be contacted. In this case, the selection of the service to invoke to obtain traffic information is based on the physical location of the phone and the Cell Phone Operator of Austria can directly deal with this request.

After a few days of meeting in Vienna she has to return to London. She therefore wants to know if the flight and tube line have any delays or planned disruptions. In this case the necessary information concerning her journey is stored within an online travel management system like TripIt.com that only authorised systems can access. In this specific case, the Cell Phone Operator she is using in Austria needs to redirect the invocation at the expense of a small roaming fee. Indeed the Cell Phone Operator wants to offer a service that is able to deal with a wide-range of locations (virtually anywhere) and it is of utmost importance that this service is available for the customers at anytime in a completely transparent manner.

Achieving these goals presents a number of technical requirements that are worth highlighting and are schematically depicted in Figure 9.1. First and foremost, offering access to such a wide-range of services offered by third parties requires a means for appropriately brokering services by dealing with data heterogeneity and supporting the selection of the most appropriate services to invoke given the location and kind of transportation used. This also highlights the need for supporting the use of diverse kinds of service technologies including WSDL but also Web APIS and RESTful ones offered directly via HTTP. Additionally, because of the need to have access to a very large amount of services it is not appropriate to embed the service selection within the process definition extensionally through a direct hard-wired inclusion of the service. Instead, an intensional definition using declarative statements regarding the suitability of services is a more appropriate solution. It is only through this manner that the process model for carrying out these activities can remain simple and that new information providers can easily be added or removed as the need arises or based on their current state, performance, etc. Finally, in order to support the portability of services it is necessary that Cell Phone Operators of remote countries can transparently redirect the request of customers of other operators or can directly deal with the request if no privately owned information is involved.

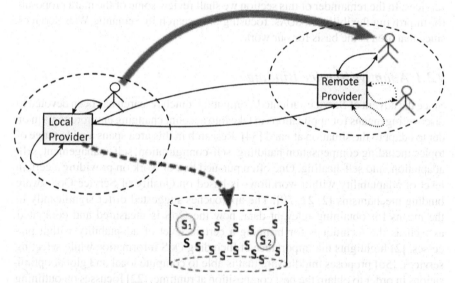

Fig. 9.1: Service portability through adaptive search
On the left is the Vienna locale, service provider, and our user. On the right, the users and providers in London. At the bottom is a service repository.

In the remainder of this chapter we describe how, by means of simple semantic annotations, it is possible to achieve these two business goals. For the sake of clarity and simplicity, we shall refer throughout the chapter to traffic report services that take as input a geographical location *location* and a human language identifier *lan-*

guage, and supply a textual summary in *language* of the traffic situation in *location*. Similarly, we shall use several ontologies to describe the services. These include the ontologies for standard parts of the semantic web, our framework, and domain specific vocabularies for traffic reporting. In particular, we use an ontology of human languages[1], and use a W3C ontology for discussing geographical location.

9.3 Background and Related Work

Web Services are software systems that offer their functionality over the Internet via platform and programming-language independent interfaces defined on the basis of a set of open standards such as WSDL, SOAP and further WS-* specifications [13]. Constructing distributed systems out of Web services is a matter of identifying suitable Web services and orchestrating them (through control and dataflow) in such a way that they achieve the desired goal. However, there exist situations, as faced in the case study that we address in this chapter, where the service to be used for execution within a concrete workflow depends on conditions that are knowable only at runtime (e.g., location of the requester), or where optimisations can be achieved by tracking certain aspects such as the overall performance exhibited by equivalent services. In the remainder of this section we shall review some of the main proposals for improving flexibility in SOAs, focusing on research in Semantic Web Services, since that area is the basis for our work.

9.3.1 Adaptive Service Binding

Since the advent of Service-Oriented Computing, much research has been devoted to discovering means for applications to take into account changing environments in order to adapt to the situation at hand [34]. Research in this area spans a wide range of topics including compensation handling, self-configuration, self-management, self-adaptation, and self-healing. One often pursued line of work on providing a certain level of adaptability within workflows is based on Quality of Service QoS aware binding mechanisms [2, 22, 50]. The approaches suggested differ significantly in the means for obtaining relevant data, how the QoS is measured and computed, as well as the techniques for bringing a certain level of adaptability within processes. [2] highlights the importance of including QoS information while selecting services. [50] proposes middleware that is able to compute local and global optimisations in order to obtain the best composition at runtime. [22] focusses on outlining how processes defined in BPEL can be enhanced with adaptive capabilities by combining it with Aspect-Oriented Programming.

The aforementioned approaches rely to a certain extent on well-known and controlled environments whereby the services that can be used are known in advance. A different point in the services space is characterised by the use of Semantic Web

---

[1] One such vocabulary is at http://www.lingvoj.org/lang/, but it does not quite fit our purpose. Since its use here is pedagogical, we take some liberties with respect to its actual content.

Services and related execution engines and machinery which aim to cater also for open environments like the Web where assumptions about data homogeneity or service availability for example cannot be made a priori. In this respect it is worth mentioning the work carried out in the METEOR-S project through the use of WSDL-S and the notion of service templates as a means to provide late-binding facilities [47]. This work is indeed closely related to ours in that we share the notion of a service template as a placeholder for describing intensionally a family of services that are suitable, and which must be retrieved and ranked at runtime. Similarly, work around WSMO [17] has proposed the use of goals within orchestrations thus allowing the process activities to be resolved and the best one invoked at runtime based on the functionality provide and other arbitrary concerns such as QoS, cost, or trust [19,32,33].

Finally, we consider context-aware systems. Although research in this field often concentrates on the distribution of sensors for gathering contextual information, its representation and processing mechanisms, their aim is to provide adaptive systems that can better tackle the situations at hand by being aware of the surrounding contextual conditions. Research in this area has therefore produced a number of architectures, conceptual models and approaches that are of particular relevance to our endeavour. The reader is referred to [4] for a survey on these matters and to [41] for a selection of methods, architectures and technologies bringing context-awareness to Web service technologies.

9.3.2 Semantic Web Services

Although service-oriented systems are highly appealing from an engineering perspective, developing them requires substantial manual effort to locate, interpret and integrate services. Consequently, Web services are mostly used within controlled environments such as large enterprises rather than on the (public) Web [11]. This is illustrated by the fact that currently there are only 28,000 Web services on the Web[2], whereas organisations like Verizon are estimated to have around 1,500 Web services deployed internally [11]. It has been argued that one possible reason for this lack of take up is that WS-* Web Services do not fully embrace the principles of the Web [11,48].

Recently, the world of Web services has changed significantly with the proliferation of Web APIS, also called RESTful services [39] when they conform to the REST architectural style [18]. This kind of service is characterised by simplicity (at least compared to WS-*) and is typically used in conjunction with Web 2.0 technologies and social networking applications. These services are usually described in natural language, on unstructured HTML pages. Attempts to introduce WSDL-style machine readable descriptions [20] have not been popular with developers. As a consequence, and despite their popularity, the development of Web applications that integrate disparate services in this manner suffers from a number of limitations similar to those we previously outlined for (standard) Web services with an increased complexity

---

[2] http://webservices.seekda.com/

due to the fact that most often no machine-processable description is available. Discovering services, handling heterogeneous data, and creating service compositions are largely manual, tedious tasks which result in the development of custom tailored solutions that use these services.

Semantic Web Services were proposed as an extension of Web services with semantic descriptions in order to provide formal declarative definitions of their interfaces, and what the services do [31]. The essential characteristic of SWS is therefore the use of knowledge representation languages with well-defined semantics, e.g., RDFS [30], OWL [35] and WSML [7] to name a few, that are amenable to automated reasoning. On the basis of these semantic descriptions, SWS technologies seek to increase the level of automation that can be achieved throughout the life-cycle of service-oriented applications which include the discovery and selection of services, their composition, their execution and their monitoring among others. Part of the research on SWS has been devoted precisely to identifying the requirements for SWS systems, and defining conceptual frameworks and architectures that cover the entire life-cycle of SWS [8, 12, 15, 17, 31, 33, 44].

The main approaches devised so far can roughly be divided into top-down and bottom-up. Top-down approaches to the development of semantic Web services like WSMO [17] and OWL-S [29] are based on the definition of high-level ontologies providing expressive frameworks for describing Web services. On the other hand, bottom-up models such as WSDL-S [1] and the Semantic Annotations for WSDL and XML Schema (SAWSDL) [14] adopt an incremental approach to adding semantics to existing Web services standards, adding to WSDL specific extensions that connect the syntactic definitions to their semantic annotations.

The landscape of Semantic Web Services is thus characterised by a number of conceptual models that, despite a few common characteristics, remain essentially incompatible due to the different representation languages and expressivity utilised as well as because of conceptual differences. For example, WSMO contains the notions of goal (to represent the client/user perspective) and mediator (to resolve heterogeneities), which have no equivalent in OWL-S. SAWSDL differs significantly from both OWL-S and WSMO, leaving aside the definition of processes and the provisioning of a high-level conceptual model, focusing instead of providing a minimal yet extensible syntactic extension on top of existing standards for describing Web services (WSDL) and their data model (XML Schema). Regardless of the concrete approach followed, the vast majority of the Semantic Web Services initiatives were based upon adding semantics to WSDL Web services. It is only recently that researchers have started focusing on Web APIs and RESTful services, the main examples being SA-REST [42] and MicroWSMO [28].

Service selection, also referred to as matching or matchmaking in several papers, has been a core research topic of the SWS community. The goal of service matchmaking is to, given a request for retrieving some *kind of* Web service, i.e., that is a family of services that meet certain criteria, identify all those Web service advertisements that match to a certain degree the request. Perhaps the best known matchmaker is Sycara et al.'s SEMANTIC MATCHMAKER [44]. It was one of several matchmakers proposed for OWL-S which matched requests according to input and output types [27, 45]. Each request's input and output types are compared pairwise with the corresponding inputs and outputs of a service description, with the comparisons resulting in per-variable matches named *exact* (the requested and offered types are the same), *plugin* (the offer is a subclass of the request), *subsumes* (the offer is a superclass of the request), and *fail* (there is no relationship). These matches are assigned numerical scores, and a service's degree of match to the original query is determined by the product of the scores for each variable.

In WSMO, the concept of a goal is used to specify problems from a client's perspective. The goals are defined using preconditions and effects, in the manner of planning operators, and through processing by heavyweight reasoners, they can be resolved with a service or orchestration of services. Examples of WSMO-based discovery engines are for instance IRS-III [12], Glue [46] or the template-based system described in [43]. The latter is quite relevant to the work presented here since it also uses the notion of templates although in this case the templates have to be structured in a hierarchy that can be exploited to speed up the search process, and therefore achieves performance improvements in controlled environments restricted to a particular domain where deep hierarchies can be defined.

Computing subsumption relations in a description logic is not a reliably fast operation, and working with the more abstract relation between goals and services is harder still. There have been some recent attempts to improve performance. The MX matchmaker treats OWL classes as keywords, trading subsumption for a vector-space similarity measure akin to information retrieval. Quality of matching is claimed to be as good as subsumption, while performing ten times faster [23].

Independently from the concrete conceptual framework used the aforementioned approaches rely on rich models that have significantly limited their uptake for two main reasons. First, they require considerable human labour for annotating the services. Secondly, these models being based on expressive knowledge representation formalisms, their complexity is such that reasoning over services descriptions is computationally demanding which in turn limits their scalability. The reader is referred to [7], [35], and [21] for details on the computational complexity of WSML, OWL, SWRL – the rule language often used in OWL-S descriptions – respectively).

In this chapter, as opposed to the research described above, we present a novel approach to providing adaptive service selection based on semantic annotations of services. The novelty lies on the use of lightweight semantic technologies which limit the expressivity of service annotations and hence the reduce the potential for carrying out highly complex service matching, in order to simplify the creation of these annotations for developers as well as to support their efficient and scalable manipulation.

9.4 Scalable Late-binding of Services based on Lightweight Semantic Annotations

In traditional workflows and business processes the execution relies on syntactically specified and rigid process models which interact with a fixed and predefined set of partner services. This rigidity impedes the provision of desirable features like the replacement of services based on their current state, the selection of those that better fit a certain context, etc. A typical approach is to modify the process models with artificial branches which exist only to work around implementation-level difficulties. Unfortunately with this approach, the resulting models are more complex, and maintaining or extending them to adapt to changing conditions becomes a harder task [36].

Our approach to this problem is based on the use of Semantic Web Services, that is of semantic annotations of services that support the application of automated machinery in order to reason about the functional and nonfunctional characteristics of services. In particular, we advocate that workflow definitions use service templates as internal activities instead of concrete and prefixed services whenever flexibility in service selection is desired. At runtime, these service templates can be bound to specific services selected on the basis of the existing conditions and informed by contextual knowledge which may include monitoring data, user location or other aspects that may affect which service is the most appropriate. Since service templates are described semantically, both the required functional and nonfunctional properties have clear semantics. This enhances the interpretation of services by humans, and more importantly, it allows service selection and data mismatches to be resolved at runtime, hence the term late-binding, as supported by Semantic Web Services middleware such as the so-called Semantic Execution Environments [16, 33].

Replacing services by service templates that define intensionally 'families of services' brings a number of benefits from a process execution perspective:

- Process models are relatively independent of the services used. If a particular service is not available the middleware can choose another functionally equivalent service without needing to change the process model. Similarly, and of particular relevance for the case study used within this chapter, should a service not be suitable due to the location of service client (e.g., the user is currently abroad), the middleware can automatically redirect the client request to the right service in a way that is completely transparent for the customer and that requires no adaptation of the client terminal (i.e., the mobile phone in our case).

- Process models are independent of the services' internal data model. The process model has its own semantically annotated data model. If the partner's data model differs from that, semantic models help to bridge the gap.

- Partner services can be selected based on business aspects. Nonfunctional information about cost, quality of service, trust and legal constraints to name a few, can be taken into account so that the selected service is the most suitable from a business perspective.

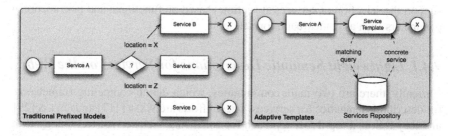

Fig. 9.2: Illustration of changes brought by our approach

The overall approach, depicted in Figure 9.2, therefore relies on the provisioning of semantic annotations for services and the corresponding storage and querying system, on the replacement of workflow activities by service templates, and on the adaptation of execution environments in order to take service templates into account and trigger the selection of appropriate services automatically. The research presented herein builds upon our previous experience [36] of using WSMO goals [17] for defining service templates within BPEL processes based on the BPEL4SWS extensions [32, 33]. The focus of this research, however, lies in an attempt to bring our technologies closer to the Web by:

• embracing current trends on services on the Web such as RESTful services and Web APIs;

• building upon existing Web standards and technologies to better support the uptake of these technologies in a Web-scale; and

• reducing the complexity of the semantic descriptions in order to support faster and more scalable service matchmaking while reducing the knowledge acquisition bottleneck faced when using rich Semantic Web Services descriptions such as WSMO [11].

In this chapter we will therefore present the technologies and methods used to achieve the goals above, leaving aside aspects such as the internals of Semantic Execution Environments, or negotiation steps [10] for the sake of clarity and space. The interested reader is referred to [16, 17, 32, 33, 36] for further details. In the remainder of this chapter we shall cover how we support the adaptive binding of services at runtime in a scalable manner by using service templates which can be automatically transformed into SPARQL queries that can interpreted by state of the art RDF stores to select suitable services efficiently. We first cover in Section 9.4.1 the formalisms used for describing services semantically using RDFS. We then show in Section 9.4.2 and Section 9.4.3 how one can use state of the art technologies from the Semantic Web to support the seamless publishing of services in a way that enables and simplifies their discovery by interested parties in a scalable manner. Finally, in Section 9.4.4 we introduce a model for describing service templates and we present a simple algorithm that can translate these into SPARQL queries to support the selection of services at runtime, based on functional and nonfunctional parameters such as contextual information.

9.4.1 Lightweight Semantic Descriptions for Services on the Web

Currently, there are two main communities, which define competing frameworks for describing semantics for services. These efforts are WSMO [17] and OWL-S [29], and they follow a top-down approach for enhancing Web service technology with semantics. In particular, they assume that the service semantic model and the actual service invocation and communication mechanisms are defined in parallel or jointly at design time. As a result, the description of a newly engineered service already comprises semantic information. Even though WSMO and OWL-S have been used in some application areas, this approach is not well suited to incrementally enhancing existing systems based on the service-oriented architecture, where thousands of WSDL-described services or Web APIs are already available on the Web or in intranets. Therefore, it is problematical to use these semantic frameworks to extend existing services.

To better address the problem of incremental or ad-hoc semantic annotation of services, we base our approach on WSMO-Lite [49], a minimal extension to SAWSDL. WSMO-Lite provides a means to create lightweight semantic service descriptions in RDFS [6] by annotating various WSDL elements in accordance with SAWSDL [14] annotation mechanism. In parallel, we use MicroWSMO [28] to annotate services that are not described in WSDL. MicroWSMO is a microformat-based language based on the same kinds of annotations as WSMO-Lite, adapted to support the annotation of HTML-based descriptions of Web APIs. Finally, we provide the minimal service model, a simple RDFS model that provides an overarching conceptual model able to capture the semantics for both Web services and Web APIs, thus allowing both kinds of services to be treated homogeneously when at selection time.

9.4.1.1 WSMO-Lite

To date, SAWSDL is the only Semantic Web Services specification that is a W3C Recommendation. It defines a set of extensions to WSDL, as well as rules for linking WSDL elements to semantic information. In particular, SAWSDL supports three kinds of annotations over WSDL and XML Schema, namely *modelReference, liftingSchemaMapping* and *loweringSchemaMapping*. These three annotation types enable links to be made from parts of a WSDL document to associated semantic elements, or to the specifications of data transformations from a syntactic representation to its semantic counterpart and vice versa. In this way, it enables the incremental addition of semantics on top of existing WSDL descriptions, providing a basis for extending results from a well-established approach. However, SAWSDL only provides simple means for connecting service elements to semantic entities and does not define any concrete service semantics such as types, formats or model for the semantic descriptions.

WSMO-Lite builds upon SAWSDL, overcoming some of SAWSDL's limitations while remaining lightweight. WSMO-Lite makes explicit the intended meaning for *modelReference* annotations without modifying SAWSDL but rather informing users on how they should structure the models their annotations point to. For instance, if the annotation is a functional categorisation, the URI the *modelReference* points to should be that of a sub-class of an instance of *wsl:FunctionalClassificationRoot* (see Listing 9.4)[3]. Similarly, should the *modelReference* point to the effect of a service, the URI should be that of an instance of *wsl:Effect*. The WSMO-Lite ontology can be used to capture four aspects of service semantics:

- The *Information Model* defines the data model. In particular, it describes the model for input and output messages and is represented by using a domain ontology, along with associated data lifting and lowering transformations.

- The *Functional Semantics* define what the service does by using functionality classification or preconditions and effects. It describes what the service can offer to its clients when it is invoked by assigning it to a particular class of service functionality, defined in a classification ontology.

- The *Behavioral Semantics* define the sequencing of operation invocations when invoking the service. The behaviour of a service can be described through a choreography or a workflow definition. However, behavioural semantics are not represented explicitly in WSMO-Lite.

- The *Nonfunctional Semantics* define any service-specific implementation or operational details such as service policies, implementation information or running environment requirements. Nonfunctional properties can include the price of a service or the Quality of Service (QoS) aspects such as performance and reliability. These are defined by using ontologies for nonfunctional properties, which should in this case be grounded on *wsl:NonFunctionalParameter*

9.4.1.2 MicroWSMO

In addition to the lightweight description of WSDL-based services, our approach supports also the adaptive use of Web APIs in business processes. MicroWSMO forms the basis for our work on semantically describing Web APIs. MicroWSMO uses microformats for adding semantic information on top of existing HTML Web API documentation, by relying on hRESTS (HTML for RESTful services) [26] for marking service properties and making the descriptions machine-processable. hRESTS provides a number of HTML classes that enable the marking of service operations, inputs and outputs, HTTP methods and labels, by inserting HTML tags within the HTML. It therefore enables, through simple injections of HTML code into Web pages, the transformation of unstructured HTML-based descriptions of Web APIs into structured services descriptions similar to those provided by WSDL.

---

[3] Throughout the chapter we assume a set of namespaces are declared for clarity and space reasons. The namespaces used can be found in the Appendix.

With the hRESTS structure in place, HTML service descriptions can be annotated further by including pointers to the semantics of the service, operations and data manipulated. Similarly to WSMO-Lite, MicroWSMO adopts the SAWSDL annotation mechanisms and uses three main types of link relations: 1) model, which can be used on any service property to point to appropriate semantic concepts identified by URIs; 2) lifting and 3) lowering, which associate messages with appropriate transformations (also identified by URIs) between the underlying technical format such as XML and a semantic knowledge representation format such as RDF. Therefore, MicroWSMO, based on hRESTS, enables the semantic annotation of Web APIs in the same way in which SAWSDL, based on WSDL, supports the annotation of Web services. MicroWSMO also adopts the WSMO-Lite ontology as the reference ontology for annotating Web APIs semantically. By doing so, both WSDL services and RESTful services, annotated with WSMO-Lite and MicroWSMO respectively, can be treated homogeneously.

9.4.1.3 Minimal Service Model

The Minimal Service Model, depicted in Figure9.3, provides a minimal and common conceptual model in RDFS for capturing the semantics of services may they be WSDL-based or Web APIs. It therefore provides the ground for treating them homogeneously when carrying out tasks such as the discovery of services. The Minimal Service Model given in Listing 9.4 builds upon a number of modules, including SAWSDL's syntactic properties, WSMO-Lite as a minimal extension to SAWSDL, and hRESTS's support for Web APIs. The Minimal Service Model defines services as having a number of *operations*, each of which have *input* and *output messages* and *faults*. Web APIs are supported through the addition of two hRESTS properties, including the *address* as a URI template, and the HTTP *method*. Finally, the Minimal Service Model is completed by the SAWSDL elements for linking semantic information through the *modelReference* and for providing lifting and lowering mechanisms.

The Minimal Service Model captures the essence of services in a way that can support service discovery, matchmaking and invocation by directly operating on the model properties. However, despite its simplicity, it is still broadly compatible with WSMO and OWL-S service models, as well as with services annotated according to WSMO-Lite and MicroWSMO principles. Although providing a formal mapping for each of these languages is out of the scope of this work, we note that the elements captured in the minimal service model are common to existing models, with the exception of the hRESTS extensions specific to RESTful services. Therefore, we base our approach for adaptive device discovery, described in the following sections, on this minimal service model.

9.4.2 Services and Annotations

In this section, we show the kinds of WSMO-Lite descriptions that might be available for the kinds of traffic report services we imagine in our use-case. In listings 9.1

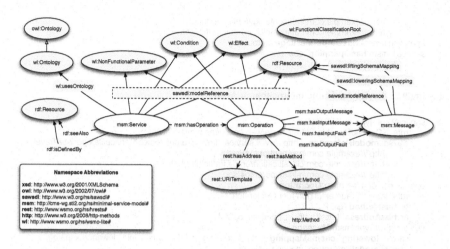

Fig. 9.3: Service models used. See Appendix for the corresponding N3 serialisation

and 9.2, we see N3 representations of the RDF resulting from processing MicroWSMO descriptions. The reader is referred to [28] for more details on how annotations can be created and how RDF can be extracted from these annotations. Common input parameters are the latitude, longitude, and language of the user, while common output parameters include the number of traffic incidents, incident names, times, resulting delays, and textual descriptions.

Listing 9.1: Traffic information service in the UK

```
1
2   service1 rdf :type msm:Service ;
3       rdfs :isDefinedBy <http://myTrafficInformation .co.uk/descriptionxmlapi.asp# trafficinfo > ;
4       sawsdl:modelReference <http://www.service–finder.eu/ontologies/ServiceCategories#Travel> ,
5           <http ://www.service–finder.eu/ontologies/ServiceOntology#AuthenticationModel> ,
6           <http ://example.com/classification/onto# trafficInformation > ,
7           <http ://example.com/mimetype/onto#xmlSupport> .
8   operation1 rdf :type msm:Operation ;
9       rdfs :label "UK Traffic Information" ;
10      hr:hasMethod "GET" ;
11      hr:hasAddress "http://myTrafficInformation .co.uk/ xmlgettrafficinfo .aspx" .
12  inputmsg rdf:type msm:Message ;
13      sawsdl:loweringSchemaMapping <http://example.com/UKTraffic–Info–lowering.xsparql> ;
14      sawsdl:modelReference <http://example.com/onto#User> ,
15          geo:long , geo:lat ,
16          <http ://www.geonames.org/ontology#Map> ,
17          <http ://example.com/geoontology/onto#Range> ,
18          <http ://example.com/imagesontology/onto#relatedImageWidth> ,
19          <http ://example.com/textontology/onto#Language> .
20  operation1 msm:hasInputMessage :inputmsg .
21  outputmsg rdf:type msm:Message ;
22      sawsdl:liftingSchemaMapping <http://example.com/UKtraffic–Info–lifting.xsparql> ;
23      sawsdl:modelReference <http://example.com/trafficontology/onto#Number> ,
24          <http ://example.com/trafficontology/onto#IncidentName> ,
25          <http ://example.com/trafficontology/onto#Created> ,
26          <http ://example.com/trafficontology/onto#Delay> ,
27          <http ://example.com/trafficontology/onto#Duration> ,
28          <http ://example.com/trafficontology/onto#Description> ,
```

```
29            <http ://example.com/trafficontology/onto#Updated> ,
30            <http ://example.com/trafficontology/onto#TrafficArea> .
31    operation1 msm:hasOutputMessage :outputmsg .
32    service1 msm:hasOperation :operation1 .
```

Listing 9.2: Service for Traffic Information in Austria

```
1
2    service2 rdf :type msm:Service ;
3         rdfs :isDefinedBy <http:// traffic .de/web-services.html#trafficinfo> ;
4         sawsdl:modelReference <http://www.service-finder.eu/ontologies/ServiceCategories#Travel> ,
5            <http ://example.com/payment/onto#Free> ,
6            <http ://example.com/classification/onto# trafficInformation > ,
7            <http ://example.com/mimetype/onto#json> .
8    operation1 rdf :type msm:Operation ;
9         rdfs :label "Staumeldungen fuer Oestereich" ;
10        hr:hasMethod "GET" ;
11        hr:hasAddress "http:// traffic .de/trafficinfoJSON" .
12   inputmsg rdf:type msm:Message ;
13        sawsdl:loweringSchemaMapping <http://example.com/DETraffic-Info-lowering.xsparql> ;
14        sawsdl:modelReference geo:long , geo:lat ,
15           <http ://example.com/onto#CurrentTime> ,
16           <http ://example.com/textontology/onto#Language> .
17   operation1 msm:hasInputMessage :inputmsg .
18   outputmsg rdf:type msm:Message ;
19        sawsdl:liftingSchemaMapping <http://example.com/DETraffic-Info-lowering.xsparql> ;
20        sawsdl:modelReference <http://example.com/trafficontology/onto#Number> ,
21           <http ://example.com/trafficontology/onto#IncidentName> ,
22           <http ://example.com/trafficontology/onto#Priority> ,
23           <http ://example.com/trafficontology/onto#Created> ,
24           <http ://example.com/trafficontology/onto#Delay> ,
25           <http ://example.com/trafficontology/onto#Description> ,
26           <http ://example.com/trafficontology/onto#Diversion> .
27   operation1 msm:hasOutputMessage :outputmsg .
28   service2 msm:hasOperation :operation1 .
```

9.4.3 Services Publication

The object of syntactic and semantic descriptions of Web services is to provide information about services in a way that can automatically be processed by machines. However, at present, these descriptions can only be retrieved through the Web of documents, which is essentially designed for human beings, or through specific interfaces to silos of services such as UDDI [9] that have failed to see significant uptake. This is particularly true for syntactic descriptions of services (although there is an RDF mapping for WSDL), but also for semantic descriptions, which have remained somewhat disconnected from current practices in the Web of Data [5].

A fundamental step for bringing services closer to the Web, thus better enabling their discovery and supporting their use, is publishing them based on current best practices on the Web. A key component within our approach is therefore a service publishing platform that plays a role similar to UDDI registries but which is based on a set of fundamentally different principles and technologies. In particular, we advocate the publishing of service annotations as Linked Data. The term Linked Data refers to a set of best practices for publishing structured data on the Web which is based on four main principles [5]:

1. Use URIs for naming things;

2. Use HTTP URIs so that also people can look up those names using Web browsers;

3. Provide information using the standards (RDF, SPARQL); and

4. Include links to other URIs, so that people and machines can discover more things.

Linked Data principles have already been adopted by a growing number of data providers, leading to an exponential growth of a Web of Data containing billions of assertions across diverse domain such as governmental data, music, and encyclopaedia knowledge. Adopting these very simple principles leads to the creation of a global data space that can be queried, browsed and combined on the fly both by machines and humans thanks to the use of standards like HTTP, RDFS, and SPARQL.

Our notion of a service repository is built around the notion of service registry always present in Service-Oriented Architectures, as well as on the Linked Data principles highlighted above. In particular, we view the service repository as a platform that facilitates the publication of semantic annotations of services on the Web as linked data, allowing humans and machines to publish, browse and discover publicly available services, using the models described earlier as the *lingua franca*. It is worth noting in this respect that we here distinguish between the actual syntactic service descriptions in WSDL, WADL or HTML, from the semantic annotations expressed according to the formalisms described previously. It is therefore possible to provide a common view over services of different kinds in a simple an convenient manner that can serve as a basis for discovering, querying and using services.

iServe[4] is our implementation of a service repository [37]. iServe provides both an interactive user interface as well as a RESTful API and a SPARQL endpoint that expose services as linked data. It uses as its core conceptual model the Minimal Service Model described previously and it currently includes a number of import mechanisms able to deal with WSDL files including SAWSDL annotations, with descriptions adopting the WSMO-Lite specific extensions, and also with MicroWSMO annotations of Web APIs. This import mechanism, illustrated in Figure 9.4, transforms the service descriptions into the appropriate terms within the Minimal Service Model and automatically generates *rdfs:definedBy*, *rdfs:seeAlso*, and *owl:sameAs* relations allowing humans and machines to discover additional information. The first relationship is established between the service annotation and the actual document describing the service (e.g., a WSDL file). It therefore allows systems to find the actual interface description definition needed for invocation after it has been determined that the service is the appropriate one to use. The *rdfs:seeAlso* relationship points to documentation and additional information about the service in case developers need it. Finally, *owl:sameAs* allows us to assert that one particular service annotation is actually the same as another one published by a third party in some other repository. In this respect it is worth noting that although currently there are no other repositories publishing services in a similar way, owl:sameAs relations

---

[4] See http://iserve.kmi.open.ac.uk

are automatically generated linking to the RDF mapping of WSDL [25] so that any application already using this approach internally can directly interact with iServe.

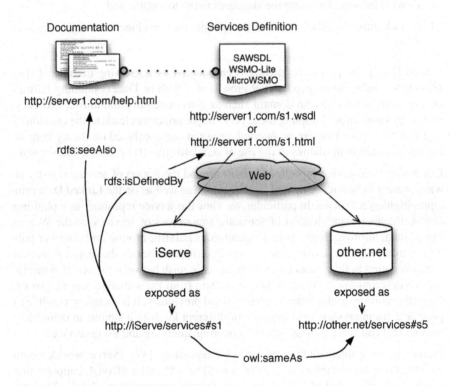

Fig. 9.4: iServe publishing process

Currently the data in iServe comes mostly from the SAWSDL Test Collection[5], OWL-S Test Collection[6] and the use cases of the EU project SOA4All. The current implementation already highlights how Web services and Web APIs can be described by means of an homogeneous (but extensible) conceptual model—the Minimal Service Model—and how they can be published as linked data, therefore better promoting their discovery based on the use of well established and adopted principles from the Web of Data. Additionally and by virtue of using existing lightweight semantic technologies such as RDFS and SPARQL, the service repository benefits from a growing body of performant and mature tools able to cater for the required scalability for dealing with large numbers of services on the Web.

---

[5] See http://www.semwebcentral.org/projects/sawsdl-tc/

[6] See http://projects.semwebcentral.org/projects/owls-tc/

9.4.4 Template-based Service Selection

The objective of creating service descriptions is so that we can later find the services, and reason about them. In this section, we are concerned with the problem of connecting a client requiring a service with a service provider. This task is known as matchmaking (in multi-agent systems) or service selection (a more recent term, common in Web services). The basic approach is for the client to create a formal description of their requirement, and for the matchmaker to compare this against the stored service descriptions to find the most appropriate matches [24].

Since our approach is centred on achieving scalability and ease of use by building on Linked Data standards, we introduce simple notions of service requests, using RDF and SPARQL. In our approach, a service request comprises a set of inputs and outputs, as well as the functional classification of a service[7]. We define RDF *service templates* which capture service requests in a similar way to the service descriptions, and transform those templates to SPARQL queries, trading expressivity for scalability. Such templates can be used operationally in workflows, acting as place-holders for late binding services; in workflow composers, enabling automated suggestion of next steps in a pipeline based on type, and enabling partial verification of correctness; in discovery engines, to find suitable services; in ranking and selection engines, to order them by suitability; and in execution engines, to supply values to service invocations.

Despite our caveat that a template is strictly less appropriate than a goal with pre- and post-conditions, the use of input and output types is actually well suited to searching for stateless services (alternatively, information processing services which are defined reasonably well in terms of a mapping from input to output), since in those cases any preconditions and effects would be only be a refinement of the typing of those inputs and outputs. Our chosen scenario of finding a traffic reporting service is one such case.

In designing these templates, we intended that they straightforwardly map into SPARQL queries over a repository of service descriptions using WSMO-Lite and the Minimal Service Model. Our templates take the following form:

```
ServiceTemplate a rdfs:Class.
    hasFunctionalClassification a rdf:Property;
    hasInput a rdf:Property;
    hasOutput a rdf:Property;
    hasPreference a rdf:Property;
    hasRequirement a rdf:Property;
```

The hasFunctionalClassification property shadows the use of a service's model reference to an object that is a subclass of FunctionalClassificationRoot. These functional classifications might be written to the UNSPSC code. For traffic information reporting, no such UNSPSC code currently exists, so services might

---

[7] A similar functionality is present in OWL-S [29] through the *serviceCategory* property, but we are not aware of any matchmaker that uses it.

instead use the appropriate DBPedia (structured information extracted out of wikipedia) [3] page to create a functional classification:

```
<http://dbpedia.org/resource/Category:Transportation_by_mode>
    rdf:type wsl:FunctionalClassificationRoot .
```

The *Requirement* and *Preference* properties are specified such that:

$$Requirement: Service \rightarrow Bool$$
$$Preference: Service \rightarrow Value$$

The intent with these is to allow the user to specify further constraints in a language of their choice, including SPARQL [38] and WSML [7]. We do not use these constraints in this chapter, but they are analogous to the pre-conditions and effects of services. In section 9.4.4.3 we will illustrate how they can be used by service providers to specify the geographical limits to the usefulness of their services.

Following our use-case, the service offered is based on a unique service template that captures a family of services that can provide traffic reports. At runtime, the service template needs only be instantiated with concrete data corresponding to the users location and the language required in order to provide all the necessary information for querying the service repository:

```
viennaTrafficRequest rdf:type st:ServiceTemplate ;
    st:hasFunctionalClassfication
        <http://dbpedia.org/page/Category:Road_traffic_management> ;
    st:hasInput [ rdf:type geo:lat; rdf:value "48.033"^^xsd:long ] ;
    st:hasInput [ rdf:type geo:long ; rdf:value "16.366"^^xsd:long ] ;
    st:hasInput [ rdf:type lang:Language ; rdf:value lang:English ] .
```

The reader should note that *Road Traffic Management* is a sub category of *Transportation by Mode* in the categorisation chosen and that Vienna is located at 48°12′31.5″N, 16°22′21.3″E.

9.4.4.1 Automatic Transformation of Service Templates to SPARQL

Services can be found by creating a SPARQL query, and in particular, queries can be derived from a service template. Since there is no explicit mediation in the model, finding exact matches for input and output types is important. We can connect these inputs to the model references from the SAWSDL and MicroWSMO.

Given our template, we want to transform it to a SPARQL query. The simplest such query (because it is the most specific) is this:

```
SELECT ?service ?operation
WHERE {
    ?service rdf:type msm:Service ;
        msm:hasOperation ?operation ;
        sawsdl:modelReference
            <http://dbpedia.org/page/Category:Road_traffic_management> .
    ?operation msm:hasInputMessage ?input ;
        msm:hasOutputMessage ?output .
    ?input sawsdl:modelReference geo:lat ;
        sawsdl:modelReference geo:long ;
```

```
        sawsdl:modelReference lang:Language .
```

This provides for services which match exactly the functional classification, and the input types. Had our original service template contained hasOutput constraints, those would have appeared in a similar way to the input types. The algorithm for constructing such queries is shown in Figure 9.5.

```
exact-match-select(template, repository) {
    query := "SELECT ?service ?operation WHERE {"
    query := query + "?service rdf:type msm:Service ;"
    query := query + "          msm:hasOperation ?operation ;"
    query := query + "          sawsdl:modelReference "
                   + template.hasFunctionalClassfication + "."
    query := query + "?operation msm:hasInputMessage ?input ;"
    query := query + "           msm:hasOutputMessage ?output ."
    for (input in template.hasInput) {
        query := query + "?input sawsdl:modelReference " + input + "."
    }
    for (output in template.hasOutput) {
        query := query + "?output sawsdl:modelReference" + output + "."
    }
    query := query + "}"
    return exectute-sparql(query, repository)
}
```

Fig. 9.5: Algorithm for converting service templates to SPARQL SELECT queries

We can also write various forms of this to account for the *exact*, *plugin*, *subsumes*, and *fail* match degrees common in the literature. This is done by the addition of subclass relations in the SPARQL queries. For instance, the following would find services which offered a *plugin* alternative to our request:

```
SELECT ?service ?operation
WHERE {
    ?service rdf:type msm:Service ;
        msm:hasOperation ?operation ;
        sawsdl:modelReference ?fcr .
    ?fcr rdfs:subClassOf
        <http://dbpedia.org/page/Category:Road_traffic_management> .
    ?operation msm:hasInputMessage ?input ;
        msm:hasOutputMessage ?output .
    ?input sawsdl:modelReference ?i1 ;
        sawsdl:modelReference ?i2 ;
        sawsdl:modelReference ?i3 .
    ?i1 rdfs:subClassOf geo:long ;
    ?i2 rdfs:subClassOf geo:lat ;
    ?i3 rdfs:subClassOf lang:Language ;
```

9.4.4.2 Match Reports

We now have a means for creating queries to discover services that match. To return the results, the natural solution is to use another RDF vocabulary which enables the labelling of each matching service with the match degree of the inputs, outputs, and functional classification.

```
st:MatchmakingResults a rdfs:Class .

st:hasServiceTemplate a rdf:Property ;
    rdfs:domain st:MatchmakingResults ;
    rdfs:range st:ServiceTemplate .

st:hasMatch a rdf:Property ;
    rdfs:domain st:MatchmakingResults ;
    rdfs:range st:Match .

st:Match a rdfs:Class .

st:MatchDegree a rdfs:Class .
        st:ExactMatch a st:MatchDegree .
        st:PluginMatch a st:MatchDegree .
        st:SubsumesMatch a st:MatchDegree .

st:hasMatchDegree a rdf:Property ;
    rdfs:domain st:Match ;
    rdfs:range st:MatchDegree .

st:hasMatchingElement a rdf:Property ;
    rdfs:domain st:Match .
```

The matchDegree property can be attached to each appropriate modelReference in the service description. Computing the match degree requires access to the class hierarchy for all the referenced types, and so can only feasibly be done at the service repository.

9.4.4.3 Checking Preconditions

The service requestor now has a set of services and operations that have matched to some degree the input and output types, and the functional classification. The client is now in a position to check that the preconditions of the services hold. Service preconditions are written as SPARQL ASK queries against the requestor's knowledge base. Essentially the same approach was applied in to OWL-S services [40].

For the purpose of evaluating the preconditions, the requestor's knowledge base will have in it only the active service template. This can be identified with the ?template rdf:type st:ServiceTemplate pattern. The rest of the precondition for the Austrian travel service is thus:

```
ASK WHERE {
    ?template rdf:type st:ServiceTemplate ;
        st:hasInputMessage ?lattitute ;
        st:hasInputMessage ?longitude ;
        st:hasInputMessage ?language ;
    ?latitude rdf:type geo:lat .
    ?longitude rdf:type geo:long .
    FILTER (?latitude < 48.5 && ?latitude > 46.5 ) .
    FILTER (?longitude < 16.6 && ?longitude > 9.6 ) .
```

The two FILTER expressions place a bounding rectangle around Austria's geographical extremities. Only a request for a traffic within that box should be matched.

9.5 Conclusions and Future Work

Service-Oriented Computing prescribes the development of systems on the basis of reusable distributed components offered as services in a language and platform independent manner. Key to the development of these kinds of systems is the discovery and selection of services, and there has therefore been a wealth of research focusing on these matters. Semantic Web Services research advocates using semantic annotations of services in order to support advanced discovery and selection techniques based on formal descriptions of both functional and nonfunctional aspects of services. On the basis of these techniques, prototypes have been developed that showcase their potential. However, Semantic Web Services technologies have been up to date based essentially on complex, high-level service ontologies and on highly expressive logics. As a consequence Semantic Web Services technologies have faced an important knowledge acquisition bottleneck and Web-scale solutions have yet to be provided.

SOA4All aims to pave the way for a Web of billions of services, overcoming the drawbacks of current Semantic Web Services technologies by using lightweight semantic annotations, existing Web standards and harnessing Web 2.0 principles. In this chapter we have focussed on the annotation of services using RDFS and a simple conceptual model. We have proposed the publication of services following a number of principles from the Semantic Web which enable easier discovery, selection and use of service annotations, and do so in a scalable manner. We have also presented the notion of service templates as declarative specifications of families of services based on restrictions over their functional or nonfunctional aspects and we have proposed their use within workflows to support the late binding of services. Finally, we have illustrated how these service templates can automatically be transformed into SPARQL queries that can be sent directly to service repositories for automatically selecting suitable services.

The work presented in this chapter are a snapshot of ongoing research that are being evaluated within three use-cases, but the results obtained thus far show already that a considerable amount of limitations currently exhibited by Web services and Semantic Web Services technologies can be mitigated to a certain extent. Further progress with respect to the generation of service annotations is expected to be achieved through the development of a fully-fledged Web-based interface for the annotation, composition and invocation of services known as the SOA4All Studio. Additionally, in the future we aim to use the benchmarking platform and test cases under development within the EU project SEALS, to carry out a comparative analysis with current service selection solutions to better account for the tradeoff between expressivity and scalability in the context of concrete domains and test-cases.

Acknowledgements This research was funded by the SOA4All project, under European Union grant FP7-215219.

9.6 Appendix

Listing 9.3: Namespaces used throughout the chapter.

```
# Standard semantic web namespaces
@prefix xsd: <http://www.w3.org/2001/XMLSchema> .
@prefix rdf: <http://www.w3.org/1999/02/22-rdf-syntax-ns#> .
@prefix rdfs: <http://www.w3.org/2000/01/rdf-schema#> .
@prefix owl: <http://www.w3.org/2002/07/owl#> .
@prefix sawsdl: <http://www.w3.org/ns/sawsdl#> .

# Minimal Service Model, WSMO-Lite, hRESTS namespaces
@prefix wsl: <http://www.wsmo.org/ns/wsmo-lite#> .
@prefix hr: <http://www.wsmo.org/ns/hrests#> .
@prefix msm: <http://cms-wg.sti2.org/ns/minimal-service-model#> .

# Service Templates
@prefix st:   <http://cms-wg.sti2.org/ns/service-template#> .

# Scenario specific
@prefix lang: <http://http://www.lingvoj.org/lingvoj#> .
@prefix geo: <http://www.w3.org/2003/01/geo/wgs84_pos#> .
```

Listing 9.4: Service models used in RDF(S) including Minimal Service Model, WSMO-Lite, hRESTS, and SAWSDL

```
1   msm:Service a rdfs:Class .
2   msm:hasOperation a rdf:Property ;
3    rdfs:domain msm:Service ;
4    rdfs:range msm:Operation .
5   msm:Operation a rdfs:Class .
6   msm:hasInputMessage a rdf:Property ;
7    rdfs:domain msm:Operation ;
8    rdfs:range msm:Message .
9   msm:hasOutputMessage a rdf:Property ;
10   rdfs:domain msm:Operation ;
11   rdfs:range msm:Message .
12  msm:hasInputFault a rdf:Property ;
13   rdfs:domain msm:Operation ;
14   rdfs:range msm:Message .
15  msm:hasOutputFault a rdf:Property ;
16   rdfs:domain msm:Operation ;
17   rdfs:range msm:Message .
18  msm:Message a rdfs:Class .
19  msm:usesOntology a rdfs:Property ;
20   rdfs:domain msm:Service ;
21   rdfs:subPropertyOf rdfs:seeAlso .
22  msm:hasFunctionalClassification a rdfs:Property ;
23   rdfs:subPropertyOf sawsdl:modelReference .
24  msm:hasNonfunctionalProperty a rdfs:Property ;
25   rdfs:subPropertyOf sawsdl:modelReference .
26  msm:hasCondition a rdfs:Property ;
27   rdfs:subPropertyOf sawsdl:modelReference .
28  msm:hasEffect a rdfs:Property ;
29   rdfs:subPropertyOf sawsdl:modelReference .
30
31  # WSMO-Lite
32  wsl:Ontology rdfs:subClassOf owl:Ontology.
33  wsl:FunctionalClassificationRoot rdfs:subClassOf rdfs:Class.
34  wsl:NonFunctionalParameter a rdfs:Class.
35  wsl:Condition a rdfs:Class.
36  wsl:Effect a rdfs:Class.
37
38  # hRESTS properties added to the above model
39  hr:Method a rdfs:Class .
```

```
40  hr:hasAddress a rdf:Property ;
41    rdfs:domain msm:Operation ;
42    rdfs:range hr:URITemplate .
43  hr:hasMethod a rdf:Property ;
44    rdfs:domain msm:Operation ;
45    rdfs:range hr:Method .
46  # a datatype for URI templates
47  hr:URITemplate a rdfs:Datatype .
48  # HTTP Methods possible methods for RESTful services
49  http:Method rdfs:subClassOf hr:Method .
50
51  # SAWSDL properties
52  sawsdl:modelReference a rdf:Property .
53  sawsdl:liftingSchemaMapping a rdf:Property .
54  sawsdl:loweringSchemaMapping a rdf:Property .
```

References

1. Akkiraju, R., Farrell, J., Miller, J., Nagarajan, M., Schmidt, M.T., Sheth, A., Verma, K.: Web service semantics - wsdl-s (2005). W3C Member Submission

2. Al-Masri, E., Mahmoud, Q.: Web service discovery and client goals.   Computer **42**(1), 104 – 107 (2009). DOI 10.1109/MC.2009.31. URL http://ieeexplore. ieee.org/search/srchabstract.jsp?arnumber=4755168&isnumber= 4755142&punumber=2&k2dockey=4755168@ieeejrns

3. Auer, S., Bizer, C., Kobilarov, G., Lehmann, J., Cyganiak, R., Ives, Z.: DBpedia: A Nucleus for a Web of Open Data. In: In proceedings of 6th International Semantic Web Conference, 2nd Asian Semantic Web Conference, pp. 722–735 (2008). DOI 10.1007/978-3-540-76298-0_52. URL http://dx.doi.org/10.1007/978-3-540-76298-0%255C_52

4. Baldauf, M., Dustdar, S., Rosenberg, F.: A survey on context-aware systems. International Journal of Ad Hoc and Ubiquitous Computing pp. 263–277 (2007). DOI http://dx.doi.org/10. 1504/IJAHUC.2007.014070. URL http://dx.doi.org/10.1504/IJAHUC.2007. 014070

5. Bizer, C., Heath, T., Berners-Lee, T.: Linked data - the story so far.   International Journal on Semantic Web and Information Systems (IJSWIS) (2009).   URL http://www.google.com/search?client=safari&rls=en-us&q=Linked+ Data+-+The+Story+So+Far&ie=UTF-8&oe=UTF-8

6. Brickley, D., Guha, R.V.: RDF Vocabulary Description Language 1.0: RDF Schema (2002). URL http://www.w3.org/TR/rdf-schema. Http://www.w3.org/TR/rdf-schema

7. de Bruijn, J.: D16.1v0.21 the web service modeling language wsml (2005). URL http: //www.wsmo.org/TR/d2/v1.3/

8. Burstein, M., Bussler, C., Zaremba, M., Finin, T., Huhns, M.N., Paolucci, M., Sheth, A.P., Williams, S.: A semantic web services architecture. IEEE Internet Computing **9**(5), 72–81 (2005). DOI http://doi.ieeecomputersociety.org/10.1109/MIC.2005.96. URL http://doi. ieeecomputersociety.org/10.1109/MIC.2005.96

9. Clement, L., Hately, A., von Riegen, C., Rogers, T.: UDDI Specification Version 3.0.2. Tech. rep., OASIS (2004)

10. Comuzzi, M., Kritikos, K., Plebani, P.: Semantic-aware service quality negotiation. In: ServiceWave '08: Proceedings of the 1st European Conference on Towards a Service-Based Internet, pp. 312–323. Springer-Verlag, Berlin, Heidelberg (2008). DOI http://dx.doi.org/10.1007/ 978-3-540-89897-9_27

11. Davies, J., Domingue, J., Pedrinaci, C., Fensel, D., Gonzalez-Cabero, R., Potter, M., Richardson, M., Stincic, S.: Towards the open service web. BT Technology Journal **26**(2) (2009)

12. Domingue, J., Cabral, L., Galizia, S., Tanasescu, V., Gugliotta, A., Norton, B., Pedrinaci, C.: Irs-iii: A broker-based approach to semantic web services.   Web Semantics: Science, Services and Agents on the World Wide Web **6**(2), 109–132 (2008).   URL http://www.sciencedirect.com/science/article/B758F- 4S1BX4N-1/2/3526a78f287ad7322cec918d2f91e46a

13. Erl, T.: SOA Principles of Service Design (2007). URL http://www.amazon.ca/exec/obidos/redirect?tag=citeulike09-20%255C&path=ASIN/0132344823
14. Farrell, J., Lausen, H.: Semantic Annotations for WSDL and XML Schema (SAWSDL). Recommendation, W3C (August 2007). URL http://www.w3.org/TR/sawsdl/
15. Fensel, D., Bussler, C.: The Web Service Modeling Framework WSMF. Electronic Commerce Research and Applications 1(2), 113–137 (2002). URL gunther.smeal.psu.edu/article/fensel02web.html
16. Fensel, D., Kerrigan, M., Zaremba, M.: Implementing Semantic Web Services: The SESA Framework (2008)
17. Fensel, D., Lausen, H., Polleres, A., de Bruijn, J., Stollberg, M., Roman, D., Domingue, J.: Enabling Semantic Web Services: The Web Service Modeling Ontology (2007)
18. Fielding, R.T.: Architectural styles and the design of network-based software architectures. Ph.D. thesis (2000). URL http://www.ics.uci.edu/%255C~%257B%257Dfielding/pubs/dissertation/fielding%255C_dissertation.pdf
19. Galizia, S., Gugliotta, A., Pedrinaci, C.: A formal model for classifying trusted semantic web services. In: 3rd Asian Semantic Web Conference (ASWC 2008). Bangkok, Thailand (2008)
20. Hadley, M.: Web application description language. Tech. rep. (2009). URL http://www.w3.org/Submission/wadl/
21. Horrocks, I., Patel-Schneider, P.F., Boley, H., Tabet, S., Grosof, B., Dean, M.: SWRL: A Semantic Web Rule Language Combining OWL and RuleML (2004). URL http://www.w3.org/Submission/SWRL/. Last Visited: April 2005
22. Karastoyanova, D., Leymann, F.: BPEL'n'Aspects: Adapting Service Orchestration Logic. IEEE International Conference on Web Services, 2009. ICWS 2009. pp. 222 – 229 (2009). DOI 10.1109/ICWS.2009.75. URL http://ieeexplore.ieee.org/search/srchabstract.jsp?arnumber=5175827&isnumber=5175786&punumber=5175785&k2dockey=5175827@ieeecnfs
23. Klusch, M., Fries, B., Sycara, K.: Automated semantic web service discovery with OWLS-MX. pp. 915–922 (2006). DOI http://doi.acm.org/10.1145/1160633.1160796. URL http://doi.acm.org/10.1145/1160633.1160796
24. Klusch, M., Sycara, K.: Brokering and matchmaking for coordination of agent societies: a survey. In: Coordination of Internet agents: models, technologies, and applications, pp. 197–224. Springer-Verlag (2001). URL http://www.dfki.de/~klusch/papers/chapter8.pdf
25. Kopecký, J.: Web services description language (wsdl) version 2.0: Rdf mapping. Tech. rep. (2007)
26. Kopecky, J., Gomadam, K., Vitvar, T.: hrests: an html microformat for describing restful web services. In: IEEE/WIC/ACM International Conference on Web Intelligence and Intelligent Agent Technology (2008)
27. Li, L., Horrocks, I.: A software framework for matchmaking based on semantic web technology. International Journal of Electronic Commerce 8(4), 39 (2004). DOI http://doi.acm.org/10.1145/775152.775199. URL http://doi.acm.org/10.1145/775152.775199
28. Maleshkova, M., Kopecký, J., Pedrinaci, C.: Adapting sawsdl for semantic annotations of restful services. In: Workshop: Beyond SAWSDL at OnTheMove Federated Conferences & Workshops (2009)
29. Martin, D., Burstein, M., Hobbs, J., Lassila, O., McDermott, D., McIlraith, S., Narayanan, S., Paolucci, M., Parsia, B., Payne, T., Sirin, E., Srinivasan, N., Sycara, K.: OWL-S: Semantic Markup for Web Services. Member submission, W3C (2004). URL http://www.w3.org/Submission/OWL-S. W3C Member Submission 22 November 2004
30. McBride, B.: The Resource Description Framework (RDF) and its Vocabulary Description Language RDFS, chap. 3, pp. 51–66 (2004)
31. McIlraith, S., Son, T., Zeng, H.: Semantic web services. Intelligent Systems, IEEE 16(2), 46 – 53 (2001). DOI 10.1109/5254.920599. URL http://ieeexplore.ieee.org/search/srchabstract.jsp?arnumber=920599&isnumber=19905&punumber=9670&k2dockey=920599@ieeejrns

32. Nitzsche, J., van Lessen, T., Karastoyanova, D., Leymann, F.: Bpel for semantic web services (bpel4sws). On the Move to Meaningful Internet Systems 2007: OTM 2007 Workshops pp. 179–188 (2007). URL http://dx.doi.org/10.1007/978-3-540-76888-3_37

33. Norton, B., Pedrinaci, C., Domingue, J., Zaremba, M.: Semantic execution environments for semantics-enabled soa. IT-Methods and Applications of Informatics and Information Technology **Special Issue in Service-Oriented Architectures**, 118–121 (2008)

34. Papazoglou, M.P., Traverso, P., Dustdar, S., Leymann, F.: Service-oriented computing: State of the art and research challenges. Computer **40**(11), 38–45 (2007). DOI http://doi.ieeecomputersociety.org/10.1109/MC.2007.400. URL http://doi.ieeecomputersociety.org/10.1109/MC.2007.400

35. Patel-Schneider, P., Hayes, P., Horrocks, I.: OWL Web Ontology Language Semantics and Abstract Syntax (2004). URL http://www.w3.org/TR/owl-semantics/. Last Visited: March 2005

36. Pedrinaci, C., Brelage, C., van Lessen, T., Domingue, J., Karastoyanova, D., Leymann, F.: Semantic business process management: Scaling up the management of business processes. In: Proceedings of the 2nd IEEE International Conference on Semantic Computing (ICSC) 2008. IEEE Computer Society, Santa Clara, CA, USA (2008)

37. Pedrinaci, C., Liu, D., Maleshkova, M., Lambert, D., Kopecký, J., Domingue, J.: iServe: a Linked Services Publishing Platform. In: Ontology Repositories and Editors for the Semantic Web at 7th Extended Semantic Web Conference (2010)

38. Prud'hommeaux, E., Seaborne, A.: Sparql query language for rdf. Recommendation, W3C (2008). URL http://www.w3.org/TR/rdf-sparql-query/

39. Richardson, L., Ruby, S.: RESTful Web Services (2007). URL http://www.amazon.ca/exec/obidos/redirect?tag=citeulike09-20%255C&path=ASIN/0596529260

40. Sbodio, M.L., Moulin, C.: SPARQL as an expression language for OWL-S. In: OWL-S: Experiences and Directions, a workshop at the 4th European Semantic Web Conference (ESWC 2007) (2007)

41. Sheng, Q., Yu, J., Dustdar, S.: Enabling Context-Aware Web Services: Methods, Architectures, and Technologies. Chapman and Hall/CRC (2010)

42. Sheth, A., Gomadam, K., Lathem, J.: SA-REST: Semantically Interoperable and Easier-to-Use Services and Mashups. Internet Computing, IEEE **11**(6), 91 – 94 (2007). DOI 10.1109/MIC.2007.133. URL http://ieeexplore.ieee.org/search/srchabstract.jsp?arnumber=4376235&isnumber=4376216&punumber=4236&k2dockey=4376235@ieeejrns

43. Stollberg, M., Hepp, M., Hoffmann, J.: A Caching Mechanism for Semantic Web Service Discovery. In: Proceedings of the International Semantic Web Conference 2007. Springer (2007)

44. Sycara, K., Paolucci, M., Ankolekar, A., Srinivasan, N.: Automated discovery, interaction and composition of semantic web services. Web Semantics: Science, Services and Agents on the World Wide Web **1**(1), 27 – 46 (2003). DOI DOI:10.1016/j.websem.2003.07.002. URL http://www.sciencedirect.com/science/article/B758F-4B4X4HF-4/2/edf27fdc23ea9094adea29fa46f65019

45. Trastour, D., Bartolini, C., Gonzalez-Castillo, J.: A Semantic Web Approach to Service Description for Matchmaking of Services. In: I.F. Cruz, S. Decker, J. Euzenat, D.L. McGuinness (eds.) Proceedings of SWWS'01, The first Semantic Web Working Symposium, pp. 447–461 (2001)

46. Turati, A., Valle, E.D., Cerizza, D., Facca, F.M.: Using Glue to Solve the Discovery Scenarios of the SWS-Challenge, pp. 185–197 (2009). URL http://dx.doi.org/10.1007/978-0-387-72496-6_11

47. Verma, K., Sivashanmugam, K., Sheth, A., Patil, A., Oundhakar, S., Miller, J.: Meteor-s wsdi: A scalable p2p infrastructure of registries for semantic publication and discovery of web services. International Journal of Information Technologies and Management **6**(1), 17–39 (2005). DOI http://dx.doi.org/10.1007/s10799-004-7773-4. URL http://dx.doi.org/10.1007/s10799-004-7773-4

48. Vinoski, S.: Putting the "web" into web services: Interaction models, part 2. IEEE Internet Computing **6**(4), 90–92 (2002). DOI http://doi.ieeecomputersociety.org/10.1109/MIC.2002. 1020331. URL http://doi.ieeecomputersociety.org/10.1109/MIC.2002. 1020331

49. Vitvar, T., Kopecky, J., Viskova, J., Fensel, D.: Wsmo-lite annotations for web services. In: M. Hauswirth, M. Koubarakis, S. Bechhofer (eds.) Proceedings of the 5th European Semantic Web Conference, LNCS. Springer Verlag, Berlin, Heidelberg (2008). URL http://data. semanticweb.org/conference/eswc/2008/papers/281

50. Zeng, L., Benatallah, B., Ngu, A., Dumas, M., Kalagnanam, J., Chang, H.: Qos-aware middleware for web services composition. Software Engineering, IEEE Transactions on **30**(5), 311 – 327 (2004). DOI 10.1109/TSE.2004.11. URL http://ieeexplore.ieee.org/search/srchabstract.jsp?arnumber= 1291834&isnumber=28776&punumber=32&k2dockey=1291834@ieeejrns

Chapter 10

Designing and Adapting Service-based Systems: A Service Discovery Framework[1]

George Spanoudakis and Andrea Zisman

Abstract This chapter describes a service discovery framework that has been developed within the EU 6th Framework projects SeCSE and Gredia. The framework supports design of service-based systems based on existing services and adaptation of service based systems during their execution due to different situations. It assumes services described from different perspectives and uses complex service discovery queries specified in an XML-based language that we have developed. The work is illustrated with the Cell Phone Operator case study.

10.1 Introduction

Service-based systems are defined as software systems that are composed of services but may also use legacy code and/or software components to provide their required functionality. The design of service-based systems has been recognized as an important topic of research in which it is necessary to have methodologies, techniques, and tools to support the development of such systems. Service integrators, developers, and providers have collaborated to support not only the development, but also the deployment and consumption of service-based systems. The de-

George Spanoudakis
City University London
Northampton Square, London, EC1V 0HB, UK
e-mail: g.spanoudakis@soi.city.ac.uk

Andrea Zisman
City University London
Northampton Square, London, EC1V 0HB, UK
e-mail: a.zisman@soi.city.ac.uk

ployment and support for adaptation of service-based systems during execution time has been recognized as necessary for these systems to continue to operate.

As an example, consider the Cell Phone Operator (CPO) case study being used in this book. In this example the CPO system is composed of several services that support different functional and non-functional aspects of the system (e.g., SMS service, voice service, email service, pay-per-view movie service, mobile phone number portability service, cost and time to use the various services). During the design of this CPO service-based system, it is necessary to be able to identify available services that can be used to support the functional and non-functional aspects of the system, and to develop design models of the system based on the characteristics of existing services. Once the CPO is deployed, it may be necessary to replace a service during execution time of the system. For example, consider a customer who moves countries for a while (change of context), and assume that the time to retrieve a movie using the current pay-per-view movie service participating in the system becomes slow due to the new location of the customer. In this case, it is necessary to identify a service that can replace the current pay-per-view movie service and conforms to the requirements of the system.

In this chapter we present a service discovery framework supporting: (a) design of service-based systems based on existing services, and (b) adaptation of service-based systems during their execution due to (i) unavailability or malfunctioning of the services they deploy, (ii) changes in the context of services they deploy or the service-based system environment, and/or (iii) emergence of new services that are superior to the services already deployed in a service-based system.

The work underpinning the framework described in this chapter has been developed within the EU 6th Framework projects SeCSE [33] and Gredia [13]. Different parts and aspects of the framework have been published in several research papers [24,25,37,38,39,40,54,55,57,58,59]. In this chapter, we present the latest unified version of the framework and demonstrate how it can be applied to support service-based system design and execution time adaptation illustrated by the case study of cell phone operators used in this book.

The design of service-based systems in the framework is based on an iterative service discovery process in which system designers can, whilst developing system design models for a service based system, specify service discovery queries representing functional and quality characteristics of services required for them, and use them to locate services that could be used in the system. Once identified and, subject to their approval by the designers, such services can be linked to the system and used as remote components by it when the system comes to operation. When designers decide to use a discovered service, its model is also automatically integrated into the design model of the system and thus generating a new version of the model. The new version of the design model may be used in further iterations to specify other service requests, identify further candidate services, and possibly interconnect them to the design as well. During this process, it is also possible to realize that certain parts of the system cannot be fulfilled by available services and, therefore, make alternative design decisions for the developing system. Examples of these decisions are concerned with the use of existing legacy code or components that could be statically linked to the system, or the implementation of new software code. This design process terminates either when new service requests derived from new versions of the models cannot identify services that match the requests or at the discretion of the designer of the system.

Execution time adaptations of service-based systems are assisted by a pro-active service discovery process in which services are identified in parallel to the execution of the system using pre-subscribed complex queries and services. The queries are identified and specified also prior to system deployment and are executed at runtime under specific conditions that make necessary the adaptation of the system. The queries locate alternative services for the ones already used by the system, which are no longer appropriate. As it is the case in the design of service-based systems, execution time service discovery can express combinations of structural, behavioural and quality conditions that should be satisfied by candidate services. In addition, they can also express context conditions (i.e., parametric conditions about characteristics of the system, its environment and its participating services that are, or could be deployed by the system, which can change frequently and dynamically at execution time). Furthermore, the execution time discovery queries supported by our framework can be executed in both pull and push modes. The former mode provides a reactive response to a runtime problem that makes the need for system adaptation necessary. The latter mode provides a means of pro-active and continuous discovery process that runs in parallel with the system aiming to identify appropriate substitute services for the ones already used by the system when the need for replacing services suddenly arises.

The support for service-based system design has been developed in the SeCSE project [33] to address challenges identified by industrial partners in the areas of telecommunications, automotive, and software in the project. The support for adaptation of service-based system has been developed in the GREDIA project [13] to address challenges identified by industrial partners in the areas of media and banking. These challenges point out the need to:

(i) Extract service discovery queries from design models of service-based systems specifying the functionality and quality properties of such systems;

(ii) Generate service discovery queries from characteristics of services that have already been deployed in systems, but may need to be replaced;

(iii) Provide a query language to support both the expression of arbitrary logical combinations of prioritised functional, non-functional, and contextual properties criteria for the required services, and similarity-based queries of the form "find a service that is similar to service X";

(iv) Match efficiently service discovery queries against service specifications and return services that may have varying degrees of match with the queries;

(v) Assist system designers to select services for a service-based system in cases where the discovery process identifies more than one candidate service satisfying a query or services that do not satisfy a query entirely;

(vi) Integrate discovered services into an iterative design process in which ser-
      vice-based systems design models may be re-formulated following the dis-
      covery of services;
(vii) Support pro-active dynamic service discovery during execution time of a
      service-based system.

The framework assumes services described from different perspectives by a set of
XML-based facets. These facets include (i) textual facets describing general information of the services in an XML format, (ii) structural facets describing operations of services with their data types using WSDL [53], (iii) behavioural facets
describing behavioural models of services in BPEL4WS [7], (iv) quality of service
facets describing non-functional aspects of services, and (v) context facets describing quality aspects of a service that change dynamically. The identification of
services based on distinct aspects provides a more accurate match between queries
and services and the consequent discovery of services with the required characteristics, as opposed to techniques that are based only on keywords or interface aspects (e.g., WOOGLE [52] and UDDI [43]), which provide less precise match.
The discovery techniques that are used in the framework to assist with both the
design and adaptation of service-based systems are based on the computation of
distances between queries and the different types of service specifications.
The remainder of this chapter is structured as follows. Section 10.2 describes an
overview of the framework to support design and adaptation of service-based systems. Section 10.3 presents the query language used in the framework. Section
10.4 describes the matching process. Section 10.5 discusses the advantages, lessons learned, and limitations of the work. Section 10.6 discusses related work on
service discovery and service-based system adaptation. Finally, section 10.7 provides concluding remarks and discussion of future work. The material presented in
the chapter is illustrated with the cell phone operator case study.

10.2 Overview of the Framework

As discussed in Section 10.1, the framework supports design and adaptation of
service-based systems. Fig. 10.1 shows the overall architecture of our framework.
As shown in the figure, the main components of the framework are: (a) *service requestor*, (b) *query processor*, and (c) *service registry intermediary*. The framework uses external service registries and is invoked by an external client application. In order to support execution time adaptation of service-based systems, the
framework uses special servers and listeners to allow notification of changes in
services and application environment. The external client applications support the
creation of service requests to be executed for both design and execution time adaptation. These service requests may contain structural, behavioural, quality, and
contextual characteristics.

The *service requestor* receives a service request from a client application. In the case of adaptation of service-based systems, the service requestor also receives context information about the services participating in a service-based system and application environment. The service requestor prepares service queries to be evaluated, organises the results of a query, and returns these results to the client application. To support adaptation, it also manages push query execution mode subscriptions, receives information from listeners about services that become available or about changes to existing services.

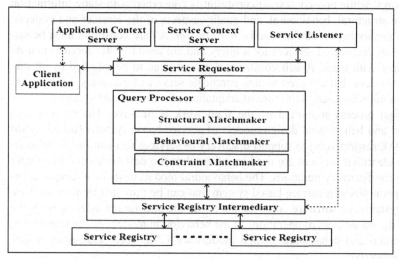

Fig. 10.1: Architecture overview of the framework

The *query processor* is responsible to parse the different parts of a query and evaluate these parts against service specifications in the various service registries. As shown in the figure, the query processor is formed by three sub-components, namely (i) structural, (ii) behavioural, and (iii) constraint matchmakers. Each of these sub-components is responsible to evaluate a different part of a query.

The *service registry intermediary* supports the use of different service registries and the discovery of services stored in different types of registries. It provides an interface to access services from various registries. The framework allows accessing services from registries organized as faceted structure, as proposed in the SeCSE project [33]. More specifically, in the registries, a service is specified by a set of XML-based facets, namely (i) textual facets, (ii) structural, (iii) behavioural, (iv) quality of service, and (v) context facets.

To support adaptation of service-based systems, the framework uses *service* and *application context servers*, and *service listeners*. The service and application context servers allow the acquisition of context information about the services and the application environment, respectively. Both context servers accept subscriptions for specific types of context information from the service requester and send updates when changes in the context of services and the application occur. The service listener is responsible to send to the service requestor notifications about new services that become available, or about changes in the descriptions of existing services. This information is extracted from external service registries through polling. The notifications are based on subscriptions for specific types of information that the service requester has made to the service listener.

The framework assumes constraints in a query to be *contextual* or *non-contextual*. A contextual constraint is concerned with information that changes dynamically during the operation of the service-based system and/or the services that the system deploys, while non-contextual constraint is concerned with static information related to structural, behavioural, and quality aspects of the services and systems. The non-contextual constraints can be *hard* or *soft*. A hard constraint must be satisfied by all discovered services for a query and are used to filter services that do not comply with them. A soft constraint does not need to be satisfied by all discovered services, but are used to rank candidate services for a query. The contextual constraints are used in the case of adaptation of service-based systems.

The design process supported by the framework is iterative. The process uses structural and behavioural design models of service-based systems (called SySM and SyBM, respectively) to support discovery of services that can fulfill the models. The identified services are used to reformulate the design models and trigger new service discovery iterations. The behavioural models describe interactions between operations of a service-based system that can be provided by web services, legacy systems, or software components, while the structural models specify the types of the parameters of operations in the behavioural models. In the framework, the structural and behavioural design models are UML class and sequence diagrams, respectively.

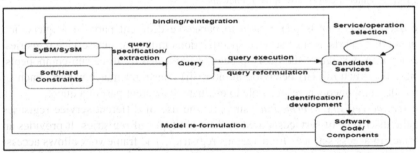

Fig. 10.2: Design process

Fig. 10.2 presents an overview of the iterative design process of the framework. As shown in the figure, queries are specified in reference to the sequence diagrams in SyBM and the classes and interfaces in SySM, and may include additional constraints about the required services. These queries are generated by any client application that is able to produce service discovery queries expressed as UML 2.0 models represented in XMI (e.g., any CASE tool that supports UML 2.0 and representation of the models in XMI). Details about the queries are presented in Section 10.3. The queries are passed to the service requestor component to be executed (see Fig. 10.1). The candidate services identified after the execution of queries by the query processor can be bound to the SySM and SyBM models by the designers of the system. When this happens, SySM and SyBM are re-formulated (e.g. by adding message data types and operations of identified services) and their new versions can be used to specify further queries for discovering additional services for other parts of the system. Queries may also be re-formulated and re-executed when the identified services are not adequate. The process can be terminated by the system designer at any time, when all the required services have been discovered, or when it is clear that further queries would not be able to identify services that have a better match with the current design models. Queries may also include hard and soft constraints expressed in an XML based language that we have developed (See Section 10.3).

The execution time adaptation process supported by the framework allows services to be identified based on both pull and push modes of query execution. The pull mode of query execution is performed to identify services (a) that are initially bound to a service-based system and their replacement candidate services, (b) as a first step in the push mode of query execution, (c) due to changes in the context of an application environment, or (d) when a client application requests a service to be discovered. The push mode of query execution is performed when the application is running and a service needs to be replaced due to any of cases (i)-(iii) described in Section 10.1. For the push mode of query execution, the framework assumes a pro-active approach in which services are identified in parallel to the execution of a service-based system based on subscriptions of application environment, services, and queries associated with these services, so that replacement services can be identified, when notification of changes in services and application environments are pushed to listeners. These notifications are supported by service and application context servers and service listeners (see Fig. 10.1).

For both design and adaptation of service-based systems, the service discovery technique is based on matching between a query and services executed in a two-phase process. The first phase consists of a *filtering* phase and the second phase consists of a *ranking* phase. In the filtering phase, hard constraints in a query are evaluated against service specifications and candidate services that comply with these constraints are identified. In the ranking phase, candidate services identified in the filtering phase are matched against structural, behavioural, and soft constraints in a query based on the computation of distances.

During design of service-based systems, the ranking phase returns n-best services for a query (n can be either specified in a query or is equal to ten by default). The designer selects from these services the ones to be used in the system. During adaptation of service-based systems, the ranking phase returns the best service for a query that is used to replace a service in the service-based system. The computation of the distances differs during the design and adaptation phases. Details of the computations and their differences are described in Section 10.4.

10.3 Query Language

In order to support service discovery queries in the framework, we have developed an XML-based language named SerDiQueL (Service Discovery Query Language [59]). It allows the specification of structural, behavioural, quality, and contextual characteristics of services to be identified or of systems being developed.

Fig. 10.3 presents the overall XML schema of SerDiQueL. As shown in the figure, a query specified in the language (ServiceQuery) has three elements representing structural, behavioural, and constraint sub-queries. The division of a query into these three sub-queries is to (i) allow the representation of these three types of information, and (ii) support the representation of queries with arbitrary combinations of these types of information. A *ServiceQuery* element also has a unique identifier, a name, and one or more elements describing different parameters for a query. A parameter element is defined by a name and a value. Examples of parameters that can be used in a query are: (a) name of the query, (b) type of the query (e.g., static, in the case of design of service-based systems or dynamic, in the case of adaptation of service-based systems), (c) mode of execution (push or pull), (d) author of the query, and (e) number of services to be returned by a query.

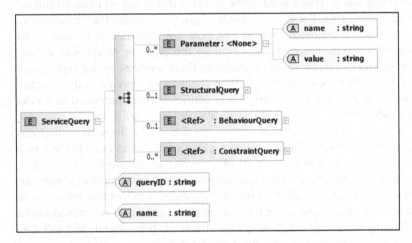

Fig. 10.3: Overview schema of SerDiQueL

10.3.1 Structural Sub-query

The structural sub-query describes structural aspects of (i) a service-based system being developed or (ii) a service participating in a running service-based system that needs to be replaced.

The structural sub-queries for case (i) use elements in SySM and SyBM design models of the system (see Section 10.2) together with a UML 2.0 profile [25] that we have developed, and it is represented as XMI documents. The profile defines a set of stereotypes for different types of UML elements such as messages in sequence diagrams, or operations and classes defining the types of arguments in the messages in the class diagrams. For example, messages in a sequence diagram may be stereotyped as: (1) *query messages* representing service operations needed in identified services; (2) *context messages* representing additional constraints for the query messages (e.g. if a context message has a parameter p1 with the same name as a parameter p2 of a query message, then the type of p1 should be taken as the type of p2); (3) *bound messages* representing concrete service operations that have been discovered in previous query executions.

In order to express a query for a service-based system being developed, system designers select an interaction from the SyBM model of the system and specify the messages in the interaction that need to be realized by service operations that are to be discovered (query messages). The designers can also specify the context messages to impose additional constraints in a query. All messages in an interaction that are not stereotyped are treated as messages irrelevant to the discovery process. Based on the selected interactions and messages, structural sub-queries for a service-based system under development are automatically generated from the class (SySM) and sequence (SyBM) diagrams.

The description of structural aspects of a service-based system is based on design models of these systems and supports the representation of operations being searched in different services together with the representation of the input and output parameters of these operations and their respective data types. This is important to assist with the matching of structural aspects of the systems with structural aspects of available services. Moreover, it supports the development of a service-based system based on the characteristics of available services instead of on requirements that may never be able to be fulfilled by existing services.

As an example of the specification of a query for case (i), consider part of the behavioural and structural design models of a Cell Phone Operator (CPO) system from the case study used in the book shown in Figures 4 and 5, respectively. As shown in Fig. 10.4, the system allows the provision of SMS, voice, and email messages; request for movies; and payment of these various services by a user of the CPO. Consider a designer of this service-based system that wants to identify a service that can provide request and payment of movies. In this case, a designer wants to find service operations that can provide implementations of the messages

    payMovie(phone:PhoneNumber, quantity:Integer):Boolean   and
    retrieveMovie(phone:PhoneNumber, info:MovieInfo):MovieStream

as specified in the diagram shown in Fig. 10.4. The designer creates a query as a copy of the sequence diagram and attaches the query message stereotype to these messages (<<asd_query_message>>). The classes representing the data types of the parameters of the two query messages, and all the classes that are directly or transitively related to them, are automatically identified and put together to formulate the structural part of the query. These classes are shown in Fig. 10.5.

The structural sub-queries for case (ii) are represented by the WSDL specification of the service to be replaced. In this case, SerDiQueL supports a complete representation of the structural aspects of a service to be identified as interface descriptions. In the framework, structural sub-queries for a service that needs to be replaced during execution time are automatically generated based on the notification that a service became malfunctioning, unavailable, or there were changes in the characteristics of the service or in the context of the application environment.

As an example, consider the CPO service-based system described above. Assume service S_{Movie} that was found during design time of the system and bound to the system. Consider S_{Movie} with operations

payment(phone:Number, serviceType:String, amount:Integer):Boolean and

getMovie(phone:Number, title:String, director:String, language:String):Movie
Suppose a user of the CPO service-based system has moved from London to Shanghai for two months. Consider that the time to retrieve movies using service S_{Movie} from Shanghai is very slow and, therefore, due to change of context, another service that provides movies via cell phones with a better performance needs to be identified and replaced in the service-based system. In this case, the structural sub-query is the WSDL specification of S_{Movie}.

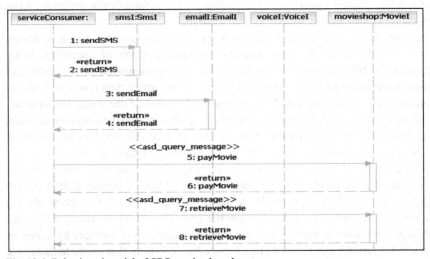

Fig. 10.4: Behavioural model of CPO service-based system

The reasons for using UML models enhanced with our UML profile specified in XMI to represent structural sub-queries during design of service-based systems are because (a) UML is the de facto standard for designing software systems and can effectively support the design of service-based systems [10,12], and (b) UML has the expressive power to represent the design models of service-based systems since it can represent modeling of software services, legacy code and software components in a system. The use of WSDL to represent structural sub-queries in the case of execution time adaptation of service-based systems is due to its wide acceptance as a service interface description language. In addition, during execution time of service-based systems, any replacement service that might be identified for an existing service in a system needs to conform to the interface of the existing service.

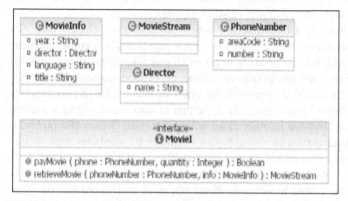

Fig. 10.5: Structural model of CPO service-based system

10.3.2 Behavioural Sub-query

The behavioural sub-queries need to allow the specification of the (1) existence of a required functionality, or a sequence of required functionalities, in a service specification; (2) order in which the required functionalities should be executed by a service; (3) dependencies between functionalities (e.g. the functionality realized by an operation always requires the existence of the functionality of another operation); (4) pre-conditions; and (5) loops concerning execution of certain functionalities.

Fig. 10.6 shows a graphical representation of the SerDiQueL's XML schema for specifying behavioural sub-queries. As shown in the figure, a behavioural sub-query is defined as (a) a single condition, a negated condition, or a conjunction of conditions, or (b) a sequence of expressions separated by logical operators. A behavioural sub-query also specifies *requires* elements.

Requires elements are used to describe the service operations that need to exist in service specifications. Every query must describe one or more required service operations, represented by *MemberDescription* elements in the query (*MemberDescription* elements can be used in various conditions and expressions in a query). A member element has three attributes, namely (a) *ID*, indicating a unique identifier for the member within a query; (b) *opName*, specifying the name of a query message (design phase) or of an operation (adaptation phase) described in the structural sub-query; and (c) *synchronous*, indicating if the service operation needs to be executed in a synchronous or asynchronous mode. The parameters and respective data types of the operations are specified in the structural sub-queries.

The existence of *requires* elements in service specifications is verified as an initial step during the execution of a behavioural sub-query rather than during the evaluation of the conditions and expressions of the query that uses these elements. This optimizes the query execution process as there is no need to evaluate any condition or expression that refers to a non-existing *requires* element.

A condition is defined as a *GuaranteedMember, OccursBefore, OccursAfter, Sequence,* or *Loop* element. A *GuaranteedMember* represents a member element (e.g., a service operation) that needs to occur in all possible traces of execution in a service. This element references requires, sequence, or loop elements. *OccursBefore* and *OccursAfter* elements represent the order of occurrence of two member elements (e.g., *Member1* and *Member2*). Note that in some cases we may require *OccursBefore(m1,m2)* whilst in other cases we may require *OccursAfter(m1,m2)*, or even need to differentiate an *OccurBefore* condition by attributes such as immediate. Hence both *OccursBefore* and *OccursAfter* elements are needed. Furthermore, they have two boolean attributes, namely: (a) attribute immediate, specifying if two members need to occur in direct sequence or if there can be other member elements in between them, and (b) attribute guaranteed, specifying if the two members need to occur in all possible traces of execution in a service. A *Sequence* element defines two or more members that must occur in a service in the order represented in the sequence. It has an identifier attribute that can be used by the *GuaranteedMember, OccursBefore, OccursAfter, Sequence,* and *Loop* elements. A *Loop* element specifies a sequence that is executed several times.

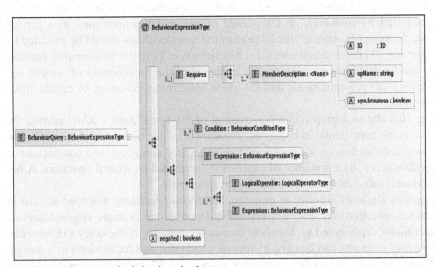

Fig. 10.6: XML Schema for behavioural sub-query

```
<tnsb:BehaviourQuery>
  <tnsb:Requires>
      <tnsb:MemberDescription ID="pay" opName="payMovie" syn-
chrounous="true"/>
      <tnsb:MemberDescription ID="retrieve" opName="retrieveMovie"
synchrounous="true" />
  </tnsb:Requires>
  <tnsb:Expression>
    <tnsb:Condition>
      <tnsb:OccursBefore immediate'"false"
                                guaranteed="false">
      <tnsb:Member1 IDREF="pay" />
      <tnsb:Member2 IDREF="retrieve" />
      </tnsb:OccursBefore>
    </tnsb:Condition>
  </tnsb:Expression>
</tnsb:BehaviourQuery>
```

Fig. 10.7: Example of behavioural sub-query in SerDiQueL

In behavioural sub-queries, expressions are defined as sequences of *requires* elements, conjunctions or disjunctions of conditions, or nested expressions connected by logical operators AND and OR. The definition of requires elements within an *expression* (E1) enables the specification of queries in which the non-existence of requires elements in a service should not invalidate its selection, if other expressions in the sub-query that are disjointed with expression E1 (i.e., expressions connected to E1 by logical operator OR) are satisfied by the service.

During the *design* of service-based systems, the interaction and sequence of messages selected by the system designers from the SyBM model (stereotyped query messages and context messages) are represented in SerDiQueL's behavioural sub-query. In order to illustrate, consider the messages *payMovie(phone:PhoneNumber, quantity:Integer):Boolean* and *retrieveMovie(phone:PhoneNumber, info:Movie-Info):MovieStream* from the example in Section 10.3.1. Fig. 10.7 shows the description of this behavioural sub-query in SerDiQueL. As shown in the figure, the *Requires* elements specify the requirement for the existence of operations *payMovie* and *retrieveMovie,* and the *OccursBefore* element defines the order of these two operations. Similar and more complex behavioural sub-queries can be specified for the execution time adaptation of service-based systems. These cases are not shown here due to space limitations.

10.3.3 Constraint Sub-query

A constraint sub-query describes different types of additional conditions, which must be fulfilled by a service-based system or by its participating services. These additional conditions may include (a) quality aspects, (b) contextual aspects, or (c) extra structural and behavioural aspects that cannot be represented in the structural and behavioural sub-queries. Examples of these additional conditions are the specification of the time or cost to execute a certain operation in a service, the receiver of a message, or the provider of a service.

As described in Section 10.2, a constraint can be classified as *contextual* or *non-contextual*. The non-contextual constraints in a sub-query can be evaluated against any type of service specification (facet) in the service registries. The contextual constraints are evaluated against *context facets*. These context facets are associated with services and describe context information of the operations in these services. Context information is specified as context operations that are executed at run-time. The framework assumes the existence of context services that provide context information (see details in Section 10.4).

A constraint sub-query is defined as a single logical expression, a negated logical expression, or a conjunction or disjunction of two or more logical expressions, combined by logical operators. A constraint sub-query has four attributes, namely (a) *name*, specifying a description of the constraint; (b) *type*, indicating whether the constraint is hard or soft; (c) *weight*, specifying a weight in the range of [0.0, 1.0]; and (d) *contextual*, a boolean attribute indicating whether the constraint is contextual or non-contextual. The weight is used to represent prioritisations of the parameters in a query for soft constraints. If the value of the attribute *contextual* is *true*, the query may contain *ContextOperand* elements.

A logical expression is defined as a condition, or logical combination of conditions, over elements or attributes of service specifications (for non-contextual constraints) or over context aspects of service operations (for contextual constraints). A condition can be negated and is defined as a relational operation (*equalTo, notEqualTo, lessThan, greaterThan, lessThanEqualTo, greaterThanEqualTo, notEqualTo*) between two operands, which can be non-contextual, contextual, constants, or arithmetic expressions.

A non-context operand (see element *NonContextOperand*) has two attributes: (a) *facetName*, specifying the name of the service specification and (b) *facetType*, specifying the type of the service specifications to which the constraint will be evaluated. The operand contains an XPath expression indicating elements and attributes in the service specification referenced in *facetName* attribute. The constraints can be specified against any element or attribute of a facet in the registries.

A contextual operand (element *ContextOperand*) specifies operations that will provide context information at runtime. More specifically, a contextual operand describes the semantic *category* of context operations instead of the signature of the operation represented by sub-element *ContextCategory*. This is due to the fact that context operations may have different signatures across different services. A contextual operand is defined by (a) attribute *serviceOperationName*, specifying the name of the service operation associated with the contextual operand, and (b) attribute *serviceID*, specifying the identifier of a service that provides the operation. The value of attribute *serviceID* is specified when the context operand provides the specification of a context operation of a known service. This is normally the case when the context operation is associated with a service-based system for which the value of a context aspect of the system needs to be dynamically identified during the evaluation of a query (e.g., location of a mobile device application). In this case, attribute *serviceID* refers to the service-based system itself. Otherwise, the value of *serviceID* is specified as "any".

A *ContextCategory* element represents the semantic category of an operation, instead of its actual signature. It is defined as a relation between two categories (*Category1* and *Category2*). These categories can be either a reference to a document or a constant. A document category (element *Document*) has an attribute type indicating if the document is an ontology or a context facet, and contains an XPath expression referencing elements in the document. In the case of an ontology document, an attribute with the URL indicating the location of the ontology that describes the context operation is used. The language can support different ontologies for describing context operation categories since it does not make any assumption of the structure and meaning of the ontologies used, apart from the fact that the ontologies need to be described in XML. A context category in a query is evaluated against context facets of candidate services. This evaluation verifies if a candidate service has a context operation with semantic category that satisfies the categories in a query.

Arithmetic expressions define computations over the values of elements or attributes in service specifications or context information. They are defined as a sequence of arithmetic operands or other nested arithmetic expressions connected by arithmetic operators. The arithmetic operators are: *addition, subtraction, multiplication*, and *division* operators. The operands can be contextual, non-contextual, constants, or functions. A function supports the execution of a complex computation over a series of arguments. The results of these computations are numerical values that can be used as an operand in an arithmetic expression.

In order to illustrate, consider the replacement of service S_{Movie} in the CPO service-based system. Assume a contextual constraint specifying that the time to receive a requested movie while in Shanghai should not be more than 60 seconds. Fig. 10.8 shows this constraint in SerDiQueL. The constraint specifies that any candidate service that can retrieve movies while the location is Shanghai (i.e., services that match operation *getMovie()* in S_{Movie}) needs to have (a) a context operation classified in the category GREDIA_RELATIVE_TIME in ontology http://eg.org/CoDAMos_Extended.xml with the result of executing this operation being less than or equal to SECONDS-60, and (b) a context operation classified in the category GREDIA_LOCATION in the ontology with the result of executing this operation being equal to Shanghai, for this service to be accepted. Other contextual and non-contextual constraints can be described in SerDiQueL during design or adaptation of service-based systems.

```
<tnsa:ConstraintQuery name="C1" contextual="true"
                      type="SOFT" weight="0.5">
 <tnsa:LogicalExpression>
  <tnsa:Condition relation="LESS-THAN-EQUAL-TO">
   <tnsa:Operand1>
    <tnsa:ContextOperand   serviceOperationName="getMovie"
                           serviceID="any">
     <tnsa:ContextCategory relation="EQUAL-TO">
      <tnsa:Category1>
       <tnsa:Document location="http://eg.org/CoDAMoS_Extended.xml"
           type="ONTOLOGY">string(/owl:Class/@rdf:ID)
       </tnsa:Document></tnsa:Category1>
      <tnsa:Category2>
       <tnsa:Constant type="STRING">GREDIA_RELATIVE_TIME
       </tnsa:Constant> </tnsa:Category2>
     </tnsa:ContextCategory> </tnsa:ContextOperand> </tnsa:Operand1>
    <tnsa:Operand2>
     <tnsa:Constant type="STRING">SECONDS-60</tnsa:Constant>
    </tnsa:Operand2>
   </tnsa:Condition></tnsa:LogicalExpression>
  <LogicalOperator>AND </LogicalOperator>
  <tnsa:LogicalExpression>
   <tnsa:Condition relation=" EQUAL-TO">
    <tnsa:Operand1>
     <tnsa:ContextOperand serviceOperationName="getMovie"
                          serviceID="any">
      <tnsa:ContextCategory relation="EQUAL-TO">
       <tnsa:Category1>
        <tnsa:Document location="http://eg.org/CoDAMoS_Extended.xml"
            type="ONTOLOGY">string(/owl:Class/@rdf:ID)
        </tnsa:Document></tnsa:Category1>
       <tnsa:Category2>
        <tnsa:Constant type="STRING"> GREDIA_LOCATION
        </tnsa:Constant> </tnsa:Category2>
      </tnsa:ContextCategory></tnsa:ContextOperand></tnsa:Operand1>
     <tnsa:Operand2>
      <tnsa:Constant type="STRING">Shanghai
      </tnsa:Constant></tnsa:Operand2>
    </tnsa:Condition></tnsa:LogicalExpression>
 </tnsa:ConstraintQuery>
```

Fig. 10.8: Example of constraint sub-query

10.4 Query Execution and Matching Process

In both design and adaptation of service-based systems, matchings between queries and services are executed by the query processor (see Fig. 10.1) in a two-
phase process. In the first phase, the query processor searches service registries in
order to identify services that satisfy the hard constraints of a query based on exact
matchings (*filtering* phase). In the second phase, candidate services identified in the filtering phase are matched against the structural, behavioural, and constraints sub-queries,
and the best candidate services for the query are identified (*ranking* phase).

The ranking phase is executed based on the computation of partial distances,
namely *structural*, *behavioural*, soft *non-contextual*, and *contextual* distances

when applicable (i.e., execution time adaptation). The partial distances computed between services and a query are aggregated into an overall distance which is then used to select the best services for a query.

The *structural* matching between a query and a service is performed by comparing (i) the signatures of query messages in the structural model of a service-based system against the signatures of the operations of WSDL specifications of candidate services, during the design of service-based systems; or (ii) the signature of the operations in the WSDL specification of a service that needs to be replaced in a service-based system against the signature of the operations of WSDL specifications of candidate services, during adaptation of service-based systems. In both cases, the structural matching is based on the comparison of graphs representing the data types of the parameters of the operations and the linguistic distances of the names of operations and parameters.

The *behavioural* matching between a query and a service is performed by comparing the behavioural specification of the services and the behavioural sub-query. In this case, the behavioural specifications of the service and the behavioural sub-query are converted into state machine models and distances between these state machines are calculated based on similarities of these state machines.

The soft constraint matching (*contextual* and *non-contextual*) between a query and a service is performed by analysing the conditions in the constraint part of a query against service specifications.

There may be some differences in the execution process of a query. These differences are due to the lack of hard, behavioural, and soft contextual and non-contextual constraints in a query, or any combinations of these constraints[2]. In cases where there are no hard constraints in a query, the filtering phase is not executed and partial distances are calculated for all the services in registries. Also if there are no behavioral or soft constraints in a query, the computation of the relevant partial distances is bypassed and the overall distance is computed by using only the partial distances of the types of constraints specified in a query. Note that structural constraints are always present in a query and, therefore, distances based on these constraints are always calculated. This is because during design of service-based systems the signatures of the types of operations to be found in services need to be specified, while during adaptation of service-based systems it is expected to have at least a WSDL description of a service to be replaced.

Other differences in the execution process of a query exist in the case when a query is to be performed to support design or adaptation of a service-based system. This difference is mainly concerned with the structural and behavioural matching processes. More specifically, during the design of a service-based system, the structural and behavioural matching processes are flexible allowing the identification of services whose structure and behaviour characteristics have dif-

---

[2] Note that during the design of service-based systems, it is not possible to consider contextual constraints in a query.

ferent degrees of similarity to those of a required service, and behaviour matchings with alternative or missing mappings between a required service and an existing service. The flexibility and alternative/missing mappings contribute to the re-
formulation of the design models of the service-based system under development
and to the design of service-based systems based on characteristics of existing services. However, during adaptation of a service-based system, the structural and
behavioural matching process requires matches with services that can be used to
substitute services in a system without disturbing the rest of the system. Therefore,
in this case, for structural matching, it is necessary to guarantee that the input information for invoking the service that needs to be replaced in the system (S)
cover the input information needed by the candidate service (S') and that the information produced by S' covers the information expected from S. For behavioural matching, the order of the different functionalities to be executed by a service needs to be preserved. Furthermore, during execution time adaptation of
service-based systems, the execution process of a query also differs for push or
pulls modes. Details of the ways of executing a query are presented below.

10.4.1 Query Execution for Design of Service-based Systems

The execution of specified queries to identify services during the design of a service-based system includes the filtering and ranking phases discussed above. During filtering phase, query execution is based on checking the satisfiability of the
hard constraints specified as part of the query by the different services that exist in
various service registries.

During ranking phase, the execution of queries is based on finding the best possible 1-1 mapping between the service operations required by a query and the operations provided by different services returned by the filtering phase or in the service
registries. The search for the best possible match is treated as an instance of the
assignment problem, i.e., for each of the alternative total 1-1 mappings (M) of required operations (RO) on to service operations (SO), a total aggregate distance is
calculated from distances between the individual (RO, SO) pairs that constitute M
(in such pairs RO is a required query operation and SO is an operation offered by
some service). The mapping that has the minimum aggregate distance is selected
as the final outcome of the process. In this process, the distance between a pair of
required and service operations (RO, SO) is computed as weighted sum of three
partial distances between RO and SO, namely the structural, behavioural and soft
non-contextual constraint distances. Fig. 10.9 presents the structural (d_{STR}), behavioural (d_{BEH}), and soft constraint (d_{SOFTC}) distances.

The structural distance between a required and a service operation is computed by
considering a linguistic distance between the names of these operations, and distances between their input and output parameters. The linguistic distance between
two operation names (see function d_{LING} in Fig. 10.9) is computed as the ratio of

tokens in the names of the two operations, for which there is no token in the other operation having a semantic relation with it in WordNet, or being identical to it (the tokenization that precedes the computation of this distance assumes that capital letters within operation names indicate the start of new tokens).

The distance between the input (output) parameters of two operations is based on finding the best possible morphism between the structures of the data types of these parameters. The computation of this morphism is based on graphs representing the input (output) parameters of the relevant operations. These graphs are formulated by a special starting node with outgoing edges which are labeled by the names of the input (output) parameters of the relevant operation and pointing to nodes representing the types of these parameters. Furthermore, for each of the input (output) parameter types T, the graph includes an edge starting from the node representing T and ending at a node representing the type of the attribute. These edges are labeled with the name of the relevant attributes whilst the nodes of the graph are labeled with the names of the relevant data types. If the type of an attribute is not a primitive one, the same construction process is followed until attributes with primitive data types are reached.

Following the construction of the graph, the structural distance between two parameter sets is computed according to the distance d_{STR} defined in Fig. 10.9. This distance is computed by finding the morphism between the edges of the graphs representing the input(output) parameters of the two operations which have the minimum aggregate distance. The latter distance is computed as the linguistic distance between the names of the two edges under comparison and the names of their source and destination nodes.

As an example of computing the signature distance between two operations, consider the operation *payMovie(phone:PhoneNumber, quantity:Integer):Boolean* in Fig. 10.4 and the operation *payment(phoneNumber: String, serviceType: String, amount:Integer): Boolean*. The linguistic distance between the names of these two operations will be $d_{LING}($ *"payMovie"*, *"payment"* $)) = 1/3 = 0.33$[3] since the names of the two operations are tokenized into the sets {"pay", "movie"} and {"payment"} and the token "movie" in the first of these sets has no semantic relation with any of the tokens in the second set whilst the tokens "pay" and "payment" have a semantic relation with each other (as "payment is the noun of the verb "pay"). Furthermore, the distance between the input parameters and the output parameters of these operations is $d_{PS}($ *In(payMovie),In(payment)* $)=(2+0.11)/4=0.527$ and $d_{PS}($ *Out(payMovie), Out(payment)* $)=0/4=0$. These distances are computed on the basis of the graphs representing the structures of the relevant parameters, which are shown in Fig. 10.10.

---

[3] In the computation of signature distances we assume that $w_1=w_2=w_3=1$.

OPERATION DISTANCE:

$d(RO,SO) = w_S * d_{STR}(RO, SO) + w_B * d_{BEH}(RO, SO)) + w_{SC} * d_{SOFTC}(RO, SO)$

STRUCTURAL DISTANCE:

$d_{STR}(RO,SO) = \quad w_N * d_{LING}(name(RO), name(SO)) + w_I * d_{PAR}(In(RO),In(SO)) + w_O * d_{PAR}(Out(RO), Out(SO))$

where

- $In(O)$ $(Out(O))$ is the set of the input (output) parameters of O

LINGUISTIC DISTANCE:

$d_{LING}(S1, S2) = \quad N1 + N2 / N$

where

- $N1$ $(N2)$ is the number of tokens in S1 (S2) which have no common synonym with a token in S2 (S1)
- N total number of tokens of S1 and S2

PARAMETER DISTANCE:

$d_{PS}(P1,P2) = MIN_{M \in Morphisms(Edges(P1), Edges(P2))} \{(\sum_{(e1,e2) \in m} d_E(e_1,e_2) + \#Edges(P1)\text{-non-in-M} + \#Edges(P2)\text{-non-in-M})$
$/ max(\#Edges(P2), \#Edges(P1)))\}$

where

- $Edges(P1)$ $(Edges(P2))$ is the graph formulated to represent the data types of the parameters in P1 (P2)
- $\#Edges(Pi)$ is the number of edges in the graph to represent the data types of the parameters in Pi
- $Morhisms(Edges(P1), Edges(P2))$ is the set of all the possible morphisms between the edges of the graph representing P1 and the edges of the graph representing P2 that covers the graph with the fewer edges
- $d_E(e_1,e_2) = w_1.d_{LING}(name(e1), name(e2) + w_2.d_{LING}(name(sourceNode(e1)), name(sourceNode(e2))) + w_3.d_{LING}(name(destNode(e1),destNode(e2)) /(w_1 + w_2 + w_3)$

BEHAVIOURAL DISTANCE:

$d_{BEH}(RO, SO, k) = 1$ *if* transitions$(SM_{SO})=\varnothing$ *or* transitions$(SM_{RO})=\varnothing$

$d_{BEH}(RO, SO, k) = MIN_{M \in Morphs^{(sk)}(SM_{RO}, SM_{SO})}$
$(\sum_{(t, t') \in M} d_{SIG}(operation(t),operation(t')) + \#transitions(SM_{RO})\text{-non-in-M} + \#transitions(SM_{QO})\text{-non-in-M}) /(MAX(length(SM_{RO}),length(SM_{QO}))$ if transitions$(SM_{SO}) \neq \varnothing$ and transitions$(SM_{RO}) \neq \varnothing$

where

- SM_{QO} is the state machine formulated by the behavioural conditions of the behavioural conditions of the query containing RO
- SM_{RO} is the state machine of the service offering the operation RO
- $Morphs^{(sk)}(SM_{RO}, SM_{QO})$) is the set of all the possible 1-1 mappings between the transitions of two paths p and q in SM_{RO} and SM_{QO} that preserve the ordering of the transitions within these paths (i.e., for all transitions t_i and t_j in p such that $t_i \prec_p t_j$ it also holds that $m(t_i) \prec_q m(t_j)$) and leave up to K transitions in p or q without counterparts
- $Length(SM_{RO})(length(SM_{QO}))$ is the length of the longest path of transitions in $SM_{RO}(SM_{QO})$

SOFT CONSTRAINT DISTANCE:

$d_{SOFTC}(RO, SO) = \sum_{C \in SOFT\text{-}CONSTRAINTS(RO)} w_C \times not\text{-}satisfied(C) / \sum_{C \in SOFT\text{-}CONSTRAINTS(RO)} w_C$

where

- $SOFT\text{-}CONSTRAINTS(RO)$ is the set of soft constraints in the query which apply to RO
- w_C is a weight expressing the significance of the constraint C for RO ($w_i > 0$),
- $not\text{-}satisfied(C) = 1$ if the constraint C_i is not satisfied by S_o, or 0 otherwise.

Fig. 10.9: Distance functions used in execution of design service discovery queries

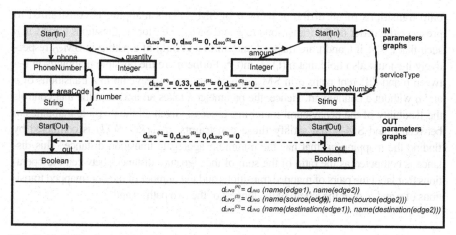

Fig. 10.10: In/Out Parameter graphs for PayMovie and Payment operations

More specifically, the distance between the input parameters of the two operations is 0.527 as there are two edges of the input graph of *payMovie* that have not been mapped onto any edges of *payment* (i.e., *phone* and *areaCode*), one edge of the input graph of *payment* that has not been mapped onto any edges of *payMovie* (i.e., *serviceType*) and two pairs of edges which have been mapped (i.e., *quantity* onto *amount* and *number* onto *phoneNumber*). The reason for mapping the edges *quantity* and *number* of the input parameter graph of *payMovie* onto the edges *amount* and *phoneNumber* of the input parameter graph of payment is because any alternative mapping would result in higher aggregate distance between the two graphs. The distance between the edge *amount* of *payment* and the edge *phone* of *payMovie*, for example, would be 0.75 as the names of the two edges as well as the names of their destination nodes do not have any semantic relation and there-fore the linguistic distances between them are equal to one in both cases. Similarly the distance between the output parameters of the operations *payMovie* and *pay-ment* is equal to zero as the two operations have the same output type.

The behavioural distance between a required query operation and a service opera-tion (see function $d_{BEH}(RO,SO, k)$ in Fig. 10.9) is computed by matching a state ma-chine representing the behavior of the interface that defines the operation in a query and the state machine of the service that provides a candidate operation for the query. The state machine of the interface that defines the required operation in the query is generated automatically from the query itself. The details of this gen-eration are beyond the scope of this chapter and are given in [40]. It should be noted, however, that this state machine always has a single path. Given these two state machines, the behavioural distance between two operations is computed by finding the best possible match between the single path p of the state machine of the query operation and the different paths of the state machine of the service (SM$_{SO}$). In the search for this match the individual transitions of p are mapped onto transitions of all different paths q of SM$_{SO}$. This mapping is constrained to preserve the order of the transitions in p and SM$_{SO}$, i.e., for all transitions t_i and t_j in p such that $t_i \prec_p t_j$ if t_i and t_j are mapped onto m(t_i) and m(t_j) of a path q in SM$_{SO}$ respectively it should also hold that m(t_i) $\prec_q$ m(t_j)[4]. Furthermore the possible mappings m between p and different paths q in SM$_{SO}$ are constrained to leave up to k transitions of p and q without a counterpart. Hence, the parameter k takes an integer value that controls the flexibility of the behavioural matching process. Given all the possible mappings m between p and SM$_{SO}$ that satisfy these constraints, $d_{BEH}(RO, SO,k)$ is computed by finding the mapping m' that has the minimum aggregate transition distance. This distance is computed as the ratio of the sum of the signature distances between the operations that label the pairs of mapped transitions and the number of the non-mapped transitions of p and q, over the length of the longest of the two paths p and q.

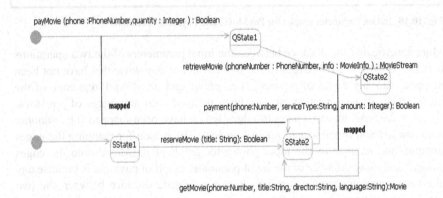

Fig. 10.11: State machines for *payMovie* and *payment* operations

As an example of the computation of $d_{BEH}(RO, SO,k)$ consider the state machines for the query and service in Fig. 10.11. Given these state machines the path morphism with the the lower aggregate distance between the two machines is the one that maps the path *(payMovie→ retrieveMovie)* of the state machine of the query onto the path *(payment →getMovie)* of the state machine of the service. The behavioural distance resulting from this mapping would be:

---

[4] $\prec_P$ is a relation indicating the order of transitions in path P and $\prec_Q$ is a relation indicating the order of transitions in an SM$_{SO}$ path Q.

$d_{BEH}(RO,SO, 0) = (d_{STR}(payMovie,payment) + d_{STR}(retrieveMovie,getMovie)) / 2$
$= ((d_{LING}(name(payMovie),name(payment)) +$
$d_{STR}(In(payMovie),In(payment)) +$
$d_{STR}(Out(payMovie),Out(payment)))/3) +$
$(d_{LING}(name(retrieveMovie),name(getMovie) +$
$d_{STR}(In(retrieveMovie),In(getMovie)) +$
$d_{SIG}(Out(retrieveMovie),Out(getMovie)))/3))/2$
$= ((0.33 + 0.66 + 0)/3 + (0 + 0.744 + 0.33)/3) /2 = 0.344$

It should be noted that other mappings between paths of these state machines are either not valid as they do not preserve the order of transitions (e.g., the mapping of *(payMovie→ retrieveMovie)* onto *(getMovie →payment))* or would not result in a minimum distance (e.g., the mapping *(payMovie→ retrieveMovie)* onto *(reserveMovie →payment))*.

10.4.2 Query Execution for Adaptation of Service-based Systems

During adaptation of service-based systems, the framework can execute queries in both pull and push modes. In the pull mode of query execution, the query requestor invokes the query processor to execute a query. The query processor executes the query and maintains services whose distance from the query does not exceed a specific threshold. The set of maintained services is sorted in ascending distance order and returned to the client application for further action.

In the push mode of query execution, the client application subscribes to the framework the services it deploys and a query for each of these services. Based on a subscribed query Q for a service S in the service-based system, the framework retrieves a set of possible candidate services that could replace S (if necessary). These candidate services are initially identified by executing the query as in the pull mode. To allow a pro-active service discovery process, the framework maintains an up-to-date version of the set of candidate services for a service S as changes in the descriptions and context of the services and/or the environment of the application are notified to the framework through the context servers and service listeners (see Fig. 10.1). The up-to-date set of candidate services is maintained in parallel to the execution of a service-based system and includes only services whose overall distance from the query subscribed for S does not exceed a given threshold. The services are sorted in ascending distance order in the set.

In the framework, the replacement of *S* in a service-based system may not take place right after modifications occur in the set of candidate services for S. This is because an immediate replacement might be inappropriate as, for example, in cases where service *S* is executing some transactions on behalf of the application, at the time when a new better service is found. The decision to stop the execution of the application in order to replace a service for which a better alternative service has been found is based on *replacement policies*. Details about the replacement policies used in the framework can be found in [26].

The distance threshold for a candidate service is specified in a query by the value of the query element Parameter, as discussed in Section 10.3. When a threshold is not specified, the framework uses a default value of 0.5.

The push mode of query execution covers four different cases. These are the cases where: (a) a service S in the system becomes malfunctioning or unavailable (Case A); (b) there are changes in the structure, functionality, quality or context of any service in the set of candidate services for S or in S (Case B); (c) there are changes in the context of the service-based system environment (Case C); or (d) new services become available or existing services have their characteristics modified (Case D). In the following, we discuss the push execution mode for each case.

Case A: In this case, service S is replaced by the first service in the set of candidate services. By virtue of the process of maintaining this set, the first service in the set is guaranteed to have the smallest distance to query Q associated with S. Following the replacement, S is removed from Set_S.

Case B: In this case, service S can be either a service in the service-based system or a service in the set of candidate services for a service in the system. Service S is evaluated against query Q to verify if it still matches the query. The new overall distance between Q and S is calculated. If S was a candidate replacement service and the distance between S and Q is below the threshold distance, S remains in the set of candidate services. The position of S in the set of candidate services may change, however. If S becomes the best replacement service in the set, S will replace a service in the system when the replacement policy permits. Otherwise, if the distance between S and Q is above the threshold, S is removed from the set of candidate services. If S is a service currently deployed by the service-based system, but is no longer the best option based on its new distance with Q, S is replaced by the first service in the set of candidate services, when the replacement policy permits the change.

Case C: In this case, a value in a context constraint in query Q is modified and a new query Q' needs to be created to reflect the new context value. The service S associated with Q that is currently bound to the system needs to be evaluated against the new context constraint in Q'. If S does not match the new query Q', the services in the set of candidate services are evaluated against Q' and a new set of candidate services may be generated. This is necessary for identifying a service S' that best matches Q' and bind it to the system, as soon as possible, so that the system can continue its execution, while the framework tries to find new services that match Q' in the service registries. Following the use of S', the framework will do an exhaustive search in registries (pull mode) to update the set of candidate services based on Q'. The same search will be executed when there are no services in the current set of candidate services that match Q'. After updating the set of candidate services, if there is a service that is better than S', this service will replace S' subject to the replacement policy.

Case D: In this case new services may appear in registries for the first time, or the descriptions of existing services in the registries that did not initially match a query Q change. After being notified of a new service S, or updated service descriptions for S, the framework evaluates S against each subscribed query Q for each service deployed in the service-based application. Depending on the distance value between S and the queries, S may be included in a set of candidate services for a service in the system or replace a service in the application, depending on the replacement policy for this service.

In any of the above cases for push mode, or in the case of pull mode of query execution, the ranking phase of the matching process between a service and a query is executed in three substages. In the first of these substages, the structural and behavioural parts of a query are evaluated against candidate services and a structural-behavioural partial distance between each of the services and the query is computed. In the second substage, the soft non-contextual constraints of a query are evaluated against the set of candidate services and a soft non-contextual partial distance is computed for each candidate service. Finally, in the third substage, the contextual constraints of a query are evaluated against the candidate services and a contextual partial distance is computed for each candidate service. At the end, the partial distances computed for each service are aggregated into an overall distance between each service and the query and the service for which this distance is below a threshold are maintained. Fig. 10.12 presents the overall distance and partial structural-behavioural distance. The soft contextual and non-contextual partial constraint distances are the same as the soft constraint distance shown in Fig. 10.9.

The structural evaluation of a query against services is executed by comparing operations in the structural sub-query with operations in structural specifications of services expressed in WSDL based on the comparison of graphs of the data types of the parameters of the operations and linguistic distances of the names of the operations and parameters. The graphs of the data types of the parameters are constructed as presented in Section 10.4.1. The matching process uses a variant of the *VF2* algorithm for detecting graph morphisms that we have previously developed for linear composition of static service discovery [55].

More specifically, a query operation Qop having an input parameter data type graph ITG_{Qop} and an output parameter data type graph OTG_{Qop} matches a service operation Sop having an input parameter data type graph ITG_{Sop} and an output parameter data type graph OTG_{Sop}, if ITG_{Sop} is a sub-graph of ITG_{Qop} and OTG_{Qop} is a sub-graph of OTG_{Sop}. In other words, a candidate service operation Sop matches a query operation Qop, if the data types of its input parameters are super-types of the input parameters of the query operation, and the data types of its output parameters are subtypes of the output parameters of the query operation. This is necessary for adaptation to guarantee that the input information assumed for invoking Qop will cover the input information needed by Sop, and the output information produced by Sop will cover the output information expected from Qop.

After computing the structural distance for each pair of query and service operations in a query Q and a service S, the framework identifies all the possible mappings between the operations in Q and operations in S in which each operation in Q is mapped onto a single operation in S.

For each of these mappings, the framework computes the behavioural distance between the mapped service and query operations based on the comparisons of paths representing the behavioural sub-query and behavioural service specification. More specifically, the behaviour matching is executed by (i) transforming behavioural service specifications into state machines, (ii) extracting all the possible paths from the generated state machine, (iii) transforming the behavioural sub-query into paths, and (iv) verifying if the path representing the behavioural sub-query can be matched against a path of the state machine of a service.

When a path representing the behavioural sub-query can be matched with a path in the state machine of a service, the behavioural distance for each pair of mappings of query and service operations in these paths is set to zero. Otherwise, the behavioural distance for each pair of mappings of query and service operations in these paths is set to one. After computing the structural and behavioural distances for all pairs of query and service operations in all possible operation mappings, the framework selects the mapping that has the minimal value for all the pairs divided by the number of operations in the query.

OVERALL DISTANCE:

$OD(Q, S) = (d_{STR\_BEH}(Q, S) + d_{NCON}(Q, S) + d_{CON}(Q, S)) / N$

where N is the number of computed partial distances

STRUCTURAL_BEHAVIOUR DISTANCE:

$d_{STR\_BEH}(Q,S) = Min(SUM(d_{SB}(Q_{opi}, S_{opj})/n)$

where

- $d_{SB}(Q_{opi}, S_{opj}) = (d_S(Q_{opi}, S_{opj}) + d_B(Q_{opi}, S_{opj})) / 2; 1 <= I <= n; 1 <= j <= m;$
- n is the number of operations in Q;
- m is the number of operations in S;
- $d_S(Q_{opi}, S_{opj})$ is the structural distance between an operation in Q and an operation in S
- $d_B(Q_{opi}, S_{opj})$ is the behavioural distance between an operation in Q and an operation in S

$d_S(Q_{opi}, S_{opj}) = (d_{LING}(Q_{opi}, S_{opj}) + d_{IN}(Q_{opi}, S_{opj}) + d_{OUT}(Q_{opi}, S_{opj})) / 3$

where

- $d_{LING}(Q_{opi}, S_{opj})$ is calculated as in Fig. 10.9
- $d_{IN}(Q_{opi}, S_{opj}) = \#UnMap\_Edges(IN\_Graph) / \#Edges(IN\_Graph)$
- $d_{OUT}(Q_{opi}, S_{opj}) = \#UnMap\_Edges(OUT\_Graph) / \#Edges(OUT\_Graph)$

$d_S(Q_{opi}, S_{opj}) = 0$ if path in the state machine of a behavioural sub-query can be mapped to a path in the stet machine of behavioural specification;

$d_S(Q_{opi}, S_{opj}) = 1$ if path in the state machine of a behavioural sub-query cannot be mapped to a path in the state machine of the behavioural specification;

Fig. 10.12: Distance functions used in execution of service discovery queries

As in the case of design of service-based systems, the evaluation of soft (non-contextual) constraints is executed by assessing constraint expressions in the constraint sub-queries against service specification facets. This evaluation takes place by retrieving the values of the XPath expressions from service specification facets and assessing arithmetic, relational and logical expressions that define the constraint using these values. The result of this evaluation is a binary value indicating whether a specific constraint is satisfied (0) or not (1). Based on the evaluation of individual constraints, a weighted soft (non-contextual) constraint partial distance is calculated (see soft constraint distance shown in Fig. 10.9).

The evaluation of contextual constraints is based on the work described in [39]. Context constraints are evaluated against context facets of candidate services. This evaluation is concerned with the runtime execution of context operations defined in the constraint sub-query and the comparison of the results of the execution of these operations with the value specified in the constraint. In the framework, context information is provided by context operations, which are associated with service operations and executed at runtime. Our work assumes the existence of context services that provide context information. These context services provide context operations that are dynamically executed in order to generate context values associated with the context operations. A service operation may have one or more context operations. A context operation may be related to one or more service operations, or a whole service-based application.

The context operations associated with a service are specified in context facets represented in XML format. A context facet specifies the service to which the facet is associated and the context operations available for this service based on semantic categories defined in terms of ontologies. In the current version of the framework we use an extended version of the CODAMOS ontology [8], as shown in the example of Fig. 10.8. However, the approach does not impose any restriction on the form of ontology used to describe semantic categories, as long as the ontology is specified in XML.

		Op1			Op2			Op3			D_{SB}
		d_S	d_B	d_{SB}	d_S	d_B	d_{SB}	d_S	d_B	d_{SB}	
C1	payment	0	1	.5							.7
	getMovie	.8	1	.9							
C2	payment	0	0	0							.0
	getMovie				0	0	0				
C3	payment	0	0	0							.13
	getMovie							.53	0	.26	
C4	payment				.8	1	.9				.9
	getMovie	.8	1	.9							
C5	payment				.8	1	.9				.7
	getMovie				0	1	.5				
C6	payment				.8	1	.9				.58
	getMovie							.53	1	.26	
C7	payment							.8	1	.9	.9
	getMovie	.8	1	.9							
C8	payment							.8	0	.4	.7
	getMovie				0	0	0				
C9	payment							.8	1	.9	.83
	getMovie							.53	1	.76	

Fig. 10.13: Structural and behavioural distances for all mapping combinations

The evaluation of a contextual constraint results in a binary value indicating whether the constraint is satisfied (0) or not (1) and the computation of a weighted contextual constraint partial distance between a query and a service.

To illustrate the query execution process and the computation of distance for execution time adaptation, consider the example in which a user of CPO service-based system has moved temporarily to Shanghai. In this case, due to change in the location (context) of the application's environment (Case C above), service S_{Movie} does not match the new context constraint and a service that matches the constraints need to be identified. Suppose that Q1 is a query describing the service that needs to be identified to replace S_{Movie} with the following characteristics:

(a) the structural sub-query is the WSDL description of S_{Movie} with operations
    payment(phone:Number, serviceType:String, amount:Integer):Boolean and
    getMovie(phone:Number, title:String, director:String, language:String):Movie
(b) the behavioural sub-query states that operation payment() needs to be executed
    before operation getMovie(), similar to the query in Fig. 10.7;
(c) the constraint sub-query as described in Fig. 10.8.

Consider $S_{MovieNew}$ a service in the set of candidate services for S_{Movie} that matches the contextual constraint of Q1 and has overall distance with Q1 below the expected threshold. Assume $S_{MovieNew}$ with the operations below and a state machine in which *Op1* is executed before *Op3* and *Op3* is executed before *Op2* (*Op1* → *OP3* → *Op2*).

Op1: payment(phone:Number, serviceType:String, amount:Integer):Boolean
Op2:getMovie(phone:Number,title:String,director:String,language:String):Movie
Op3:listRelatedMovies(phone:Number,title:String,director:String,language:String
    ):String

Fig. 10.13 shows the structural (d_S) and behavioural (d_B) distances for all possible combinations of mappings of pairs of operations in Q1 (d_{SB}) and $S_{MovieNew}$ and the structural_behavioural distance (D_{SB}) for each combination. As shown in this figure, the behavioural distances for the mappings in combinations 2, 3, and 8 are zero, since in these combinations the mappings of the query and service operations guarantee the order specified by the behavioural condition in the query. More specifically, in combination 2, the query operation payment is mapped to service operation Op1, the query operation *getMovie* is mapped to service operation Op2, and Op1 occurs before Op2 in the state machine of the service. Similar situations occur in (a) combination 3, in which payment is mapped to Op1, *getMovie* is mapped to Op3, and Op1 occurs before Op3 in the state machine of the service; and (b) combination 8, in which payment is mapped to Op3, *getMovie* is mapped to Op2, and Op3 occurs before Op2 in the state machine of the service. In all other combinations, the behavioural distances are set to 1 since the service operations mapped to payment and *getMovie* query operations do not preserve the order specified by the behavioural condition of the query. For example, in combinations C4, C7, and C6, payment is mapped to a service operation that occurs after the service operation to which query operation *getMovie* is mapped. In this example the best mapping is the one corresponding to combination 2.

10.5 Discussion

The framework that we have presented in the preceding sections provides a common basis for supporting both design time and execution time adaptation of service-based systems based on service discovery.

In particular, the discovery of services during the design of service based systems needs to be compatible with established system design specification languages and processes. This means that it should enable the specification of service discovery queries in ways that are conceptually close to design specification languages in order to make it easy to specify the discovery queries during the design phase of the software development life cycle and derive discovery conditions for the services to be discovered from design models. Furthermore, it should be possible to create representations of the discovered services in the same language that has been used to specify the design model which has driven their selection, and integrate the representations of the services that the designers decide to use consistently into these models.

It should also be noted that, from a matching point of view, the discovery process should be able to offer varying degrees of flexibility as such degrees might be appropriate and required at different stages of the system design process depending on the maturity of the ongoing design model. In early stages of the system design process, for instance, it is very likely to require a high degree of matching flexibility in discovery in order to ensure that no services which could be potentially useful for a system are missed due to strict matching. Later in the design process, however, when the design model of a system is more likely to have taken a rather elaborate and stable form, the degree of flexibility in matching may need to be reduced in order to ensure that the key assumptions of the design model and the constraints that it defines for the system are preserved by any of the services that can be located through the discovery process. In general, the degree of matching flexibility correlates negatively with the maturity of the design model: the more mature the design model less flexibility is required and vice versa.

The discovery framework that we have presented in this chapter addresses these requirements as it supports the graphical specification of service discovery queries in reference to design models of service based systems expressed in UML, the automatic expansion of these queries with parts of the specification of the design model which are relevant to the required services, the transformation of the expanded queries into queries that are expressed in a common executable query language, the execution of the queries, and the transformation of the descriptions of the located services back into UML. The discovery framework provides a range of features that enable designers to control the flexibility of the matching process including the abilities: (a) to distinguish between hard and soft constraints that should be satisfied by the located services and allow the generation of results that satisfy the latter type of constraints only partially, (b) to define the weight that each soft constraint should have in the matching process, (c) to opt between dif-

ferent types of structural matching between the types used in the operation signatures in queries and services (e.g., strict subgraph matching vs. detection of non
overall structure preserving morphisms between these types), and (d) to opt between different types of matching for query and service behavioural models.

Our framework could provide more comprehensive support for service discovery
during system design subject to certain enhancements. The first of these enhancements is support for verifying that the design model generated from integrating the
descriptions of the discovered services with the original design model used in the
discovery process satisfies certain properties (e.g., avoidance of deadlocks). The
results of verification analysis could be used to decide which of the discovered
services should be integrated into the system. The verification process could also
be used in order to support the specification of discovery queries in subsequent iterations. If the conjunction of a service model and a design model is found to vio-
late a property (e.g. avoidance of deadlocks), and the violation can be attributed to
certain elements in the model of the service, a subsequent query could be formulated with conditions that would filter out services having these elements.

The discovery of services during the execution time adaptation of service-based
systems needs to support different situations that may trigger the need for adapting
the systems. In this respect, the framework that we described in this chapter provides the required support for (i) unavailability of malfunctioning of a service, (ii)
changes in the characteristics of a service, (iii) changes in the context of a service
or the application's environment, and (iv) availability of a service that is superior
to one being used in the system. Moreover, the language to allow for the specification of queries should be able to express complex and different types of constraints. Services are described from different perspectives and, therefore, in order
to guarantee a better precision during the identification of a service to replace a
service on a running service-based system, it is necessary to consider combinations of these different perspectives.

Although our experience has demonstrated that the discovery of services based on
different perspectives increases its precision, it is not possible to guarantee that
services will always be described in terms of their structural, behavioural, and
quality characteristics. Therefore, it is necessary to provide ways to infer the behaviour of services based on monitoring of these services.

Also for execution time adaptation of service-based systems another critical factor
is the performance of the service discovery process. This factor is often neglected
in the literature. Our measure for addressing this factor is the pro-active discovery
approach. In this approach, which is realized by our framework, services are continually identified in parallel to the execution of the system and pointers to those
of them that can replace existing system services are maintained so as to be able to
rebind to them immediately if the need arises. Based on this pro-active approach,
our framework provides considerable reduction in the time required for identifying
replacement services (see [56] for experimental results).

Some limitations of the adaptation process provided by the framework include the
need to support changes in service-based systems that are not only concerned with

the replacement of a service by another service, but that consider (a) replacement of a service by a composition of services, (b) replacement of a group of services by a single service or another composition of service, (c) changes in other parts of a service-based system workflow (e.g., variables, conditions, loops). Adaptation of service-based system should consider other aspects that may require adaptation apart from (i)-(iv) above such as dynamic evolution and changes of business activities that underpin and need to be supported by the service-based system, as well as dynamic evolution of user requirements and demands.

10.6 Related Work

Two areas of research related to the work presented in this chapter, namely service discovery and service-based system adaptation, are reviewed below.

Service discovery has been a main strand of research in service oriented computing. The different approaches to service discovery can be classified based on the *core algorithmic aspects* of the search process that they use into (i) keyword, (ii) model, and (iii) semantics based approaches. Some approaches support also context based service discovery.

Keyword based service discovery approaches specify service requests as sets of keywords and are implemented predominantly as part of service search engines. Examples of such engines include Seekda [34] and Strikeiron [41]. Seekda offers a search facility that looks into textual and interface (i.e. WSDL) descriptions of services. Seekda allows also the application of predefined filters on discovered service results (e.g country or service provider). Both these search engines provide browsing facilities for discovery and continually updated fixed types of searches based on criteria such as the frequency of service usage. Keyword based searches are also deployed in active service registries such as AWSR [42]. AWSR searches for RSS data feeds providing information about services in different web-sites, combines them together, and offers them in new "syndicated" data feeds. Similarly, text-based requirements specifications are matched with textual descriptions of services to drive the discovery process in [49]. The latter approach uses also term disambiguation based on WordNet Overall, keyword based approaches are easy to implement, conform to the paradigm of information retrieval over the Internet, and are more natural and easier to use from an end user perspective. However, they tend to have low precision and recall and are unable to support complex querying conditions regarding interface, behaviour, or quality of services.

In model based service discovery approaches, queries and services are described in some form of structured models without using ontologies and semantic matchmaking techniques. In [14], for example, service discovery is based on the use of behavioural service models represented in WSCL [54] and matching these models with graphs representing users requirements based on graph matching. The work in [44] proposes QoS-based selection. A goal-based model that considers re-use of predefined goals, discovery of relevant abstract services described in terms of capabilities, and contracting of concrete services to fulfill requesting goals has been proposed in [21]. Other approaches deploy graph transformation rules [17,20], or behavioural matching [14,16,27,35]. The approach in [16] uses abstract behavioural models of services. In [15] and [36], functional and quality crosscutting concerns of components and services are specified as aspects, and discovery is based on a formal analysis and validation of aspect based descriptions. The work in The use of behavioural specifications expressed in BPEL and a tree-alignment algorithm to identify query-service matchings is used in [27].

The approach described in [24] supports the specification of service discovery queries using system design models expressed in UML and uses graph matching techniques. In [30], the authors propose USQL, an XML-based language to represent syntactic, semantic, and quality of service search criteria. An extension of USQL that incorporates behavioural models expressed as UML sequence diagrams has been proposed in [31]. An XML based service query language is also used in [54,37] for service discovery. The queries expressed in this language can cover service interface, behaviour and QoS characteristics and can be specified by system developers to discover replacement services for systems at runtime. The query language proposed in [32] is used to support composition of services based on user goals. In [5] the authors propose BP-QL a visual query language for business processes.

Some of the model based approaches are hybrid as they deploy both keyword-based lexical matching and model matching. WSDL-M2 [23] uses lexical matching to calculate linguistic similarities between concepts, structural matching to evaluate the overall similarity between composite concepts, and combines vector-space model techniques with synonyms and semantic relations based on WordNet. The work in [51] combines WordNet-based techniques and structure matching for service discovery. The work in [45] uses four similarity assessment methods for service matching.

Model based approaches enable the specification of semantically richer queries and can produce results of higher precision than keyword based approaches. These advantages arise when services that have descriptions in the form of structured models assumed by the approaches are available. However, this is not always the case. Therefore, these approaches are often non applicable especially in situations where normal users are searching for services to support them, rather than to build some "system" out of them. On the other hand model based approaches work better for system designers who might have, complete or partial, system design models providing the basis for specifying model based service discovery queries.

The semantic based approaches assume services described in terms of structured models that may incorporate logical conditions expressing behavioural and quality service properties, annotated by ontologies. These ontologies are used to signify the semantics of services, providing a basis for detecting semantic similarities between services as well as between services and queries. Several techniques have been developed using semantic approaches including [1,17,19,21,22]. METEOR-S [1], adopts a constraint driven service discovery approach in which service requests are integrated into the composition process of a service-based system. In

[17], service discovery is based on matching requests specified in a variant of Description Logic (DL). The work in [21] supports explicit and implicit service semantics and uses logic based approximate matching and Information Retrieval (IR) techniques. In [35] a query language based on first-order logic that focuses on properties of service behaviour signatures specified in OWL is used to support the discovery process. Approaches for service discovery based on service capabilities have been proposed in [28,50]. The work in [50] uses DAML-S to describe service capabilities, while in [28] services are described in OWL. In [50] service requests are matched against service advertisement. The approach considers four degrees of matching, namely exact, plugin, subsumes, and fails. The work in [28] reduces these four degrees of matching to three degrees (exact, inclusive, and weak), and considers discovery of pervasive services based on context and QoS characteristics. The semantic service discovery category includes also many approaches that have been developed to support context aware service discovery such as [6,48].

Semantic service discovery approaches are normally expected to be more precise than their model and keyword based counterparts. This expectation, however, is not plausible unless ontologies are accurate and consistent. Generally, there is lack of appropriate service ontologies and semantic based approaches are limited to those cases where there are adequately described services. This limitation is also due to the fact that semantic approaches are more difficult to use, as they require the specification of some complex logic-based queries. Similarly, these approaches require substantial investment from service providers to provide complex service models, annotate them in reference to existing ontologies, and maintain service descriptions when ontologies evolve.

Context oriented service discovery approaches are found in [5,6,9,39,48]. These approaches may use matching techniques similar to those described above, but differ on the automatic generation of discovery queries from service deployment context. In [9], context information is represented by key-value pairs attached to the edges of a graph representing service classifications. This approach does not integrate context information with behavioural and quality matching, and context information is stored explicitly in a service repository that must be updated following context changes. In [6] queries, services, and context information are expressed in ontologies. The work in [5] focuses on user context information. The approach in [48] locates components based on context-aware browsing. In this approach, the interaction of software developers with the development environment is monitored and candidate components that match the development context based on signature matching are identified and presented to developers for browsing. The above approaches support the use of context conditions in service discovery but do not fully integrate such conditions with behavioural criteria. They also have limited applicability since they depend on the use of specific ontologies for the expression of context conditions. An approach that uses other discovery criteria (service interface and behaviour) without assuming the use of a particular ontology is presented in [39]. Context oriented service discovery approaches are useful when the criteria for service discovery are related to the deployment context of the required service and their main strength arises from their ability to construct automatically queries with context discovery conditions and execute them in a seamless way. The drawback of such approaches is that they often do not take into account other discovery conditions and if they do these conditions need to be specified manually.

Recently, some approaches that support **adaptation of service-based systems** started to appear. The dynamic binding approach described in [4] provides binding and reconfiguration rules to support evolution of service compositions during run-time. The work supports four types of rules, namely: (a) rule to discover services based on defined constraints and preferences and to bind the best identified service; (b) rule to bind to a service from a list of candidate services defined during design time of the composition; (c) rule to delete or modify a binding to point to another service; and (d) rule to stop the execution of the composition.

A self-healing approach for service compositions based on monitoring rules and reaction strategies is proposed in [3]. Examples of reaction strategies, i.e., actions taken by the system when monitoring expressions are not verified, include the re-execution of the same service invocation, the selection of a new service, the creation of a composition of services that can execute the behaviour of the faulty interaction or changes in the way that the process is monitored (i.e., less strict). Another self-healing approach is found in the PAWS framework [2], which also uses monitoring and recovery actions. Examples of PAWS recovery actions include retrying/redoing the process task, substituting the problematic service by a candidate service, or executing a compensation action.

The VieDAME framework [29] uses an aspect-oriented approach to allow adaptation of service-based systems for certain QoS criteria based on alternative services. A service participating in the system can be marked as replaceable to indicate that alternative services can be invoked instead of the original one, when necessary. Policies are used to indicate alternative services. In [18], the authors propose PROSA, a pro-active adaptation approach based on online testing.

10.7 Conclusions and Future Work

In this chapter we presented a framework to support design and execution time adaptation of service-based systems based on service discovery. The work presented in this chapter unifies the results of two EU F6 projects in the area of service-oriented computing, namely SeCSE [33] and Gredia [13] projects. The work has been developed based on the challenges identified by industrial partners in both projects in the areas of telecommunications, automotive, software, media, and banking. Different characteristics of predecessors of the unified framework focusing on design and execution time service discovery have been discussed in earlier publications (see Section 10.1). This chapter, however, presents the unified version of the framework for the first time, and uses the Cell Phone Operator system case study of this book to illustrate how the framework works, hence making it easier for the reader to appreciate how it compares with alternative approaches. Several evaluations of different aspects of the framework have been conducted and reported elsewhere (e.g. in [58,40]). These evaluations measure the framework in terms of the recall and precision that it achieves in service discovery as well as the efficiency of the service discovery processes that it implements both at design time and at execution time. Overall, as we have reported in the cited papers, the results of these evaluations have been very positive.

Currently, we are extending the framework to address some of the points that we discuss in Section 10.5. In particular, we are extending the framework to support: (a) discovery based on behavioural service operation composition, (b) the verification of design models after introducing into them models of discovered services, (c) pro-active negotiation of service level agreements as part of the execution time service discovery process, and (d) other forms of adaptation of service-based systems triggered by changes in business activities and user desires.

References

1. R. Aggarwal, K. Verma, J. Miller, and W. Milnor. Constraint Driven Web Service Composition in METEOR-S, Int. Conf. on Services Comp. 2004.
2. Ardagna, D., Comuzzi, M., Mussi, E., Pernici, B., Plebani, P.: PAWS: A Framework for Executing Adaptive Web-Service Processes. IEEE Software, 24 (6), (2007).
3. Baresi, L., Ghezzi, C., Guinea, S.: Towards Self-Healing Compositions of Services. Studies in Computational Intelligence, v. 42, Springer (2007).
4. Baresi, L., Di Nitto, E., Ghezzi, C., Guinea, S.: A Framework for the Deployment of Adaptable Web Service Compositions. Service Oriented Computing and Applications Journal (to appear).
5. C. Beeri, A. Eyal, S. Kamenkovich, and T. Milo. Querying Business Processes. 32nd International Conference on Very Large Data Bases, VLDB, Korea, September (2006).
6. F. Bormann, et al, Towards Context-Aware Service Discovery: A Case Study for a new Advice of Charge Service", 14th IST Mobile and Wireless Communications Summit, 2005.
7. BPEL4WS.http://www128.ibm.com/developerworks/library/specification/ws-bpel/
8. CoDAMoS. www.cs.kuleuven.ac.be/cwis/research/distrinet/projects/CoDAMoS/ontology/
9. S. Cuddy, M. Katchabaw, and H. Lutfiyya. Context-Aware Service Selection Based on Dynamic and Static Service Attributes. IEEE Int. Conf. on Wireless and Mobile Computing, Networking and Comm., 2005.
10. Deubler M., Meisinger M., Kruger I. Modelling Crosscutting Services with UML Sequence Diagrams. 8th Int. Conf. on Model Driven Engineering Languages and Systems, 2005
11. J. Dooley, A. Zisman, G. Spanoudakis. Runtime Service Discovery for Grid Applications. Book chapter in Grid Technology for Maximizing Collaborative Decision Management and Support: Advancing Effective Virtual Organizations, 2009.
12. Gardner T. UML Modelling of Automated Business Processes with a Mapping to BPEL4WS. *In 2nd European Workshop on OO and Web Services (ecoop), 2004.*
13. GREDIA. www.gredia.eu.
14. D. Grirori, J.C. Corrales, and M.Bouzeghoub. Behavioral Matching for Service Retrieval, International Conference on Web Services, ICWS 2006, USA, September 2006.
15. J. Grundy and G. Ding. Automatic Validation of Deployed J2EE Components Using Aspects. IEEE 16th International Conference on Automated Software Engineering, USA, 2001.

16. R.J. Hall and A. Zisman. Behavioral Models as Service Descriptions, Int. Conf. on Service Oriented Computing, 2004
17. J.H. Hausmann, R. Heckel and M. Lohman. Model-based Discovery of Web Services, Int. Conf. on Web Services, 2004.
18. Hielscher, J., Kazhamiakin, R., Metzger, A., Pistore, M.: A Framework for Proactive Self-Adaptation of Service-based Applications Based on Online Testing, 1st Eur. Conf. Towards a Service-Based Internet, ServiceWave, LNCS 5377, 2008.
19. W. Hoschek. The Web Service Discovery Architecture, IEEE/ACM Supercomputing Conf., 2002.
20. U. Keller, R. Lara, H. Lausen, A. Polleres, and D. Fensel. Automatic Location of Services, European Semantic Web Conference, 2005.
21. M. Klein and A. Bernstein. Toward High-Precision Service Retrieval. IEEE Internet Computing, 30-36, 2004.
22. M. Klusch, B. Fries, and K. Sycara. Automated Semantic Web Service Discovery with OWLS-MX, Int. Conf. on Autonomous Agents and Multiagent Systems, 2006.
23. Kokash N., van den Heuvel W.J., D'Andrea V. Leveraging Web Services Discovery with Customizable Hybrid Matching, Int. Conf. on Web Services, ICWS 2006, 2006.
24. A. Kozlenkov V. Fasoulas F. Sanchez G. Spanoudakis A. Zisman. A Framework for Architecture-driven Service Discovery, International Workshop on Service Oriented Software Engineering (IW-SOSE'06), ICSE, China, 2006.
25. Kozlenkov A., Spanoudakis G., Zisman A., Fasoulas F., Sanchez F. Architecture-driven Service Discovery for Service Centric Systems, International Journal of Web Services Research, special issue on Service Engineering,, 4(2):81-112, 2007
26. K Mahbub and A. Zisman, Replacement Policies for Service-based Systems, 2nd Workshop on Monitoring, Adaptation and Beyond (MONA+), Stockholm, November 2009.
27. R. Mikhaiel and E. Stroulia, Interface- and Usage-aware Service Discovery, 4th Int. Conf. on Service Oriented Computing (ICSOC), 2006.
28. B. Mokhtar S., Georgantas N., Preuveneers D., Issarny V., and Berbers Y. EASY: Efficient semantic Service discovery in pervasive computing environments with QoS and context support. Journal of Systems and Software 81: 785-808, 2008.
29. O.Moser, F. Rosenberg, S. Dustdar, Non-Intrusive Monitoring and Service Adaptation for WS-BPEL, 17th Int. World Wide Web Conference, 2008.
30. M. Pantazoglou, A. Tsalgatidou, and G. Athanasopoulos. Discovering Web Services in JXTA Peer-to-Peer Services in a Unified Manner. 4th International Conference on Service Oriented Computing (ICSOC), 2006.
31. M. Pantazoglou, A. Tsalgatidou, and G. Spanoudakis, G.: Behavior-aware, Unified Service Discovery. In Proceedings of the Service-Oriented Computing: a look at the inside Workshop, SOC@Inside'07, Austria, September, 2007.
32. M. Papazoglou, M. Aiello, M. Pistore, J. Yang. XSRL: A Request Language for web services, http://citeseer.ist.psu.edu/575968.html
33. SeCSE. Secse.eng.it/pls/secse/ecolnet.home.
34. Seekda . [Online]. Available at: http://seekda.com/
35. Z. Shen and J. Su. Web Service Discovery based on Behavior Signatures. IEEE Int. Conf. on Service Computing, 2005.
36. S. Singh, J. Grundy, J. Hosking, J. Sun. An Architecture for Developing Aspect-Oriented Web Services, 3rd European Conf. in Web Services, 2005.
37. G. Spanoudakis G., A. Zisman, A. Kozlenkov: A Service Discovery Framework for Service Centric Systems, 2005 IEEE Conference on Services Computing (SCC 2005), 2005.
38. G. Spanoudakis and A.Zisman. UML-based Service Discovery Tool, 21st IEEE International Conference on Automated Software Engineering Conference, ASE, Japan, 2006.
39. G. Spanoudakis, K. Mahbub, and A. Zisman. A Platform for Context-Aware Run-time Service Discovery, IEEE Int. Conf. on Web Services (ICWS 2007), USA, 2007
40. G. Spanoudakis and A. Zisman. Discovering Services during Service-based System Design using UML, IEEE Transactions of Software Engineering (to appear).

41. Strikeiron, [Online]. Available: http://strikeiron.com/
42. M. Treiber and S. Dustdar, Active web service registries, *IEEE Internet Computing*, 11(5): 66–71, 2007.
43. UDDI. www.uddi.org.
44. X. Wang, T. Vitvar, T. Kerrigan, and I. Toma, "A QoS-Aware Selection Model for Semantic Web Services", 4th Int. Conf. on Service Oriented Computing, ICSOC, USA, 2006
45. J. Wu and Z. Wu "Similarity-based Web Service Matchmaking". IEEE Int. Conf. on Services Computing, SCC, 2005.
46. WSDL. http://www.w3.org/TR/wsdl
47. XQuery. http://www.w3.org/TR/xquery/
48. Y. Ye and G. Fischer. Context-Aware Browsing of Large Component Repositories. IEEE 16th Int. Conf. on Automated Software Engineering, ASE, USA, 2001.
49. K. Zachos, N.A.M Maiden, S.Jones and X.Zhu, 'Discovering Web Services To Specify More Complete System Requirements', 19th Conf. on Advanced Information System Engineering, (CAiSE), 2007.
50. Paolucci M., Kawamura T., Payne T.R., and Sycara K. "Semantic Matching of Web Services Capabilities". Int. Semantic Web Conference, Italy, 2002.
51. Wang Y. and Stroulia E. "Semantic Structure Matching for assessing Web-Service Similarity", 1st Int. Conf. on Service Oriented Compusting, 2003.
52. WOOGLE. http://www.gujian.net/woogle/
53. WSDL. http://www.w3.org/TR/wsdl..
54. WSCL. Web Services conversation language. http://www.w3.org/TR/wscl10
55. A. Zisman, K. Mahbub, and G. Spanoudakis. A Service Discovery Framework based on Linear Composition, 2007 IEEE International Conference on Services Computing (SCC 2007), USA, July 2007.
56. Zisman A., Spanoudakis G., Dooley J.: A Framework for Dynamic Service Discovery, 23rd IEEE/ACM International Conference on Automated Software Engineering, 2008.
57. A. Zisman, J. Dooley, G. Spanoudakis. Proactive Runtime Service Discovery, IEEE 2008 International Service Computing Conference (SCC '08), Hawaii, 2008.
58. A. Zisman and G. Spanoudakis. UML-based Service Discovery Framework, 4th International Conference on Service Oriented Computing, ICSOC, Chicago, 2006.
59. A. Zisman, G. Spanoudakis, J. Dooley. A Query Language for Service Discovery, 4th International Conference on Software and Data Technologies - ICSOFT, Bulgaria, 2009.

Chapter 11
VRESCo – Vienna Runtime Environment for Service-oriented Computing

Waldemar Hummer, Philipp Leitner, Anton Michlmayr, Florian Rosenberg, and Schahram Dustdar

Abstract Throughout the last years, the Service-Oriented Architecture (SOA) paradigm has been promoted as a means to create loosely coupled distributed applications. In theory, SOAs make use of a service *registry*, which can be used by providers to publish their services and by clients to discover these services in order to execute them. However, service registries such as UDDI did not succeed and are rarely used today. In practice, the binding often takes place at design time (for instance by generating client-side stubs), which leads to a tighter coupling between service endpoints. Alternative solutions using dynamic invocations often lack a data abstraction and require developers to construct messages on XML or SOAP level. In this paper we present *VRESCo*, the *Vienna Runtime Environment for Service-oriented Computing*, which addresses several distinct issues that are currently prevalent in Service-Oriented Architecture (SOA) research and practice. VRESCo reemphasizes the importance of registries to support dynamic selection, binding and invocation of services. Service providers publish their services and clients retrieve the data stored in the registry using a specialized query language. The data model distinguishes between abstract *features* and concrete service implementations, which enables grouping of services according to their functionality. An abstracted message format allows VRESCo to *mediate* between services which provide the same feature

Waldemar Hummer
Vienna University of Technology, Austria e-mail: waldemar@infosys.tuwien.ac.at

Philipp Leitner
Vienna University of Technology, Austria e-mail: leitner@infosys.tuwien.ac.at

Anton Michlmayr
Vienna University of Technology, Austria e-mail: michlmayr@infosys.tuwien.ac.at

Florian Rosenberg
CSIRO ICT Centre, GPO Box 664, Canberra ACT 2601, Australia e-mail: florian.rosenberg@csiro.au

Schahram Dustdar
Vienna University of Technology, Austria e-mail: dustdar@infosys.tuwien.ac.at

but use a different message syntax. Furthermore, VRESCo allows for explicit *versioning* of services. In addition to functional entities, the VRESCo service metadata model contains QoS (Quality of Service) attributes. Clients can be configured to dynamically rebind to different service instances based on the QoS data. The paper presents an illustrative scenario taken from the telecommunications domain, which serves as the basis for the discussion of the features of VRESCo.

11.1 Introduction

In the course of the last years, software engineering research and practice have put remarkable focus on the Service-Oriented Architecture (SOA) [20] paradigm, which propagates the use of services – autonomous applications made available in a computer network using standardized interface description and message exchange – as a means to create decoupled, distributed, composite applications in heterogeneous environments. *Web Services* [29] represent the most common way of implementing SOAs. Conceptually, SOA involves three main actors: 1) *service providers* implement services and make them available at a certain location (endpoint) in the network; 2) *service registries* store information about services, and providers can publish their services in such registries; 3) *service consumers* discover (find) services by querying a service registry, bind to the obtained service references and execute the services' operations. This model of three collaborating actors is often referred to as the *SOA triangle*. It has been argued that currently the SOA triangle is actually *broken* [16], since the binding between consumer and service provider often happens at design-time and service registries are rarely used in practice. This is largely due to the limited success of service registry standards such as UDDI [19].

Furthermore, dynamic binding and invocation of services is often only supported for services having the same syntactical (or technical) interface. Since there is no standard mechanism to describe the logical equivalence of service operations using service metadata, service consumers are experiencing difficulties determining whether two service implementations actually perform the same task. Even if clients are aware of the concrete service endpoints that are available for a certain task, the problem of different syntactical interfaces remains. One possibility would be to provide input message templates for all possible service versions at design time. However, a more dynamic and flexible approach to mediation between diverse interfaces is desirable. The same applies to cases in which different versions of one and the same service exist. So far, service *versioning* is not directly supported by service registries such as UDDI. An end-to-end solution for service versioning, which allows to transparently switch to the latest version of a service, is desirable. Dynamic service selection and binding should also be possible based on other non-functional attributes, such as the availability or response time.

In this chapter we address some of the issues and shortcomings that are prevalent in current SOA research and practice. We present *VRESCo*, the *Vienna Runtime Environment for Service-oriented Computing*. The discussion of the capabilities of the

VRESCo framework is based on an illustrative example scenario. The scenario contains a number of challenges for Service Oriented Computing (SOC). We identify and describe these issues and subsequently present appropriate solutions based on VRESCo. VRESCo has in part been developed within the FP7 Network of Excellence project S-Cube, within work package WP-JRA-2.3 (Self-* Service Infrastructure and Discovery Support). Within S-Cube, Vienna University of Technology is the beneficiary responsible for the development of the VRESCo prototype.

The remainder of this paper is structured as follows. In Section 11.2 we describe the example scenario that serves as the basis for the discussion of VRESCo. Section 11.3 comprises the main part of the paper, in which we describe the concepts and features of VRESCo. In this part, we always try to establish a link between the abstract concepts and the reference implementation of the scenario. In Section 11.4 we discuss existing work related to VRESCo. Since the VRESCo framework embraces a number of rather distinct research areas, the related work discussion can only focus on a few selected aspects. The paper concludes with a summary and final remarks in Section 11.5.

11.2 Example Scenario

To demonstrate the capabilities of the VRESCo framework, we consider an example scenario taken from the telecommunications domain. The scenario models a process that allows customers to port a phone number from their current CPO (cell phone operator), say *CPO1*, to another operator, say *CPO2*. The idea behind number porting is that customers are able to choose freely between providers of telecommunication services, without having to give up the phone number of their existing contract. When a customer decides to switch to provider CPO2, she signs the new contract and is temporarily assigned a new phone number (`TempNumber`). In the following, the customer (or, in fact, the new provider CPO2 acting on behalf of the customer) instructs her old provider, CPO1, to issue the number porting process and transfer the existing number (`DesiredNumber`) to provider CPO2.

Figure 1 illustrates the scenario process as well as the internal and external services that are involved. For the sake of brevity, error handling routines are not depicted in the figure. However, each process activity includes reasonable integrity checks concerning the input parameters and the current execution state. Input to the process are two phone numbers, the existing number with CPO1 (`DesiredNumber`), and the temporary number with CPO2 (`TempNumber`) and the time for which the number porting is scheduled.

The first step in the process is to contact a *CRM* (Customer Relationship Management) *Service* in order to look up the customer that is associated with `Desired-Number`. Secondly, the partner CPO is determined dynamically. For that purpose, each CPO operating on the market publishes a *CPO Service* that can be used to query whether a certain number belongs to that CPO. The one CPO answering with a positive response is the partner for this process execution. Next, the *Number Porting*

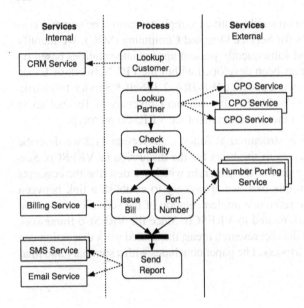

Fig. 11.1: Example scenario

Service of the partner CPO is invoked to check the portability status. In case porting is not possible at the time, appropriate measures need to be taken. Assuming that no error has occurred, the process can now execute two activities in parallel: performing the actual number porting with the partner *Number Porting Service* and issuing a bill using the internal *Billing Service*. As soon as both activities are finished, a report is sent to the customer via the internal *Email Service* and one instance of the (replicated) *SMS Service*.

11.2.1 Involved Web Services

Table 1 lists the Web services involved in the scenario, as well as the operations that are provided by these services.

Since the *CRM Service* is a core element not only in the number porting process, but in the IT architecture of the telecommunications provider as a whole, its requirements have changed in the past and will continue to evolve in the future. Not only the behavioral aspects change, but the renewed implementations often employ a different service interface. This raises the demand for explicit service *versioning* support.

For the *CPO Service* and the *Number Porting Service*, one instance (replica) exists for every CPO involved in the scenario. However, the replicas are not entirely identical: although they require the same (abstract) parameters and generate the same result, the concrete syntax (i.e., XML schema) of the exchanged messages is slightly different for each CPO.

Table 11.1: Web services involved in the example scenario

CRM Service			
Operation: GetCustomer	Input	Number:	PhoneNumber
	Output	MatchingCustomer:	Customer
CPO Service			
Operation: IsRegisteredNumber	Input	Number:	PhoneNumber
	Output	IsRegistered:	boolean
Number Porting Service			
Operation: CheckPortability	Input	TempNumber:	phone number
		DesiredNumber:	phone number
	Output	PortingPossible:	porting status
Operation: SchedulePorting	Input	TempNumber:	phone number
		DesiredNumber:	phone number
		ScheduledTime:	timestamp
	Output	Result:	porting result
Billing Service			
Operation: IssueBill	Input	TheCustomer:	Customer
		ServiceToBill:	PortingResult
Notification Services (Email Service, SMS Service)			
Operation: NotifyCustomer	Input	TheCustomer:	Customer

Consider the operation *SchedulePorting* of the *Number Porting Service*. The schemas of the different input messages for three operators (CPO1, CPO2, CPO3) are illustrated in Figure 11.2. The data contained in each of the messages is the existing *temporary number*, the *desired number* and the *time* that the number porting shall be scheduled for. For CPO2 and CPO3, the *country code* (e.g., *43* for Austria) and the *area code* (e.g., *686*) of the phone numbers need to be specified separately, while for CPO1 this information is included in the phone number string (e.g., *"0043 686 1234567"*). Since CPO2 expects only one CountryCode argument, it is expected that the temporary number and the desired number are from the same country. The scheduled time is expressed as a timestamp and is of type string for CPO1 and of type long for CPO2 and CPO3. Similarly, the CheckPortability operation of the three CPOs has slightly different message schemas, which will not be discussed in more detail for the sake of brevity.

The *SMS Service*, which is heavily used across the overall system, is replicated in several instances. In order to maximize throughput, the requests to this service should be distributed to the deployed replicas. Hence, the request for SMS notification at the end of the number porting process should be handled by the service instance which currently shows the best performance.

11.2.2 SOC Challenges

To sum up, the presented number porting scenario addresses the following SOC challenges:

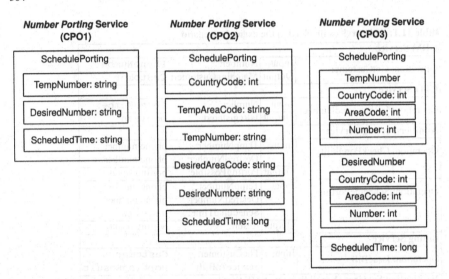

Fig. 11.2: Input messages of operation *SchedulePorting*

- **Service Metadata**: It is desirable to have a data model for describing the services that participate in the system. The description should cover both functional and non-functional characteristics. Functional attributes include the services' technical interface in the form of its operations and their input and output parameters. Non-functional characteristics concern *Quality of Service* (QoS) aspects such as the performance, security or price of a service. To account for services which perform similar or identical tasks, the description of the abstract functionality provided by a service should be separated from the definition of concrete endpoints. This is particularly required for the replicated versions of the *SMS Service* and the different versions of the *Number Porting Service*.
- **Service Versioning**: When services evolve over time, it is important that new versions of a service can be published and easily integrated into the existing process. Ideally, the integration should happen automatically and transparently, and it should be possible to either always bind to the latest version of a service or to explicitly switch back to older versions of a service. In the scenario, this is particularly important for the *CRM Service*, which exists in different versions and is subject to ongoing changes.
- **Service Interface Mediation**: Each CPO participating in the example scenario uses a slightly different input message schema for the operation `Schedule-Porting` of the *Number Porting Service*. The demand for transparently exchanging endpoints of this operation results in the necessity for mediation between service interfaces. To that end, the commonalities of the different concrete interfaces provided by CPO1, CPO2 and CPO3 have been identified and combined in an abstract interface description of this operation. For instance, the abstract interface specifies that the `SchedulePorting` operation requires

two telephone numbers and one timestamp (see Table 11.1). Based on the abstract interface definition, it should be possible to define for each concrete implementation how the elements of the abstract interface can be mapped to the elements of the concrete interface. After defining the mapping at design time, the conversion should be conducted automatically at runtime.

- **Dynamic Service Invocation**: Since hardwired solutions of service invocations are inflexible and usually fail in case of even the smallest modification to the system (such as changing the value of an XML namespace or extending an XML schema with an additional element), it is advisable to reach a maximum level of dynamicity. Ideally, the message exchange should be expressed in an abstracted, high-level way and the actual invocations and message transformations should be performed by an underlying framework.

- **Service Rebinding**: Related to service versioning and dynamic invocation, rebinding denotes the capability of a client to bind to a new service or service interface. Rebinding may happen at different occasions – either in *periodic* intervals, *on demand* or *event-based*. For instance, the *CRM Service* is frequently changed and hence its clients' binding should be reconsidered periodically. Furthermore, the scenario is dynamic in the sense that the version of an existing *Number Porting Service* may change and that new partner CPOs may join the market or existing CPOs may cease to exist. As soon as any changes in the structure of the system arise, clients shall be notified of the modifications and rebind to the target service(s).

- **QoS-Based Service Selection**: The *SMS Service*, which is used to send a notification to the customer at the end of the number porting process, exists in several instances to serve the high demand for this functionality. To offer the clients a good performance of this service, requests should be distributed among all deployed replicas. The decision which replica to use is based on QoS (Quality of Service) characteristics, e.g. the availability of the service and the response time of the operation *NotifyCustomer*.

11.3 The VRESCo Solution

In the following we present the VRESCo framework, based on a reference implementation of the *number porting* scenario described in Section 11.1. This section is divided into several subsections, each of which addresses a particular aspect of the SOC challenges mentioned in Section 11.2. Furthermore, the VRESCo features are applied to the concrete solution of the example scenario.

11.3.1 System Overview

As has been mentioned in the introductory section of this chapter, the VRESCo platform is an effort to compensate issues and shortcomings in current SOA solutions. VRESCo strives to recover the "*broken*" SOA triangle [16] by focusing on the use of service metadata published in a registry, as well as dynamic binding and invocation of services.

An overview of the VRESCo architecture is depicted in Figure 11.3. The system is implemented in C# and makes use of the *Windows Communication Foundation* (WCF) [11]. The *VRESCo Runtime Environment* is a server application that is invoked using the *VRESCo Client Library*. The interfaces of the server components are exposed as Web services and the communication between clients and the VRESCo runtime uses the SOAP [28] messaging protocol.

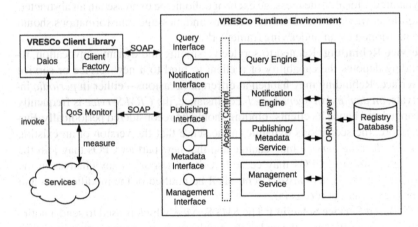

Fig. 11.3: VRESCo architecture overview, adapted from [15]

The *VRESCo Runtime Environment* is made up of different sub-components:

- The *Query Engine* allows to search for any entity that is stored within the runtime. To that end, a specialized query language (*VRESCo Query Language*, VQL) is offered, which will be further discussed in Section 11.3.3.
- With the aid of the *Notification Engine* clients are able to subscribe for notification of events that occur during execution of the runtime [13].
- The *Publishing/Metadata Service* offers two interfaces, the *Metadata Interface* for adding entries to the *metadata model* and the *Publishing Interface* for registering the description of a service implementation using the *service model*. The distinction between these to models will be clarified in Section 11.3.2.
- The *Management Service* is responsible for storing user information and handling the user access rights.

Additionally to the aforementioned parts, the VRESCo runtime employs a fifth core component, the *Composition Engine*. However, a discussion of the composition mechanism is out of the scope of this paper and the interested reader will find a detailed description in [22]. All communication is secured using an *Access Control* layer that checks user credentials (username, password), handles encryption and applies signatures to the exchanged messages.

On the client side, Daios [9], a framework for dynamic and asynchronous service invocation, is used to conduct the message exchange with the involved Web services. Daios uses an abstracted message format, the *Daios Message*, which provides for protocol-independence and support for both SOAP and REST based services. The dynamic messaging approach will be briefly presented in Section 11.3.6. The *Client Factory* is used to instantiate proxy objects that communicate with the interfaces of the VRESCo Runtime Environment. Since these interfaces are exposed as Web services, SOAP is used as the messaging protocol between clients and the runtime.

Finally, since VRESCo allows for selection and composition of services based on *Quality of Service* (QoS) attributes, a *QoS Monitor* [14] is deployed as a standalone component, which regularly measures the availability, performance and accuracy of the target Web services. The QoS Monitor feeds back the acquired measurement values to the VRESCo runtime via the *Publishing Interface*. The runtime aggregates the stored measurements and calculates average values.

11.3.2 Metadata Model and Service Model

VRESCo uses a *metadata model* to describe functionalities offered by Web services in an abstract way. A *category* is a named entity that describes the general purpose of services and serves as an umbrella item for all other entities in that domain (e.g., the VRESCo category of our example scenario is named `TelcoSystem`). A category contains an arbitrary number of *features*, which describe a concrete action in the system. In the scenario, a feature named `PortNumber` describes the action of actually performing the porting with a target partner CPO. As illustrated in Figure 11.4, the base element in the model is the abstract *Concept*, which is specialized by the three sub-entities *Data Concept*, *Predicate* and *Feature*. All concept entities are composable, i.e., a concept can be derived from another concept. *Data concepts* define the data types that occur in the system and are either atomic (string, number, etc.) or composed of other data concepts. For instance, in the *number porting* scenario we make use of a data concept named `PhoneNumber`, which itself consists of three elements named `CountryCode`, `AreaCode` and `Number`.

Additionally, the metadata model allows for the definition of *Preconditions* and *Postconditions* that need to be fulfilled when a feature is executed. Both types of conditions are associated with a number of *Predicates*, which may each have multiple *Arguments*. The arguments are described by an associated data concept. Two types of predicates are distinguished: *Flow Predicates* indicate constraints related to the data flow such as data required or produced by a feature (predicates `requires` and `produces`); *State Predicates* express global constraints that need to be fulfilled. For a more detailed description of the metadata model we refer to [15].

The *service model* constitutes the information about concrete services managed by VRESCo. A *service* is available in one or more *revisions*. *Revisions* are the basis for

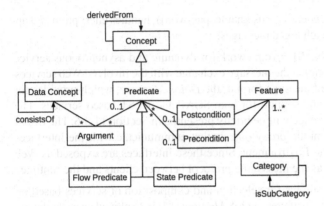

Fig. 11.4: Service metadata model, adapted from [15]

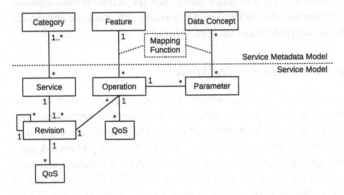

Fig. 11.5: Mapping between service model and metadata model, adapted from [15]

service versioning, which will be discussed in more detail in Section 11.3.4. Figure 11.5 depicts the mapping between the service metadata model and the (concrete) service model. *Services* are mapped to *categories*, a service *operation* is one concrete implementation of a *feature* (note that one *feature* may be implemented by several different *operations*) and operation *parameters* are mapped using *data concepts*. The *mapping function* between the latter is the basis for the VRESCo service mediation, which will be further discussed in Section 11.3.7.

In addition to the functional characteristics of services, VRESCo also saves non-functional attributes in the form of *QoS* attributes. Operation-specific QoS data are attributes such as *response time* or *accuracy*, whereas attributes such as *latency* apply to a service revision. A more detailed description of QoS attributes is given in Section 11.3.5.

11.3.3 Service Querying

The *VRESCo Querying Language* (VQL) constitutes an interface to query the data stored in the registry. VQL queries are based on the entities and relations of the data model presented in Section 11.3.2. In that sense, the query language abstracts from the concrete database schema that is used to store the model entities. Following the Query Object Pattern [6], VQL provides an API to programmatically construct queries from a set of *criteria*. Criteria are defined either as *mandatory* using the function **Add** or as *optional* using the function **Match**. Mandatory criteria must be fulfilled for all elements of the result set that is obtained by executing the query, whereas optional criteria are treated differently depending on the *querying strategy*:

- The *EXACT* querying strategy treats all criteria as mandatory, regardless of whether they are **Add** or **Match** criteria.
- With *PRIORITY* querying, each **Match** criterion is prioritized using a numeric *weight* attribute. The higher its weight, the more importance a criterion receives during the selection process of the query engine. The final result is sorted by the sum of priority values. For instance, a **Match** criterion with priority weight 4 takes precedence over the sum of two criteria with weights 1 and 2, because $4 > (1 + 2)$.
- The *RELAXED* strategy is a specialized case of *PRIORITY* querying, where the priority weight of each **Match** criterion is 1. This method simply distinguishes between mandatory and optional parameters and sorts the final result list based on the number of optional (**Match**) criteria that are fulfilled.

Upon execution, VQL query objects are internally converted to an according SQL query string and finally executed on the underlying database.

```
1  var querier = VRESCoClientFactory.CreateQuerier("username", "password");
2  var query = new VQuery(typeof(Service));
3  query.Add(Expression.Eq("Category.Features.Name", "PortNumber"));
4  query.Add(Expression.Eq("Revisions.IsActive", "true"));
5  var list =
6      querier.FindByQuery(query, QueryMode.Exact) as IList<ServiceRevision>;
7
8  // create client proxy for each Number Porting Service
9  foreach(var service in list) {
10     query = new VQuery(typeof(ServiceRevision));
11     query.Add(Expression.Eq("Service.ID", service.ID));
12     query.Add(Expression.Eq("Tags.Property.Name", "LATEST"));
13     DaiosProxy proxy = querier.CreateRebindingProxy(query,
14         QueryMode.Exact, 1, new PeriodicRebindingStrategy(1000*60*60));
15     ...
16 }
```

Listing 11.1: VQL Example Query Using EXACT Strategy

Listing 11.1 illustrates an initialization routine of the number porting scenario which obtains the references to the *Number Porting Service*s of the involved CPOs and creates a client for each instance. Firstly, a *Querier* instance is created with the aid of the VRESCo client factory. For the creation of the VQuery object in line 2, a parameter is used to specify the expected return type of the result (`Service`). Lines 3 and 4 add criteria to the query, one related to the name of the feature the service implements (needs to contain the string *"PortNumber"*) and the second mandating that at least one revision of this service needs to be active. The query uses an *EXACT* query strategy and hence treats all criteria as mandatory. In lines 5 and 6 of the code listing, the query is executed and the result is received as a list of services. Subsequently, the code loops over all result entities and creates a new `VQuery` that expects `ServiceRevision` results (line 10). The criterion in line 11 is used to have the service identifier (`ID`) of the result match the `ID` of the service in the current loop execution. Line 12 specifies that only the latest version of a service should be returned (more details on modeling service versions with VRESCo is given in Section 11.3.4). Finally, the constructed query object serves as the basis for creating a `DaoisProxy` that is utilized to perform the dynamic service invocations later on (see Section 11.3.6). More sophisticated VQL examples that include alternative querying strategies and `Match` criteria will follow in the remaining parts of this chapter.

11.3.4 Service Versioning

Just as any other IT artifact may evolve over time, Web services are also subject to changes made by the service providers. For example, services may be extended by new functionalities, adapted to changed environments or restructured to better fit the overall IT architecture. The process of services being modified over time is collectively referred to as service *evolution*. When a service evolves, usually the older versions of this service are still available in order not to break the operability of existing clients. Hence it is an important requirement for service registries to handle service evolution and to document the changes of service interfaces. Current registries such as UDDI [19] do not directly support different versions of the same service.

The distinction between *services* and *revisions* in the VRESCo service model allows for explicit versioning of services [8]. The service model defines *tags*, which describe a revision. VRESCo defines six default revision tags, while custom tags can also be added by service providers. Table 11.2 lists the default tags, their meaning and who they are assigned by. The tags `INITIAL`, `HEAD` and `LATEST` are automatically assigned by the VRESCo runtime, whereas all other tags are added manually by the provider.

Relationships between service versions can be visualized as a *service version graph*, where the nodes constitute service revisions and directed edges point from a revision node to all its successor revisions. Figure 11.6 depicts the relation between the revisions of the *CRM Service*. The first version (*v1*) is tagged `INITIAL`. For the second version, the `Customer` data type has been extended by an additional field and the implementation has been thoroughly tested such that *v2* deserves the tag `STABLE`. Version 3 has been implemented as a WCF service [11] – making use of the integrated security and encryption framework – and is therefore tagged *wcf*. Ver-

Table 11.2: Predefined service revision tags

Tag	Description	Assigned by
INITIAL	The first version of this service	VRESCo
STABLE	A well-tested production-level service version	provider
HEAD	The most recent version in a branch	VRESCo
LATEST	The most recent version in the entire version graph; implies HEAD	VRESCo
DEPREC	The version is deprecated and should not be used anymore	provider
OFF	The version has been taken offline and is not available anymore	provider

sion 4, on the other hand, is an unsecured version of the CRM Service, realized with JAX-WS [1]. Finally, revision *v5* represents an extension of the WCF implementation. This is the last revision in the WCF branch and also the most recent version in the version graph.

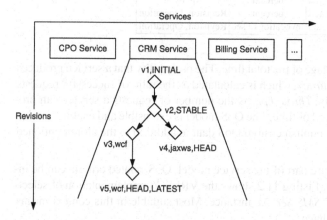

Fig. 11.6: *CRM Service* version graph

11.3.5 QoS-Based Service Selection

As mentioned in the *number porting* scenario description (see Section 11.2), the *SMS Service*, which is used to send a notification to the customer at the end of the number porting process, is replicated (i.e., exists in several instances) to serve the high demand for this functionality. Ideally, the requests should be equally distributed to all replicas to avoid the situation that one service instance becomes overloaded.

The VRESCo runtime stores QoS data that apply to both service *revisions* and *operations*. The QoS information may be either added manually using the *Management Service* or measured automatically with the aid of the *QoS Monitor*. VRESCo cur-

---

[1] https://jax-ws.dev.java.net/

rently defines the QoS attributes that are listed in Table 11.3 [15]. While *Price*, *Reliable Messaging* and *Security* are static values that are manually entered by service providers, the remaining attributes are *calculated* by the QoS Monitor. *Latency* denotes the (average) time required to transport a request over the network. *Response Time* is the sum of latency for request and response plus the execution duration of the service operation. *Availability* is the time during which the service is up and running,

Table 11.3: Predefined QoS attributes

Attribute	Type	Unit	Applies To
Price	static	$ / invocation	Revision, Operation
Reliable Messaging	static	{true, false}	Revision
Security	static	{None, X.509}	Revision, Operation
Latency	calculated	ms	Revision
Response Time	calculated	ms	Operation
Availability	calculated	percent	Revision
Accuracy	calculated	percent	Revision, Operation
Throughput	calculated	invocations / sec	Revision, Operation

expressed as the percentage of the total time. The probability that a service produces a valid result is the *Accuracy*, which is calculated as the ratio of successful requests to total requests. Finally, *Throughput* is the number of requests a service can process during a given period of time. The QoS model is extensible and enables service providers to define and publish custom QoS data in addition to the aforementioned QoS attributes.

Since the QoS entities are part of the service model, QoS-related criteria can be included in VQL queries. Listing 11.2 shows the VRESCo implementation of selecting the "most suitable" *SMS Service* instance. Most suitable in this context means that the service should have

1. most importantly, a high availability ($> 90\%$),
2. the smallest possible response time,

   a. less than 100 ms (priority weight 3), or
   b. less than 200 ms (priority weight 2), or
   c. less than 500 ms (priority weight 1);

3. if possible, an accuracy of at least 80%.

We assume that the combination of points 2 and 3 has the same weight as point 1. Listing 11.2 displays the VQL query construction necessary to achieve this specific service selection. The `Add` criterion in line 2 mandates that the service name must include the String *"SMSService"*. The `Match` operation in the following two lines specifies that with a priority weight of 5 the availability should be greater than 0.9 (90%). Note that the '&' operator is a shortcut for an `And` operation. With the aid of the following 3 statements, a response time of less than 100, 200 or 500 ms is targeted, with a priority weight of 1 each. Therefore, in sum, the priority weight of a response time of less than 100 ms is 3 and the priority weight of a response time of less than 200 ms is 2.

```
1   var query = new VQuery(typeof(ServiceRevision));
2   query.Add(Expression.Like("Service.Name", "%SMSService%"));
3   query.Match(Expression.Eq("QoS.Property.Name", "Availability") &
4               Expression.Gt("QoS.DoubleValue", 0.9), 5);
5   query.Match(Expression.Eq("QoS.Property.Name", "ResponseTime") &
6               Expression.Lt("QoS.DoubleValue", 100.0), 1);
7   query.Match(Expression.Eq("QoS.Property.Name", "ResponseTime") &
8               Expression.Lt("QoS.DoubleValue", 200.0), 1);
9   query.Match(Expression.Eq("QoS.Property.Name", "ResponseTime") &
10              Expression.Lt("QoS.DoubleValue", 500.0), 1);
11  query.Match(Expression.Eq("QoS.Property.Name", "Accuracy") &
12              Expression.Ge("QoS.DoubleValue", 0.8), 2);
13
14  var list =
15      querier.FindByQuery(query, QueryMode.Priority) as IList<ServiceRevision>;
16  var bestServiceInstance = list[0];
17  ... // perform SMS notification using bestServiceInstance
```

Listing 11.2: VQL Query Using QoS Attributes

Assume that five *SMS Service* instances are deployed in the example scenario. A illustrative snapshot of QoS values at a certain point in time is given in Table 11.4. Values that fulfill the QoS criteria named above are printed in bold text. *Total Score* is the sum of priority weights of those QoS criteria that are fulfilled by a service. *SMS Service 1* is ranked first since it has the highest total score of 8 points. Services 2 and 5 are ranked second with 7 points each, and the services 4 (5 points) and 3 (4 points) take positions 3 and 4, respectively.

Table 11.4: Snapshot of QoS characteristics of SMS service instances

Service	Availability	ResponseTime	Accuracy	Total Score	Rank
SMS Service 1	**0.91**	**413 ms**	**0.80**	5 + 1 + 2 = 8	1
SMS Service 2	**0.95**	**194 ms**	0.78	5 + 2 + 0 = 7	2
SMS Service 3	0.81	**156 ms**	**1.00**	0 + 2 + 2 = 4	4
SMS Service 4	0.85	**96 ms**	**0.85**	0 + 3 + 2 = 5	3
SMS Service 5	**0.97**	527 ms	**0.93**	5 + 0 + 2 = 7	2

The VRESCo query engine internally performs the same calculation: for each Match criterion m in a query with *PRIORITY* (or *RELAXED*) query strategy, it determines for each element e in the universal set (in this case, all ServiceRevision entities whose name contains the string *"SMSService"*) whether e fulfills criterion m, and adds the priority value of m to the score of e. As mentioned in Section 11.3.3, this calculation is actually performed by constructing a corresponding SQL statement, which is executed on the underlying DBMS. The final result is ordered by decreasing score of the elements. Hence, after execution of the query, the variable list in Listing 11.2 contains the service revision objects in the order of their QoS score. The first element of the list is assigned to the variable `bestServiceInstance`, a reference to *SMS Service 1*, which is subsequently used to perform the SMS notification.

11.3.6 Dynamic Service Invocation

Web Service invocations in VRESCo are executed using the *Daios* framework [9]. In contrast to many other Web service client frameworks that rely on code generation and client-side stubs to invoke services (such as Apache Axis 2 [2]), Daios seeks to provide *stub-less* communication with Web services. Furthermore, the Daios framework is *protocol-independent* in the sense that it transparently distinguishes and handles SOAP and REST invocations. This is achieved by using an abstracted *Daios message* format, which describes request and response messages in a high-level way, leaving protocol-specific details to the lower, internal layers of Daios. In the following, we briefly present the dynamic binding capability of VRESCo and discuss the message-centric invocation approach of Daios.

11.3.6.1 Dynamic Binding

The ability of clients to dynamically bind to services is often claimed to be one of the key advantages of SOA. However, in practice binding often happens at design time using generated stubs. Daios overcomes this issue and provides a service invocation framework that is build upon the dynamic invocation principle. The process of binding to a service involves several steps. Firstly, the client needs to retrieve and parse the service interface description, or *service contract*. WSDL is the standard description language for Web services that use SOAP [28] as the messaging protocol, whereas WADL [24] (Web Application Description Language) is often used to describe REST-based services. Typically both WSDL and WADL parsing involves processing XML schema definitions (XSD) that define the data types of the exchanged documents. Next, a service *proxy* is created from the in-memory representation of the service contract. When the client issues an invocation, the provided input is matched with the message definitions contained in the service contract.

The frequency and occasion at which binding takes place determine the accuracy of the proxy, but also influence the runtime performance since rebinding causes a certain overhead. VRESCo distinguishes the following rebinding strategies:

- `Fixed`: Fixed proxies perform binding upon creation but never rebind to the target service. They are used in scenarios where rebinding is not required.
- `Periodic`: With this strategy, the proxy reconsiders the binding periodically in fixed intervals, which is inefficient if the frequency of invocations is low.
- `OnInvocation`: This strategy causes the proxy to update its binding prior to every service invocation. This ensures that the binding is always up to date but obviously results in a large overhead.

---

[2] http://ws.apache.org/axis2/

- **OnDemand:** If rebinding happens upon client request, the overhead is reduced in comparison to **Periodic** and **OnInvocation**, with the drawback that the binding is not always up to date.
- **OnEvent:** This rebinding strategy combines the advantages of all strategies by making use of the VRESCo *Event Notification Engine* [13]. Clients enter subscriptions that define in which situations rebinding should take place. If rebinding is due, the VRESCo runtime triggers a corresponding event notification. A disadvantage of this strategy is that clients need to expose a callback service in the network.

The implementation of the number porting scenario makes use of different rebinding strategies. The proxy for the *CRM Service* is updated periodically every hour (**Periodic**), since this service is subject to frequent changes. A **Periodic** strategy is also applied for the *Number Porting Service*. Because the *Email Service* and the *Billing Service* are very stable and have not evolved over the last years, the message exchange with these services is conducted using a **Fixed** client. In order to select the best-performing instance of the *SMS Service* in each execution of the number porting process, an **OnInvocation** proxy is used for invoking the **Notify** operation. A thorough performance evaluation of the different rebinding strategies has been carried out in [15].

11.3.6.2 Message-Centric Communication

Daios follows a message-oriented approach, i.e., client developers do not "invoke operations" but send and receive messages to and from the service. Daios uses a special message format which abstracts messages from their XML representations. The Daios message represents objects as a collection of name/value pairs. The value of one such pair entry may be either 1) a simple type (string, integer, ...), 2) an array of simple types or 3) a message or an array of messages (recursive construction).

```
1   DaiosProxy proxy = ...;  // get proxy for service of partner CPO
2
3   var request = new DaiosMessage();
4   var tempNumber = new DaiosMessage();
5   tempNumber.Set("CountryCode", 43);
6   tempNumber.Set("AreaCode", 686);
7   tempNumber.Set("Number", 1234567);
8   var desiredNumber = new DaiosMessage();
9   desiredNumber.Set("CountryCode", 43);
10  desiredNumber.Set("AreaCode", 677);
11  desiredNumber.Set("Number", 87654321);
12  request.Set("TempNumber", tempNumber);
13  request.Set("DesiredNumber", desiredNumber);
14  request.Set("ScheduledTime", 1267124400);
15
16  DaiosMessage response = proxy.RequestResponse(request);
```

Listing 11.3: Construction of Daios Messages

Listing 11.3 shows how a request to the operation *SchedulePorting* of the *Number Porting Service* is constructed using Daios. The service selection and proxy creation has been illustrated in Listing 11.1 in Section 11.3.3. Now we assume that the process execution has just determined the partner CPO in the activity *Lookup Partner* and that in line 1 of Listing 11.3 we obtain a reference to the Daios proxy for this partner. To construct the desired request message, three Daios messages are instantiated: a "container" Daios message named `request` and two message instances `tempNumber` and `desiredNumber`. In lines 5-7 and 9-11, respectively, the simple values `CountryCode`, `AreaCode` and `Number` are set. The recursive construction of Daios messages is illustrated in lines 12 and 13.

Once the DaiosMessage has been constructed, the `DaiosProxy` instance is used to perform a synchronous service invocation (see line 15 in Listing 11.3). Note that this proxy follows a `Periodic` rebinding strategy and reconsiders its binding every 60 minutes in order to always bind to the most recent version of the service (see Listing 11.1). Besides the "request response" invocation flavor, Daios also supports asynchronous communication ("fire and forget", "poll object" and "callback"). The achievement of the Daios framework is that all information necessary to construct the final SOAP message (qualified operation names, XML namespaces, etc.) is transparently collected from the target service's WSDL document in the background. Analogously, the SOAP response from the service is internally converted back to the high-level Daios message format. In Section 11.3.7 we will discuss the internals of service invocations in VRESCo and how transformations of input and output messages are performed using a *Mediator Chain*.

11.3.7 Service Mediation

The *Number Porting Service* instances of the three different CPOs participating in the example scenario have the same logical interface in terms of which information needs to be provided by a calling endpoint, but the services differ in their syntactical interface (i.e., the schema of the input messages). In VRESCo terms, the three services provide the same (abstract) *features*, but implement a different concrete *operation* interface. Hence, if service endpoints are to be exchanged transparently, there is a need to map the interfaces to one another. This mapping can be easily achieved using the *VRESCo Mapping Framework* (VMF), which provides capabilities to map between input and output parameters of features and operations stored in the registry.

The VMF architecture is illustrated in Figure 11.7. At design time, or *mapping time*, service providers use the *Mapper* component to enter the mapping information into the mapping database via the *Metadata Service*. The mapping information comprises 1) the (interfaces of the) abstract *features* that are available, 2) the (interfaces of the) *operations* a service offers, 3) which operation implements which feature and 4) how operation interface and feature interface are mapped to one another.

Having published the mapping functions for the operations of all three CPOs, the endpoints for feature `PortNumber` can be dynamically exchanged at *execution time*. Clients simply provide their input in the format that is dictated by the feature's interface. The VRESCo client library then transparently converts the input such that

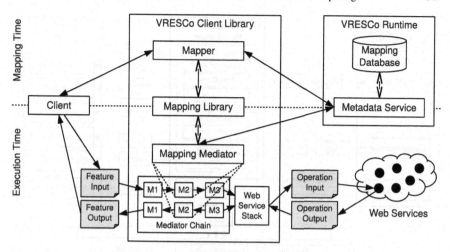

Fig. 11.7: VMF architecture

it matches the interface of the target operation. To that end, *Mapping Mediators* are plugged in to the client library as a part of the *Mediator Chain*. Each mediator that is part of this chain may perform modifications to the incoming and outgoing messages. Converting a high-level feature input or output message to its equivalent message on operation level is referred to as *lowering*, whereas the opposite is called *lifting*. The *Mapping Mediator* retrieves the lowering and lifting information from the *Metadata Service*. When outgoing messages are handed through the mediator chain, the *Mapping Mediator* performs the lowering before the message is finally serialized to SOAP and sent via the *Web Service Stack*. Incoming messages are firstly deserialized and travel back through the mediator chain in the opposite direction.

The concrete interface mediation concerning the service operation *SchedulePorting* is depicted in Figure 11.8. The *feature* `PortNumber` is stored in the VRESCo metadata model. The metadata model defines that the feature expects the input data *TempNumber*, *DesiredNumber* and *ScheduledTime*. The type of the parameters is defined in the model as *data concepts*: in the case of *TempNumber* and *DesiredNumber* the type is *PhoneNumber* (which contains sub-elements *CountryCode*, *AreaCode* and *Number*), and the type of *ScheduledTime* is *long*. The telecommunication operators CPO1, CPO2 and CPO3 provide a *SchedulePorting* operation, each of which has a slightly different interface (see Section 11.2.1). To create the mapping between the *feature* parameters and the *operations'* parameters, VMF provides a number of *Mapping Functions*. Mapping Functions may be defined for both input and output parameters. Currently, the following Mapping Functions are supported:

- **Assign** functions link one parameter to another parameter of the same data type.
- Parameters may be assigned **constants** of simple data types.

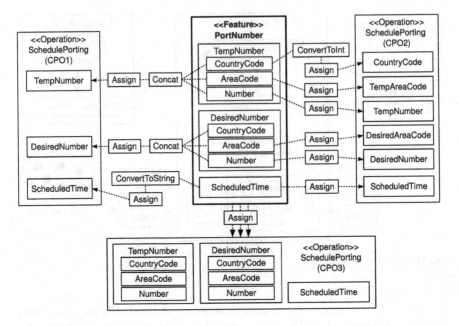

Fig. 11.8: Interface mapping for *SchedulePorting* operations

- Simple data types may be **converted** to other simple types. For example, *con-vertToInt* converts a given value to an *integer* (if possible) and the *convert-ToString* function creates a string representation of its input value.
- The set of **array** functions provides for creation of arrays and the access to elements at certain positions.
- Functions such as *Concat* or *Substring* allow for **string manipulation**.
- **Mathematical** operations are supported for *numeric* and *boolean* data types.
- Additionally, more **complex mappings** may be defined directly in C# code. The mapping code is stored in VRESCo as plain text and gets executed upon request using *CS-Script* [3], a scripting engine for C#.

Listing 11.4 contains a code excerpt that shows how mapping functions can be added to the VRESCo runtime. In the listing, the mapping between the service operation *SchedulePorting* of CPO1 and the feature `PortNumber` is implemented. In line 4, a `Mapper` object is created that mediates between the feature and the operation. The mapper allows direct access to the input (and output) parameters of both the feature and the operation. In lines 6 and 7, the parameters are stored to the variables `fInput` and `oInput`. Starting from line 9, the actual mapping functions are constructed. As indicated in Figure 11.8, the mapping functions are applied in a chain, where the result of one function becomes the input of another function. In this example, the "elementary" mappings are two `Concat` (string concatenation) functions

---

[3] http://www.csscript.net/

and one `ConvertToString` function (compare lines 9-22). The results of these functions serve as input to an `Assign` function for each of the three parameters of the operation *SchedulePorting* of CPO1.

```
1   var metaPubl = VReSCOClientFactory.CreateMetaDataPublisher("user", "pass");
2   var feature = ...;       // get 'PortNumber' feature
3   var operation = ...;     // get 'SchedulePorting' operation of CPO1
4   var mapper = metaPubl.createMapper(feature, operation);
5
6   IList<MappingElement> fInput = mapper.FeatureInputParameters;
7   IList<MappingElement> oInput = mapper.OperationInputParameters;
8
9   var concat1 = new Concat();
10  concat1.AddInputElement(fInput[0].Children[0]);
11  concat1.AddInputElement(fInput[0].Children[1]);
12  concat1.AddInputElement(fInput[0].Children[2]);
13  concat1 = mapper.AddFeatureToOperationFunction(concat1);
14
15  var concat2 = new Concat();
16  concat2.AddInputElement(fInput[1].Children[0]);
17  concat2.AddInputElement(fInput[1].Children[1]);
18  concat2.AddInputElement(fInput[1].Children[2]);
19  concat2 = mapper.AddFeatureToOperationFunction(concat2);
20
21  var toString = new ConvertToString(fInput[2]);
22  toString = mapper.AddFeatureToOperationFunction(toString);
23
24  mapper.AddFeatureToOperationFunction(new Assign(concat1.Result, oInput[0]));
25  mapper.AddFeatureToOperationFunction(new Assign(concat2.Result, oInput[1]));
26  mapper.AddFeatureToOperationFunction(new Assign(toString.Result, oInput[2]));
27
28  metaPubl.AddMapping(mapper.GetMapping());
```

Listing 11.4: Creating the Mapping for Operation *SchedulePorting* of CPO1

Finally, the metadata publisher is used to store the constructed mapping instructions in the VRESCo runtime. Registering the mapping for operation *SchedulePorting* of the remaining operators CPO2 and CPO3 works analogously. CPO2 requires only one parameter to be converted to *integer* using the function `ConvertToInt`, the remaining input message parts can be simply copied using the `Assign` function. The mapping for CPO3 is straight-forward since its operation *SchedulePorting* and the `PortNumber` feature are identical in their interface.

11.4 Related Work

In this section we point to existing work that is related to VRESCo. We focus our discussion on the areas of service registries and service metadata, as well as service mediation and dynamic invocation.

In the area of Web service registries, a number of approaches and standards exist. UDDI [19], which was originally proposed as a core Web service standard, models characteristics of services (in the form of `businessService`, `binding-Template` and `tModel`) as well as identities of service providers (`business-Entity` contains metadata about a publisher and `publisherAssertion` de-

scribes relations between parties). The technical model (tModel) of UDDI supports mainly unstructured data, whereas the VRESCo data model is well-defined
and distinguishes between the *metadata model* and the *service model*. UDDI had
very limited success and was never fully adopted by the industry, a claim which is
supported by the fact that public UDDI registries of Microsoft, SAP and IBM were
eventually shut down in 2005. The set of specifications collectively described as
ebXML (Electronic Business using XML) [4] enables enterprises to conduct electronic
business over the Internet. Amongst other concepts, ebXML defines a *Registry Information Model* [17] and a *Registry Services* [18] standard. Similar to UDDI, the
ebXML data model is rather unstructured, reducing the service description to a collection of links to its technical specification, such as the WSDL document. Furthermore, no distinction is made between abstract service features and concrete service
implementations or instances. IBM's *WebSphere Service Registry and Repository*
(WSRR) [7] uses a more structured information model, with the ability to automatically generate model entities (called *logical derivations*) from *physical documents*
of well-known formats such as WSDL, XSD or WS-Policy. As opposed to VRESCo,
WSRR has limited support for metadata versioning in the sense that logical derivations are not manipulable and hence not versionable.

Table 11.5: Comparison of related registry approaches

Category		UDDI	ebXML	WebSphere	VRESCo
Service Metadata:	Unstructured	✓	✓	✓	~
	Structured	~	~	✓	✓
Service Querying:	Query Language / API	✓	✓	✓	✓
	Type-Safe Queries	✕	✕	~	✓
Service Versioning:	Service Model Versioning	✕	✓	✓	✓
	Metadata Versioning	✕	✓	~	✕
	End-to-End Support	~	~	✕	✓
Quality of Service:	Explicit QoS Support	✕	✕	~	✓
	QoS Monitoring	✕	✕	✕	✓
Dynamic Service Invocation:	Binding & Invocation	✕	✕	~	✓
	Mediation	✕	✕	✓	✓

The results of the comparison between VRESCo and related approaches are summarized in Table 11.5. Of all discussed approaches, VRESCo is the only framework that provides end-to-end versioning support, which allows to seamlessly rebind and invoke different service revisions are runtime. All mentioned registries
allow for querying using a specialized Query language or an API that operates on
the datamodel entities, respectively. However, type-safe queries are not supported by
most approaches since usually querying is performed on the underlying unstructured
model using SQL or the like. Explicit support for non-functional, QoS-related service metadata is not available with UDDI or ebXML. WebSphere offers basic QoS
support by means of integration of WS-Policy documents as well as user-defined

---

[4] http://www.ebxml.org/

classifications metadata. However, this approach is limited to static attributes such as security, price or reliable messaging, and leaves out important performance-related characteristics such as the availability of a service or the response time of an operation. In addition to UDDI and ebXML, a number of other standards and approaches in the area of service metadata [2] exist. For instance, OWL-S [26] is an ontology for describing semantic Web services [12] with the aim of automatic Web service discovery, invocation and composition. SAWSDL [27] attempts to include semantic annotations directly into WSDL documents, which describe the service interface. SAWSDL enriches WSDL by semantic models on XML schema level as well as interface and operation level. SAWSDL also uses *lifting* and *lowering* of messages using XSLT transformation. However, it must be emphasized that the VRESCo metadata model addresses enterprise scenarios where metadata is considered a valuable business asset and does therefore not compete with semantic Web approaches, which aim at disclosing all metadata. Furthermore, VRESCo logically and physically separates the service description (e.g., in the form of WSDL) from the metadata description. Related to metadata description is the problem of runtime querying for services that match certain requirements. The authors of [30] present a Web service query algebra based on a formal model of service and operation graphs. The model also includes QoS parameters and allows for defining constraints in the form of inter-service and intra-service dependencies. The query language uses algebraic operators on service functionalities (*functional map* operator), QoS (*quality select* operator) and compositions (*compose* operator). Upon execution of a query, optimization techniques are applied to select the best service execution plan. This work is different to VRESCo since it focuses on the formal service model and the query algebra as well as its optimizations, whereas VRESCo constitutes a runtime for service management and querying. The API of VQL queries is based on the Query Object pattern [6] rather than on formal predicates and clauses. Furthermore, optimizations are left to the underlying database management system.

Obviously, pure registries such as UDDI and ebXML do not support dynamic binding, mediation and invocation. WebSphere supports service mediation using *mediation streams*, a sequence of processing steps that are executed when an input message arrives. Inside mediation streams, a set of mediation primitives can be used to change the format and content of messages. In contrast to VRESCo, mediation streams are general purpose interceptors that are also used to log messages, perform database lookups and so forth, whereas mediation in VRESCo is tailored to define a mapping between abstract features and concrete operations. Of the previously discussed frameworks, integration of dynamic binding and invocation is only implemented by VRESCo. WebSphere does provide the prerequisites for dynamic endpoint selection and for dynamically exchanging the message transport protocol (e.g., HTTP, JMS), but the degree of abstraction does not reach the same level as with the Daios messaging approach, where even the messaging protocol itself (e.g., SOAP, REST) can be transparently switched. Dynamic binding has also been addressed by other approaches. For example, Di Penta et al. [4] present WS-Binder, a framework that enable dynamic binding of services within WS-BPEL [23] processes. In their approach, proxies are used to separate abstract services and concrete instances. Similarly, the autors of [21] present a solution to model bindings in the JOpera system using reflection. In contrast to VRESCo, both frameworks focus mainly on service composition environments.

In the area of service mediation, most approaches to resolving interface incompatibilities use an adapter-based solution [3, 10]. Whereas these adapters are principially similar to the mediators in VRESCo, they are more decoupled from the clients. The mediators approach allows to easily integrate existing domain knowledge, also in the form of more complex mediation concepts (such as mediation based on semantic service metadata), which is not always simple to achieve using adapters. Besides syntactic mediation of service messages [25], other related work focuses on mediation on business protocol level. The authors of [1] identify and characterize different interoperability patterns of business-level interfaces and protocols, and propose possible solutions. In [5], a set of operators is defined to tackle the problem of behavioral service interface adaptation. The behavioral interface is seen as *"a collection of control dependencies defined over a set of message exchanges"*. The paper also provides a graphical notation for the interface transformation algebra that is put forward. In contrast to the mentioned approaches, the VRESCo runtime mediates structural differences of service interfaces, but does not consider mediation on message exchange level.

11.5 Conclusion

One of the key promises of SOC is that it provides for loosely coupled distributed applications based on the publish-bind-find-execute cycle. However, SOC practice often falls short of keeping this promise due to the lack of service metadata, service querying possibilities, explicit QoS support, and solutions for dynamic binding and interface mediation. In this paper we have described *VRESCo*, the *Vienna Runtime Environment for Service-oriented Computing*, which provides a solution for some issues and shortcomings that are prevalent in current SOA research and practice. The challenges addressed by VRESCo have been identified and illustrated based on a *number porting* example scenario. First and foremost, in an attempt to "recover the broken SOA triangle" [16], VRESCo constitutes a service *registry* that is used by providers to store information about services in a (meta-)data model. The distinction between abstract *features* (*metadata model*) and concrete service implementations (*service model*) allows to group service instances that provide an identical functionality. VRESCo enables clients to query the stored information using the specialized query language VQL in order to dynamically select an endpoint for their invocations. The selection may be based on *functional* criteria which concern the interface (or service contract), but also on *non-functional* criteria in the form of *QoS* attributes. The Daios framework employs an abstracted message format and is used in VRESCo to realize *dynamic* and protocol-indendent *invocations*. The VRESCo data model supports explicit *versioning* of service revisions, operations and parameters. User-defined and default *tags* describe the features of a service revision and its position in the *version graph*. With the aid of mapping functions, the VRESCo runtime mediates between service instances which perform the same task but differ in their technical interface. The VRESCo framework covers several distinct aspects of SOC practice and research. The result of our related work review is that similar solutions in each partial research direction exist, but that VRESCo constitutes a unique combination of service computing concepts and techniques.

Acknowledgements The research leading to these results has received funding from the European Community's Seventh Framework Programme [FP7/2007-2013] under grant agreement 215483 (S-Cube).

References

1. Benatallah, B., Casati, F., Grigori, D., Nezhad, H.R.M., Toumani, F.: Developing Adapters for Web Services Integration. Advanced Information Systems Engineering **3520/2005**, 415–429 (2005)
2. Bodoff, D., Ben-Menachem, M., Hung, P.C.K.: Web Metadata Standards: Observations and Prescriptions. IEEE Softw. **22**(1), 78–85 (2005). DOI http://dx.doi.org/10.1109/MS.2005.25
3. Cavallaro, L., Di Nitto, E.: An approach to adapt service requests to actual service interfaces. In: SEAMS '08: Proceedings of the 2008 international workshop on Software engineering for adaptive and self-managing systems, pp. 129–136. ACM, New York, NY, USA (2008). DOI http://doi.acm.org/10.1145/1370018.1370041
4. Di Penta, Massimiliano and Esposito, Raffaele and Villani, Maria Luisa and Codato, Roberto and Colombo, Massimiliano and Di Nitto, Elisabetta: WS Binder: a framework to enable dynamic binding of composite web services. In: SOSE '06: Proceedings of the 2006 international workshop on Service-oriented software engineering, pp. 74–80. ACM, New York, NY, USA (2006). DOI http://doi.acm.org/10.1145/1138486.1138502
5. Dumas, M., Spork, M., Wang, K.: Adapt or Perish: Algebra and Visual Notation for Service Interface Adaptation. Business Process Management **4102/2006**, 65–80 (2006)
6. Fowler, M.: Patterns of Enterprise Application Architecture. Addison-Wesley Longman Publishing Co., Inc., Boston, MA, USA (2002)
7. International Business Machines Corporation (IBM): WebSphere Service Registry and Repository. http://www.ibm.com/software/integration/wsrr/ (2002)
8. Leitner, P., Michlmayr, A., Rosenberg, F., Dustdar, S.: End-to-End Versioning Support for Web Services. In: SCC '08: Proceedings of the 2008 IEEE International Conference on Services Computing, pp. 59–66. IEEE Computer Society, Washington, DC, USA (2008). DOI http://dx.doi.org/10.1109/SCC.2008.21
9. Leitner, P., Rosenberg, F., Dustdar, S.: DAIOS - Efficient Dynamic Web Service Invocation. IEEE Internet Computing **13**(3), 72–80 (2009)
10. Lin, B., Gu, N., Li, Q.: A requester-based mediation framework for dynamic invocation of web services. In: SCC '06: Proceedings of the IEEE International Conference on Services Computing, pp. 445–454. IEEE Computer Society, Washington, DC, USA (2006). DOI http://dx.doi.org/10.1109/SCC.2006.13
11. Löwy, J.: Programming WCF Services. O'Reilly (2007)
12. McIlraith, S.A., Son, T.C., Zeng, H.: Semantic Web Services. IEEE Intelligent Systems **16**(2), 46–53 (2001). DOI http://dx.doi.org/10.1109/5254.920599
13. Michlmayr, A., Rosenberg, F., Leitner, P., Dustdar, S.: Advanced event processing and notifications in service runtime environments. In: DEBS '08: Proceedings of the second international conference on Distributed event-based systems, pp. 115–125. ACM, New York, NY, USA (2008). DOI http://doi.acm.org/10.1145/1385989.1386004
14. Michlmayr, A., Rosenberg, F., Leitner, P., Dustdar, S.: Comprehensive qos monitoring of web services and event-based sla violation detection. In: MWSOC '09: Proceedings of the 4th

International Workshop on Middleware for Service Oriented Computing, pp. 1–6. ACM, New York, NY, USA (2009). DOI http://doi.acm.org/10.1145/1657755.1657756

15. Michlmayr, A., Rosenberg, F., Leitner, P., Dustdar, S.: End-to-End Support for QoS-Aware Service Selection, Binding and Mediation in VRESCo. IEEE Transactions on Services Computing (TSC) (2010). (forthcoming)

16. Michlmayr, A., Rosenberg, F., Platzer, C., Treiber, M., Dustdar, S.: Towards recovering the broken SOA triangle: a software engineering perspective. In: IW-SOSWE '07: 2nd international workshop on Service oriented software engineering, pp. 22–28. ACM, New York, NY, USA (2007). DOI http://doi.acm.org/10.1145/1294928.1294934

17. Organization for the Advancement of Structured Information Standards: OASIS/ebXML Registry Information Model v2.0. http://www.oasis-open.org/committees/regrep/documents/2.0/specs/ebrim.pdf (2002)

18. Organization for the Advancement of Structured Information Standards: ebXML Registry Services. http://www.oasis-open.org/committees/regrep/documents/2.5/specs/ebrs-2.5.pdf (2003)

19. Organization for the Advancement of Structured Information Standards: UDDI Version 3.0.2. http://www.oasis-open.org/committees/uddi-spec/doc/spec/v3/uddi_v3.htm (2004). URL \url{http://www.oasis-open.org/committees/uddi-spec/doc/spec/v3/uddi_v3.htm}. Visited: 2010-01-20

20. Papazoglou, M.P., Traverso, P., Dustdar, S., Leymann, F.: Service-Oriented Computing: State of the Art and Research Challenges. Computer **40**(11), 38–45 (2007). DOI http://dx.doi.org/10.1109/MC.2007.400

21. Pautasso, C., Alonso, G.: Flexible Binding for Reusable Composition of Web Services. In: Proceedings of the 4th International Workshop on Software Composition (SC'2005). ACM (2006)

22. Rosenberg, F., Celikovic, P., Michlmayr, A., Leitner, P., Dustdar, S.: An End-to-End Approach for QoS-Aware Service Composition. In: EDOC '09: Proceedings of the 2009 IEEE International Enterprise Distributed Object Computing Conference (edoc 2009), pp. 151–160. IEEE Computer Society, Washington, DC, USA (2009). DOI http://dx.doi.org/10.1109/EDOC.2009.14

23. for the Advancement of Structured Information Standards, O.: Web Services Business Process Execution Language Version 2.0. http://docs.oasis-open.org/wsbpel/2.0/OS/wsbpel-v2.0-OS.html (2007)

24. (Sun Microsystems, Inc), M.H.: Web Application Description Language. http://www.w3.org/Submission/wadl/ (2009). URL http://www.w3.org/Submission/wadl/. Visited: 2010-02-15

25. Szomszor, M., Payne, T.R., Moreau, L.: Automated syntactic medation for web service integration. In: ICWS '06: Proceedings of the IEEE International Conference on Web Services, pp. 127–136. IEEE Computer Society, Washington, DC, USA (2006). DOI http://dx.doi.org/10.1109/ICWS.2006.34

26. (W3C), W.W.W.C.: OWL-S: Semantic Markup for Web Services. http://www.w3.org/Submission/OWL-S/ (2004)

27. (W3C), W.W.W.C.: Semantic Annotations for WSDL and XML Schema. http://www.w3.org/TR/sawsdl/ (2007)

28. (W3C), W.W.W.C.: SOAP Version 1.2 Part 1: Messaging Framework (Second Edition). http://www.w3.org/TR/soap12/ (2007). URL http://www.w3.org/TR/soap12/. Visited: 2010-02-15

29. Weerawarana, S., Curbera, F., Leymann, F., Storey, T., Ferguson, D.F.: Web Services Platform Architecture: SOAP, WSDL, WS-Policy, WS-Addressing, WS-BPEL, WS-Reliable Messaging and More. Prentice Hall PTR, Upper Saddle River, NJ, USA (2005)

30. Yu, Q., Bouguettaya, A.: Framework for web service query algebra and optimization. ACM Trans. Web **2**(1), 1–35 (2008). DOI http://doi.acm.org/10.1145/1326561.1326567

Glossary

Understanding the glossary

To provide unambiguous descriptions of terms used in this book, the glossary terms and corresponding descriptions are selected from S-Cube Knowledge Model (S-Cube KM)[5] whenever applicable. The sources of descriptions are cited when they are from third party publications. The terms without citations are written by the authors of this book.

The S-Cube KM provides multiple definitions to one term according to the *Domain Layer* and *Cross-cutting issue* in which the term is applied. When the terms are selected from S-Cube KM, their domain layer and cross-cutting issue are also presented for clarity. The acronyms used in S-Cube KM domain layer and cross-cutting issue are listed as follows:

- Engineering and Design (KM-ED)
- Adaptation and Monitoring (KM-AM)
- Quality Definition, Negotiation and Assurance (KM-QA)
- Business Process Management (KM-BPM)
- Service Composition and Coordination (KM-SC)
- Service Infrastructure (KM-SI)
- Generic (domain independent)

Terms

Actor Domain Layer: *generic*. Cross-cutting issue: *KM-ED*. Actors in Tropos and i* are organizational units, roles, positions or other systems [Bresciani et al. 2004].

Adaptable Service-based Application Domain Layer: *KM-SC*. Cross-cutting issue: *KM-ED*. Adaptable Service-based Application is an application that is designed

---

5 http://www.s-cube-network.eu/km

to make possible the selection of the running service at run-time. This kind of application is also designed to modify at run-time the structure of the composition schema.

Adaptability Domain Layer: *KM-SI*. Cross-cutting issue: *generic*. Adaptability is the ability of a computing component to adapt itself to changes in the environment. Adaptability can be considered as a proper subset of self-*.

Adaptation Domain Layer: *generic*. Cross-cutting issue: *KM-AM)*. Adaptation is a process of modifying service-based applications in order to satisfy new requirements and to fit new situations dictated by the environment on the basis of Adaptation Strategies designed by the system integrator [PO-JRA-1.2.1].

Adaptation Mechanism Domain Layer: *generic*. Cross-cutting issue: *KM-ED*. Adaptation Mechanism is the tool and mechanism provided by the underlying platform in different Functional Layers of Service-based Application that allow for the implementation of various Adaptation Strategies. [PO-JRA-1.2.1],

Adaptation Strategy Domain Layer: *generic*. Cross-cutting issue: *KM-ED*. Adaptation Strategy is the means through which adaptation is accomplished. Examples of adaptation strategies are re-configuration, re-binding, re-execution, re-planning, etc. [CD-IA-1.1.1].

Auditor The person who is authorized to examine and verify whether business processes are compliant.

Bounded Context The delimited applicability of a particular model. Bounding contexts gives team members a clear and shared understanding of what has to be consistent and what can develop independently. [Evans04]

Business Policies Domain Layer: *KM-BPM*. Cross-cutting issue *generic*. Business Policies describe laws and regulations that must be satisfied by an enterprise's business model. They include conditions that must be met in order to move on to the next stage of a process. These conditions are often defined in a textual manner and may be machine readable.

Business Process Domain Layer: *KM-BPM*. Cross-cutting issue: *generic*. A Business Process is a Process used to achieve a well-defined business outcome and is completed according to a set of procedures. The key elements in this definition are that a business process may span organizations and may typically involve both people and systems. A business process includes both automated and manual tasks. A (business) process view implies a horizontal view on a business organization and looks at processes as sets of interdependent activities designed and structured to produce a specific output for a customer or a market [Davenport, 2004]. A business process defines the results to be achieved, the context of the activities, relationships between the activities, and the interactions with other processes and resources, and users. Business processes can be measured, and different performance measures apply, like cost, quality, time and customer satisfaction. A business process may receive events that alter the state of the process and the ordering of activities. A business process may produce events for input to other applications or processes. It often invokes applications to perform computational functions, and it may post assignments to human work lists to request actions by human actors. A Business Process is a collaborative service that is closely linked to a business purpose [NEXOF-RA]

Business Process Execution Domain Layer: *KM-BPM*. Cross-cutting issue: *Generic*. Business Process Execution refers to the deployment and execution of a business process within a BPM execution engine (usually a part of BPM Software Suite). The BPM execution engine executes process instances by delegating work to humans and automated applications as specified in the process model [Leymann and Roller, 2000; Papazoglou and Ribbers, 2006].

Business Process Modeling Domain Layer: *KM-BPM*. Cross-cutting issue: *generic*. Process models are needed to help business managers and analysts understand actual processes and enable them, by visualization and simulation, to propose improvements. Business process modeling tools provide a shared environment for the capture, design and simulation of business processes by business analysts, managers, architects and other IT professionals. Process models are generally shown in graphical form for defining or building a business process. The key elements of a process model are individual activities performed, the events that trigger actions, the ordering of activities, the business rules used to support decision making and execution flow, as well as exception handling and error handling mechanisms. Modern business process modeling tools include business process analysis functionality of capturing, designing, and modifying business processes and their properties, resource requirements, such as definition and selective enforcement of process standards. They also facilitate the expression of business process views at different levels of abstraction depending on authorization, functional responsibility and the level of detail desired. Process modeling is a modeling-only environment, not an execution environment. It can however support simulation. To support simulation, the models must also embrace characteristics such as skills, availability and costs of the people, and other resources that perform the process. [Papazoglou & Ribbers, 2006], [Leymann 2000]

Business Protocol Domain Layer: *KM-BPM*. Cross-cutting issue: *generic*. A Business Protocol specifies the possible message exchange sequences (conversations) that are supported by a business process, either from a local or global point of view, respectively referred to as orchestration- and choreography business protocols [Mancioppi et al, 2008]. Business protocols can be specified using notations such as BPELlight [Nitzsche et al, 2007], [Nitzsche et al, 2008], and more generally any formalism that describes timed languages between and among participants made of message exchanges.

Compliance Conformity in fulfilling compliance requirements.

Compliance Requirement A constraint or assertion that results from the interpretation of the compliance sources. It may be defined in various levels of abstraction.

Compliance Risk The risk of impairment to the organization's business model, reputation and financial condition (resulting) from failure to meet compliance requirements.

Compliance Rule An operative definition of a compliance requirement.

Compliance Rule Violation A dissatisfaction of a compliance rule with respect to a compliance target or compliance target instance.

Compliance Source A document that is the origin of compliance requirements.

Compliance Control A statement that describes the restraining or directing influence to check, verify, or enforce rules to satisfy one or more compliance requirement – at the business level.

Context Domain Layer: *generic*. Cross-cutting issue: *KM-ED*. Context refers to the physical and social situation in which a Service-based Application or a service is embedded. It is defined by any information that can be used to characterize the situation of an entity - be it a person, a place or a physical or computational object - this is because of the way this information is used in interpretation rather than because of its intrinsic properties.[CD-IA-1.1.1].

Context Map A representation of the Bounded Contexts involved in a project and the actual relationships between them and their models. [Evans04]

Customization Domain Layer: *generic*. Cross-cutting issue: *KM-ED*. Customization refers to the design and creation (by an author, for a specific requirement) of content that meets a user's specific needs; it is static until changed. [PO-JRA-1.1.1].

Design for Adaptation Domain Layer: *generic*. Cross-cutting issue *KM-ED*. Design for Adaptation is a design process specifically defined to take adaptation into account. It should incorporate into the system under development all those features that enable the system to meet adaptation requirements from very early design stages up to and including execution.

Design Pattern A description of communicating objects and classes that are customized to solve a general design problem in a particular context. [Gamma95, p. 3]

Domain A sphere of knowledge, influence, or activity. [Evans04]

Domain-Driven Design An approach to software development that suggests that (1) For most software projects, the primary focus should be on the domain and domain logic; and (2) Complex domain designs should be based on a model.

Dynamic Binding Domain Layer: *KM-SI*. Cross-cutting issue: *KM-AM*. Dynamic Binding provides the foundation for adaptation in service infrastructures by matching client requests to services in a dynamically changing service environment.

Dynamic Invocation Domain Layer: *generic*. Cross-cutting issue: *generic*. Dynamic Invocation is the execution of a service whose interface is first known at run time.[CD-IA-1.1.1]

Evolution Domain Layer: *generic*. Cross-cutting issue: *KM-AM*. Evolution of a service-based application is a long-term history of continuous modifications of the SBA after its deployment in order to correct faults, to improve performance or other attributes, or to address a modified environment.

Failure Domain Layer: *generic*. Cross-cutting issue: *KM-QA*. The inability of a system or system component to perform a required function within specified limits. Service Failure occurs when the delivered service deviates from its correct behaviour, determined by its specification or SLA, so it implies that at least one external state of the system deviated from the correct service state.

Formal Specification Domain Layer: *KM-BPM*. Cross-cutting issue *KM-AM*. A formal model that describes relevant aspects of Web service behavior during execution, event monitoring, adaptation and coordination requirements.

Goal Domain Layer: *generic*. Cross-cutting issue: *KM-ED*. A stakeholder's Goal is an objective, which should be achieved by the future system. Goals represent the actors strategic interests (intentions) of the future system.

Hard Goal Domain Layer: *generic*. Cross-cutting issue: *KM-ED*. A Hard Goal is any goal, which has clear cut criteria to decide whether the goal is satisfied or not [Bresciani et al. 2004]. {Synonym: Goal}

Mashup Web mashups are Web applications developed using contents and services available online. [Yu09]

Monitoring Domain Layer: *KM-SC*. Cross-cutting issue: *KM-AM*. Monitoring in Service Compositions refers to checking whether certain predefined properties over the composition model are satisfied when the composition is executed [JRA-1.2.1].

Monitoring Mechanisms Domain Layer: *generic*. Cross-cutting issue *KM-AM*. Monitoring mechanisms are techniques, tools and functionalities for the continuous observation and detection of relevant run-time events.

NEXOF-RA An activity of finding and identifying a service that might fulfill user requirements. [NEXOF-RA]

On-the-Fly Service Composition Domain Layer: *KM-SC*. Cross-cutting issue *KM-AM*. On-the-Fly Service Composition is an adaptation technique that assembles a set of services, associating these with workflow steps as and when these are executed. New services can seamlessly replace failed services in the composition.

Plan Domain Layer: *generic*. Cross-cutting issue: *generic*. Plans represent activities carried out by some actor to satisfy goals or to satisfice soft-goals [Bresciani2004]. {Synonym: Task}

Planning Domain Layer: *generic*. Cross-cutting issue *generic*. Planning is the process of finding a sequence of actions (from a repertoire of possible actions), that lead to a goal or a desirable state.

Proactive Adaptation Domain Layer: *generic*. Cross-cutting issue: *KM-ED & KM-AM*. Proactive Adaptation prevents future problems that may happen in a SBA by proactively identifying and handling their sources. Proactive adaptation aims to modify SBA before a deviation will occur during the actual operation and before such a deviation can lead to problems.

Post-Mortem Adaptation Domain Layer: *generic*. Cross-cutting issue: *KM-ED*. Post-Mortem Adaptation modifies or evolves the SBA at design time or when it is stopped. [CD-JRA-1.1.2] GEN: Adaptation

Proactive Adaptation Domain Layer: *generic*. Cross-cutting issue: *KM-ED*. Proactive Adaptation prevents future problems that may happen in a SBA by proactively identifying and handling their sources. [CD-JRA-1.1.2] GEN: Adaptation

Process Model Domain Layer: *generic*. Cross-cutting issue: *KM-ED*. A process model is a precise description of the software process. It serves three main purposes:

1. It facilitates understanding and communication.
2. It supports process management and improvement.
3. It may serve as a basis for automated support.

A process model is a simplification of reality

QoS-Aware Service Composition Domain Layer: *KM-SC*. Cross-cutting issue: *generic*. Quality of Service-Aware Service Composition is a form of service composition that is based on and attempts to improve the overall Quality of Service (QoS) of the composite service, such as execution time, reliability, availability or cost.

Quality of Service Level Domain Layer: *generic*. Cross-cutting issue: *KM-QA*. Quality of Service (QoS) Level defines the different modes in which a system can be. Depending on, e. g., available resources, a different execution level can be jumped to if continuing the execution in the current one is not possible. The sub-metamodel defines the abstract classes to represent levels, transitions between them, and when those transitions have to take place [IA-1.1.1]. {Synonym: QoS Level}

Reactive Adaptation Domain Layer: *generic*. Cross-cutting issue: *KM-AM*. Reactive adaptation refers to the modification in reaction to the changes already occurred [JRA-1.2.2].

Rebinding Domain Layer: *generic*. Cross-cutting issue: *KM-ED*. Rebinding implies the replacement of a binding with another one. Rebinding can happen at design time, deployment time, and runtime.[CD-IA-1.1.1]

Repository A mechanism for encapsulating storage, retrieval, and search behavior which emulates a collection of objects. [Evans04]

Requirement Domain Layer: *generic*. Cross-cutting issue: *KM-ED*. A Requirement is a goal under the responsibility of the future system.

Requirements Analysis Domain Layer: *generic*. Cross-cutting issue: *KM-ED*. In the Requirements Analysis the goals are decomposed in sub-goals and the best strategies to satisfy each goal are individuated; this activity produces a set of functional requirements that will be validated to check potential conflicts among the requirements (Requirement Validation). [CD-JRA-1.1.2].

Requirements Engineering Domain Layer: *generic*. Cross-cutting issue: *KM-ED*. Requirements Engineering is one activity in the software development lifecycle, which aims to identify, document, agree upon and verify the purpose of the system to be. [CD-JRA-1.1.2].

Robustness Domain Layer: *generic*. Cross-cutting issue *KM-QA*. Robustness is a feature of components and functionalities to behave in an expected fashion in anomalous or exceptional situations.

Self-Adaptation Domain Layer: *generic*. Cross-cutting issue: *KM-AM*. Self-Adaptation requires that all adaptation steps, decisions, and actions are performed by the SBA autonomously. This also assumes that all the necessary mechanisms to enact adaptation strategies are built into the application. When the adaptation process assumes any form of human intervention, one deals with human-in-the-loop adaptation [CD-JRA-1.1.2].

Self-Configuration Domain Layer: *KM-SI*. Cross-cutting issue: *generic*. Self-Configuration is called the ability of a computing component to configure itself in accordance with high-level policies that specify what is desired not how it is to be accomplished. [AutonomicVision]

Self-Optimization Domain Layer: *KM-SI*. Cross-cutting issue: *generic*. Self-Optimization is called the ability of a computing component to seek ways to improve its operation, identifying and seizing opportunities to make itself more efficient in performance or cost [IA-1.1.1; Kephart and Chess, 2003]. {Synonym: Self-Optimising}

Semantic Web Services Domain Layer: *KM-SC*. Cross-cutting issue: *generic*. Semantic Web Services are those Web Services that are defined using rich formal specifications of their capabilities, based on ontologies and the general infrastructure offered by the Semantic Web. [PO-JRA-2.2.1].

Service Domain Layer: *generic*. Cross-cutting issue: *generic*. Software services are not just pieces of software; instead, they represent the functionality that the underlying pieces of software offer. Rather than building a software system from scratch, or developing it by selecting and gluing together off-the-shelf components, now designers can realize applications by composing services, possibly offered by third parties. This shift from adopting the piece of technology (the software) to using the functionality (the service) offers us a valuable tool to design those software systems that we call service-based applications at a higher level of abstraction, possibly building new value-added composed services. Services have taken the concept of ownership to the extreme: not only, as off-the-shelf components, their development, quality assurance, and maintenance are under the control of third parties, but they can even be executed and managed by third parties. [DiNitto et al. 2008]

Service-based Application Domain Layer: *generic*. Cross-cutting issue: *KM-ED*. A Service-based Application is composed by a number of possibly independent services, available in a network, which perform the desired functionalities of the architecture. Such services could be provided by third parties, not necessarily by the owner of the service-based application. Note that a service-based application shows a profound difference with respect to a component-based application: while the owner of the component-based application also owns and controls its components, the owner of a service-based application does not own, in general, the component services, nor it can control their execution [JRA-1.1.1]. {Synonym: SBA}

Service-based Application Construction Domain Layer: *KM-SC*. Cross-cutting issue: *generic*. The process of SBA Construction may be manual if the service developer defines an executable process (workflow) composed of concrete or abstract services using an appropriate service composition specification language; it may be model-driven if service orchestration models are generated from more abstract models; and it may be automated if the executable SBA is automatically generated using the available service models. [CD-JRA-1.1.2]

Service Binding Domain Layer: *generic*. Cross-cutting issue: *KM-ED*. Service Binding is the process of associating a service request to a service offer. Binding can happen at design time, deployment time, and runtime. [CD-IA-1.1.1].

Service Choreography Domain Layer: *generic*. Cross-cutting issue: *generic*. Service Choreography is the collaborative processes involving multiple services where the interactions between these services are seen from a global perspective. [Barros 2005]

Service Composition Domain Layer: *KM-SC*. Cross-cutting issue: *generic*. Service Composition is a combination of a set of services for achieving a certain purpose. Different service composition types can be distinguished, in particular: service orchestration, service choreography, service wiring, and service coordination. Often service composition is used as synonym for the more special term service orchestration. [PO-JRA-2.2.1]

Service Coordination Domain Layer: *KM-SC*. Cross-cutting issue *generic*. Service Coordination is a form of service composition in which a distributed activity is created by temporarily grouping a set of service instances that follow a coordination protocol. At the end of the activity a coordinator decides on the outcome of the protocol and disseminates the result to the participating services. WS-Coordination is an example of a specification that supports coordination of Web services.

Service Description Domain Layer: *generic*. Cross-cutting issue: *KM-ED*. A service description is a set of documents that describe the interface to and semantics of a service. It defines the message formats, datatypes, transport protocols, and transport serialization formats that should be used between the requester agent and the provider agent. It also specifies one or more network locations at which a provider agent can be invoked, and may provide some information about the message exchange pattern that is expected. In essence, the service description represents an agreement governing the mechanics of interacting with that service. [W3C]

Service Discovery Domain Layer: *KM-SI*. Cross-cutting issue: *KM-ED*. Service Discovery is the process of finding services that match the requirements of the service requestor. Runtime service discovery is an important ingredient for self-adaptation. [CD-IA-1.1.1] ETC: self-adaptation.

Service Level Agreement Domain Layer: *generic*. Cross-cutting issue: *KM-QA*. A Service-Level Agreement (SLA) is a formally negotiated agreement between two parties. It is a contract that exists between customers and their service provider, or between service providers. It transcripts the common understanding about services, priorities, responsibilities, guarantee, etc. with the main purpose to agree on the level of service. For example, it may specify the levels of availability, serviceability, performance, operation or other attributes of the service like billing and even penalties in the case of violation of the SLA.

Service Mediation Domain Layer: *generic*. Cross-cutting issue: *generic*. Service Mediation is the process of interception and modification of messages that are exchanged between services.

Service Orchestration Domain Layer: *generic*. Cross-cutting issue: *generic*. A Service Orchestration is the description of the interactions in which a given service can engage with other services, as well as the internal steps between these interactions (e.g., data transformations). [Barros 2005]

Service-oriented Software Engineering Domain Layer: *generic*. Cross-cutting issue: *KM-ED*. Service-oriented software engineering (SOSE) deals with theories, principles, methods, and tools for building enterprise-scale solutions as the collaboration of loosely-coupled application services that provide particular business functionality and are distributed within and across organizational boundaries [Stojanovic2005]. An enterprise-scale solution can be understood as both an SBA and a pool of services. SYN: SOSE

Service Registry Domain Layer: *KM-SI*. Cross-cutting issue: *generic*. A Service Registry is a repository that contains Web service related meta information (e.g. Web service descriptions). [CD-IA-1.1.1].

Service Runtime Domain Layer: *KM-SI*. Cross-cutting issue: *KM-AM*. A Service Runtime Environment provides features (e.g., logging) that enables the monitoring of individual services that are executed. Adaptions (e.g., replacements) are also supported by the Service Runtime Environment.

Service Specification Domain Layer: *generic*. Cross-cutting issue: *KM-ED*. A Service Specification is usually defined by the Service Developer/Provider and may include both functional and non-functional information such as information on the service interface, the service behavior, service exceptions, test suites, commercial conditions applying to the service (pricing, policies, and SLA negotiation parameters) and communication mechanisms. [SeCSE]

Soft Goal Domain Layer: *generic*. Cross-cutting issue: *KM-ED*. Soft Goals are goals which do not have clear cut criteria to decide whether the goal is satisfied or not. In contrast to hard-goals, soft-goals can only be partially fulfilled (satisfied).

Task Modeling Domain Layer: *generic*. Cross-cutting issue: *KM-ED*. Task Modeling is the description of the structured sets of activities that a user has to perform – often in interaction with a system influenced by its contextual environment – in order to attain goals.

Ubiquitous Language A language structured around the domain model and used by all team members to connect all the activities of the team with the software. [Evans04]

Validation Domain Layer: *generic*. Cross-cutting issue: *generic*. The aim of Validation is to check if a system being built or already built is the right one. Validation typically involves the final user / client and is context dependent: the environment in which the system is to be installed / executed has to be taken into account, as well as HCI issues. It is, therefore, difficult to formalize it fully, and it partly is a subjective process.

Value Object An object that describes some characteristic or attribute but carries no concept of identity. [Evans04]

Workflow Domain Layer: *generic*. Cross-cutting issue *generic*. A workflow is a representation of a business process in whole or part, consisting of a series of interconnected steps that define a sequence of operations.

References

[AutonomicVision] J.O.Kephart, D.M. Chess: The vision of autonomic computing, IEEE Computer N 36 pp 41-50, 2003

[Barros 2005] Alistair Barros and Marlon Dumas and Phillipa Oaks. A Critical Overview of the Web Services Choreography Description Language (WS-CDL). BPTrends. March 2005

[Bresciani et al. 2004] Bresciani, P., Perini, A., Giorgini, P., Giunchiglia, F., Mylopoulos, J.: Tropos: An agent-oriented software development methodology. Autonomous Agents and Multi-Agent Systems 8(3), 203ñ 236 (2004)

[Cappiello et al 2008] C. Cappiello, B. Pernici, Quality-aware design of repairable processes, Int. Conf. on Information Quality, ICIQ, Boston, Nov. 2008.

[CD-IA-1.1.1] Comprehensive overview of the state of the art on service-based systems.

[CD-JRA-1.1.2] "Separate design knowledge models for software engineering and service based computing".

[DiNitto et al. 2008] Elisabetta Di Nitto, Carlo Ghezzi, Andreas Metzger, Mike Papazoglou and Klaus Pohl. A journey to highly dynamic, self-adaptive service-based applications. In Automated Software Engineering, 2008.

[Evans04] Eric Evans. Domain-Driven Design: Tackling Complexity in the Heart of Software. Addison- Wesley, 2004.

[Gamma95] Erich Gamma, Richard Help, Ralph Johnson and John Vlissides, Design Patterns: Elements of Reusable Object-Oriented Software, Addison-Wesley, 1995.

[IA-1.1.1]Andrikopoulos, V., Fairchild, A., van den Heuvel, W.J., Kazhamiakin, R., Leitner, P., Metzger, A., Nemeth, Z., di Nitto, E., Papazoglou, M.P., Pernici, B., Wetzstein, B.: Comprehensive overview of the state of the art on service-based systems. http://www.s-cubenetwork. eu/results/(2008)

[JRA-1.1.1] Andrikopoulos, V., Bertoli, P., Bindelli, S., Nitto, E.D., Gehlert, A., Germanovich, L., Kazhamiakin, R., Kounkou, A., Pernici, B., Plebani, P., Weyer, T.: State of the art report on software engineering design knowledge and survey of hci and contextual knowledge. http://www.scube- network.eu/results/ (2008)

[JRA-1.2.1] Benbernou, S., Cavallaro, L., Hacid, M.S., Kazhamiakin, R., Kecskemeti, G., Poizat, J.L., Silvestri, F., Uhlig, M., Wetzstein, B.: State of the art report, gap analysis of knowledge on principles, techniques and methodologies for monitoring and adaptation of SBAs. http://www.s-cube-network.eu/results/ (2008)

[JRA-1.2.2] Hielscher, J.; Metzger, A.; Kazhamiakin, R.: Taxonomy of Adaptation Principles and Mechanisms. http://www.s-cube-network.eu/results/ (2009)

[JRA-2.1.1] Andrikopoulos, V., Benbernou, S., Bitsaki, M., Danylevych, O., Hacid, M., van den Heuvel, W., Karastoyanova, D., Kratz, B., Leymann, F., Mancioppi, M., Mokhtari, K., Nikolaou, C., Papazoglou, M., Wetzstein, B.: Survey on business process management. http://www.s-cube-network.eu/results/(2008)

[Kephart and Chess, 2003] Kephart, J.O., Chess, D.M.: The vision of autonomic computing. IEEE Computer 36(1), 41ñ50 (2003)

[Leymann and Roller, 2000] Leymann, F., Roller, D.: Production Workflow - Concepts and Techniques. PTR Prentice Hall (2000)

[Mancioppi et al, 2008] Michele Mancioppi, Manuel Carro, Willem-Jan van den Heuvel, Mike P. Papazoglou: Sound Multi-party Business Protocols for Service Networks. ICSOC 2008:302-316

[NEXOF-RA] Glossary. Visited: 03.02.2009. http://www.nexof-ra.eu/node/202

[Nitzsche et al, 2007] Jörg Nitzsche, Tammo van Lessen, Dimka Karastoyanova, Frank Leymann: BPEL light. BPM 2007:214-229

[Nitzsche et al, 2008] Jörg Nitzsche, Tammo van Lessen, Frank Leymann: Extending BPEL light for Expressing Multi-Partner Message Exchange Patterns. EDOC 2008:245-254

[Papazoglou and Ribbers, 2006] Papazoglou, M.P., Ribbers, P.M.A.: e-Business: Organizational and Technical Foundations. J. Wiley & Sons (2006)

[PO-JRA-1.1.1] A. Rockley, P. Kostur, and S. Manning, Managing Enterprise Content, New Riders, 2003.

[PO-JRA-1.2.1] State of the Art Report, Gap Analysis of Knowledge on Principles, Techniques and Methodologies for Monitoring and Adaptation of SBAs

[PO-JRA-2.2.1] Overview of the State of the Art in Composition and Coordination of Services

[SeCSE] "SeCSE Project", http://www.secse-project.eu/.

[Stojanovic2005] Service-oriented software system engineering: challenges and practices, Zoran Stojanovic and Ajantha Dahanayake Idea Group Publ., (2005)

[Yu09] Jin Yu, Boualem Benatallah, Fabio Casati and Florian Daniel, IEEE Internet Computing, 5 (12), p. 44-52, 2009

[W3C] Booth D., Haas H., McCabe F., Newcomer E., Champion M., Ferris C., Orchard D., Web Services Architecture, http://www.w3.org/TR/ws-arch/

Index